ANGLISTIK UND ENGLISCHUNTERRICHT

Herausgegeben von
Gabriele Linke
Holger Rossow
Merle Tönnies

Band 80

JANA GOHRISCH
ELLEN GRÜNKEMEIER (Eds.)

Listening to Africa

Anglophone African Literatures
and Cultures

Universitätsverlag
WINTER
Heidelberg

Bibliografische Information der Deutschen Nationalbibliothek
Die Deutsche Nationalbibliothek verzeichnet diese Publikation
in der Deutschen Nationalbibliografie;
detaillierte bibliografische Daten sind im Internet
über *http://dnb.d-nb.de* abrufbar.

Herausgeber:
Prof. Dr. Gabriele Linke
PD Dr. Holger Rossow
Prof. Dr. Merle Tönnies

ISBN 978-3-8253-6119-8
ISSN 0344-8266

Dieses Werk einschließlich aller seiner Teile ist urheberrechtlich geschützt. Jede Verwertung außerhalb der engen Grenzen des Urheberrechtsgesetzes ist ohne Zustimmung des Verlages unzulässig und strafbar. Das gilt insbesondere für Vervielfältigungen, Übersetzungen, Mikroverfilmungen und die Einspeicherung und Verarbeitung in elektronischen Systemen.

© 2012 Universitätsverlag Winter GmbH Heidelberg
Imprimé en Allemagne · Printed in Germany
Druck: Memminger MedienCentrum, 87700 Memmingen

Gedruckt auf umweltfreundlichem, chlorfrei gebleichtem
und alterungsbeständigem Papier

Den Verlag erreichen Sie im Internet unter:
www.winter-verlag.de

Contents

Dike-Ogu Chukwumerije:
  Mister Man, Don't Teach Me Nonsense (poem) — 9

Jana Gohrisch and Ellen Grünkemeier:
  Listening to Africa: Anglophone African Literatures and Cultures. Introduction — 11

GENERAL ISSUES

Kirsten Rüther:
  On the Book Shelf in My Study. Approaching African Literatures and Cultures from an Historian's Perspective — 23

Anne Schröder:
  Voices from Africa. The English Language in Africa — 41

Melanie Klein:
  Between History, Politics and the Self. Photographic Portraiture in Contemporary Art from Africa — 69

EAST AFRICA

Doreen Strauhs:
  Anglophone East African (Women's) Writing since 2000. *Femrite* and *Kwani Trust* — 93

Claudia Böhme:
  'Action, Cut and Roll!' The Language Question in the Tanzanian Film Industry — 121

Uta Reuster-Jahn:
  Am walking on the way kuiseti future yangu. The Use of
  English in Bongo Flava Music in Tanzania   145

WEST AFRICA

Dike-Ogu Chukwumerije:
  Writing and Publishing in Nigeria. An Author's Perspective   175

Dike-Ogu Chukwumerije:
  The Revolution Has No Tribe (poem)   181

Rainer Emig:
  Doing Business in West Africa. The Case of Ghana   183

Susanne Gehrmann:
  Re-Writing War in Contemporary Nigerian Fiction. From
  Biafra to Present Times   209

Anke Bartels:
  Remembering the Past, Changing the Present. Anglophone
  Women Playwrights from West and South Africa   239

SOUTH AFRICA

Henning Marquardt:
  Literary History and the Publishers. South African Mission
  Presses and Secular Publishing from the 1920s to the 1940s   263

Riaan Oppelt:
  Dialogues between 'Old' and 'New' in Contemporary South
  African Theatre   285

Russell Harold Kaschula:
  Teaching Oral Literature in the 21st Century   313

RESEARCH AND TEACHING

Ellen Grünkemeier:
   Teaching South Africa. Histories, Literatures, Cultures   335

Jana Gohrisch:
   Teaching West Africa. Histories, Literatures, Cultures   355

Dike-Ogu Chukwumerije:
   Enduring Images (poem)   377

Henning Marquardt:
   Anglophone Africa. A Chronology of Events and Texts   379

Henning Marquardt:
   Annotated Bibliography   395

Contributors' Addresses   403

Dike-Ogu Chukwumerije (Abuja)

Mister Man, Don't Teach Me Nonsense

Mister Man, I am tired of your ignorance
If you don't know, say so
But don't tell me I have no history
Did Vasco da Gama build Kumbi Saleh?
Where was Livingstone when the men from Nok
Were blazing new trails through the heart of Africa?

If you want to tell me about commerce
Why do you begin so far away in Europe?
Did gold – that indispensable aid of ancient trade –
Did gold not come over the Sahara on roads built by black hands?
Around the Cape, were the Europeans not surprised;
Africans drinking water from Chinese porcelain?

If you want to tell me about democracy
Why do begin so far away in Greece –
As if the Pierian springs were not off shoots of the Nile?
There were city states in Hausa land; city states in Swahili country
More than enough to feed your lectures
Teach me of participatory power but as an example use the Khoisan

If you want to tell me about freedom
Why do you begin so far away in France or Boston?
Before France – tell me about Palmares – the black state in Brazil
Tell me about the maroons who won freedom for slaves in Jamaica!
Tell me about Queen Nzinga who refused, with her blood, to sell her people
Tell me about the great battle of Mbwila!

If you want to tell me about empires and kingdoms
Why do you begin so far away in Rome?
Will you not discuss Kush and Nubia?
I am longing to hear of Egypt – the fountain of modern civilization
Tell me of Kimbundu, Kongo, Luba and Kikonja
Tell me of the Shona kings that built Great Zimbabwe

That is all I ask of you –
Think twice before you repeat the text book
Who can grow on a pack of lies?
My people are struggling to grasp knowledge
Because it is cloaked in alien forms
In foreign motifs

I am tired of you tele-guided wisdom
Your inherited structure of organized half-truths
There are enough proverbs in Africa to fill your mouth
Quote Achebe, Quote Thiong'o, Quote Gordimer
Stop reciting this lifeless monologue of blind learning
Mister Man, don't teach me nonsense

Dike-Ogu Chukwumerije has kindly allowed us to reprint this poem from his collection *The Revolution Has No Tribe. Contemporary Poetry on African History, Culture and Society*, London, 2008, pp. 17-18.

Dike-Ogu Chukwumerije is an Abuja Literary Society (ALS) Poetry Slam Champion and the winner of the maiden edition of The African Poet Nigeria (TAPng) National Poetry Slam Competition. He is a lawyer, with a postgraduate degree in Development from the School of Oriental and African Studies (SOAS), London. A dedicated literary advocate and social activist, his works show a fine balance between his intellectual interests and his creativity, as a writer. He has self-published several books, including the highly acclaimed poetry collection, *The Revolution Has No Tribe*. One of his novels, *The African American*, was longlisted for the 2012 Wole Soyinka Prize for Literature. He lives in Abuja with his family.

Jana Gohrisch & Ellen Grünkemeier (Hanover)

Listening to Africa:
Anglophone African Literatures and Cultures.
Introduction

Compared to other postcolonial regions, Africa is less well represented in German school and university curricula. To address this imbalance, our collection seeks to promote the presence of literatures and cultures from Anglophone Africa by providing (university) teachers and students with ideas, material and recommendations for further reading. With this number, *anglistik & englischunterricht*, the German journal dedicated to the teaching of English at school and university, suggests listening to Africa. After a volume on the Caribbean (2007) and one on India (2009) it is the third volume on postcolonial literatures and the first one to focus on a whole continent which opens up possibilities *and* limits the endeavour at the same time. Taking into account an entire continent sounds presumptuous, Eurocentric and even colonial: who would dream of editing a single book on the broad variety of European literatures and cultures? Why do we nevertheless choose such an approach to Africa? Moreover, why do we concentrate on Anglophone Africa, leaving aside the wealth of material produced in hundreds of other African languages?

There are two major reasons for us to undertake the venture despite these concerns and challenges. First of all, we value the inherent opportunities of this large-scale approach and wish to survey the great range of cultural practices performed in varieties of English, a language well accessible to our readership. Our issue of *a&e* is targeted at university and high school teachers in Germany as well as at advanced university students enrolled in English Studies programmes, the majority of whom want to become teachers themselves. In most English departments, African literatures and cultures are – if at all – taught as part of English literature classes. Yet, there are also English departments that have long specialised in postcolonial literatures in English and can therefore offer thematically and geographically diversified courses and lecture series on Africa. At some German universities, there are African Studies departments whose programmes include literatures and cultures in African languages (such as Amharic, Bambara, Hausa, Sotho or Swahili) as well as in English and French. Their students may also be interested in the material assembled here because we included papers that look at the regional interaction between the languages, especially in East African music and film as well as in South African poetry. Moreover, this volume features an extensive linguistic overview of English in Africa to enable the readers to analyse the specific use of English in the literary and cultural texts.

The title metaphor of 'Listening to Africa' alludes to the continued importance of – the ever changing – oral genres and practices alongside the written material. The essays are dedicated to different genres and regions, foregrounding new and mediated forms of orality in films and theatre performances, praise poetry and music. To challenge the dominance of literary studies in the postcolonial field and to enable a dialogue about Africa across the disciplines, we solicited contributions from other academic domains such as linguistics, history and art history. The articles provide surveys rather than in-depth studies of individual artists or works but will point out how to use the material in teaching.

Secondly, listening to English-speaking voices from Africa will allow the readers to engage directly with African self-images, concepts and ideas. This, in turn, will help to contend the wide-spread – and largely negative – stereotypes about Africa which level out regional, cultural and historical differences. This is the subject matter of Dike-Ogu Chukwumerije's poems "Mr Man, Don't Teach Me Nonsense" that opens our book and of "Enduring Images" that concludes it.[1] The self-assured speaker of the first poem angrily charges a generic Western man for churning out nonsensical clichés about Africa, "half truths" and "blind learning",[2] that will be accepted no longer. Using the categories of Western political discourse, she or he lists African and diasporic achievements in history, commerce, democracy and freedom, empires and kingdoms. Nevertheless, in German (and many international) mainstream media, Africa is still mainly associated with war, crime and violence, poverty, hunger and streams of refugees. It is presented as predominantly tribal, patriarchal and democratically deficient, i.e. as politically and economically underdeveloped and thus in need of Western aid. These images permeate the dominant discourse and resurface, for example, in German school books for geography and English as a Foreign Language (EFL). Over the last twenty years, the German EFL curriculum has been considerably extended and now comprises, in addition to Britain and the United States, Australia, New Zealand and India. Africa, however, remains marginalised. It is difficult to generalise about the curriculum in a country with a federal education system, but let us illustrate our point with a school book used in the federal states of Berlin and Brandenburg, *English G1 für Gymnasien. Band A 5* (2010).[3] This grade 9 school book dedicates one unit (out of four) to Australia (Unit 1) and one to "Life in the big city" (Unit 3) illustrated by Hong Kong, Johannesburg (the "city of contrasts") and Mumbai. There are accompanying exercises that include the school system in New Zealand, travelling in Australia, a text about the British-Asian leading actor in *Slumdog Millionaire*, one about a white musician from South Africa and one about *Tsotsi*, a prize-winning film set in post-apartheid South Africa (adapted from Athol Fugard's novel). On the one hand, the school book mentions the harsh living conditions in the slums of Mumbai and Soweto underlining them by photographic images. On the other hand, however, it implicitly proposes middle-class lives and upward social mobility as the desirable norm, exemplifying them by *Slumdog Millionaire*, a feature film set in India rather than Africa.

For university teachers of African literatures and cultures, the under-representation of Africa in school[4] means that students will arrive with relatively little knowledge about Africa and rely on their largely unacknowledged stereotypes instead of critically engaging with and reflecting on the course material.

Listening to Africa offers both material and methodologies for studying it that will allow teachers and students to become aware of the stereotypes, to question and negotiate them and, ideally, to transcend them. The essays approach their subjects from different disciplinary and (trans)national perspectives. The disciplines comprise African Studies including literature, culture and film studies, English and Anglophone Studies with their sub-disciplines of linguistics, literature and culture, art history as well as historiography. Culturally, the majority of the contributors have a German academic background with expertise gained while researching in Africa. In addition, scholars from South Africa write about genres and practices that are best studied from a locally informed perspective such as Xhosa poetry and South African theatre. We are very glad to have been able to win the Nigerian poet and novelist Dike-Ogu Chukwumerije to describe his experience of writing and publishing in Nigeria and Britain and to allow us to print three poems from his latest collection. The articles are grouped in five sections beginning with general issues such as an historian's approach to literature, a sociolinguistic survey of African Englishes and an essay on contemporary photography. The following sections correspond to the linguistic classification of African Englishes with sections on West Africa, East Africa and South Africa. We conclude with a service section on research and teaching which contains two essays on the methodologies of interdisciplinary teaching of South and West African literatures and cultures at Leibniz University of Hanover where historians and literary and cultural scholars have a long tradition of joint instruction. Moreover, the section supplies readers with annotated bibliographies and teaching guides as well as a chronology of African cultural history.

What is special about this collection of essays compared to other recent books on Africa, especially within the German academic context? As African literatures and cultures are mainly taught in English Studies programmes in the context of postcolonial literatures, German publications tend to present surveys of this field with at least one chapter dedicated to Africa.[5] The latest trend is transnational Anglophone Studies, accounting for globalisation and its impact on literatures and cultures in English.[6] Catering explicitly to both high school and university teachers, the most recent books do not only suggest reading material but provide teaching aids as well. Thus, *Teaching the New English Cultures and Literatures* (2010) contains two essays on South Africa, the only representative of Africa in the school curriculum.[7] In the section on English-speaking cultures around the world, which is organised by regions, Gisela Feuerle discusses South African short stories and suggests (obviously tested) assignments for individual and group work to explore "Young People in Literature and Society".[8] In the section on the new English literatures, Laurenz Volkmann reads J. M. Coetzee's canonical and award-winning novel *Disgrace* (1999) as a "Disturbing Literary Representation of the New South Africa" concentrating on issues of education, race relations and language.[9] Both essays highlight the central theoretical and methodological problem that all texts about Africa (as indeed, all literature) posit to both professional and non-professional readers: the relationship between literature and reality.

In his article on "African Novels and the Question of Theory", included in Gaurav Desai's collection *Teaching the African Novel* (2009), Olakunle George summarises four central approaches that have been applied to African novels, i.e. formalism, Afrocentrism, Marxism and poststructuralism.[10] He looks at their merits and demerits in historical context "suggesting that it is more promising to think of theory as itself a product of history and culture, very much like novels and poems".[11] He gives credit to poststructuralism because it introduced into the criticism of African literature "the critique of notions of African authenticity as well as the view of literature as a transparent medium that can give us direct knowledge of past or present African realities".[12] Among the uses of poststructuralism in the classroom he mentions that

> [i]t makes possible a mode of reading that does not limit itself to pronouncing whether or not a novel is authentically African (as Afrocentric criticism sometimes does) or emancipatory in some untheorized sense (as Marxist criticism sometimes does).[13]

One of the stereotypes students often bring to the study of African literatures and cultures sees Africa as fixed in 'tradition' as opposed to their own – unacknowledged – 'modernity'. Depending on the type of tradition in question, it may put readers off or intrigue them. Thus, the alleged 'closeness to nature' will probably attract them because it suggests a wholeness of experience long lost in the modern West. The openly patriarchal traditions, however, are more likely to cause unease. Nevertheless, both reactions are rooted in the same stereotypical belief in an 'unspoiled', 'authentic' and 'original' Africa.[14]

The volume has been inspired by cultural studies approaches that understand cultural products as part of a historical moment and thus as embedded in a variety of discourses with which they interact. Literature and cultural artefacts do not 'mirror' or 'reflect' any 'given' reality but juxtapose and negotiate conflicting perceptions of realities, interweaving them with desires and even utopian ideas.[15] To study them, it is worthwhile to turn to the production and reception of popular culture, such as music or cinema, to take postcolonial studies further into postcolonial cultural studies, as Simon Featherstone has suggested.[16] Moreover, the contributions to this issue account for Africans as agents – both as producers of cultural artefacts and as fictional characters within plays, song lyrics, films or novels.[17] They investigate the power structures past and present within and, sometimes against, which creative artists work and which re-appear in the works themselves, asking to be appreciated by the readers, viewers or beholders. Cultural studies approaches always pay attention to the historical dimension of texts and cultural artefacts to be analysed on three levels: the moment of production, the moments of reception when first released and when actually studied (for example in a German EFL classroom or university literature class) as well as the temporal settings of texts, films or photographs. Discussions need to pay attention to the interaction of these historical moments: (university) teachers and students should ask themselves why a specific aesthetic means has been used at this particular point in time and in this particular place. To illustrate this understanding of literary and cultural products, we reflect on our own teaching experience with historians at the end of the book. This feature as well as the diversity of the material and the contributing scholars set this issue of *a&e* apart from other publications in the field.

While literary and cultural studies are the central concern of our volume, the opening part is dedicated to neighbouring disciplines that provide further perspectives on Africa. The articles on history, linguistics and art shed light on the interdisciplinary field of African studies. As a researcher and lecturer in African history, KIRSTEN RÜTHER explores the interfaces of history and literature. Taking issue with the common understanding of history as 'background information', she argues that historical narratives produce meaning about the past, which is why they are not unlike literary texts. By discussing various sources and texts, she outlines how historians can approach African literatures and cultures. ANNE SCHRÖDER, who has an academic background in English Studies and linguistics, outlines the characteristic features of African varieties of English, focussing on phonology, morphology and syntax, vocabulary and pragmatics. She introduces selected models to describe the different Englishes spoken around the world and especially in Africa. To illustrate her arguments, she studies literary texts from Cameroon. The art historian MELANIE KLEIN analyses the role of (self-)portraiture in the history of African photography. Starting with the pioneering work of Samuel Fosso who was born in Cameroon and then moved to the Central African Republic, she goes on to examine photographs by Kudzanai Chiurai (from Zimbabwe, now living in Johannesburg) and by Nomusa Makhubu (from South Africa). She investigates in what ways these artists use (self-)portraiture to represent the self as well as historical or current political issues.

DOREEN STRAUHS's contribution on recent East African (women's) writing in English opens the section on East Africa. Her article combines a sociological and a literary studies point of view and argues that literary non-governmental organisations such as *Kwani Trust* in Kenya and *Femrite* in Uganda have shaped the countries' literary landscapes. In online and print publications, the writers experiment with different styles influenced by electronic media (such as blogging, email and SMS) and with different language varieties, thus creating new literary trends. Focussing on Tanzania, the African studies scholars Claudia Böhme and Uta Reuster-Jahn are equally concerned with the choice of language in contemporary cultural products. In her analysis of video films, CLAUDIA BÖHME discusses the ways in which Swahili and/or English are used. To set the ground for her investigation, she sketches the history of film production in Tanzania, traces (colonial) language policies and ponders on language as a marker of identity. UTA REUSTER-JAHN examines an emerging genre of the Tanzanian music scene, namely a form of hip-hop called Bongo Flava. The songs combine the local and the global: they draw on Tanzanian music styles, contexts and languages (especially Swahili); simultaneously, they provide templates for youth identity that connect youth cultures in Tanzania with those in the United States and Jamaica. On the basis of selected examples, she shows how and with what effects English loan words are incorporated into Swahili lyrics.

The section on West Africa opens with a special feature of this volume: based on his own experience and perspective as a writer, DIKE-OGU CHUKWUMERIJE reflects on the literary landscape and publishing in Nigeria. His novel *The African-American* was long-listed for the 2012 Wole Soyinka Literature Prize in Africa and his self-published poetry collection *The Revolution Has No Tribe*, from which we reproduce three poems, is organised around themes such as history, democracy, underdevelopment and Africans in the diaspora. With his contribution on

Ghana as a business location, RAINER EMIG looks at (West) Africa from another angle. Using his expertise in English literary and cultural studies, he confronts the stereotypical perception of Africa in the Western world. He scrutinises Ghanaian newspaper articles and other local sources as well as Western perspectives in order to explore and evaluate different opinions on Ghana's economic conditions and prospects. The Biafra War (1967-70) has been one of the most prominent topics in Nigerian literature, which is why SUSANNE GEHRMANN dedicates her article to representations of this civil war. Approaching the issue through the lens of African literary studies, she pays particular attention to child soldiers as protagonists and narrators. Starting from Ken Saro-Wiwa's influential *Sozaboy*, she moves on to recent rewritings by the diasporic third-generation authors Uzodinma Iweala, Chris Abani, Biyi Bandele, Chimamanda Ngozi Adichie and Helon Habila. Compared to the previous contributions, ANKE BARTELS deals with a different genre, namely African theatre, with a special focus on women playwrights. The article brings together her main research interests, which are postcolonial literatures (especially from Africa) and 20th-century drama. Summarising the genre's history, she distinguishes between African and Western theatre standards and techniques. This overview sets the ground for her analysis of gender-related issues in selected plays by Ama Ata Aidoo from Ghana, Julie Okoh from Nigeria, Sindiwe Magona and Muthal Naidoo from South Africa. As this list shows, her survey links the book's sections on West and South Africa. Bartels concludes with an annotated list of recommended further reading on African (women) playwrights, which will prove particularly helpful for newcomers to this field. Henning Marquardt provides a similar but more general bibliography at the end of the volume.

The contributions by Henning Marquardt and Riaan Oppelt are both concerned with apartheid, though in different ways. With his focus on the 1920s to 1940s, HENNING MARQUARDT studies a period that has often been over-shadowed by the academic interest in apartheid literature and has therefore been marginalised in South African literary history. Yet, these early decades deserve critical attention because they have shaped the country's literary scene of political writing. Taking into account the different publishing agendas and target audiences, he investigates how publications by missionary and secular presses attend to themes of urban and rural life, war, indigenous communities and miscegenation. Looking at theatre during and after apartheid, the South African literary scholar RIAAN OPPELT provides an overview of plays and genres, including the rarely studied Afrikaans and 'Coloured' theatre. While theatre used to be divided in the 'old' South Africa between a theatre of rebellion and a theatre of the establishment, the strands have merged in the 'new' South Africa. As his contribution makes evident, contemporary theatre is no longer preoccupied with the past but also engages with immediate socio-political and cultural concerns. In his contribution on contemporary oral poetry, RUSSELL KASCHULA argues that digital media have had a strong impact on this genre. Modern technology helps to capture and circulate African poetry so that students and teachers from around the world can get access to a wide corpus of oral poetry, including rap, slam and *izibongo*, i.e. Xhosa oral poetry. Based on his expertise in African language studies, especially in isiXhosa and oral literature, Kaschula provides a case study on the poems by the late Bongani Sitole, whose collection *Qhiwu-u-u-la!! Return to the Fold!!* contains selected poems in both isiXhosa and English.

In keeping with the agenda of *anglistik & englischunterricht*, the final section continues the enquiries into research and teaching. It provides case studies and material for further reading in order to promote the presence of African literatures and cultures at schools and universities. Like the historian Kirsten Rüther, ELLEN GRÜNKEMEIER and JANA GOHRISCH explore the intersections of history and literary studies, but – given their academic background in English literary and cultural studies – they approach the issue from another angle. Reflecting on their experiences with interdisciplinary co-teaching, they provide concrete examples of university courses on South and West Africa that were based on the expertise of lecturers and students from the English and the History departments at the Leibniz University of Hanover. The issue concludes with two documents compiled by Henning Marquardt: the chronology of events and texts provides a general frame of reference; the annotated bibliography comprises entries on African (literary) history, on African literatures, films and music and on teaching resources. Students, teachers, university lecturers and everyone else who is interested in African voices will thus encounter many suggestions on how to approach Anglophone African literatures and cultures.

As editors, we would like to thank the contributors for their interest in this interdisciplinary venture and the work they have put into their respective papers. Moreover, we extend our thanks to the series editors, Gabriele Linke, Holger Rossow and Merle Tönnies, who entirely trusted our choice of topic, scholars and focus. Last but not least, we thank Henning Marquardt for his work that went far beyond technical editing which he performed with absolute reliability, patience and carefulness.

Hanover, October 2012

Jana Gohrisch and Ellen Grünkemeier

Notes

1 Chukwumerije (2008: 17-18, 80). As a service for his Western readers Chukwumerije provides an extended glossary with details on African history, geography and other issues.
2 Chukwumerije (2008: 18).
3 *English G1 für Gymnasien. Band A 5*, Berlin, 2010. Like Klett's *Green Line* school book (for high schools) in North Rhine-Westphalia, Cornelsen's *English G1 für Gymnasien* for Berlin and Brandenburg and North Rhine-Westphalia has the USA as its topic in grade 8 and moves on to general issues such as human rights and environmental issues in grade 10.
4 There are, however, additional resources that teachers can employ such as the volumes published in Langenscheidt's Viewfinder Series for pupils up to grade 10: *The Postcolonial Experience. Decolonizing the Mind* (2006) compiled by Michael Mitchell with excerpts from short stories and other texts by postcolonial writers, among them three South Africans. With *South Africa. The Rainbow Nation at the Cape* (2009), Claudia Drawe edited a volume exclusively on South Africa. This may go well with the *Green Line* grade 10 school book for North Rhine-Westpahlia that has multiethnic Britain and South Africa for its postcolonial topics. The 'new' South Africa features also in *Camden Town 6* (published in 2005 by Schöningh). Rather than present other Anglophone African countries, *The New Summit. Text and Methods* (2009), edited by Engelbert Thaler for high schools in Lower Saxony, mentions Kenya only in a chapter on globalisation. The result of this cursory glance at school books is sobering: if they contain Africa at all,

it is South Africa after apartheid that is deemed interesting while 'the rest' of the continent is silenced.
5 Döring (2008), Eckstein (2007), Jansohn (2002).
6 Antor (2006), Schulze-Engler & Helff (2009).
7 Eisenmann, Grimm & Volkmann (2010).
8 Feuerle (2010: 46).
9 Volkmann (2010: 165-182).
10 George (2009: 20).
11 *Ibid.* 32.
12 *Ibid.* 30-31.
13 *Ibid.* 31.
14 See also Döring (2008: 111).
15 Volkmann, too, warns of the "realist fallacy", which he defines as "the tokenistic concept that a single novel can be regarded as 'representative' of a country's reality or that the reality depicted in the novel is actually the one reality of the country in question" (Volkmann 2010: 168). Drawing on an earlier publication (by Brumfit and Carter, 1986), he states that texts select elements of reality and then "combine them into a new concept or model of reality which exists only within the text" (*Ibid.*). Volkmann then underlines the creative activity of the readers who shape the texts along their own realities and needs. Given the wide-spread stereotypes of Africa, however, we have to be aware of the fact that students bring them to the texts as well, finding them supported rather than refuted due to the selective reading process that values things known over those unknown.
16 Featherstone (2005: 8).
17 See also Coundouriotis (2009: 63).

Bibliography

Antor, Heinz (Ed.): *Inter- und Transkulturelle Studien. Theoretische Grundlagen und interdisziplinäre Praxis*, Heidelberg, 2006.
Camden Town 6, Paderborn, 2005.
Chukwumerije, Dike-Ogu: *The Revolution Has No Tribe. Contemporary Poems on African History, Culture and Society*, London, 2008.
Coundouriotis, Eleni: "Why History Matters in the African Novel". – In Gaurav Desai (Ed.): *Teaching the African Novel*, New York, 2009, pp. 53-69.
Desai, Gaurav (Ed.): *Teaching the African Novel*, New York, 2009.
Döring, Tobias: *Postcolonial Literatures in English*, Stuttgart, 2008.

Drawe, Claudia (Ed.): *South Africa. The Rainbow Nation at the Cape*, Berlin, 2009.

Eckstein, Lars (Ed.): *English Literatures Across the Globe. A Companion*, Paderborn, 2007.

English G1 für Gymnasien. Band A 5, Berlin, 2010.

Eisenmann, Maria, Nancy Grimm & Laurenz Volkmann (Eds.): *Teaching the New English Cultures and Literatures*, Heidelberg, 2010.

Featherstone, Simon: *Postcolonial Cultures*, Edinburgh, 2005.

Feuerle, Gisela: "Teaching South African Literatures. A Diversity of Writings and Experiences". – In Maria Eisenmann, Nancy Grimm & Laurenz Volkmann (Eds.): *Teaching the New English Cultures and Literatures*, Heidelberg, 2010, pp. 43-57.

George, Olakunle: "African Novels and the Question of Theory". – In Gaurav Desai (Ed.): *Teaching the African Novel*, New York, 2009, pp. 19-36.

Jansohn, Christa (Ed.): *Companion to the New Literatures in English*, Berlin, 2002.

Mitchell, Michael (Ed.): *The Postcolonial Experience. Decolonizing the Mind*, Berlin, 2006.

Schulze-Engler, Frank & Sissy Helff (Eds.): *Transcultural English Studies. Theories, Fictions, Realities*, Amsterdam & New York, 2009.

Thaler, Engelbert (Ed.): *The New Summit. Text and Methods*, Paderborn, 2009.

Volkmann, Laurenz: "Disturbing Literary Representation of the New South Africa". – In Maria Eisenmann, Nancy Grimm & L. V. (Eds.): *Teaching the New English Cultures and Literatures*, Heidelberg, 2010, pp. 165-182.

Kirsten Rüther (Vienna)

On the Book Shelf in My Study.
Approaching African Literatures and Cultures from an Historian's Perspective

1. Introduction

This is a reflection on, rather than a systematic exploration of, the boundaries between African history and literature. These boundaries exist, but there is ample opportunity to cross them. Even though I am not a scholar of literatures and cultures myself, as an historian of Africa and as a passionate reader I engage with this intersection quite regularly. In fact, my academic exposure to African literatures and cultures occurred through the two editors of this volume when, a couple of years ago, we taught a sequence of interdisciplinary seminars on topics to be explored from both historical and literary perspectives.[1] In many ways, hence, this is a highly personal reflection, especially as I have taken the literary examples to which I will refer in the course of this article just from the book shelf in my study. There, in the course of the past twenty years, novels (rather than plays, films or poems) have piled up either according to the uncoordinated logics of simple reading pleasure or subsequent to excellent recommendations of friends and colleagues. In what is to follow I will indicate how historians have engaged with the field of literature. I will also point to some achievements which have been reached when interdisciplinary research teams, comprising scholars of history as well as of literature, engaged with research questions and topics of joint interest.

In my capacity as a lecturer and researcher of African history I am particularly concerned with the analysis of change in, and transformations of, African societies over time. I share this interest with many of my colleagues in the highly interdisciplinary field of African studies which comprises a variety of expertises such as, to name but a few, languages, literature, anthropology, politics – and history. As an historian of Africa with a particular inclination towards social and cultural history I have long been interested in exchange and cooperation with colleagues who engage in the fields of literature and culture.

Against this backdrop, let me briefly explain my understanding of interdisciplinarity. Basically, interdisciplinary ventures capture efforts to address topics and research questions from more than one disciplinary perspective. Rather than to argue about methodology the aim is to engage with different research questions in order to use the oral and documentary record of a society in innovative ways so as to improve understandings or to change paradigms in the writing of history and in conducting research in other disciplines. Interdisciplinarity is not about teaching historical methods to others who are not versed in this art. It is about letting these others participate in one's research agendas and, in turn, about gaining insight into the research questions with which others concern themselves. Sometimes the impulse to such exchange and cooperation results from a certain frustration with the current state of one's own discipline, for instance, when pertinent questions cannot be answered in a satisfactory manner, when debates stagnate, or when one is limited by the circumscribed ways of using data and empirical material. African history has benefited from various such interdisciplinary research engagements. In South Africa particularly, my primary area of research, over the past few years an interdisciplinary research project between historians, archaeologists, anthropologists and linguists on precolonial and early colonial history has shifted research paradigms in South African history and archaeology.[2]

In fact, while historians of Africa share an interest in the analysis of culture and society with disciplines such as the social sciences and anthropology, the fields of cultural expression and textual analysis represent research areas where historians particularly benefit from linking up with scholars of literature. Moreover, ever since social and cultural historians have embarked on revealing the multiperspectivity of historical dynamics, historians of Africa have changed their ways of narrating history. Many have learnt to devote much effort to capture as explicitly as possible narratives of experience. To work with such narratives implies to present topics from a possibly broad range of historical agents' views. Scholars of African literatures and historians of

Africa engage with the same material, for instance, with narratives of the past, the self or of society. However, they have dealt with different functions of such materials. While some historians are on the search for alternative ways of narrating history, literary texts capture, albeit in fictional guise, perspectives and experiences related to, rather than reflective of, social change. This provides good reason to elaborate on such texts from historical as well as from literary perspectives.

Here I will show how as an historian I approach several selected literary texts, not to offer an analysis of them (as to do this I would not be qualified), but to understand them as impulses for raising questions within my own art. Subsequent to this introduction, I will devote a second section of this article to sources and texts. As I will show, many of the narratives and personal accounts that historians use, create and assemble as sources resonate with African literature to the effect that textual analysis as conducted by scholars of literature enhances our understanding of these primary materials. I will especially focus on historians' approaches to documentaries and life histories as these provide two major bodies of historical sources with which historians engage and which border on both history and literature. I will also address projects in which, by reading primary texts, interdisciplinary research groups made use of each others' expertise and jointly managed to raise and answer questions about crucial transformations in African societies.

There is a conventional understanding of history as providing a frame, context and thematic depth for present interactions and entanglements which unfold between groups and individuals, and for the personal experience of people more generally. According to such notion, history also ought to provide a background and orienting structure against which the artistic expression of societies takes place, even though, of course, any artistic product by definition transcends the boundaries of history. Frequently historians feel a degree of unease about such conventions because, even though history is about evidence and, to some extent, about what happened, it is not necessarily about the 'truth' or 'facts' and always more than just 'background information'. Like other publicly accessible narratives, historical narratives are interrelated with the cultural expression of the time and spatial location of their producers. They endow the past with meaning and, in this capacity, bear a relationship to literature.[3] Historians have taken this as a challenge to reflect upon the kind of narrativity the history they write adheres to. Meanwhile many historians give high priority to the provision of more than one point of view. They attempt to uncover the agency of women, workers, peasants, criminals and many other groups whose voices and perceptions have long been relegated to the shadow of history and have effectively been subdued especially within the context of writing political and national histories. Even the history of Africa, hard to believe as to now, has not necessarily been a history of African agency.

In the end, however, history is an art which goes beyond mere multiperspectivity. It consolidates, at least to a certain extent, the variety of views it digs out and tries to propose a 'general' or 'overall' argument. To my understanding this constitutes a crucial difference to how literature works. In this article, therefore, a third section will take up the issue of how history moves between multiperspectivity and general argument about social change or, to put it differently, how historians try to capture perspectives which relate to social change. The section will concern itself with how an engagement with literary texts can be crucial to understanding history from more than just a circumscribed disciplinary perspective and prod my profession with new questions. In fact, a number of historians and literary writers actually share research interests. As the narratives of history and literature may overlap substantially and as both can be concerned with the explanation and the interpretation of the African past, there are instances in which historians and literary writers give each other the cue. At times this happens in a spirit of cooperation, but at others it happens in a spirit of competition. The third section will therefore also suggest to read in conjunction certain texts of distinct genres. Sometimes texts of different making offer joint or conflictual narratives on history and society.

2. *Sources and Texts*

As a social historican with a strong inclination towards culture and multiperspectivity I have a particular interest in narrative sources and various kinds of written and spoken text.[4] I am generally concerned with using as broad a range of evidence as possible. After all, these sources constitute the empirical data from which representatives of my profession reconstruct social practices, and on the basis of which we interpret transformations or engage with historiographical and theoretical debates. As a result, historians carefully assemble source material from various archives. More importantly, they figure out procedures of reading, assessing and contextualising the assembled material. It takes students of history many years to learn to use them in the pursuit of their respective research questions.

In recent decades notions of what constitutes an archive have changed fundamentally. No longer do historians rely on the official documentation of the state, the church or other political institutions only. Of course, they still work with official records kept in such institutions which in their own way represent encounter zones between the public, professional users and the spheres of former, or ongoing, power and authority. To uncover in such archives the perspectives of the marginalised and unprivileged always constitutes a challenge as one has to read with, and against, the classificatory system.[5] Similarly, to name but one further example, mission archives provide huge bodies of material to be explored in detail.[6] Working with these texts it is, of course, crucial to read 'against the grain'. Probably not everybody would go as far as to treat missionary texts as "inscribed forms of oral tradition".[7] If, however, one wants to treat missionary texts like that, a great deal more is necessary to decode them than understanding these texts as mere representation. One would, for instance, have to read them against the intellectual world of missionaries and the social practice of mission encounters as well as against African cultural practice and the converts' larger world view. Furthermore, one would have to politically and socially contextualise the representations captured in these texts. As one author, Richard Roberts, put it, "representations [themselves] have distinctive histories, but [...] without attention to how humans act on them, or in spite of them, representations are hollow explanations for historical change".[8] In any way, and to return to the case of missionary texts, the genres of historical sources overlap and it would be an oversimplification to neatly separate so-called mission perspectives from perceived local ones.

The body of sources consulted for a particular topic may comprise spoken texts such as interviews and, probably to a lesser extent, oral traditions.[9] Whereas oral traditions tend to reproduce – shiftingly – dominant and authoritative interpretations of the past, interviews in which more recent experiences become the focus of inquiry, frequently collected as part of oral history projects, try to recover the experience of people who have been hidden from history (as their experience was not kept in any of the official archives). Of course, depending on which people are selected for interviewing, oral material is biased as well.[10] Usually it has to be counterprovided with written archival evidence. If necessary, historians work with the local press and the 'grey' material of NGOs or other activist groupings. The local press has long been an under-explored source, but this is beginning to change. Not only does it provide a rich source to be tapped for information, but, more interestingly, it is a source which pieces together text and illustration, thus showing how the worlds of journalism, neighbourhood information and advertising intersect and conflict.

In addition, historians work with personal letters and other material assembled in so-called tin trunks.[11] These are boxes or containers in which people keep letters, newspaper clippings, photographs, diaries and many other personal belongings they assembled over the course of their lives or inherited from family and friends. Historians also use travelogues and published journals.[12] Many more sources handed down in textual form are possible to imagine. Against the background of such broad empirical basis it can be useful to sort out approaches to texts in conjunction with experts on textual analysis – I am thinking of scholars of African languages, literatures and cultures. Anthropologist Karin Barber edited an excellent volume on many of Africa's "hidden histories" in which scholars of various academic backgrounds engage jointly with African people's everyday uses of literacy by exploring their repertoires for social activities.[13] The spread of literacy caused, and accompanied, one of the most crucial historical transformations of African societies, and it is highly interesting to understand how African men and women contoured a sense of self and personhood by resorting to literacy. Connected with this is the question why these processes of change took place at a certain moment in history. Not only does the volume show how, in their everyday lives, African people created, used, approached and appropriated the medium of text on a personal level or on a level which shaped their self-conception as persons; it also explores the making of reading cultures, publics and the press in African societies. Furthermore, it focuses on the ways in which people worked with text as a social or political strategy of distinction and empowerment, how they organised themselves and how they contributed to the emergence of new genres. Especially in the fields of popular literature, personal writing and genres not originally intended for publication, as well as in the analysis of the local press, enormous benefit can be derived from an interdisciplinary understanding of individuals' and particular social groups' experiences and uses of textual media in history. Barber's volume also provides reproductions of original texts such as letters, obituaries, newspaper clippings and journal extracts, many of which were translated from various African languages into English for the purpose of this publication. They are now accessible to English readers and demonstrate the richness of reading and writing in Africa.

The volume achieves even more: to work and cooperate in interdisciplinary fashion around a notion of literature, writing and literacy opens up the preconceived category of 'literature' which, as a concept and a term, was not originally derived from African cultural practice and expression, oriented more stringently towards orality and performance. In fact, as African societies' encounters with writing, written literature and literacy occurred in the context of religious change and colonialism, it is crucial to problematise the notion of 'literature' in order to move beyond the description of African history and cultural practice as one of aberration, deficit and difference.

For reasons of teaching, especially for teaching on an introductory level, I do not exclusively watch out for texts which are literary in the strict sense. I also look for texts which *resemble* both literary and academic texts. I search for texts which resonate with academic issues but which, at the same time, challenge stereotypes that are relevant to students who grew up in an environment where knowledge about African societies is scarce. The texts are meant to create space for new images and a first differentiated understanding of social dynamics. For 'newcomers' to African history, texts which are not purely academic are very helpful as they help sharpen the students' sense of regional differences within Africa and of a general timeframe. In this regard, especially in the initial phase of 'encountering Africa' on an academic level, exposure to documentaries and life histories can be important. They provide a terminology different from the ones in the media or in the world of advertising, and yet intersect with everyday rather than academic language. Jonny Steinberg's *Three Letter Plague*, for instance, provides such an engaging reading experience.[14] The documentary, in which an academically working journalist, or a journalistically inclined academic, engages with the question why Sizwe, a young man in South Africa, does not test for HIV/AIDS. It explores Sizwe's ponderings against the background of debates carried out in the secondary literature. Notes and further reading at the end of the text channel readers to the academic base of Steinberg's writing.

In a different way, I also appreciated the memoir of the Nigerian historian Toyin Falola. In a funny, poetic and appealing language *A Mouth Sweeter than Salt* describes a childhood of the 1950s and 1960s.[15] A broad range of historical themes are woven into the narrative, even though they are not fully explored in the fashion of a professional historian. Students, whose first encounter with Nigeria might be based on this narrative, certainly feel challenged to explore the political aspects of the period of Nigeria's independence and hopefully resort to academic reading in such an endeavour.

Life histories crafted in a colonial context are particularly interesting for other reasons.[16] Many of them were produced in a joint effort between one (black) person who narrated his or her life and another (white) person who converted the spoken account into a written one, who arranged and sometimes even published the narrative. In African history, this is an important text form. Very frequently the lives and voices of (historical) Africans reach us in entangled and partly subdued fashion. Against the backdrop of an abundance of such narratives I will comment on only a few of them. Margaret McCord's and Katie Makanya's narrative on a young South African woman who in the late 1890s, as a member of an African choir, travelled to Great Britain and who, back in South Africa, married and worked in the Durban hospital of Dr. James McCord, introduces its readers to the South African worlds of colonialism, apartheid, medicine and labour migration – to name but a few.[17] Katie who sang to Queen Victoria and who could have stayed in Britain decided to return to the country of her birth where she wanted to start a family. The narrative records how she married, moved between Johannesburg and Durban and, in the hospital of Dr. McCord, assisted the doctor in organising the ward, in treating the patients and explaining the medicines to them. It would be a futile exercise to disentangle the voices of Katie and her biographer, and the insistent reader may have to recognise that her or his quest for the supposed authenticity of an African voice will never be answered convincingly. And yet *The Calling of Katie Makanya* remains an illuminating text for historical investigation. In other texts voices such as Katie Makanya's would not even glimmer through and illuminate topics such as travelling to Victorian Britain or working in the health sector in 20th-century South Africa. The text resonates with a way of presenting African people's lives in fictional contexts. For this reason the view of literary experts on the account would certainly enrich and sharpen the historical interpretation of the source.

Another life story in which voices are intertwined in even more intricate ways is, for instance, Mary F. Smith's, Michael Smith's and Baba of Karo's narrative on a Muslim Hausa woman's biography and on her outlooks on life.[18] *Baba of Karo: A Woman of the Muslim Hausa* captures the world and secluded voice of a woman whom the anthropologist's wife was equipped to approach, not the male anthropologist himself. Baba of Karo, who had been born in 1877, had a lot to tell to the young Mary Smith when they met in 1949. To endow with academic legitimacy the outcome of these women's encounters the anthropologist husband added an "introduction" of 24 pages which itself reveals many of the gender dynamics at work in European, US-American and academic contexts.[19] As problematic as these mediated narratives are as sources for historical analysis, they remain important texts in which voices became entangled and from which – in the context of a general lack of sources – historians draw conclusions concerning social transformations and transcultural conversations at least tentatively.

Many such texts have attracted attention from authors eager to revisit them for historical or literary investigation. Some texts have been republished with interdisciplinary combinations of introduction and afterword to make them more easily accessible to modern readers. *Zulu Woman*, a narration of the life of Christina Sibiya, wife of the Zulu king Solomon, is such a text in case. Marcia Wright, an historian, and Liz Gunner, a scholar of literature and culture, prepared the text originally composed by Rebecca Reyher, an organiser of the National Woman's Party in the US and a feminist journalist.[20] In fact, not much information is available on the domestic lives of African kings. For this reason alone the manuscript is invaluable.

Another text revisited more recently would be *Black Hamlet*. The text was prepared for re-publication by the joint team of Saul Dubow, an historian, and Jacqueline Rose, a scholar of English literature.[21] It records a sequence of conversations which took place in 1920s Johannesburg between Chavafambira, a Manyika herbalist, diviner and migrant labourer from Zimbabwe, and Wulf Sachs, a recently immigrated Jewish psycholanalyst from Lithuania. The voice of Chavafambira remains largely hidden, and yet it is one of the first texts providing a black African man with a voice and an inner world. *Black Hamlet* resonates with debates which are still in full swing. It touches upon the possibilities and the limits of intercultural dialogue and, more generally, it addresses the ambiguous cultural translations at work. Chavafambira's and Sachs's encounter was intercultural as well as intra-professional. It brought together two men whose opportunities in South Africa were heavily shaped by the racism of their time. In this regard the narrative inspires and informs debates about the nature of South African racism and its textual representation, but also about intersecting fields of health-related professionalism.

These few examples taken from the book shelf in my study can be made productive for a fruitful cooperation between scholars of history, literature and culture. They demonstrate that there is an ongoing interest in rereading historical texts and in relating them to issues of academic debate relevant in more than one Africanist discipline.

3. Capturing Perspectives which Relate to Social Transformations. Historical and Alternative Narrations

Current research tendencies indicate that in the years to come considerably more research will be done on topics relating to issues of migration and mobility. Historians of Africa will face the challenge to connect historical perspectives to research conducted by the social and political sciences on more recent phenomena. In this context it could be worthwhile to take into consideration fiction which deals with experiences of migration and mobility. Some of the novels by Tahar Ben Jelloun on leaving and returning migrants might be especially instructive. Jelloun's novels are set in Morocco, where young people leave for Europe or where they wait to be able to leave. It is also a setting to which 'successful' migrants return in old age.[22]

As regards the assessment of the historical dimension of such current phenomena, there is a number of novels on the book shelf in my study which could be considered. Take, for instance, the novels *Mine Boy* by Peter Abrahams or *Blanket Boy's Moon* by Peter Lanham and A.S. Mopeli-Paulus, set, in the first case, in South Africa and, in the second, in Lesotho. In both settings labour migration to the South African gold mines provides the common theme.[23] Labour migration in South Africa is, of course, a topic of its own and does not immediately link up to the Moroccan experience so prevalent in these days. South African labour migration takes place between city and countryside, within the country and, regionally, across national borders. And yet, both the 'Moroccan' as well as the 'South African' experience revolve around the insecurity of labourers once they arrive in a new place. The novels are about efforts to create a family and a sense of respect around oneself.[24] As an historian I would be interested to learn whether and how scholars of literature are interested in the topic of migration as well. If this was the case they should perhaps seize the opportunity to detect in such texts topics of mutual concern.

In the history of many African societies particular forms of migration and mobility have been caused by the implications of war and exile. Browsing along the book shelf my eyes stop at Nuruddin Farah's *Links*. The text features a Somali refugee to the United States who, after many years in exile, returns to visit his mother's grave and who struggles to cope with the business of family and home in a setting in which he now feels like a stranger.[25] Again, the topics of war and exile do not immediately connect with those forms of migration which result from the need to earn wages in Europe or South Africa. In an interdisciplinary research venture on long-term dynamics of mobility and migration in African societies, texts such as these – and many others – would be worth consulting in order to grasp the cultural expression of such fundamental social experiences.

As far as the selection of such texts is concerned I must remark on the various languages in which African literatures are being produced. Most historians of Africa would be aware of the fact that if they approach literature they ought not to reduce themselves to approaching African literature in English only. To study the history of Africa requires an engagement with more than just one language introduced in the course of colonialism. Works by authors such as the Algerian literary writer, historian and film maker, Assia Djebar, or António Lobo Antunes, military doctor of the colonial Portuguese army, psychiatrist and literary writer, enlarge the often artificially constricted Anglophone perspective on Africa's social transformations and remind one that the history of Anglophone Africa at time connects, but also contrasts, with the history of Francophone and Lusophone African countries.[26] As an historian I was struck by the multiperspectivity explored in Djebar's and Antunes's texts. They render civil wars and other harsh conflicts intelligible from a variety of viewpoints, sometimes dramatically intersecting and conflicting with each other, in the case of Antunes's *Guten Abend ihr Dinge hier unten* radically competing with one another to the extent that no voice succeeds in dominating the other but that, concomitantly, no voice is in a position to claim for itself the space it would need to be recognised as a coherent view. To an historian with a strong inclination to present various view points, these texts, by using a broad range of stylistic devices, breathtakingly convey not only the inner conflicts and the wretchedness of characters in ways difficult to achieve for historians. They challenged my understanding of historical narratives which, as explained in the introduction, are usually characterised by a clear tendency to consolidate conflicting views at least in the concluding remarks. But coping with insecurity, conflict and marginalisation may require innovative ways of presenting historical narratives. Certainly for social and cultural historians the ability of literary writers to portray the unresolved experience people have had in wars provides stimulating incentives. They challenge us to engage, within our discipline, with the task and desire to convey and leave open such unconcluded, and inconclusive, experiences which we encounter in our source material as well.

If historians approach African literature and culture, they at times rub shoulders with the artists themselves. Two examples of historians engaging with the art of literary writing may be illustrated here. The first is about an historian's and a literary writer's disjoined presentations of one important marker of a country's past. It is about rivalling interpretations of the Zimbabwean past as embodied in Solomon Mutswairo's literary and David N. Beach's historical rendering of the story of Mapondera, a Shona social bandit.[27] In Zimbabwe's prolonged history of anti-colonial struggle this man who lived from about 1840 to 1904 became an important figure in the Zimbabwean national consciousness. In about 1894, two years before the First Chimurenga, the Shona and Ndebele people's resistance movement against the rule of the British South Africa Company, Mapondera embarked upon activities as a social bandit. He and a large group of allies fought a pitched battle with the Rhodesian colonial authorities seven years later, in 1901. For this he was tried and imprisoned. Mutswairo's decision to present this story as a novel rested on his intention to celebrate "a true story and not a mythical figment" as it "would make more provocative reading than if cast as a 'plain history'". He adds that "the scenes are as truthfully imagined as possible".[28] Shortly after this publication Beach embarked on an effort to capture and rescue from lore and imagination the "history" of a man and the "facts" and "events" of a century which, to his mind, were currently being "prettified".[29] He considered it his duty as an historian to put straight some distorted knowledge about an important moment in the making of modern Zimbabwe. More than 440 footnotes adjoining a text of some 60 pages and an extended index of places, people, rulers and "dynasties" turn the text into what Beach designs as factual history. In fact, Mapondera's story had entered public consciousness in various forms. Both Mutswairo and Beach responded to this and created their own narratives of the past – none of them immediately faithful to the oral remembering people might have shared about Mapondera among themselves. Thus, a writer and an historian entered a debate about the past of a society they live in. It proves especially rewarding to read the two texts in conjunction so as to grasp the political debate which lies beyond the story of the two texts.

A different dynamic of an historian's and a literary writer's art adjoining each other can be found in some of the texts by Nigel Penn and André Brink. One of them a South African historian, the other a South African writer, they both engage with archival sources and foreground the narrative. Nigel Penn, for instance, rendered the account of the 18th-century Cape brewer Willem Menssink and thus placed the readers of his text between the blurred boundaries of a novel and a kind of history focused on the micro-level and on the sphere of the everyday.[30] Willem Menssink's story covers that of a Dutch brewer who, at the initiative of the Dutch East India Company, was shipped to the Cape in 1694 in order to improve beer brewing. He was married twice and had a number of relationships with slave women. His favourite slave woman and a number of menfolk around her attempted to murder his wife and were subsequently executed. Menssink, in turn, was divorced and expelled from the Cape elite. Penn provides a multilayered account of a constellation of people and endows a small number of 18th-century Cape characters with a history who otherwise would have gone unnoticed. He fits in layers of structural information where the source basis of an otherwise well-documented episode of Cape history become thin. And he 'goes literary' as far as possible.

Corresponding efforts of a writer 'going historical' can be found in André Brink's works such as *Praying Mantis* or *Instant in the Wind*.[31] One account fictionalises the life of Cupido Kakerlak, an 18th-century intermediary figure, a Khoikhoi who converted to Christianity. After his conversion, Cupido started to preach independently from the missionaries. He had great success but later lost his community. The other novel, also set in the 18th-century Cape, tells the story of a runaway slave, Adam Mantoor, who beyond the frontier of the Cape settlement meets Elisabeth Larsson, accompanying her Swedish husband-explorer into the Karoo desert, where he died. In the desert the slave and the white woman manage to survive and to love each other. On their return back to the Cape Colony and, this time, beyond the boundary of the desert, however, their relationship is doomed to break due to racism from which the two cannot escape in the Cape. *Praying Mantis* ends with a "note", i.e. three pages on which Brink refers to the sources and secondary literature he consulted. *An Instant in the Wind* is also based on material stored in Cape and London archives. Different from what a historian can do, Brink endows his protagonists with inner voices and lets them lead monologues where the source material remains silent on such perspectives. This way crucial gaps are filled in. In a context of white domination, both Brink and Penn provide the marginalised with unfragmented, linear and coherent narrative.

4. Conclusion

I have shown how as an historian I engage with literary texts and, in the pursuit of shared research questions, with colleagues from other Africanist disciplines who are interested in African societies' engagement with literature, culture and social change. It is more than worthwhile to cross the boundaries between the disciplines. We come from different angles but share an interest in texts, in their making and in the ways they relate to social transformation. Against this backdrop it is also highly productive to interrogate one another about our respective goals in 'teaching Africa' at university level.

The forms of instructing each other can be multifaceted. They can be traced in interdisciplinary research ventures. They can also be found in a mutual exploration of each others' narrative conventions and archives, and thus in assessing the conditions of ascribing meaning to stories, characters, historical structures and events.

Notes

1 Approaching the issue through the lens of literary and cultural studies, Grünkemeier and Gohrisch provide a perspective that corresponds to this article. In the interdisciplinary classes we dealt with the following literary texts: Magona (1998), Reyher (1999 [first published in 1948]) and Plaatje (1978 [first published in 1930]). For a discussion on Magona and Reyher, see the article by Grünkemeier; Plaatje is addressed in Marquardt's contribution to this volume.
2 Mulaudzi, Schoemann & Chirikure (2010). See also the special issue of *Journal of Southern African Studies* (2012) on South Africa's 500-Year-Initiative.
3 White (1973).
4 Historians also work with quantitative or serial data. In this case they are likely to provide a particular focus on structural history (which is a kind of history concerning itself with structures of change rather than with the agency of individuals). Many historians explore visual material. They often work with a wide notion of what constitutes a 'text'. These are sources, however, which for reasons of economy I will not consider in this contribution.
5 For an engagement with these archives and the strategies to detect in them 'counter'-narratives such as gender-based perspectives of history, see, for instance, Burton (2004).
6 Attwell (1999), De Kock (1996), Rüther (2012).
7 Hunt (1999: 23).
8 Roberts (1999: 392).
9 Working with oral traditions was important when the academic writing of African history started off in the 1950s. For various reasons not to be

commented upon here reference to, and use of, this source had to be modified in fundamental ways. See the still magisterial introduction by Vansina (1961).
10 For an introduction, see Perks & Thomson (1998).
11 For an excellent history based on tin trunk documents, see Krüger (2009).
12 There is a huge body of literature on travelogues and travel writing. Here I want to leave the reader with one splendid reference only, Fabian (2001).
13 Barber (2006).
14 Steinberg (2008).
15 Falola (2004).
16 In her contribution to this volume, Strauhs also explores life narratives.
17 McCord (1995).
18 Smith (1954).
19 *Ibid.* 11-34.
20 Reyher (1999).
21 Sachs (1996), originally published in London in 1937, republished as *Black Anger* in Boston in 1947 and 1957 and, as a mass market paperback, in 1969. There is no immediate reference as to why the original book title refers to Hamlet. Certainly the narrative as provided by Wulf Sachs presents the story of a tragic figure 'doomed' to fail. As the title of the republished manuscript indicates, however, there were other contexts in which Chafavarimba's life might be interpreted.
22 Ben Jelloun (2001), (2006).
23 In his contribution to this volume, Marquardt also analyses *Mine Boy* with regard to labour migration.
24 Abrahams (1946), Lanham & Mopeli-Paulus (1953).
25 Farah (2003).
26 Antunes (2005), Djebar (1996).
27 Beach (1989), Mutswairo (1983).
28 Mutswairo (1983: 4).
29 Beach (1989: 5).
30 Penn (1999: 9-72).
31 Brink (2006), (1976).

Bibliography

Abrahams, Peter: *Mine Boy*, London, 1946.
Antunes, António Lobo: *Guten Abend ihr Dinge hier unten*, München, 2005. [orig. *Boa Tarde às Coisas Aqui Baixo*, Lissabon, 2003, unavailable in English]
Attwell, David: "Reprisals of Modernity in Black South African 'Mission' Writing", *Journal of Southern African Studies* 25:2, 1999, 267-285.
Barber, Karin (Ed.): *Africa's Hidden Histories. Everyday Literacy and Making the Self*, Bloomington, 2006.
Beach, David N.: *Mapondera. Heroism and History in Northern Zimbabwe 1840-1904*, Gweru, 1989.
Brink, André: *An Instant in the Wind*, London, 1976.
---: *Praying Mantis*, London, 2006.
Burton, Antoinette: "Archive Stories. Gender in the Making of Imperial and Colonial Histories". – In Philippa Levine (Ed.): *Gender and Empire,* Oxford, 2004, pp. 281-293.
Djebar, Assia: *Algerian White. A Narrative*, Paris, 1996.
Fabian, Johannes: *Im Tropenfieber. Wissenschaft und Wahn in der Erforschung Zentralafrikas*, München, 2001.
Falola, Toyin: *A Mouth Sweeter Than Salt. An African Memoir*, Ann Arbor, 2004.
Farah, Nuruddin: *Links*, New York, 2003.
Hunt, Nancy Rose: *A Colonial Lexicon of Birth Ritual, Medicalization, and Mobility in the Congo*, Durham & London, 1999.
Ben Jelloun, Tahar: *A Palace in the Old Village*, London, 2001.
---: *Partir*, Paris, 2006.
De Kock, Leon: *Civilising Barbarians. Missionary Narrative and African Textual Response in Nineteenth-Century South Africa*, Johannesburg, 1996.
Krüger, Gesine: *Schrift – Macht – Alltag. Lesen und Schreiben im kolonialen Südafrika*, Köln, 2009.
Lanham, Peter & A.S. Mopeli-Paulus: *Blanket Boy's Moon*, London, 1953.
Magona, Sindiwe: *Mother to Mother*, Boston, 1998.
McCord, Margaret: *The Calling of Katie Makanya*, London, 1995.
Mulaudzi, M., M. H. Schoeman & S. Chirikure: "Continuing Conversations at the Frontier", *South African Historical Journal* 62:2, 2010, 219-228.
Mutswairo, Solomon: *Mapondera. Soldier of Zimbabwe*, Harare, 1983.
Penn, Nigel: *Rogues, Rebels and Runaways. Eighteenth-Century Cape Characters*, Cape Town, 1999.

Perks, Robert & Alistair Thomson (Eds.): *The Oral History Reader,* London & New York, 1998.

Plaatje, Sol: *Mhudi.* Ed. Stephen Gray, Portsmouth, 1978. [first published in 1930]

Reyher, Rebecca Hourwich: *Zulu Woman. The Life Story of Christina Sibiya.* Eds. Marcia Wright & Liz Gunner, Pietermaritzburg, 1999. [first published in 1948]

Roberts, Richard: "Representation, Structure and Agency. Divorce in the French Soudan during the Early Twentieth Century", *Journal of African History* 40: 3, 1999, 389-410.

Rüther, Kirsten: "Through the Eyes of Missionaries and the Archives They Created. The Interwoven History of Power and Authority in the Nineteenth-Century Transvaal", *Journal of Southern African Studies* 38:2, 2012, 369-384.

Sachs, Wulf: *Black Hamlet*, with a new Introduction by Saul Dubow and Jacqueline Rose, Baltimore & London, 1996.

Smith, Mary F.: *Baba of Karo. A Woman of the Muslim Hausa*, London, 1954.

Steinberg, Jonny: *Three-Letter Plague. A Young Man's Journey Through a Great Epidemic*, Jeppestown, 2008.

Vansina, Jan: *De la tradition orale: essai de méthode historique*, Tervuren, 1961. [transl. into English in 1965]

White, Hayden: *Metahistory. The Historical Imagination in Nineteenth-Century Europe*, Baltimore & London, 1973.

Anne Schröder (Bielefeld)

Voices from Africa.
The English Language in Africa[1]

1. Introduction

Aptly referred to as "a living laboratory of languages",[2] Africa is the most linguistically complex of all the continents: the home of a great number of indigenous languages and several former colonial languages, in addition to contact languages such as pidgins and creoles or so-called mixed languages. The language situation in Africa is therefore an important key to understanding the cultural richness and diversity of this continent; at the same time it can serve as a starting point for the investigation of more general (socio-)linguistic topics such as language variation, language contact and the development of national language varieties as well as the connection of language to identity issues.

"The presence of English […] in Africa […] is due to several historical events,"[3] the nature of which have led to different types, varieties and uses of African English. In this paper, I will first present models, categorisations and uses of English around the world as they are frequently discussed in the relevant literature and apply these to the African context. I will also give an outline of the most characteristic linguistic features of African varieties of English, followed by a discussion of language use in literary texts. Finally, these issues will be illustrated by taking the linguistic situation and literary texts from Cameroon as an example.

2. Models, Categorisations and Uses of English

2.1 English as a Native Language, English as a Second Language and English as a Foreign Language

One way of describing the range of Englishes spoken around the world is to classify them according to the (official) status the language has in different countries. Thus, we differentiate between nations in which English is spoken as a native language, i.e. ENL-COUNTRIES, and those in which English is spoken as a second language, i.e. ESL-COUNTRIES. In addition, there are countries in which English is spoken as a foreign or as an international language, i.e. EFL- or EIL-COUNTRIES. Typical examples of ENL-countries are the UK, the USA or Australia, i.e. nations where the majority of the population have English as their mother tongue and acquire the language in childhood from their parents. ESL-countries are typically former British colonies, where English assumes important intra-national functions (e.g. as an official language alongside indigenous national languages) and is usually acquired through formal language teaching. In EFL- or EIL-countries English is widely taught in the educational system but does not usually serve any intra-national function. However, the abbreviations ENL, ESL and EFL/EIL can be used to refer both to different countries and to different types of speakers of English, and different types of speakers may be found in any individual country, irrespective of its classification, i.e. we may have ENL-speakers in an ESL-country.

If this classification is applied to the African continent, one quickly comes to realise that all three categories are present. Generally speaking, we find few ENL-speakers in Africa; only Liberia is usually listed among the African ENL-countries because of its "sizable minority of black ENL speakers" – descendants of US-American freed slaves.[4] But we also find English spoken as a native language by white British settlers and their descendants in Zimbabwe, Kenya, Namibia and – most importantly – in South Africa. These countries are usually also classified as ESL-countries, ESL being "[b]y far the most important category of English in Africa",[5] because most English speakers in Africa will have acquired the language via formal instruction and not as a mother tongue from their parents. Finally, many African countries have acknowledged the world-wide importance of English and use English in the media and in secondary or tertiary education; their inhabitants therefore "strive to acquire it for its international usefulness" as a foreign language, e.g. in Egypt and Ethiopia.[6] However, especially in the African context, "ENL, ESL, EIL, and EFL are [...] best seen as a continuum [...], which is artificially, but not arbitrarily, divided into crude categories".[7] In most African countries, the number of English speakers – be they ENL, ESL or EFL-speakers of English – will not exceed twenty percent of the population and is most likely to be well below that, so that for the majority of the (rural) African population English remains an unknown language.

2.2 The Three Concentric Circles of English

Another – albeit similar – way of categorising the varieties of English around the world, and hence in Africa, is Kachru's model of three concentric circles, according to which the following three speech communities are differentiated: (1) INNER CIRCLE-communities, speaking English as a native language, (2) OUTER CIRCLE-communities, speaking English as a second language, and (3) EXPANDING CIRCLE-communities, speaking English as a foreign language.[8] Probably the most important difference between this model and the previous one is in terms of norms and standards: (1) is regarded as NORM-PROVIDING, (2) as NORM-DEVELOPING and (3) as NORM-DEPENDENT, thus challenging the primacy of native Englishes and viewing "Outer Circle countries as developing norms of their own".[9] Kachru argues that English belongs to all its users and that British rules of grammar and pronunciation therefore need not be strictly followed.[10]

2.3 The Dynamic Model of the Evolution of Postcolonial Englishes

One of the more recent models of World Englishes, and possibly the most useful to describe the varieties of Englishes in Africa, is Schneider's Dynamic Model of the Evolution of Postcolonial Englishes, which takes into account the historical development of English varieties, the dynamics of language contact and identity construction.[11] Schneider argues that varieties of English around the world basically follow the same evolutionary process, during which the (linguistic) differences between immigrant settler communities and the indigenous population decrease and eventually become blurred. This evolutionary process consists of five developmental phases, at which social, political, historical and linguistic parameters are considered in the model:

- PHASE ONE 'FOUNDATION' sees the introduction of the English language to a new territory as a lingua franca, e.g. through trade, missionary activities or long-term settlement. The settler community and the indigenous population constitute separate communities, the former identifying itself as part of the original British nation. The different English dialects current among the settlers come into contact, forming a new stable koiné.[12] Contacts between the settlers and the indigenous population are restricted, but in this phase marginal minority bilingualism may occur, as some members of the indigenous population may serve as interpreters. The borrowing of indigenous lexical items into the English language, for local flora and fauna or place names, is the first linguistic effect and change.
- In PHASE TWO 'EXONORMATIVE STABILISATION', the colonial situation stabilises politically under British rule. The English language is firmly established as the language of administration, law and education. But despite the existence of a local variant increasingly influenced by lexical borrowings from indigenous languages and the koinéisation process, the reference variety is still the one spoken in the 'mother country', which therefore still determines the formal norms. Among the indigenous population (elite) bilingualism increases and especially among children of mixed ethnic origin, a hybrid local identity, best described as 'local-plus-English', may emerge. Similarly, the settler group still views itself primarily as an outpost of the British nation but increasingly – because of the colonial experience – also develops a sense of being 'English-plus-local'.
- PHASE THREE 'NATIVISATION' is the most important and interesting phase because it marks a transition both in terms of identity construction for the groups involved and of the status of the newly developing variety of English. As the ties with Britain are increasingly weakened, usually resulting in the colony gaining independence, the settler and the indigenous communities start

perceiving themselves as parts of the same national community coexisting in the same territory. Contacts between the two groups increase, bilingualism in the indigenous group is common and may sometimes even result in language shift. This leads to important structural changes at all levels of linguistic description: massive lexical borrowing, the development of a discernable local accent and new morphological and syntactic structures and thus a new variety of English, shared by both communities. However, at this stage a 'complaint tradition' may also develop among more conservative language users, who resent 'falling standards' of English.
- Post-independence PHASE FOUR 'ENDONORMATIVE STABILISATION' is characterised by an increased recognition of a positively-evaluated new linguistic norm, which is becoming codified in dictionaries and grammatical descriptions. The new variety of English is accepted by its speakers as an expression of a new identity and adopted, for instance, in literary representations. The two population strands join to form one, increasingly pan-ethnic nation.
- Finally, PHASE FIVE 'DIFFERENTIATION' will see the emergence of various ethnic, regional or social dialects of the new English variety as the young nation redefines itself as consisting of different subgroups.

Schneider has applied his model to a number of African nation states, most notably South Africa, Kenya, Tanzania, Nigeria and Cameroon.[13] For the latter four countries he concludes that they "have all reached phase 3 and appear to be undergoing a phase of nativisation, in some cases a vibrant one, right now".[14] While in Kenya, Nigeria and Cameroon the nativisation process and thus the structural nativisation is fairly advanced, Tanzania seems not to have moved so far into phase three and to have been "stuck" there.[15] As far as South Africa is concerned, this country has made it well into phase four, "although it is not justified to talk of a single, stabilised variety, and an endonormative orientation is highly disputed at best".[16] The transition from phase three to phase four also implies the substitution of the label 'English in X' to 'X English', i.e. a change of status from an ill-defined variant of English to a distinguishable variety of its own, possibly on equal terms with other varieties such as British and American English.[17]

2.4 Mixed Languages and Language Mixing

In addition to the creation of new varieties of English, the language contact situation in many African regions has led to the creation of new contact languages, which may involve extreme restructuring or pervasive mixing of linguistic structures. In Gambia, Sierra Leone, Liberia, Ghana, Nigeria and Cameroon, along the West African coast, we find English-based PIDGINS. These are highly simplified and reduced languages with a very restricted vocabulary and basic grammar rules, which are primarily used for trade and which are typically nobody's mother tongue. They usually developed in language contact situations without widespread bi- or multilingualism, which necessitated the creation of such a medium of communication as a lingua franca. If these languages are acquired as first languages, they usually develop into CREOLES with more complex linguistic structures and the full range of linguistic uses. In the multilingual African context, however, varieties of pidgin have expanded into fully functional languages as means of inter-ethnic communication without necessarily becoming mother tongues. In West Africa today, such an expanded pidgin, also referred to as West African Pidgin English (WAPE) is "more widespread [...] than is English as a second language".[18]

More recently, in multilingual and multiethnic urban settings in developing African states, the creation of a number of MIXED LANGUAGES can be observed. Mixed languages are languages incorporating "large portions of an external vocabulary into a maintained grammatical frame," and thus the lexicon and the grammatical structure can be traced back to the different source languages, from which they are usually taken in large chunks.[19] Unlike pidgins or creoles, these languages develop in language situations with widespread bi- or multilingualism. They are therefore not really needed as medium of communication but "arise instead within a single social or ethnic group because of a desire, or perhaps even a need, for an in-group language,"[20] and are frequently "deliberate and conscious creations".[21] These languages seem to function as indicators of a newly developed and independent (hybrid) ethnic identity and therefore fulfil important functions in the ecolinguistic environment of African urban centres.[22]

To complicate matters further, almost all African speech communities are marked by a high degree of CODE-SWITCHING, i.e. the alternating use of several languages and the transfer of linguistic elements of one language into another within a conversation, either between sentences or even within sentence boundaries. This may involve only the insertion of single words or else of phrases and entire sentences, which sometimes makes it difficult to draw a boundary between lexical borrowing and code-switching.[23] In addition, mixed languages, as described in the previous paragraph, are also frequently described as constituting a continuum of CODE HYBRIDISATION with code-switching at one pole and fully crystallised mixed languages at the other.[24] There are several reasons why people code-switch: for instance a change in the conversational situation, such as a new participant with a different linguistic background joining the conversation, or the introduction of a new topic. Code-switching therefore serves a variety of functions. These may be more referential (quoting someone or the recital of a proverb etc.) or affective (expressing solidarity, identity or social distance, signalling authority etc.) and they may serve inclusionary or exclusionary purposes.[25] Finally, if code-switching occurs between different varieties of the same language, e.g. between Standard English and a more localised African variety, or between genetically related languages, e.g. between Cameroonian English and WAPE, it is much more difficult to pinpoint individual switches or to identify and describe particular characteristics of either variety.

3. *Features of African Varieties of English*

Most linguistic descriptions of African varieties of English distinguish between Southern, East and West African varieties of English. Frequently, similar colonial heritages, the pattern of African first languages or the similarity of linguistic features allow varieties of English to be grouped accordingly, although the heterogeneity even within these categories is usually stressed in the relevant publications. SOUTHERN AFRICAN VARIETIES would comprise the varieties of English spoken in South Africa, Namibia, Botswana and possibly Zambia and Zimbabwe. However, detailed descriptions of the varieties spoken outside South Africa are rare or non-existent and what Bowerman says for ENL-varieties in these countries is probably true for other varieties of English as well: "The term 'White South African English' is applied to the first language varieties of English spoken by White South Africans, with the L1 English variety spoken by Zimbabweans and Namibians, mainly of British descent, being recognised as offshoots."[26] The Englishes found in Gambia, Sierra Leone, Liberia, Ghana, Nigeria, Cameroon could be referred to as WEST AFRICAN ENGLISH(ES). And while some linguists believe West African English to have "been recognised as an independent regional variety of English,"[27] others doubt "that [it] already exists as a formally recognised regional variety" although it may be emergent.[28] Descriptions of EAST AFRICAN ENGLISH(ES) usually focus on the Englishes spoken in Kenya, Uganda and Tanzania, "which are often seen as the core of East Africa," whereas the Englishes used in e.g. Malawi, Somalia, Ethiopia, Mauritius and the Seychelles tend to be disregarded.[29]

While the English of African ENL-speakers is usually very close or almost identical to other native varieties of English at the morpho-syntactic level, phonological and lexical differences may exist.[30] The latter are mostly triggered by language contact phenomena and predominantly include borrowings from indigenous or other contact languages, to refer to local toponymic or cultural particularities. Examples of this are *impi* ("African warrior band") borrowed from Zulu, or *veld* ("flat, open country") and *kraal* ("African village"), both borrowed from Afrikaans into South African English (SAE).[31] We also find a few English lexical particularities such as *robot* ("traffic light"), *reference book* ("identity document") or *bioscope* ("cinema").[32] African ENL varieties, especially White South African English (WSAE) can be comparatively close to British English even at the phonological level. Or, as Trudgill and Hannah put it:

> [A]ccents are phonologically very close to RP [Received Pronunciation], phonetically there are differences: the 'mild' accents differ somewhat from RP, while the 'broad' accents differ considerably from RP. The 'mild' accents tend to be found at the top of the social scale, particularly amongst older speakers. (RP is an accent which still has some prestige in these countries, but there has been a very marked decline in this prestige in the past fifty years or so.)[33]

Similarly, Bowerman distinguishes between 'cultivated', 'general' and 'broad' varieties of WSAE, the first approximating RP and being associated with the upper class, the second with the middle class and the latter with the working class and/or people of Afrikaans descent.[34] This last variety would probably also qualify as an ESL variety. However, it seems that these categories are becoming increasingly difficult to distinguish as WSAE is expanding "to younger middle class members of other ethnic groups".[35] Very generally speaking, South African ENL is phonetically comparatively close to Australian and New Zealand English varieties.[36]

Most African varieties of English are ESL varieties, although even in countries in which English is used only as an official language, we find – especially in the educated upper classes – people speaking it as a mother tongue. However, even their English will be marked by local forms at all levels of linguistic description. These nativised or indigenised varieties are all marked by particular local traits, but they also share many features, which makes them recognisably 'African'. Only some of the most important phonological, morpho-syntactic and lexical characteristics of African Englishes can be outlined here; detailed phonological and morpho-syntactic descriptions of individual varieties can be found in Mesthrie (2008a), while Kachru *et al.* (2009) or Trudgill and Hannah (2008) provide accessible surveys of the three broader categories, i.e. Western, Eastern and Southern African English(es) respectively.[37]

3.1 Phonology

Most varieties of African English have a decisively reduced phoneme inventory when compared to native varieties. Thus, differences made, e.g. in Received Pronunciation (RP), tend to be levelled down and phonemes may have merged. Examples of this are:

- reduction from a twelve to a five vowel system;[38]
- long and short vowels are not differentiated;[39]
- diphthongs tend to be monophthongised;[40]
- central vowels tend to be avoided, schwa /ə/ is frequently absent;[41]
- vowels in heavy final syllables or in the penultimate are lengthened.[42]

Figure 1 and Figure 2: Correspondences between vowels in RP and in West African and East African English[43]

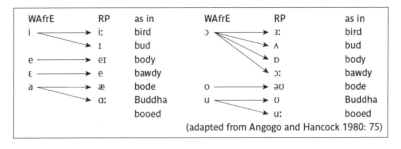

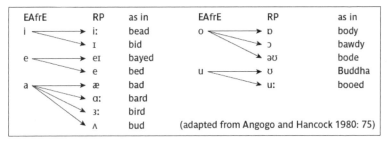

In addition, in African Englishes we frequently find that:

- dental fricatives /θ/ and /ð/ tend to be avoided; they may be replaced by plosives /t/ or /d/ or by alveolar fricatives /s/ and /z/;[44]
- /r/ and /l/ may merge to an intermediate sound; this is particularly true for speakers with a Bantu L1 background;[45]
- consonant clusters are usually simplified, especially in word final position;[46]
- we may find spelling pronunciations, e.g. with words ending in *-mb* or *-ng*;[47]
- rhythm is syllable-timed rather than stress-timed;[48]
- stress allocation may be different in a number of words.[49]

3.2 Morphology and Syntax

With regard to morpho-syntax, the following observations have been made:
- verbs may not always be inflected for tense or number;[50]
- there is an avoidance of complex tense and aspect forms;[51]
- the continuous form is extended to stative verbs;[52]
- there is a variant use of particles in particle verbs, i.e. the omission, the substitution or the addition of particles;[53]
- there is no infinitival *to* after some verbs;[54]
- plural *-s* is extended to non-count and mass-nouns;[55]
- there is an avoidance of redundant plural inflections, e.g. after numerals;[56]
- articles are omitted in front of nouns;[57]
- gender is not distinguished in personal pronouns;[58]
- resumptive pronouns are used in relative clauses;[59]
- tag questions are invariant;[60]
- comparatives or superlatives are formed without inflection;[61]
- adjective and adverb forms are conflated;[62]
- negative yes/no questions are confirmed by an answer in the positive.[63]

3.3 Vocabulary

Not surprisingly, all ESL varieties of African English also exhibit particularities at the lexical level. They are, for example, frequently heavily influenced by the various local indigenous languages, although individual loan words cannot be generalised to all African Englishes, but are specific to particular localities. This is especially true for food terms, which are highly culture-specific. Thus, "Tanzania's *ugali* is Uganda's *posho* or Zimbabwe's *sadza*," all terms for a staple food dish.[64] More widely used borrowings are *matatu* ("taxibus"), borrowed from Swahili into East African English,[65] or *akara* ("bean cake") and *juju* ("witchcraft", "talisman") as well as *chop* ("food"), borrowed into West African English from Yoruba and Pidgin respectively.[66] Sometimes these may even form compounds with English lexemes, as in *akara ball* or *juju music*[67] and *chop bar*.[68] In addition, all African Englishes use

English words in word-formation processes, such as affixation, reduplication or compounding, thus coining complex lexemes that are largely unknown to speakers of other (native) varieties of English. Examples of such African innovations are *co-wives* ("wives of the same husband"), *slow slow* ("slowly" or "very slow") or *bush meat* ("game"), all frequent in most West African Englishes.[69] English words may also have undergone semantic changes in African Englishes, possibly exhibiting a wider or narrower range of meanings. Thus in West Africa *amount* may also mean "money", *corner* may also refer to "a bend in the road" and *to hear* includes the meaning of "to understand".[70] Finally, we find loan translations from indigenous languages, e.g. *next tomorrow*, a calque on Yoruba *otunla* (lit. "new tomorrow"), meaning "day after tomorrow".[71] Though not easily generalisable, these calques, borrowings, new word-formations and semantic changes impart an 'African flavour' to these varieties of English, as they reflect "the sociolinguistic millieux [sic] in which English is spoken".[72]

3.4 Pragmatics

With regards to pragmatics, it is most important to be aware of different greetings and forms of address. In West African Englishes we find *How now?* and in East Africa *Are you all right?* rather than "How are you?"[73] Furthermore, Schmied points out that "if the addressees or partners in communication have a title or are known by an honorary name it is often used even by close friends" and "correct forms of address demonstrate respect for the human being, hence their usage is deeply rooted in behavioural norms".[74] Thus, professors, and even teachers or lecturers, are usually addressed as *Prof* or *Professor*, elderly people senior in age can be referred to as *Ma*, *Pa* or *Chief* and as *Old man* etc. It is also customary to begin a longer communication by enquiring about the wellbeing of the conversation partners and their extended families. Thus, questions concerning the health of closer relatives (parents, children, spouses) are usually asked and brief answers are expected before other matters are discussed.[75] Finally, idiomatic phrases and the frequent use of proverbs also distinguish African English discourse from other varieties of English. As aptly summarised by Schmied, it is important to be aware of these different politeness strategies.

> 'Preserving face' is extremely important in many African cultures [...]. Culture-specific differences in the interpretation of such conventions and strategies can lead to misunderstandings and can even generate negative cultural stereotypes, as for instance [...] stereotyping of the 'whites are hectic, Zulus are lazy' type [...].[76]

As the discussion of the various features of African Englishes, and thus of the nativisation or the indigenisation of English in Africa, very clearly shows, the English language has been given an 'African' imprint. Despite the fact that English was originally introduced by the colonisers and may thus be perceived as a language of oppression and cultural alienation, some researchers believe that this language is no longer foreign to African indigenous cultures, but rather an adequate means for the preservation, expression and conveyance of African world views and identities.[77]

4. Language in Literature

At least since independence, the question of whether the English language is an adequate means of expression of African identities and thus of literary expression has been a prominent one among writers. "Whereas elsewhere language in literature attracts attention and debate only in terms of the artistic effectiveness of its use, in Africa the major point of contention is in what language or languages the literatures may legitimately be expressed."[78] The most forceful and probably best-known opponent of the use of English is Ngũgĩ wa Thiong'o, who declared in 1986 that "African literature can only be written in African languages".[79] However, another – equally well-known – author claimed as early as 1965 that "the English language will be able to carry the weight of my African experience";[80] Achebe's famous statement "I have been given this language and I intend to use it"[81] has since become programmatic for African literatures written in English. Today, we can simply take the literary use of English as a fact and as one important parameter in phase four of Schneider's model, described above. African literature in English has become an important part of postcolonial literatures, and its success has not least "been achieved through the fresh and vigorous approach of African writers to the use of English in creative literature".[82]

In linguistic terms, Angogo and Hancock distinguish the following four types of African authors writing in English:[83]

1. African-born Europeans, ENL-speakers (e.g. Nadine Gordimer, Alan Paton);
2. ENL-speakers (e.g. A.D. Banks-Henries, Alice Perry-Johnson);
3. ESL-speakers (e.g. Chinua Achebe, Wole Soyinka);
4. EFL-speakers (e.g. Marigold Don-Ameche, H. Maxwell, Amos Tutuola).

Similarly, Sand and Skandera distinguish between ADAPTATIONISTS ('those who appropriate English') and (NEAR-)STANDARD ENGLISH WRITERS, and they introduce a further category, the CREOLE WRITERS, i.e. authors "who have decided to write exclusively in the local creole as an expression of their own national or cultural identity".[84] Zabus also mentions PIDGINISATION as one of the methods used by African authors to indigenise the English language and to make it a (more) suitable means of African literary expression.[85] The other three modes of indigenisation discussed by Zabus are: RELEXIFICATION, i.e. the translation from an indigenous language into English; CUSHIONING, i.e. the use of an indigenous word aligned with its equivalent in English; and CONTEXTUALISATION, i.e. the provision of sufficient context to render cushioning unnecessary. A typology of African literature in English is proposed by Schmied, who discusses the language in African literature according to whether authors deliberately deviate from Standard English (StE) and whether they are conscious of this deviation or not.[86] However, I fully agree with Sand and Skandera that any categorisation of literary texts based on language use "runs the risk of being a crude oversimplification, [and] the boundaries between the categories must be seen as fuzzy and permeable".[87]

The English language as used in literary texts is very likely to deviate considerably from (Standard) British usage. Therefore a number of the features of African English discussed in the previous sections will inevitably also be present in literary language, although "most of the linguistic features that characterise the postcolonial varieties are either *over*represented or *under*represented in literary texts".[88] Thus, literary texts cannot be taken as authentic representations of linguistic realities, since "writers are usually not linguists and their view of the world and communicative processes is not based on scientific analysis but on participant observation, allied with linguistic creativity"[89] and possibly prejudice. Nevertheless, looking at literary texts from a linguistic perspective may prove useful and produce interesting insights for linguists and literary scholars alike.

5. *An Example. Cameroon*

In many publications, Cameroon is referred to as 'Africa in miniature', because this country "is not only a crossroads on the African continent on a sociological and economic level, but also on a linguistic level",[90] and much of what has been discussed in the previous sections can be exemplified by looking at this country in more detail.

Located in West Africa, on the Bight of Biafra, between Equatorial Guinea and Nigeria, and also having common frontiers with Gabon, the Republic of Congo, the Central African Republic and Chad, Cameroon is among the more densely populated African countries. It is also one of the most linguistically diverse countries on the African continent. In addition to the two official languages, French and English, there are approximately two-hundred eighty indigenous languages spoken at the local level, out of which seven or eight, as well as Cameroon Pidgin English (CamP), have attained the status of regional lingua francas.[91] In addition, most urban centres show a great multilingual and multicultural complexity, which has produced a mixed language, composed of French, English, Pidgin and various local indigenous languages. This language is referred to as Camfranglais, and it has become a marker of solidarity and identity for urban Francophone youths, comparable to CamP for Anglophone adolescents.[92] Schematically, the linguistic situation in Cameroon can be illustrated as follows:

Figure 3: The Linguistic Situation in Cameroon

Local level	Indigenous languages
	CamP and Camfranglais (in urban areas)
Regional level	Indigenous languages of wider communication (e.g. Duala, Bulu, Ewondo, Ewondo Populaire, Mungaka, Fulfulde)
	CamP
	(English and French)
National level	English, French, CamP
International level	English, French (CamP/WAPE with other West African countries)

Thus, languages at the local level are used as in-group languages and as symbols of solidarity, while languages functioning at the regional level are used for inter-ethnic communication. Unlike most other African countries, Cameroon has not established any of these indigenous languages as a national language, and hence the official (and former colonial) languages are the only means of national communication, but CamP is also sometimes used (although not officially). CamP may also be unofficially used for communication at the international level, if other West African and thus WAPE-speaking people are involved.[93]

Cameroon could be classified as an ESL-country, although four fifths of the population are actually Francophone and thus are more likely to be EFL-speakers. Cameroon is therefore located between the EXPANDING and the OUTER CIRCLE in Kachru's model described above, and it has attained phase three in the DYNAMIC MODEL. However, Schneider suggests "that strictly speaking the evolutionary trends described in the Dynamic model operate fully only in the Anglophone, Northwest and Southwest provinces".[94] His case study gives a concise overview of Cameroon's colonial history, showing very clearly that a large number of factors have made this country a rich (linguistic) resource: missionary activities, the establishment of a Pidgin, the country's colonisation – first by the Germans and subsequently by the French and the British, the partition of the country under these two colonial powers after World War I, the competition between the two official languages (or rather between Anglophone and Francophone Cameroonians) and the existence of a stigmatised pidgin.[95] It is hardly surprising that this does not fail to leave its imprint in the national literature.

Zabus believes that the novel provides "an adequate testing terrain for the practice of indigenization – the novel being a flexible, polysemic form that can [...] incorporate other genres and other registers as well,"[96] which makes the use of other languages and language varieties plausible. Particularly, in dialogues and passages with direct speech writers attempt to represent the linguistic realities and thus the multilingual repertoire of their protagonists. This is what Zabus refers to as 'synchronic practice' which, "with its representational thrust, seeks to revise the improbable use of the metropolitan French or English in early West African literature".[97]

The following extracts from *No Way to Die,* a novel about the disappointments in the life of a young artist by the Cameroonian writer Linus T. Asong, exemplify this.[98] While the narrative text shows few differences from other varieties of Standard English, the direct speech reflects aspects of African English:

```
1    Footsteps behind me, or it was what like that? Yes, they were footsteps.
2    I turned:
3        "Good even Denniz."
4        It was Mossah. Some people are born to die together. That I meet a
5    man in prison by accident, then we leave at the same time, get work at
6    the same time and live in the same quarter?
7        "Evening Mossah," I responded.
8        "No work for you agen sa?" he asked. "Since tri days today, nobody
9    to hear ya smell at the jobside?"
10       "Not been there," I told him."I could not."
11       "You sick?"
12       I did not answer. Would answering keep Mossah quiet? Unless you
13   didn't know the man you are talking about.
14       [...]
15       "You wan to draw dat here or how?"
16       "Finished. I have finished."
17       Mossah went over to where I was standing and looked at the canvas
18   for a while. I knew what he was seeing: a single dark column painted to
19   stand against a background that began with a deep green at the bottom
20   and ended with a blue layer to the upper section. [...]
21       "But dis make no sense Denniz," he told me.
22       According to him it made no sense. [...] My end was their
```

23	beginning, I thought again.
24	After staring at the canvas for another whole minute Mossah said:
25	"And you buy the paint!"
26	Why should he be surprised? Unnecessary. I told him flat:
27	"I make nothing Mossah, except the drawing."
28	Mossah was wearing a jumpa that reached over his knees [...].

Of the phonological features listed in section 3.1 above, we find, for instance: monophthongisation of a diphthong, e.g. in 1.8 *agen* ("again"), avoidance of a central vowel, e.g. in 1.8 *sa* ("sir"), substitution of a dental fricative by a plosive, e.g. in 1.8 *tri* ("three"), 1.15 *dat* ("that"), 1.21 *dis* ("this") and simplification of consonant clusters, e.g. in 1.15 *wan* ("want"). The author may have been unaware of his spelling of *jumpa* (1.28), possibly reflecting the avoidance of schwa; this is all the more interesting as it is used in the narrative text. At the morpho-syntactic level, we can note the avoidance of complex tenses (1.8, 1.25), copula deletion (1.11, *you sick*), the unusual formation of an interrogative (1.8) and the negation without an auxiliary (1.21). Elsewhere in the same novel, we find omissions of third person singular -*s* inflection as in *He know everybody* (*Ibid*. 19), the use of a universal question tag as in *This month not so, doctor?* (*Ibid*. 23) and the grading of an ungradable, *That was the onliest one* (*Ibid*.), all occurring in direct speech. Similarly in direct speech we also find clear instances of CamP use, as in *Papa give we chop, papa we want chop* ("Papa, give us food, papa, we want food") (*Ibid*. 16) or *Ah! Na blackman-o!* ("Ah! It's a black person!") (*Ibid*. 17).

However, among Anglophone Cameroonians one would expect far more use of CamP, but this could make a novel unintelligible to readers unfamiliar with this language. Zabus notes that "pidgin English is gradually becoming extinct as a stylistic device in the West African europhone novel," despite the fact that she believes a creolised variety of English "to be the ideal medium to escape the dichotomy between the target and the source language and fill 'the space between' the sociolinguistic and the literary situation".[99] With Ngũgĩ wa Thiong'o, I believe that "drama is closer to the dialectics of life than poetry and the fiction".[100] How the multilingual repertoire of Cameroonians can be used for literary purposes is well illustrated in the works of the Cameroonian playwright Bole Butake, probably the best-known and most popular dramatist in Cameroon.

For example, in his play, *Lake God,* which has the 1986 Lake Nyos gas disaster as a topic, Butake uses English and CamP side by side.[101] English is used to represent the local indigenous language, while CamP may be spoken by characters to distance themselves from their interlocutors. This can be illustrated by the following scene, at the beginning of the play:

1	Shey Bo-Nyo:	Keep your hands off me, you scoundrels. I will see
2		the Fon. He must listen to me. The white man has
3		brought trouble to the land. He has killed our gods
4		and the Fon is impotent.
5	Doggo:	Shurrup! You dis crissman.
6	Kinchin:	You wan see Fon for weti?
7	Shey Bo-Nyo:	I must warn the Fon. I say lay off your hands! Sons of
8		bitches and prostitutes! It is an abomination for the
9		Fon to surround himself with thugs and sons of
10		whores and people who will kill us and destroy the
11		land.
12	Fon:	Why is he always accusing me?
13	Father Leo:	Typical behaviour of the mad. They always have an
14		obsession. Something they cling to. Something they
15		repeat all the time. I wouldn't pay any attention. What
16		trouble have I brought to this village? The church has
17		brought new life and progress to this village. And yet
18		he says the white man will kill people and destroy the
19		land. Sheer madness.
20	Doggo:	We go show you say we be akwara woman dem
12		pickin. Tekam!
22		[...]
23	Fon:	Those idiots will kill the old man. All bulk and no
24		brains.[102]

Although Doggo and Kinchin, the guards of the Fon, understand Shey Bo-Nyo, the diviner and priest of Lake God, they prefer to answer him in CamP (l.5 and l.6), either because they are not fluent in the particular indigenous language that he is using or because they would like to impress their interlocutor by using a different code, adding authority to their statements and possibly code-switching for exclusionary purposes. The Fon's comment on his guards' intellectual capacities (l.23-24) may indicate that their using CamP is in fact meant to suggest their lack of education. However, when the Fon himself (described as an educated man) needs to communicate with somebody from a different ethnic background – in the following scene it is Dewa, a Fulani cattle keeper – he also has to have recourse to this inter-ethnic means of communication.

1	Fon:	Good. That makes twenty thousand francs. I have
2		spoken. He is ready to pay you now. (to Dewa) No bi
3		you gettam twenty tosand fo dere?
4	Dewa:	Yes, Mbe. Me gettam. Allah de! Me tink sey me go
5		sellam leke five cow befo me pay da chop. Allah de!
6	Fon:	You go muf two cow fo you nyun puttam for me
7		nyun. Woman cow wey get leke three year so dat
8		small tam dem get belle. You don hear fine, fine?
9	Dewa:	Me don hear, Mbe. Kai, wusai Allah don go?
10	Fon: (to women)	What do you say?
11	Nkasai:	The cattle and their owners must go!
12		[...]
13	Fon:	Give me de money. I go lef back pay dem. (Dewa
14		hands over the money). You fit go now. Pass fo dis
15		sai. (to one of the guards) You go with him as far as
16		the stream. (to other guard) And you make sure no
17		one gets in here, you understand?[103]

The Fon switches easily between CamP and the local language, here represented by English, and uses CamP for inter-ethnic communication, while the local language serves as a means of communication between him and his subordinates (the guards and the women). Butake uses several of the techniques mentioned above to make English resemble the local language. Thus, *I have spoken* (l.1-2) and *you understand* (l.17) might be phrases directly translated from the indigenous language. In the passages with CamP, we also find many characteristics of this language: preverbal markers to indicate tense and aspect, i.e. *don* (l.8, l.9) for perfectivity, *go* (l.4, l.13) for future/anteriority; copula *bi* (l.2); the modal auxiliary *fit* ("can/be able to") (l.14), copula *de* (l.4), complementiser *sey* (l.4), relativiser *wey* (l.7), serial verb constructions (l.13) and in the scene above (l.20-21) a genitive by juxtaposition *akwara woman dem pickin* ("child(ren) of whores"). There are also lexical items such as *chop* ("food"), *hear* ("to understand"), *belle* ("pregnant"). The representation of CamP and its uses are thus highly realistic.[104] The inconsistent spelling is to be expected since CamP orthography has not been codified.

It is, however, more important to note that in some scenes the use of CamP can also be interpreted as signalling modernity or a hybrid identity. Whereas its use is clearly context-driven in the conversation between the cattle keeper and the chief, it can also be used for affective purposes. Because it is usually an urban phenomenon and is only used in rural areas as an inter-ethnic means of communication (as seen above), CamP also makes its way into the communication between the educated chief of the village and his equally educated wife, the headmistress of the village school:

1	Angela:	[...] When my parents told me, 'Don't marry a graffi man,
2		especially the son of a chief' I refused to listen.
3	Fon:	Angie, na weti don happen?
4	Angela:	I know you want children. I know you want to marry
5		another woman, their queen. And which graffi man ever
6		had only one wife? But for Father Leo, you would have
7		married their queen long ago.
8	Fon:	That's not true, Angie! If no graffi man ever had only one
9		wife, then I am the first and history will bear me witness.
10		[...][105]

These two protagonists seem to see themselves trapped between tradition and the expectations of the people towards their leader and their educated, Christian background. CamP being a non-traditional, non-rural and hybrid code may therefore be perceived as an appropriate means of expression of their 'Euro-African' identity.

6. *Concluding Remarks*

A firm knowledge of the linguistic ecology of the African continent is a prerequisite for a full apprehension and understanding of the cultural richness expressed in the manifold literary texts it has produced. "The African [...] 'contact literatures' adopt all the linguistic and cultural processes – and transfers – that are present in languages in contact."[106] Much as linguists are aware of the importance of literary creativity in a newly developing variety of English and hence its inclusion as a parameter, e.g. in the Dynamic Model described above, literary scholars also can profitably take into account language variation and the linguistic characteristics of African varieties of English.

Notes

1 I would like to thank Naomi Hallan and Till Meister for providing comments on an earlier version of this article.
2 Schmied (1991: 205).
3 Mesthrie (2008b: 23).
4 Skandera (2002: 94).
5 *Ibid.* 97.
6 Schneider (2011: 30).
7 Skandera (2002: 102).
8 Kachru (1992: 355-366).
9 Schneider (2011: 32).
10 *Ibid.*
11 See Schneider (2007: chapter 3), Schneider (2008) and Schneider (2011: 33-35).
12 A koiné is a compromise dialect formed in dialect contact situations, usually as a result of dialect levelling.
13 See Schneider (2007: 173-218) and Schneider (2008).
14 Schneider (2008: 299).
15 *Ibid.* 292.
16 Schneider (2007: 188).
17 See *Ibid.* 50.
18 Mesthrie (2010a: 518).
19 Winford (2003: 24). See also Thomason (2001: 196-198).
20 Thomason (2001: 198).
21 Matras (2000: 81).
22 For details see Schröder & Rudd (forthcoming).
23 There is a huge body of literature on code-switching. A comprehensive introduction is given in Matras (2009: Chapter 5).
24 See Schröder & Rudd (forthcoming).
25 For comprehensive overviews of the reasons for and functions of code-switching, see Appel & Muysken (2005: 118-121), Holmes (2001: 34-44) or Gramley (2008: 317-322).
26 Bowermann (2008a: 164).

27 Wolf & Igboanusi (2003: 69).
28 Ominiyi (2009: 182).
29 Schmied (2009: 188).
30 Most notably, Liberian Settler English, spoken by descendants of the African-Americans who immigrated to Liberia in the 19th century, constitutes an exception to this. See Singler (2008a, 2008b) for a description of this variety.
31 Trudgill & Hannah (2008: 36).
32 *Ibid*.
33 *Ibid*. 22.
34 Bowerman (2008a: 164).
35 *Ibid*. 175. See also recent research by Rajend Mesthrie on this point (e.g. Mesthrie 2010b, Mesthrie 2009).
36 See Bowerman (2008a) and Trudgill & Hannah (2008) for details.
37 For details and examples, please consult the references indicated.
38 See Mesthrie (forthcoming).
39 See Schmied (1991: 59).
40 See Mesthrie (forthcoming), Schmied (1991: 59).
41 *Ibid*.
42 See Mesthrie (forthcoming).
43 Figures taken from Gramley (2012: 317, 320). Schematic comparisons of vowel differences can also be found in Schmied (1991: 61) and Angogo & Hancock (1980: 75). See also Mesthrie (forthcoming) for a comparison of West African, Southern African and East African English vowel systems.
44 See Schmied (1991: 58).
45 See Trudgill & Hannah (2008: 132), Schmied (1991).
46 See Trudgill & Hannah (2008: 129), Schmied (1991: 61-62).
47 See Trudgill & Hannah (2008: 129).
48 See Schmied (1991: 64).
49 See Trudgill & Hannah (2008: 129), Schmied (1991: 63).
50 See Schmied (1991: 65).
51 *Ibid*. 66.
52 See Mesthrie (forthcoming), Schmied (1991: 67).
53 See Mesthrie (forthcoming), Schmied (1991: 67-68).
54 See Trudgill & Hannah (2008: 130), Schmied (1991: 69).
55 See Mesthrie (forthcoming), Trudgill & Hannah (2008: 130), Schmied (1991: 69-70).
56 See Schmied (1991: 69).
57 *Ibid*. 71.
58 See Mesthrie (forthcoming), Schmied (1991: 71-72).

59 See Mesthrie (forthcoming), Trudgill & Hannah (2008: 130), Schmied (1991: 72-73).
60 See Trudgill & Hannah (2008: 131), Schmied (1991: 73).
61 See Mesthrie (forthcoming), Trudgill & Hannah (2008: 130).
62 See Schmied (1991: 72).
63 See Mesthrie (forthcoming), Trudgill & Hannah (2008: 131), Schmied (1991: 73).
64 Schmied (1991: 79).
65 *Ibid.* 77.
66 Igboanusi (2010: 44).
67 Gramley (2012: 317).
68 Trudgill & Hannah (2008: 131).
69 Gramley (2001: 136).
70 Igboanusi (2010: 50), Trudgill & Hannah (2008: 131).
71 Igboanusi (2010: 230), Gramley (2001: 136).
72 Bokamba (1991), quoted in Gramley (2001: 136).
73 Angogo & Hancock (1980: 77).
74 Schmied (1991: 91-92).
75 *Ibid.*
76 *Ibid.* 93.
77 See e.g. Wolf (2001: 304-305), Wolf (2003: 20).
78 Owomoyela (1993: 347).
79 Ngũgĩ wa Thiong'o (1986: 27).
80 Achebe (1965: 30).
81 *Ibid.*
82 Schmied (1991: 123).
83 Angogo & Hancock (1980: 86).
84 Sand & Skandera (2000: 138).
85 Zabus (2007).
86 Schmied (1991: 123). See Schmied (1991: 123-130) for details and a discussion of some examples.
87 Sand & Skandera (2000: 135).
88 *Ibid.*, original emphasis.
89 Schmied (1991: 133).
90 Bot Ba Njock (1966: 6), my translation.
91 See Schröder (2003).
92 See Schröder (2007), Schröder & Rudd (forthcoming).
93 See Schröder (2003) for details.
94 Schneider (2007: 212).
95 *Ibid.* 212-218.

96   Zabus (2007: 5).
97   *Ibid.* 16.
98   Asong (1993: 2-5). Further references to this edition will be included in the text.
99   Zabus (2007: 203).
100 Ngũgĩ wa Thiong'o (1986: 54).
101 In 1986, the lake suddenly emitted a large carbon dioxide-cloud, which asphyxiated many people and livestock in nearby towns and villages.
102 Butake (1999: 9-10).
103 *Ibid.* 18.
104 For a comprehensive description of the characteristics of CamP, see Schröder (forthcoming).
105 Butake (1999: 35).
106 Kachru (2008: 574).

Bibliography

Achebe, Chinua: "English and the African Writer", *Transition* 18, 1965, 27-30.
Angogo, Rachel & Ian Hancock: "English in Africa. Emerging Standards or Diverging Regionalisms?", *English World-Wide* 1, 1980, 67-96.
Appel, René & Peter Muysken: *Language Contact and Bilingualism*, Amsterdam, 2005.
Asong, Linus T.: *No Way to Die*, Bamenda, 1993.
Banda, Felix: "The Scope and Categorization of African English. Some Sociolinguistic Considerations", *English World-Wide* 17:1, 1965, 63-75.
Bot Ba Njock, Henri Marcel: "Le problem linguistique au Cameroun", *L'Afrique et l'Asie* 73, 1966, 3-13.
Bowermann, Sean: "White South African English. Phonology". – In Rajend Mesthrie (Ed.): *Varieties of English 4. Africa, South and Southeast Asia*, Berlin, 2008a, pp. 164-176.
---: "White South African English. Morphology and Syntax". – In Rajend Mesthrie (Ed.): *Varieties of English 4. Africa, South and Southeast Asia*, Berlin, 2008b, pp. 472-487.
Butake, Bole: *Lake God and Other Plays*, Yaoundé, 1999.
Gramley, Stephan: *The Vocabulary of World English*, London, 2001.
---: "Code-Switching". – In S. G. & Vivian Gramley (Eds.): *Bielefeld Introduction to Applied Linguistics. A Course Book*, Bielefeld, 2008, pp. 313-327.

---: *The History of English. An Introduction*, London, 2012.
Herbert, Robert K. (Ed.): *Language and Society in Africa. The Theory and Practice of Sociolinguistics*, Witwatersrand, 1992.
Holmes, Janet: *An Introduction to Sociolinguistics*, 2nd ed., Harlow, 2001.
Huber, Magnus & Manfred Görlach: "Texts. West African Pidgin English", *English World-Wide* 17:2, 1996, 239-258.
Igboanusi, Herbert: *A Dictionary of Nigerian English Usage*, Berlin, 2010.
Kachru, Braj B.: "Teaching World Englishes". – In B. B. K. (Ed.): *The Other Tongue. English Across Cultures*, 2nd ed., Urbana, 1992, pp. 355-366.
---: "World Englishes in World Contexts". – In Haruko Momma & Michael Matto (Eds.): *A Companion to the History of the English Language*, Malden, 2008, pp. 567-580.
Kachru, Braj B., Yamuna Kachru & Cecil L. Nelson (Eds.): *The Handbook of World Englishes*, paperback edition, Malden, 2009.
Kamwangamalu, Nkongo M.: "South African Englishes". – In Braj B. Kachru, Yamuna Kachru & Cecil L. Nelson (Eds.): *The Handbook of World Englishes*, paperback edition, Malden, 2009, pp. 158-171.
Kirkpatrick, Andy (Ed.): *The Routledge Handbook of World Englishes*, London & New York, 2010.
Lanham, L. W.: "English in South Africa". – In Richard W. Bailey & Manfred Görlach (Eds.): *English as a World Language*, Ann Arbor, 1993, pp. 324-352.
Lucko, Peter, Lothar Peter & Hans-Georg Wolf (Eds.): *Studies in African Varieties of English*, Frankfurt, 2003.
Matras, Yaron: "Mixed Languages. A Functional-Communicative Approach", *Bilingualism. Language and Cognition* 3:2, 2000, 79-99.
---: *Language Contact*, Cambridge, 2009.
Mazrui, Alamin M.: *English in Africa. After the Cold War*, Clevedon, 2004.
---: "English in Africa". – In Haruko Momma & Michael Matto (Eds.): *A Companion to the History of the English Language*, paperback edition, Malden, 2011, pp. 423-430.
Mazrui, Ali A.: *The Political Sociology of the English Language. An African Perspective*, The Hague & Paris, 1975.
Mesthrie, Rajend (Ed.): *Varieties of English. Volume 4. Africa, South and Southeast Asia*, Berlin, 2008a.
---: "Introduction. Varieties of English in Africa and South and Southeast Asia". – In Rajend Mesthrie (Ed.): *Varieties of English. Volume 4. Africa, South and Southeast Asia*, Berlin, 2008b, pp. 23-31.
---: "Deracialising the GOOSE Vowel in South African English. Accelerated Linguistic Change Amongst Young, Middle Class Females in Post-Apartheid South Africa". – In Thomas Hoffmann & Lucia Siebers (Eds.):

World Englishes. Problems, Properties and Prospects. Selected Papers from the 13th IAWE Conference, Amsterdam, 2009, pp. 3-18.

---: "Contact and African Englishes". – In Raymond Hickey (Ed.): *The Handbook of Language Contact*, Malden & Oxford, 2010a, pp. 518-537.

---: "Socio-Phonetics and Social Change. Deracialisation of the GOOSE Vowel in South African English", *Journal of Sociolinguistics* 14:1, 2010b, 3-33.

---: "English in Africa. A Diachronic Typology". – In Alexander Bergs & Laurel Brinton (Eds.): *English Historical Linguistics. Vol. II*, Berlin & New York, forthcoming 2012.

Ngũgĩ wa Thiong'o: *Decolonizing the Mind. The Politics of Language in African Literature*, London, 1986.

Ominiyi, Tope: "West African Englishes". – In Braj B. Kachru *et al.* (Eds.): *The Handbook of World Englishes*, paperback edition, Malden, 2009, pp. 172-187.

Owomoyela, Oyekan: "The Question of Language in African Literature". – In O. O. (Ed.): *A History of Twentieth-Century African Literatures*, Lincoln, 1993, pp. 347-368.

Sand, Andrea & Paul Skandera: "Linguistic Manifestations of Hybridity in Literary Texts from Africa and the Caribbean". – In Therese Steffen (Ed.): *Crossover. Cultural Hybridity in Ethnicity, Gender, Ethics*, Tübingen, 2000, pp. 135-150.

Saro-Wiwa, Ken: "The Language of African Literature. A Writer's Testimony", *Research in African Literatures* 23:1, 1992, 153-157.

Schmied, Josef: *English in Africa. An Introduction*, London, 1991.

---: "East African Englishes". – In Braj B. Kachru *et al.* (Eds.): *The Handbook of World Englishes*, paperback edition, Malden, 2009, pp. 188-202.

Schneider, Edgar W.: *Postcolonial English. Varieties around the World*, Cambridge, 2007.

---: "Towards Endonormativity? African English and the Dynamic Model of the Evolution of Postcolonial English". – In Kenneth Harrow & Kizitus Mpoche (Eds.): *Language, Literature and Education in Multicultural Societies. Collaborative Research on Africa*, Newcastle, 2008, pp. 283-305.

---: *English Around the World. An Introduction*, Cambridge, 2011.

Schröder, Anne: *Status, Functions, and Prospects of Pidgin English. An Empirical Approach to Language Dynamics in Cameroon*, Language in Performance 27, Tübingen, 2003.

--- (Ed.): *Crossing Borders. Interdisciplinary Approaches to Africa*, Afrikanische Studien 23, Münster, 2004.

---: "Camfranglais. A Language with Several (Sur-)Faces and Important Sociolinguistic Functions". – In Anke Bartels & Dirk Wiemann (Eds.):

Global Fragments. (Dis)Orientation in the New World Order, Cross/Cultures 90, Amsterdam, 2007, pp. 281-298.

---: "Cameroon Pidgin English". – In Susanne Michaelis *et al.* (Eds.): *Atlas of Pidgin and Creole Language Structures, Vol. II. The Language Surveys*, Oxford, forthcoming.

Schröder, Anne & Philipp W. Rudd: "Language Mixing and Ecology in Africa. Focus on Camfranglais and Sheng". – In Ralph Ludwig, Peter Mühlhäusler & Steve Pagel (Eds.): *Linguistic Ecology and Language Contact*, Cambridge, forthcoming.

Singler, John Victor: "Liberian Settler English. Phonology". – In Rajend Mesthrie (Ed.): *Varieties of English 4. Africa, South and Southeast Asia*, Berlin, 2008a, pp. 102-114.

---: "Liberian Settler English. Morphology and Syntax". – In Rajend Mesthrie (Ed.): *Varieties of English 4. Africa, South and Southeast Asia*, Berlin, 2008b, pp. 385-415.

Skandera, Paul: "A Categorization of African Englishes". – In D. J. Allerton *et al.* (Eds.): *Perspectives on English as a World Language*, Basel, 2002, pp. 92-103.

Spencer, John (Ed.): *The English Language in West Africa*, London, 1971.

Thomason, Sarah G.: *Language Contact. An Introduction*, Edinburgh, 2001.

Todd, Loreto: "The English Language in West Africa". – In Richard W. Bailey & Manfred Görlach (Eds.): *English as a World Language*, Ann Arbor, 1993, pp. 281-305.

Trudgill, Peter & Jean Hannah: *International English. A Guide to the Varieties of Standard English*, 5th ed., London, 2008.

Winford, Donald: *An Introduction to Contact Linguistics*, Malden, 2003.

Wolf, Hans-Georg: *English in Cameroon*, Berlin, 2001.

---: "The Contextualization of Common Core Terms in West African English. Evidence from Computer Coprpora". – In Peter Lucko, Lothar Peter & H.-G. W. (Eds.): *Studies in African Varieties of English*, Frankfurt, 2003, pp. 3-20.

Wolf, Hans-Georg & Herbert Igboanusi: "A Preliminary Comparison of Some Lexical Items in Nigerian English and Cameroon English". – In Peter Lucko *et al.* (Eds.): *Studies in African Varieties of English*, Frankfurt, 2003, pp. 69-81.

Zabus, Chantal: *The African Palimpsest. Indigenization of Language in the West African Europhone Novel*, 2nd enlarged ed., Cross/Cultures 4, Amsterdam, 2007.

Melanie Klein (Berlin)

Between History, Politics and the Self. Photographic Portraiture in Contemporary Art from Africa

1. Introduction

In 1975, an adolescent boy was playing dress up with clothing of various origins at the back of a photographic studio in Bangui, capital of the Central African Republic. After applying make-up and imitating images he found in commercial catalogues from France, he posed and took photographs of himself. Inspiration would later come from fashion magazines and record covers from Europe and Africa. This moment in the history of African photography was extraordinary due to this photographer's pioneering role in self-portraiture, which actually anticipated, prompted and still influences the genre's development today.[1] Additionally, his actions explore and position the self through style, costume and role-play in a way to which many can relate.[2]

The extensive variety of Samuel Fosso's early photographic self-portraits exemplifies such exploration. It is important to keep in mind that engaging in such practices would have put one in a precarious situation during the reign of Jean-Bédel Bokassa, when extravagant clothing was forbidden.[3] Fosso's way of memorializing those years seems to recall an almost cathartic process. The audacious pictures in French magazines, he explained in an interview, "made me want to produce the same kind of image. I posed in front of my camera and, for the first time, I felt alive. I was healthy. I became an adult. It was kind of a rite of passage."[4] Fosso's oeuvre and the versatile character of its development have been discussed extensively. His work is located within African studio photography from the 1990s, when the emphasis was laid – in a rather ethnological manner – on cultural and social aspects that generally marked investigations into this category.

Okwui Enwezor, theorist, curator and director of *Haus der Kunst* in Munich since 2011, highlights Fosso's impact on the genealogy of modern African imagery in all its facets:

> In an uncanny anticipation of postmodern photographic conventions [...] he remade his studio in the after hours of his commercial work into a space of self-mimicry, idealization and theatricalization. In fact, the studio took on an aspect of the burlesque stage of preening, posing, dissimulating, masking and performing an extended ballad of self-adoration and the exploitation of sexual release. [...] His work may yet be one of the earliest examples of a considered commentary on contemporary African masculinity, gender, identity and sexuality, all of which come off rather as ambiguous depictions.[5]

Furthermore, Olu Oguibe, professor for art theory at the Institute for African American Studies at the University of Connecticut states:

> [E]ven in those early photographs, Fosso's staged auto-portraits were already symbolic on a social and historic scale that was larger than mere adolescent self-regard. They were already constructed to capture the spirit of a moment as African societies completed their transition from a unique, pre-colonial milieu to a modern global epoch.[6]

In the following years, the aesthetic quality of Fosso's images has been spotlighted in accordant publications and exhibitions and thoroughly discussed by Ingrid Hölzl (2008). She positions Fosso's oeuvre within the matrix of photographic index theory[7] and focuses on its self-referential traces that range from his early self-portraits as "proof of life"[8] to the representation of fictional and historical characters as self-photography. Hölzl acknowledges the prominent role of the photographer as author[9] who, in an "autoportraitistic pact"[10] between producer and viewer, actually performs the self-portrait apart from what can be discerned in the finished photograph. With regard to self-portraiture as an index term, she suggests an extension of it towards an autobiographical marker.[11] In this spirit, Fosso's works – as we will see – blur the categorical divisions between the body, the self, the role and the fiction to a surprisingly high degree.

When looking generally at studio photography from Africa, one must also take into account the dynamics of authorship. In Fosso's self-portraits those dynamics are distinctly definable. They are shifted towards the sitter's representational gesture of staging the self, as can also be seen in commissioned works by Seydou Keïta in which "authorship slipped back and forth between client and artist and sometimes straddled intention and serendipity".[12]

An additional factor of early studio photography as we perceive it today is the viewer, both African and Western, who is involved in constantly changing the context of viewing and resulting interpretation that is far from any final conclusion. Bigham (1999: 65) writes:

> As Keïta becomes a generative point for the perception of other African photographers, his authorship encompasses far more than an individual oeuvre. His celebration as a canonical figure is precipitous, occurring in the absence of a broad understanding of the art history of West African portrait photography and without evidence of how and to what extent his work has been significant to other practitioners.

The autoportraitistic pact of those early images was later relocated from the local to a more global significance,[13] initiated by a rather singular photographer like Fosso as self-portraitist or, conversely, established between studio clients and their families, friends and acquaintances.[14] Protagonists in contemporary art – where those dimensions amount to something like a generic amalgam of different visual traits such as historical convention, artistic style and aesthetic perception – seem to play with the possibilities that this amalgamation reveals and thus open up fresh perspectives on a field still negotiated fervently by many disciplines.

In this essay I will discuss two later series of Fosso's works, which can be considered both a foundation and reference point for portraiture and self-portraiture in contemporary photography from Africa that connects with historical investigation and political commentary. I will then turn to Kudzanai Chiurai, who uses the genre to address current political issues. Finally, I discuss the work of Nomusa Makhubu, who – in a seemingly antithetical way – explores human existence through imagining the distorted body. These examples reveal only a small part of the variety that can be found in present photographic portraiture, but nevertheless provide a basic understanding of such artistic strategies in

Africa today. I chose the above examples to provide a diverging interpretation of both portraiture and Fosso's legacy. They not only differ in terms of scrutinising gendered constructions but also concerning the employment of varying stylistic and technical strategies. They mark opposite ends of different photographic trajectories. In particular, I will look at the parameters that are used to describe and thus reformulate conditions of actual identities within the domain of power relations and memory. These parameters appear to explore and extend the techniques used by the first generation of African photographers. They seem to redirect the possibilities and destinations of photographic portraiture and further disrupt assumptions, especially when it comes to the autoportraitistic pact, the identity of the photographer, the photographer as sitter and the audience's way to read the images.

2. Samuel Fosso. Exploring and Allocating the Self in History

Samuel Fosso was born in Cameroon in 1962. His turbulent childhood led him to a village in Nigeria where his mother's family lived. Due to the outbreak of the Biafran War[15] in 1967, they had to hide in the countryside for three years and found their hometown entirely destroyed upon return. They had also lost several family members. Fosso speaks of these experiences of losing a childhood – also in a very literal sense since there are no pictures left of him or his relatives – as one of his leitmotifs in later creative output.[16] In 1972 he was taken to Bangui where his uncle had opened a small footwear company. Fosso worked in his uncle's factory and household until he could persuade his uncle to allow him to take an apprenticeship for a few months at the studio of a Nigerian photographer. When his uncle noticed Fosso's talent, he bought him the necessary technical equipment for setting up his own studio, which Fosso then opened in 1975 at the age of thirteen.

In his teenage years Fosso witnessed the increasingly despotic dictatorship of one of the most eccentric and bizarre heads of state on the African continent, Jean-Bédel Bokassa. In an interview with Fosso, Guido Schlinkert compares the disturbing images of Bokassa's public appearances with the depiction of 'freaks' by Diane Arbus – photographs of people whose existence seems almost surreal.[17] Her images of children in particular refer to the distant war in Vietnam with a playful yet frightening earnestness such as *Child with Toy Hand Grenade in Central Park* of 1962 and *Boy with a Straw Hat Waiting to March in a Pro-War Parade* of 1967.[18] With this quite far-fetched comparison concerning the images' protagonists and different aesthetic approaches, Schlinkert nevertheless addresses Bokassa's seemingly infantile self-expression. The African statesman, having only basic education, crowned himself emperor of Central Africa. His self-staging can be understood as exemplary for certain authoritarian conduct anywhere in the world and seems to have influenced not only Fosso in one of his later works, namely *The Chief who Sold Africa to the Colonialists*, but also more current thematisations of modes of African leadership. With a cynical twist, Schlinkert examines certain mental states through the analogy of the dictator's infantilisation of his fellow citizens needing to be caned.[19] Images of Bokassa as emperor, depicting the underlying tension between childlike and cruel behaviour, were surely inspired by the pomposity of European courts, which made Bokassa appear as a caricature of colonial rule.[20] However, in being compared to Arbus's freaks, Bokassa becomes a petulant and spoilt child, who lacks any sense of reality, erects an imaginary world, fancies itself omnipotent and erases any voice of resistance.

In contrast to official imagery, the photographic studio provided a space for the celebration of life apart from politics and the constant fear of suppression. Hölzl discusses Valentin Y. Mudimbe, philosopher, linguist and historian, writing on African studio photography, and states:

> African portrait photography as popular cultural technique does not know any anti-colonial manifests, any idealisations of African tradition as defined by Senghor, Nkrumah or Nyerere and any myth-making of the African authentic of Mobutu, Amin or Bokassa to support their megalomania. It only knows hybridity, actuality and commerciality.[21]

Yet, the appalling combination of immaturity, mythologisation and megalomania in the behaviour of leaders such as Bokassa was to be an issue in Fosso's later work, several years after his self-portraits were 'discovered' by the French curator Bernard Descamps in 1993. Here, Fosso captured new thematic domains utilising the medium of typical studio photography. The studio's privacy became a space of historical exploration.

In a series that was commissioned by the Parisian department store Tati,[22] Fosso assumes different roles, for example one in which he represents *The Chief who Sold Africa to the Colonialists*. Although his photograph is not "explicitly political" and does not directly refer to dictators of the post-independence era, it nevertheless "can express anger and indignation".[23] The colourful impression of the work together with strikingly harmless attributes such as the sunflowers – in the place of weapons or a sceptre – jewellery, backdrops of ornamental cloth, and Fosso's lightly vested body suggest an enjoyably exotic and almost jaunty scene, which only reveals its underlying context when reading the title. Only then does the viewer become aware of the historical implications of Fosso's display. All the innocent toys are transformed into tools of concealed terror, particularly regarding the absurdity and bitter reality of dictatorial self-staging.[24] Over time, even Fosso himself classifies his work in differing ways and hence consciously mirrors such variations, especially in images like *The Chief who Sold Africa to the Colonialists*.[25]

Fosso handles the topic with an irksome humour that inevitably recalls Charlie Chaplin's *The Great Dictator* of 1940. However, while Chaplin created the film before the war ended and could not have made it with the knowledge of "the actual horrors of the German concentration camps",[26] Fosso, being a contemporary of the postcolonial era, creates a figure, a *pars pro toto*, which stands for a whole set of incidences affiliated with certain chiefs and their now well-documented role in history. Oscillating between associations of cuteness and ruthlessness, between ineptitude and incalculability, Fosso can be included in the history of satire.[27] He subtly dismantles the image of African colonial leaders with their alleged powerlessness, authentic traditions[28] and profitable complicity, and thus allocates his humorous intervention to the more complex realm of Western ideological constructions as well as concealed African histories. All in all, "humour plays multiple roles in helping us experience the full extent of our humanity, which in turn helps us come to terms with the present and the past".[29]

Coming back to the question of self-referentiality, it is unclear how much of a real or an imaginary Fosso we can find in this particular image, or how much historical linkage can be traced. The image appears critical of historical events as well as self-critical. Hölzl suggests that "Fosso interprets but does not incarnate the characters"[30] and thus represents fictional personalities. Since those characters are not named, but typified, Fosso comments on something unreal – with the use of his disguised yet recognisable body – and things exaggerated and invented that nevertheless symbolically offer a projection screen for the above mentioned laughter and revenge, yet also stands in for dreams and desires as in other photographs of the series. As an author, Fosso arranges these scenes. As a model he is completely available for representing people that interest him.[31] He withdraws the self and emphasises the body as a stage to comment on a thematic trajectory rather than an autobiographic one.

In his work *Le Rêve de mon Grand-Père* of 2003, specific personal experiences play a crucial role. The autobiographic referent is explicitly denominated through the title and an imaginary but simultaneously possible self, which relates to his grandfather's will for Fosso to become a healer and leader. Fosso states: "I borrow an identity. In order to succeed I immerse myself in the necessary physical and mental state. It's a way of freeing me from myself. A solitary path. I am a solitary man."[32] In referring to the immersion of the self into the potentiality of a personal role and the act of freeing himself – in a temporary sense, from the former practice of self-representation or in a more literal sense, from the generational burden of continuing one's ancestral traditions – Fosso unfolds his potential as artist or author. He juggles with what Hölzl calls the blurring of the "borderline between the autonomous and the heteronymous".[33] Also, the "solitary" gesture constructs the author as something similar to the genius that autonomously mediates between reality and the audience. Fosso cleverly follows the solitary path in stripping off the self in favour of the manifestation of a figure with autobiographical traits. He simultaneously strengthens the artistic self in becoming not only an ingenious actor but also the autonomous director of constructions around an inherited history.[34] Hölzl's interpretation of the images as "a self-vision, a series of self-photographs that do not reflect an actual life [...] but a virtual (possible) self",[35] are not contradictory to what can be called autobiographical traits. Both perspectives complement each other because they both point towards a potentiality – which Fosso develops in his later works – and designate the various methods of negotiating processes of identification. They manoeuvre through past and present and thus inform a virtual as well as an actual self.

In his recent series *African Spirits* of 2009, Fosso continues to play with an immersion of the self. He now actually incarnates the characters. Not only does Fosso assume the roles of black celebrities, politicians, cultural leaders and athletes such as Malcolm X, Angela Davis, Martin Luther King, Kwame Nkrumah, Miles Davis and Muhammad Ali, among others, he also re-enacts the iconic images with which they are associated.

Re-enactment is a peculiar phenomenon. In popular culture re-enactors adopt an alien identity in an attempt to reach the most authentic effects concerning the credibility of the re-enacted event.[36] The dissolution of the self into the new character often measures the degree of this credibility. However, in the sense of historical or temporal genuineness, social context, natural setting or the actors' identities, everything is imitation and nothing is real. The only quasi-authentic evidence can be found in the materiality of the re-enacted scene and the protagonists' performative achievement, which corresponds to the possibility of permanent improvement.[37] This applies to Fosso's artistic path as well. The effort of his astonishing conversion into personalities of African and African-American history is documented on the Internet as a making of-video on *YouTube*. Here, it becomes evident again that the photographs are, above all, self-portraits as Fosso activates the release of the camera himself.[38] Accordingly, the series is alternatively titled "auto-portraits" or "self-portraits" in several magazines and other publications without mentioning the names of the characters, although it is not clear whether Fosso himself added these subtitles to his *African Spirits*, or if this is an external positioning of the work within the apparent homogeneity of the self-portrait oeuvre.

Fosso's re-enactments go beyond their equivalent in popular culture and thus become more complex and ambivalent. Whereas pop culture follows a straight line towards the greatest possible authenticity, the artist seems to use the dissolution of his individual identity to fathom possibilities of self-portraiture between reference to the self and historical characterisations. Although Fosso disappears behind the characters, he nevertheless remains the artistic authority relating to the production of their images. The body as representational instrument remains under his aegis. Yet, the pictorial icons actually remain in their recognisable orchestration as well. In short, Fosso exhausts the boundaries between self-expression and self-disguise, between subjective and objective imagery and uses the immersive state of the self as both personal freedom and artistic autonomy. This interplay can be read as a comment on people's relation to the world in flux. The self is (in) history, and history informs the self.

So what is it that confronts us in Fosso's work – apart from the obliteration of the singularity of self in the here and now and the dissemination of historical events and icons within his performances? Although Fosso's photographs are still considered self-portraits and reflect his ongoing pleasure in role-play, they also address memory and collective iconography. In *African Spirits* he does not invent a role as in *The Chief who Sold Africa to the Colonialists*. Fosso appropriates already existing images that add a trace of the self to that prominent disguise, particularly if spectators are not familiar with these specific subjects. At the same time, however, he takes us along a journey through the cultural and political iconography of African and African-American history. It becomes a game of retrieving these icons and their accordant biographies. The reference to Fosso's artistic identity as self-portraitist and author essentially becomes an instrument for establishing the photographs as common property and anchoring them in a particular present. Fosso's body is used as representational plane, his status as author is employed to revive memory. With this work, Fosso does not dismiss self-referentiality but instead connects it with the past or, as Hölzl explains: "In not mentioning the names of the portrayed persons he appropriates their personality and achievement as part of his own cultural identity".[39] In this sense, it is not only the blurring of borders between the autonomous and the heteronymous as mentioned above, but also between past and present. Fosso comments on possible connections between historical as well as visual heritage.

3. *Kudzanai Chiurai. Directing Political Subjects*

Relating to Samuel Fosso's development as self-portrait photographer, Kudzanai Chiurai's photographs appear in line with the satirical representation of African politicians that can be found *inter alia* in Fosso's earlier work.

Kudzanai Chiurai was born in Harare in 1981. At the University of Pretoria he became the first black student to graduate with a Bachelor in

Fine Arts. A biography on the website of a Johannesburg art gallery states that he was banned from Zimbabwe because of his irreverent depiction of President Robert Mugabe.[40] In an interview with the BBC he spoke of his involvement in politics as an exile, having left his home city for South Africa in 1999. "I used to paint flowers", he explains, referring to his coming of age.[41]

Chiurai can be considered a shooting star in the international art scene with exhibitions in the United States, Great Britain, Australia, Denmark, Norway and Finland and with art enthusiasts such as Elton John owning *The Minister of Education* and other pieces. This photograph is part of his series *Dying to be Men*, which was displayed at his sixth solo exhibition at the Goodman Gallery in Cape Town in 2009.

The difference between Fosso and Chiurai is the latter's status as an author only. Chiurai is neither a self-portraitist nor a photographer. For the depiction of *The Black President* and his cabinet of ministers he collaborated with a photographer and a stylist, while YFM radio's DJ Siyabonga Ngwekazi played all characters.[42] Chiurai acknowledges that "the tradition with this kind of work has been for the artist to use their own image in the shots".[43] Yet, Chiurai is not interested in a self-referential trace. Firstly, he orchestrates his photographs with references to occurrences and material associations that particularly address the ambivalence of political reality in Africa between modernity and tradition as well as corruption, vanity, megalomania and violence. *The Minister of Health*, for example, dons a stethoscope as well as several skulls strung together with braided ropes and attached feathers and fur, recalling the practices and tools of *sangomas* or traditional healers in South Africa. *The Minister of Defence* holds both a machine-gun and an object resembling an African sceptre or fly-whisk. Other ministers wear fur coats, light their cigars with money or carry a gun. They all appear to concurrently inhabit the visual realm of African studio photography with its postmodern approach to representing fashion and material culture as well as referencing the continual representation of African leaders and US-American hip-hop culture in African art. All those dimensions, however, are rearranged here.[44] Whereas protagonists of studio photography neglected what was considered traditionally African, especially concerning clothes and other cultural symbols, Chiurai adopts it for his acrimonious visual commentary, as the ridicule of politicians derives directly from this antagonistic approach. The title of the whole series also suggests continuative interpretations of power and masculinity.

In working with this artistic legacy, Chiurai takes the eclecticism of studio photography even further. In this sense, he becomes a curator of the images rather than creator of a self-exploring project like that of Samuel Fosso. Although the photographs are in fact carefully concerted and aesthetically ambitious artworks, Chiurai seems nevertheless to be a collector of items and director of poses that together produce effects similar to the dark humour of satirists like Fosso or Chaplin. His 'studio photography' actually goes beyond any self-referential connotations and investigates socio-political affairs in general.

The background of Chiurai's images directly refers to the studio practice of Seydou Keïta, with his "ever-changing textile backdrops".[45] Enwezor also notes that "[w]ith the bold patterns of his draperies, however, Keïta subverted that sense of identification with the Western ideal and instead rooted his portraits in the immediacy of the African environment [...]."[46] Later, he writes:

> Though he was clearly in command of his compositional techniques, and carefully staged and designed every effect in his photographs, for him the photographic portrait was instead an instrument of two things: first, of social and cultural analysis, and second, of self-fashioning and myth-making.[47]

Within the photographic language of African studio photography, Enwezor declares Keïta's ornamented and painted backgrounds to be inventive and singular achievements.[48] He also writes that the draperies together with props were used as aesthetic and compositional tools to underline the sitters' status and comment on their position within society. Keïta's images were, in fact, commissions by an emerging Malian middle class from 1949 until the closing of his studio in 1964 and do not serve any political purpose.

It becomes all the more interesting to find contemporary artists like Kudzanai Chiurai following in his footsteps and deconstructing the visual myths of leadership. He constructs them as subjects of irony within the intimate space of the photographic studio. The ministers in Chiurai's images seem to overestimate their own capabilities, and yet they are clearly placed – perhaps trapped – on the fantastic and ultimately undefined stage of the portrait-making procedure. They are neither the characters Fosso plays nor images of leaders that are depicted within historical scenes or propagandistic orchestrations. Instead, Chiurai seems to intrepidly arrange his protagonists using the rich archive of (art) history for inspiration.[49] He easily takes up motifs of older photographic practices in Africa as well as those of popular culture in the United States. Kehinde Wiley and David LaChapelle are among the major artistic influences mentioned by Chiurai himself.[50] However, with the method of eclectically curating characters, types and scenes through culture and time, Chiurai opens up negotiations on the sincerity and respectability of his subjects. Their connectivity with different visual trajectories, which are indeed never arbitrary but instead derive from a volume of entangled narratives, puts them into perspective. While Fosso blurs the borders between the self and beleaguered history, Chiurai investigates the entanglement of visual culture in general and points it towards questions of masculinity, propaganda and political representation. Through their obviously composed and ridiculed character, his high gloss ministers are at once dazzling and susceptible to manipulation and vacuity.

4. Nomusa Makhubu. Negotiating the Archive

Both Samuel Fosso and Kudzanai Chiurai portray concrete and identifiable characters, be they fictional, historical or self-referential; the former oscillating between biographical traces, social phenomena and historical legacy through his self-exploration and the latter composing visual traditions that address representations of power and authority. Nomusa Makhubu's approach adds yet another formal as well as intellectual possibility to the exploitation of portraiture in dealing with the body, the self and the visual archive.

Makhubu is a young emerging artist born in South Africa in 1984. She studied at Rhodes University and is currently pursuing a PhD in history of art and visual culture. She has won several prizes and has been exhibited in South Africa and abroad. With reference to her self-portrait project, Makhubu explains:

> It will be comprised of images that disfigure the self-portrait while trying to re-place it to an identifiable axis. There is usage of old (South)

African photography. My self-portrait becomes lost within images that have centred debates about the black female body within constructs of culture and socialisation.[51]

In her work Makhubu also sets similar parameters as those discussed above with regard to Fosso and Chiurai. Like Fosso she uses her own body as a stage for an investigation of the self by means of historical images that hint at a colonial heritage as well as a deliverance of the self through disappearance.

Like Chiurai she arranges visual traces to reshape stereotypes that are imparted – in her case – by colonial documentary photography[52] and the accordant perceptions and prejudices. Yet, Makhubu finds other ways to use these artefacts and ideas. Her strategy of disguise is neither that of inventing and mocking fictional characters that comment on political representation nor is it mimicking historical icons to locate the self within a temporal continuum. Instead Makhubu entangles and layers visual trajectories and thus creates a disturbing effect.

In layering chromatic shots of her own body with historical black-and-white slides of African women that are projected on a screen behind her, the whole self-portrait index becomes distorted and appears as something freakish, something that can be linked to disability and deformation. The demarcation between artistic self and historical material is not easily discerned because Makhubu readjusts her posture to the figures in the background photographs, and both bodies merge into one another. In addition, the light and contours of the projection adjust to the artist's body without losing their perceptibility. The corporeal condition – represented by Makhubu's body – is not disguised, mocked or relativised but rather technically connected to the concrete historical index. The spectators do not ask themselves if what they see is a gifted actor playing a role and conjuring up certain associations and memories. They try to separate the visual elements and find out which components belong to which image. Whose mouth is this and whose nose? Where does the arm fit in and where the pattern of the skirt? In dressing herself with historic images rather than masquerading, Makhubu avoids self-reference and establishes a broader space within which the audience can explore different interpretations.

The works' titles directly reference historical documents. In Makhubu's *Lover*, for example, the same concept can be found as in an old photograph titled "Zulu Girl Waiting for her Lover". In another photograph, which is titled in isiXhosa *Omama Bencelisa* ("Mothers Breastfeeding"), we can see the words "*Kafir* mothers"[53] in the background image. Yet, the titles can also be applied to Makhubu's self-portrait when she refers to *Ntombi* ("girl") and *Ubuhle* ("beauty").

Using a simple technical method, Makhubu comments on the historical representation of bodies, especially female bodies, and its impact on present-day perceptions. Questions remain as to what kind of photographic commentary is at work here, and how parameters of self-reference and visual traces of a former colonial establishment are arranged to trigger what effects. Richard Powell, for example, took up the term "modern ancestorism"[54] with reference to the photographer Doris Ulmann who, in the early 20th century, documented rural people and their daily life in South Carolina. He aligns her work with the "primitivism" of the Harlem Renaissance. He writes:

> To the undiscerning this modern cult of the primitive was a throwback to an earlier tradition of "plantation" art and "colonialist" literature. Yet Ulmann's photographs were a radical way of looking at something old and familiar: a view infused with respect, awe and [...] a modern "ancestorism".[55]

Powell employs this notion to describe baptisms in African-American communities depicted in Ulmann's photographs in conjunction with "ancestorism", referring to religious practices that engage with the spirit of deceased relatives. Although Makhubu does not directly address any religious beliefs, she nevertheless uses visual documents of ancestral social life. Rather than utilising the art-historical archive in El Baroni's sense,[56] Makhubu works with an archive that was produced by agents of colonial powers and formed Western impressions of African identities. The "radical way" of promoting "respect and ancestorism" is carried forward photographically in the sense that Makhubu opens up new visual perspectives with images that represent myopic viewpoints.

To comprehensively explain Makhubu's work, another concept can be applied. Susanne Gehrmann speaks of the production of autoethnographies in literature which are not "individual intro- and retrospections"[57] but thematise the self as being located within social structures.[58] Makhubu, too, incorporates depictions of people into her self-portraits who could be her relatives, ancestors or just markers of a common historical heritage. Even if the self-referential gesture still remains dominant, it informs negotiations about the influences of such a heritage on today's identities rather than simply visually implementing ethnographic scrutiny.

Yet, apart from the fact that Makhubu explores the self and self-portraitistic instruments, her work can also be looked at from a different angle. The inclusion of her body in the projections also changes the historical documents due to the changed context. They become individualised and are entrained into a present that attempts to transcend stereotypes and subvert them by exposing personal or alternative stories. Assumptions are altered. In this sense, the personal takes on another, more complex dimension in the self-portrait as well as the historical photograph.

5. Summary

This essay on African photographic portraiture between history, politics and the self has explored the continuities and changes in a genre that was famously established by Samuel Fosso, a photographer born in Cameroon and working in Bangui, Central African Republic. In his early works he pioneers self-portraiture by negotiating images of Africans from French magazines. He uses his body to question European stereotypes and transforms his studio into a space of historical exploration. He satirically exposes the absurdity of Bokassa's dictatorial self-fashioning and later moves on to re-enact personalities of African and Afro-American history. His images are both self-portraits and products of self-referential role-play that comment on the production of icons and images and visually connect the past and the present.

I have shown how younger artists from Zimbabwe, such as the international shooting star Kudzani Chuirai, and from South Africa, as Nomusa Makhubu, negotiate the achievements of first-generation artists such as Fosso. Chiurai is less a photographer himself but an artist who works together with photographers to take the eclectic studio photography even further. Combining characters, types and scenes across space and time, he becomes a curator of images rather than a creator like Fosso. Reminiscent of Keïta from Mali and of Fosso, he deconstructs the visual myths of leadership and discusses the forms of male political leadership. Nomusa Makhubu is mainly concerned with visual representations of the black female body. Like Fosso she uses the body as a stage to investigate the self and like Chuirai she employs visual traces of the past reshape stereotypes. But unlike the two, Makhubu reworks photographs from the colonial archive, merging them with representations of her own body so that it becomes impossible to tell the two apart.

The three artists examined in detail prove the vitality of African portraiture that has long since developed its own tradition with which younger artists engage. It remains to be seen how the influence of global interchange will impact African artists in the future.

Notes

1   This is at least the current state of research also underlined by Olu Oguibe (2008: 52) who writes that "no art photographer has worked longer – or spent more time – with images of himself than Bangui studio master Samuel Fosso".
2   The notion of the self is an intensely discussed concept. It hovers between the deconstruction of homogeneous and hegemonically positioned subjects and the reconstruction of the agency of subjects that were and are considered the Others of those hegemonic selves, their opposition or alterity. The legitimisation of this practice derives from the belief that the self is a fiction.

    David Hume was one of the first philosophers who acknowledged the self as a product of what the body feels and experiences within a certain context. The embedding of the self in social contexts, language and discourse has since been elaborated upon further, especially by Jacques Derrida and Michel Foucault. It is this relational character of the self which is investigated by the artists' work discussed in my essay. For a first introduction see, for example, Edgar and Sedgwick (2002).
3   Jean-Bédel Bokassa (1921-1996) seized power through a military coup in 1965. He established himself by purges and then with help of personal guards as well as nationalistic propaganda. In 1976 he changed the constitution in order to replace the republican system by a monarchy and crowned himself emperor in 1977. The former support of the French government diminished until Bokassa was finally overthrown in 1979, during one of his travels abroad, because of the increased oppression of his

own people and the unpredictability of his political moves (Speitkamp 2007: 412).
4   Schlinkert (2004: 35).
5   Enwezor (2004: 17).
6   Oguibe (2008: 53).
7   The index in photography describes the causal and material trace of the respective object or subject on the actual photograph.
8   This is my translation of "Lebensbeweis" (Hölzl 2008: 222), a term that seems even more plausible as Fosso used his self-portraits to let his grandmother in Nigeria know that he was alive and healthy.
9   Apart from the relativisation of the author's status as the exclusive producer of meaning in poststructuralist thought, a photographic self-portraitist like Fosso strengthens the relevance of an author precisely because he arranges and performs the self as a constantly alterable image and also activates the camera's automatic release button. In this sense, "any text [or image] written by someone considered to be an author [or photographer] may acquire additional significance precisely because of this authorship" (Edgar & Sedgwick 2002: 29).
10 Hölzl makes productive Philippe Lejeune's theory of the autobiographic pact for visual forms of self-expression to explain the identity of photographer and the photographed as being produced by a reading or viewing contract between artist and viewer. The autoportraitistic pact and its accordant signature as self-portrait is thus an argument for the aforementioned identity, not its authentication (2008: 165).
11 See Hölzl (2008: 132).
12 Bigham (1999: 58).
13 Hölzl (2008: 181) points to the investigation of photography from Africa in European ethnographic scholarship from the 1990s onwards.
14 See also Lamunière who writes that "to their clients, sitting for a portrait and then displaying it at home or sending it to family and friends was a potent means of self-definition at a time of considerable social change" (2001: 11).
15 The Biafran conflict from 1967 to 1970 emerged due to a perceived disproportionality within the federal structure of society from 1960 onwards. The densely populated north of Nigeria contributed the majority of members of parliament whereas the social elites of the Yoruba and Igbo in the south felt themselves numerically under-represented. After a failed coup by Igbo officers and their subsequent persecution by the military from the north, the Igbo proclaimed their region as the independent state of Biafra. In 1970, however, Biafra had to submit to the military superiority of the federal

troops. (Speitkamp 2007: 386-388) For literary negotiations of the Biafra war, see Susanne Gehrmann's contribution to this volume.
16 See Schlinkert (2004: 29).
17 After a career in fashion photography with her husband Allan, Arbus started taking photographs of New York's bleak areas – wax museums or flophouses – in the late 1950s. She then turned towards people not commonly visible in public visual culture that was dominated by documentary or commercial photography in magazines like *Life* or *Look*. The special effect of Arbus's intimate portraits of handicapped persons, transvestites or circus performers resulted from their marginalisation within society. Their surreal appearance stems from the contrast with a hegemonic reality mediated through glossy magazines as well as from Arbus's selection of scenes that capture the unfamiliar ambivalence between roughness and tenderness.
18 Schlinkert (2004: 31).
19 In associating the habit of punishments and beatings "with the notion of parental authority as it was constituted in colonial times" Jean-Francois Bayart, for example, describes Jean-Bédel Bokassa as the "great presidential flogger, 'Papa' Bokassa" (2000: 257).
20 Speitkamp (2007: 414).
21 My translation of "Die afrikanische Porträtfotografie als populäre Kulturtechnik kennt keine antikolonialen Manifeste, keine Idealisierungen der afrikanischen Tradition eines Senghor, Nkrumah oder Nyerere und keine den eigenen Größenwahn unterstützenden Mythologisierungen des Afrikanisch-Authentischen eines Mobutu, Amin oder Bokassa. Sie kennt nur Hybridität, Aktualität und Kommerzialität." (Hölzl 2008: 178-179)
22 The series was commissioned on the occasion of Tati's 50th birthday, a discount shop that is mainly visited by African migrants (Hölzl 2008: 202).
23 Fosso quoted in Schlinkert (2004: 51).
24 It would have been interesting here to compare reactions of different spectators within different contexts which might have provided another indicator for an artwork's ever-changing position and function.
25 In a recent interview Fosso states that this particular picture "really sums up what I am trying to say about African-ness, about western clichés. And it's ironic." This statement seems to be an extension of what he addressed as an expression of anger in an earlier discussion. Also, he connects the photograph to recent, postcolonial issues rather than to a critique of colonial slavery – as might be perceived by a Western audience – when he says that "it's about the history of the white man and the black man in Africa. Because they may try to cover it up these days, [...], but underneath it's still the same." Fosso points out how such images can change meaning. A self-

critical dimension comes into play when he emphasises again the autobiographical marker – in a very general form this time – and mentions that "I am an African chief [...]. I am all the African chiefs who have sold their continent to white men." (Henley 2011)

26 Reimer (2009).
27 As defined, for example, by Alexander Kozintsev (2010: 22) as "an unnatural hybrid of laughter and anger".
28 With this I refer to the constructed and, in the course of colonisation, contested character of tradition that Eric Hobsbawm, for example, calls "invented tradition". He writes: "'Invented tradition' is taken to mean a set of practices, normally governed by overtly or tacitly accepted rules and of a ritual or symbolic nature, which seek to inculcate certain values and norms of behaviour by repetition, which automatically implies continuity with the past." (Hobsbawm 1983: 1)
29 Reimer (2009).
30 Hölzl (2009: 43).
31 Schlinkert (2004: 51).
32 *Ibid.* 25.
33 Hölzl (2009: 43).
34 See also Ostermann (2002: 117).
35 Hölzl (2009: 47).
36 See also McCalman & Pickering (2010).
37 Protagonists of re-enactment are proud of their "absolute authenticity". Their hobby requires extensive historical research and an exact replication of the material culture involved. (Lemhöfer 2011)
38 Here, Hölzl (2010) very clearly differentiates between the self-portrait in Fosso's earlier works and the self-photograph of the series *African Spirits*. For her, his imitation of icons of African culture can be defined as photography without the intention to self-portraiture, when the referent of the image is not the photographer himself. That the demarcation of a self-portraitistic intention is indeed a difficult task is especially apparent in Fosso's oeuvre, where one receives the impression that he always consigns a self-referential trace. As Hölzl recognises with regard to *African Spirits*, Fosso's individual signature is at least visible as author and actor of the scenes when she detects "significant" (2010: 125) departures from the original models. I do not want to discuss at this point whether Fosso's latest series can be theorised as self-portraiture, portraiture or self-photography. I am more interested in the visual references that expand into his images and therefore call his works photographs.

39 My translation of "Indem er die Namen der Dargestellten nicht nennt, eignet er sich [...] deren Persönlichkeit und Leistung als Teil seiner eigenen kulturellen Identität an." (Hölzl 2010: 126)
40 See Goodman Gallery (2012).
41 Harding (2011).
42 Barnett (2011).
43 Jacobs (2009).
44 For further reading see Bell (1996) or Bazin (1995).
45 Enwezor (2010: 31).
46 *Ibid.*
47 *Ibid.*
48 In an article on the question of authorship in Seydou Keïta's work, Elizabeth Bigham also addresses the sitters' possible roles in its production in addition to the construction of Keïta's autonomy as an artist from the 1990s onwards. She (1999: 57) writes: "Indeed, one can argue that they [the photographic subjects] not only provided the photographs' literal content but also engaged in their own transformations into aesthetic images." For another brief analysis of Keïta's use of African print fabrics see also Cezar Bartholomeu (2011).
49 In an interview with Hassan Khan, for example, Bassam el Baroni differentiates today's artistic practices by their relationship to art history. Although it seems to be difficult to establish clear-cut categories of what can be perceived as fine art and contemporary art, Baroni nevertheless introduces the idea of "art history as an archive" to explain contemporary art's link to knowledge production and the "grand 'global' Culture of many cultures" (Khan 2011).
50 Kudzanai Chiurai and Kehinde Wiley were both, for instance, mentioned in separate articles in the South African pop culture magazine, *One Small Seed*, in 2011. Although Wiley – with his heroic portraits of prominent black men and black adolescents in Harlem and in urban spaces throughout the world – pursues completely different matters, his and Chiurai's use of ornamental backgrounds as well as their formal approaches are similar. This journey of Seydou Keïta's draperies in particular – also applied by Wiley – in visual culture seems to become more and more wide-spread and diversified.
51 See Nomusa Makhubu's listing of her exhibition at Alliance Française on *Artthrob* in 2008.
52 For a deeper insight into colonial photography and its context see Albrecht (2004).

53 The term *Kafir* or *Kaffir* derives from the Arabic word for disbeliever and, in South Africa and other African countries, was used offensively to describe black people.
54 Powell (1997: 25).
55 *Ibid.*
56 Khan (2011).
57 Gehrmann (2004: 11).
58 See also Heewon Chang who defines the autoethnographic approach as that which "should be ethnographic in its methodological orientation, cultural in its interpretive orientation, and autobiographical in its content orientation" (2008: 48).

Bibliography

Albrecht, Michael (Ed.): *Getting Pictures Right. Context and Interpretation*, Köln, 2004.
Artthrob: "Nomusa Makhubu at Alliance Française", *Archive* 131, July 2008, <http://www.artthrob.co.za/08jul/listings_cape.html#af>, accessed 12 June 2012.
Barnett, Laura: "Photographer Kudzanai Chiurai's Best Shot", *The Guardian Online*, 10 July 2011, <http://www.guardian.co.uk/artanddesign/2011/jul/10/photography-kudzanai-chiurai-best-shot>, accessed 22 May 2012.
Bartholomeu, Cezar: "African Photography in the Gilberto Chateaubriand Collection". – In Museu de Arte Moderna (Ed.): *Fotografia Africana Coleção Gilberto Chateaubriand*, Rio de Janeiro, 2011, pp. 12-47.
Bayart, Jean-Francois: "Africa in the World. A History of Extraversion", *African Affairs* 99, 2000, 217-267.
Bazin, Hugues: *La Culture Hip-hop*, Paris, 1995.
Bell, Clare: *In/sight. African Photographers 1940 to the Present*, New York, 1996.
Bigham, Elizabeth: "Issues of Authorship in the Portrait Photographs of Seydou Keïta", *African Arts* 32:1, 1999, 56-67.
Chang, Heewon: *Autoethnography as Method*, Walnut Creek, 2008.
Edgar, Andrew & Peter Sedgwick (Eds.): *Cultural Theory. The Key Concepts*, London, 2002.
Enwezor, Okwui: "Popular Theatre. Photography and Difference". – In Maria Francesca Bonetti & Guido Schlinkert (Eds.): *Samuel Fosso*, Milan, 2004, pp. 14-19.

---: "Gesture, Pose, Mimesis. Seydou Keïta's Portraits". – In O. E. (Ed.): *Events of the Self. Portraiture and Social Identity*, Göttingen, 2010, pp. 31-33.
Fell, Sarah Jayne (Ed.): *One Small Seed. The South African Pop Culture Magazine* 19, 13 March 2011, <http://www.onesmallseed.com/2011/03/issue-19-online/>, accessed 12 June 2012.
Gehrmann, Susanne: "Vom Entwerfen des Ich im Erinnern des Wir. Überlegungen zur Autobiographik in Afrika", Inaugural Lecture, Berlin, 2004, pp. 3-44, edoc-Server der Humboldt-Universität zu Berlin.
Goodman Gallery: "Kudzanai Chiurai", *Goodman Gallery*, 2012, <http://www.goodman-gallery.com/artists/kudzanaichiurai>, accessed 22 May 2012.
Harding, Andrew: "Zimbabwe's Kudzanai Chiurai. Can Art Change Africa", *BBC News Africa*, 24 October 2011, <http://www.bbc.co.uk/news/world-africa-15429299>, accessed 22 May 2012.
Henley, Jon: "Photographer Samuel Fosso's Best Shot", *The Guardian Online*, 19 June 2011, <http://www.guardian.co.uk/artanddesign/2011/jun/19/photographer-samuel-fosso-best-shot>, 22 May 2012.
Hobsbawm, Eric: *The Invention of Tradition*, Cambridge & New York, 1983.
Hölzl, Ingrid: *Der Autoporträtistische Akt. Zur Theorie des Fotografischen Selbstporträts am Beispiel von Samuel Fosso*, München, 2008.
---: "Self-Portrait, Self-Vision. The Work of Samuel Fosso", *Nka. Journal of Contemporary African Art* 24, 2009, 40-47.
---: "Inszeniertes Selbst. Der Fall Samuel Fosso". – In Lars Blunck (Ed.): *Die Fotografische Wirklichkeit*, Bielefeld, 2010, pp. 117-127.
Jacobs, Katharine: "Kudzanai Chiurai at Goodman Gallery Cape", *Artthrob*, 2009, <http://www.artthrob.co.za/Reviews/Review-of-Dying-to-be-Men-by-Katharine-Jacobs-at-Goodman-Gallery-Cape.aspx>, accessed 22 May 2012.
Khan, Hassan: "Interview with Bassam el Baroni", *Artterritories*, 005 Trail, 2011, <http://www.artterritories.net/?page_id=2063>, accessed 22 May 2012.
Kozintsev, Alexander: *The Mirror of Laughter*, New Brunswick, 2010.
Lamunière, Michelle: "You Look Beautiful Like That. The Portrait Photographs of Seydou Keïta and Malick Sidibé". – In M. L. (Ed.): *You Look Beautiful Like That. The Portrait Photographs of Seydou Keïta and Malick Sidibé*, New Haven & London, 2001, pp. 11-43.
Lemhöfer, Anne: "Reenactment in Minden. Jeder Knopf Stimmt", *Die Zeit* 46, 10 November 2011, <http://www.zeit.de/2011/46/Interview-Minden>, accessed 22 May 2012.
McCalman, Iain & Paul A. Pickering: *Historical Reenactment. From Realism to the Affective Turn*, Basingstoke, 2010.

Obolo, Pascale: "Making of Samuel Fosso's African Spirits", *Patras Planelle Tisserand Editions*, *YouTube*, 2008, <http://www.youtube.com/watch?v=HJGd4DnyZYc>, 22 May 2012.

Oguibe, Olu: "In the Beginning was the Self. Self-Portraiture in Samuel Fosso's Art Photography", *Foam Magazine* 17, 2008, 52-54.

Ostermann, Eberhard: *Die Authentizität des Ästhetischen. Studien zur Ästhetischen Transformation der Rhetorik*, München, 2002.

Powell, Richard L.: "Jazz Age Harlem and Beyond". – In R. L. P. & David A. Bailey (Eds.): *Rhapsodies in Black. Art of the Harlem Renaissance*, Berkeley, Los Angeles & London, 1997, pp. 16-33.

Reimer, Robert C.: "Does Laughter Make the Crime Disappear? An Analysis of Cinematic Images of Hitler and the Nazis 1940-2007", *Senses of Cinema* 52, 2009, <http://sensesofcinema.com/2009/52/does-laughter-make-the-crime-disappear-an-analysis-of-cinematic-images-of-hitler-and-the-nazis-1940-2007/>, accessed 22 May 2012.

Schlinkert, Guido: "Transformer". – In Maria Francesca Bonetti & G. S. (Eds.): *Samuel Fosso*, Milan, 2004, pp. 22-55.

Simbao, Ruth Kerkham: "The Thirtieth Anniversary of the Soweto Uprisings. Reading the Shadow in Sam Nzima's Iconic Photograph of Hector Pieterson", *African Arts* 40:2, 2007, 52-69.

Speitkamp, Winfried: *Kleine Geschichte Afrikas*, Stuttgart, 2007.

Galleries

Chiurai: Goodman Gallery, http://www.goodman-gallery.com
Fosso: Jack Shainman Gallery, http://www.jackshainman.com
Makhubu: Erdmann Contemporary, http://www.erdmanncontemporary.co.za

Doreen Strauhs (*Bonn*)

Anglophone East African (Women's) Writing since 2000.
Femrite and *Kwani Trust*

1. Introduction. Why Study Anglophone East African Writing?

This article will provide an overview on literary themes, aesthetics, writers and publishing dynamics in Anglophone East African (women's) writing since 2000.[1] Following a brief insight into the relevance of Anglophone East African (women's) writing and its history, the discussion of selected literary texts will illustrate the extent to which literature is interrelated with immediate local environments and life realities. Examining these texts and structures of the literary scene from this region in greater detail, this article also proposes recommendations for primary sources and secondary reading to this field. In particular, this contribution will focus on literatures from Kenya and Uganda, for in both countries the literary NGOs (LINGOs) *Femrite* and *Kwani Trust* have been trend-setting as sites of literary innovation and as publishing organs. Many of their associated contributors such as Binyavanga Wainaina, Yvonne Owuor, Muthoni Garland, Monica Arac de Nyeko or Goretti Kyomuhendo have gained international reputation and are currently celebrated among the best-known writers from the region. *Femrite* and *Kwani Trust* offer a platform for established as well as upcoming writers to experiment with form, media, content and language both in online and print publications, thereby giving birth to new literary trends and styles that have started to refashion and broaden the canon of East African writing in English.

To cultural outsiders, studying these contemporary literatures can contribute to a sound understanding of the continent and its peoples in times when the image of Africa is still conflicting. Very recently, Binyavanga Wainaina, a Kenyan author and co-initiator of *Kwani Trust*, wrote for BBC news in response to the "Kony 2012" campaign:[2]

> Let us imagine that Africa was really like it is shown in the international media. Africa would be a country. Its largest province would be Somalia. Bono, Angelina Jolie and Madonna would be joint presidents, appointed by the United Nations. European aid workers would run the Foreign Affairs Office, gap year students from the UK the Ministry of Health and the Ministry of Culture would be run by the makers of the Kony 2012 videos.[3]

Binyavanga Wainaina argues that the world has got its image of Africa very badly wrong.[4] Given this general lack of understanding, it is more than worthwhile to study (recent) writing from these countries at high school and university levels. Students, teachers and lecturers can thus raise their awareness for Africa and African perspectives.

2. Production Sites of East African Literature in Historical Perspective

To recall the set-up of the Anglophone literary landscapes in Kenya and Uganda at this point certainly will be helpful as to contextualise the discussion of agency and narrative that this article examines. Between the late 1940s and the late 1990s, the literary worlds in Kenya and Uganda consisted of at least six large frameworks within and from which Anglophone writers were acting, writing and speaking: (1) university literature departments (at Makerere and Nairobi University), (2) the indigenous and multinational publishing industry (i.e. producing textbooks as well as books that were considered 'popular' literature), (3) exiled authors, (4) journalism (i.e. newspaper columns like "Whispers"[5]), (5) the theatre (i.e. campus theatre, open air theatre or pub theatre) and (6) LINGOs (LINGOs of the 1960s: *Transition*, *Mbari*, *Chemchemi* and present LINGOs such as *Femrite* and *Kwani Trust*). These literary frameworks were highly interconnected. In terms of their transnational and trans-institutional set-up, writers would move from one framework to another or be involved with one framework more than with another at various stages of their career both within their countries as well as increasingly across territorial borders.[6] With the beginning of the new millennium and the increased accessibility of the Internet, a seventh framework has additionally emerged with (7) the World Wide Web, providing a plethora of opportunities for self-promotion and publishing.[7] Among all of these frameworks, LINGOs are not new to the region. Yet, due to the shift of non-African funding and development aid into the NGO-sector, these literary agencies have been on the rise across the continent with their literature being more easily accessible to cultural outsiders through online distribution[8] and online ordering systems. As Marie Krüger remarks in her book *Women's Literature in Kenya and Uganda* (2011), *Kwani Trust* and *Femrite* along with their various contributors have dramatically reshaped the East African literary scene for more than a decade.[9]

Over the past twelve years, these LINGOs and their associated writers have enriched the literary landscapes inside and outside their countries with publications of global interest and accessibility[10] – more so than any other existing African literary NGO. Founded by aspiring creative writers in 2002, *Kwani Trust* meanwhile has released six volumes of its flagship publication, the literary journal, *Kwani?*,[11] and ten mini booklets, the *Kwanini*. At the same time, its affiliated writers have continued to stir a global interest in Anglophone Kenyan writing with essays, short stories and poetry collections published on websites and short story anthologies or newspapers world-wide apart from the *Kwani Trust* imprint. Binyavanga Wainaina's satirical essay "How to Write About Africa", for instance, circulated on the Internet as spam in 2006 and triggered several video responses on *YouTube*. Essays later compiled in the *Kwanini After the Vote* (2008) had previously been published in *The New York Times*.

By the time Wainaina's essay was circulating on the World Wide Web, *Femrite*, founded by female university lecturers from Makerere University in 1995, had already released over fourteen print publications including novels, short story and poetry anthologies as well as life-writing collections. Simultaneously, *Femrite*'s members have triggered debates about creative writing from Uganda with their short stories and novels apart from the *Femrite* publishing imprint. Some of these works have already appeared in transnational publishing houses. Doreen Baingana's short story collection, *Tropical Fish*, compiled in 2005, has seen local print runs in the USA, Kenya, Nigeria and South Africa. In 2007, Goretti Kyomuhendo reached global attention with her fourth adult novel, *Waiting*, released by the Feminist Press, USA. Having won the Caine Prize in 2007, Monica Arac de Nyeko provoked a controversial debate about homosexuality in Uganda with her short story "Jambula Tree", previously published in Ama Ata Aidoo's collection of *African Love Stories* (2006). Among the African LINGOs focussing on women's writing, *Femrite* has been the only African LINGO that has contributed to the women's writing scene on the continent with such outreach and diversity.[12]

As non-profit organisations, these LINGOs operate in a sector between public, i.e. governmental, institutions and for-profit business enterprises. Given their primary focus on literature, LINGOs belong to the field of arts and culture within the non-profit sector. LINGOs are largely dependent on external funding, yet in their actions they are usually financially independent from their local governments. As is common for NGOs, the LINGOs' organisational structures are also characterised by flat hierarchies and a great number of volunteers. LINGOs are organisations that explicitly have the production and promotion of literature, most notably fiction, poetry and creative non-fiction, at the core of their interests and use creative writing as their major tool of expression. They exist largely to generate programmes and services that are of benefit for others in support of nurturing literary talent, literary awards, literary productivity and literacy in national and local languages. In terms of their communal work, LINGOs aim at promoting creative writing and reading for the individual and society through literary workshops, reading events and conferences as well as writing competitions and publications. As the producers, initiators and creators of such programmes and services, LINGOs situate themselves outside the university context in order to attract an audience that is not necessarily involved with academic research. Most importantly, LINGOs differ from NGOs in the sector of Theatre for Development, since the literature produced and promoted by LINGOs and their associated authors is at least not openly content-tailored as to suit specific donor interests in development policy, such as HIV/AIDS prevention. LINGOs are instead open to any kind of innovative literary creativity as long as it is in line with the LINGOs' individually established agenda. LINGOs can have their own publishing companies, which are mostly registered under the company law with their local governments, and under which they publish literature by their members, associates or people who have produced literature that fits the LINGOs' agendas. As publishing ventures, LINGOs are usually small-scale publishing outfits, which is largely due to their low economic capital, their specific literary agendas and their primary focus on the organisation of literary activities and events. In order to emerge, exist and evolve as locally established, legally recognised and ultimately influential actors in public, LINGOs generally depend on a certain level of socio-political leeway in their local societies.

Given that they are dynamic networks of heterogeneous groups of writers, it is useful to imagine LINGOs such as *Femrite* and *Kwani Trust* as force-fields and sites of struggles, in which positions of greater authority can change – to echo Pierre Bourdieu – "considerably depending on different periods,"[13] as authors withdraw while others arrive. Individuals with their own writing style or ideas on the LINGOs' literary mission influence the construct of the LINGO to varying degrees. The publications by *Kwani Trust* and *Femrite* therefore display a great diversity offering novels, novellas, short stories, visual narratives, testimonials and poetry anthologies. By using electronic media such as blogging, email and SMS and promoting language varieties such as Sheng and Engsh[14] in all of their publications, *Femrite* and *Kwani Trust* as well as their writers moreover contribute to the development of a flexible notion of literature in the region.

3. Kwani Trust. *Experimenting with Fictional Writing in Blog, Email and SMS*

When asked about the importance of the Internet and the interaction of art and literature in Kenya, Binyavanga Wainaina highlighted in October 2006:

> The biggest movement so far has been the group of the bloggers – the blogging community and its growth is phenomenal and inside there are poets and politics, commentators, guys linking information about what is going on in the banks of Kenya. Expression left the printed page a while ago and one of the things that *Kwani?* is trying to do is to make interaction between those spaces and trying to find out how to make those things exciting. One of our marketing tools for instance is SMS which brings people to our readings. We've been very careful to use all

these kinds of media. We've once had a love story by SMS in long Sheng that everyone is screaming about.[15]

In Kenya, electronic media and social web spaces on the Internet as well as SMS technology enjoy a growing popularity that cuts across ethnic, social, religious and personal backgrounds, although this holds more true for the urban population with a certain level of literacy and a certain level of access to electronic facilities as well as socio-economic means. *Kwani Trust* has consistently worked towards disintegrating the borders between online and offline communication by incorporating and exploring email, blogging and SMS technology as narratives for literary expression since its first issue and most prominently in *Kwani? 04*, released in 2007.[16] In her article "Kwani? Exploring New Literary Spaces in Kenya", Dinah Ligaga highlights the example of the "Vain Jang'o Letter", a creative email correspondence published under the title "Fw.Fw.". Wainaina introduces the email as follows: "A year or so ago, I received this forward, a story in 'Engsh' by an anonymous Kenyan. I sent it around; it was very funny, but annoying – written by a major wannabe, so Muthoni and I decided to respond."[17] While keeping its original form, Wainaina and Garland transform the message into a creative two-part narrative – written by a Luo man and a response by a Gĩkũyũ woman. Both characters use the email mode in order to tackle the ethnic differences and personal perceptions of their private encounter.

In "Fw.Fw.", the Luo author of the anonymous mail becomes Vain Jang'o. To cultural outsiders, this reads like a real name, but it actually is a telling name functioning as an ironic remark on the writer's personality: "Jang'o is a sheng word used to refer to Luo men in general who are often known for their materialistic, flamboyant and showy nature that projects them as vain,"[18] Ligaga points out. The first part of the narrative contains the original email in which Vain Jang'o presents himself as a well-situated and sophisticated man who stresses his desired self-image by showing off his ability of speaking Engsh. In the narration, his usage of Engsh has a humorous connotation considering the fact that he would want to use the language to underline his personality as a Jang'o.[19]

While "chilling in Cactus," a posh bar in Nairobi Westlands, "[t]he other Sato [Saturday]",[20] Vain Jang'o spots a girl he wants to impress because her outward appearance appeals to him. This impression, however, crumbles when he talks to her: "Kwanza [Firstly]," he points out, "the baby has a deep rural Okuyu [Gĩkũyũ] accent you know the one where the Rs and Ls are kabisa [totally] interchanged. Oh no!"[21] Vain Jang'o continues to talk about the woman whose accent and lack of education gets him disinterested. The second part of the narrative contains the response by the girl justifying herself in Engsh and dismantling Vain Jang'o's fake demeanour. It becomes clear that the girl is not "'a brainless bimbo' that Vain Jang'o patronizingly looks down upon, [...] [but actually] a beautiful girl from Kiambu,"[22] who has a clear sense of her social status, the environment around her and the goals she wants to achieve in the future. In her analysis of "Fw.Fw.", Lillian Kaviti from Nairobi University adds that

> [a]s the story unfolds, both Vain Jang'o and the girl betray a hidden contempt for each other based on negative stereotypical attitudes the Luo and Gĩkũyũ communities are assumed to harbour towards each other.[23]

Both characters in this story therefore use Engsh to present themselves.[24]

The title of the piece, "Fw.Fw.", short for 'forward', already points at electronic mail language as well as at the fact that its content has already been forwarded at different times.[25] On page, the message and its response appear as an open window of an email programme identifying Binyavanga Wainaina and Muthoni Garland as the recipients "@Binyavanga@bin.com @Muthoni@G.com",[26] thereby visually emphasising the email mode and introducing Wainaina and Garland as the authors of the fictitious response. Wainaina and Garland illustrate that "e-mail allows personal narratives to be told in public while still remaining paradoxically private".[27] Instead of confronting the Gĩkũyũ girl directly, Vain Jang'o shares his private impressions of the girl afterwards (via email) with anonymous recipients who in turn forward the email to others (like Wainaina and Garland). As a result of this forwarding, the mail becomes public while still remaining specifically private in terms of its content. The email format transcends the personal sphere and invites the public for a response. This invitation for the response of others is deliberately planned by Vain Jang'o. His rhetorical question "[G]uess what gentlemen?"[28] thus reveals that Vain Jang'o intended to share his private experience with male recipients of the email like in an open letter. The fictitious response by the Gĩkũyũ woman, Ligaga argues, could therefore also be read as a response which such an email might invite from the online community, and one could add that this then invites even unexpected responses from women, who were not originally addressed by Vain Jang'o.

In "Fw.Fw.", Garland and Wainaina therefore highlight the ways in which Kenyans channel private issues informally in times when digital technology impacts personal lives decisively, by adopting the email mode and the usage of Sheng and Engsh for writing fiction. Through its usage of Engsh and the tackling of ethnic tensions between Luo and Gĩkũyũ as well as frictions between people with higher and lower education, the narrative provides a sense of life in today's Kenya. The incorporation of the email mode in *Kwani?* dissolves the borders between online and offline media. These borders dissolve the moment *Kwani Trust* decides to bring the narration into the printed form of its literary magazine that also circulates in public – similarly to email communication in the online world. In doing so, *Kwani Trust* not only gives insights into possible life situations in today's Kenya, but also heightens the significance of considering email as a space that – as in the case of Wainaina's "How to Write About Africa" in 2006 – can inhabit pieces that can either be read or indeed be intended as pieces of creative expression from Kenya and hence are worth considering in order to grasp a more comprehensive picture of contemporary literature from Kenya.

This merging of online and offline media is further pursued in *Kwani? 03* containing the Sheng love story in SMS by Roger Akena and in *Kwani? 05 Part Two* including a great number of SMS messages from the post-election violence as well as with blogging in *Kwani? 04*. The fourteen blog entries in *Kwani? 04* include a range of non-fictional essays as well as fiction. With such deliberate incorporation of email, SMS and blogging as well as oral codes such as Sheng and Engsh, *Kwani Trust* promotes a flexible notion of literature. The LINGO and its contributing writers demand that the very definition of what counts as literature as well as the sites where literature is created and the ways an audience deals with creative expression need to be re-defined. To this LINGO, the digital media inhabit creativity just as much as print media do. In opposition to print media, digital media allow for a world-wide and instant marketing of texts and also invite an audience from Kenya and around the world that otherwise might not engage with literature in print, but that is drawn to creative expression by the currently prominent digital formats of email, SMS or blogging. Thus, *Kwani Trust* and its published writers contribute to a renewed understanding of literature and the places where it thrives.

4. Femrite. *Promoting Women's Rights through Fiction*

When *Femrite* was founded in 1996, the promotion of women's writing was a very new step in Uganda's literary scene.[29] Other literary agents, like Fountain Publishers, one of the oldest publishers in Uganda, were rather doubtful in the beginning when looking at *Femrite*, not knowing what to expect. *Femrite* and Fountain Publishers began to cooperate, for instance, with the publication of literary material such as Goretti Kyomuhendo's novel *Secrets No More* (1996) and Mary Karooro Okurut's novel *The Official Wife*, printed by Fountain Publishers in 2003 and later sold and promoted electronically by *Femrite*.[30] *Femrite* members did not perceive their project as a laughing matter. Strong-minded, they set out in order to change the literary canon as well as the power relationships in the literary world through the visibility of female writing. Like *Kwani Trust*, *Femrite* thus also joined the struggle over authority as a counterforce to the established status-quo in the literary field.

In ways similar to the novels *Secrets No More* and *The Official Wife*, Susan Kiguli's poem "I am Tired of Talking in Metaphors", published in the poetry collection of *The African Saga* (1998) criticises the behaviour of men in Ugandan society. Being a brief text, this poem can easily be used as an introductory piece to Ugandan women literature at both high school as well as university levels.

> I Am Tired of Talking in Metaphors
>
> I will talk plainly
> Because I am moved to abandon riddles.
> I will tell you how we held our heads
> In our hands
> Because the owl hooted throughout the night

And the dogs howled as if in mourning:
We awaited bad news
We received it
Our mother blinded in one eye
Crippled in the right leg
Because she did not vote
Her husband's candidate.

I will remind you
Of the time the peeled plantains
Stood upright in the cooking pot
We slaughtered a cock
Anticipating an important visitor
We got her:

Our daughter – pieces of flesh in a sack –
Our present from her husband.

No, I will not use images
I will just talk to you:
I do not fight to take your place
Or constantly wave my fist in your face.

I refuse to argue about
Your "manly pact"
With my father –
Buying me for a bag of potatoes and pepper

All I want
Is to stop denying Me
My presence needs no metaphors
I am here
Just as you are.
I am not a machine
For you to dismantle whenever you whim
I demand for my human dignity.[31]

Kiguli wrote the poem following the presidential elections in 1996. At that time, she talked to women who had been forced to follow their husbands' political opinions.[32] In the poem, the female lyrical persona claims a right of political self-determination questioning patriarchy at the same time. The poem begins with the description of the violence that women experience at the hands of their husbands; simultaneously, it highlights the anxiety women go through in anticipation of this violence. Although the pain as well as the violence are voiced, they are not articulated in any accusatory manner. Interestingly enough, these aspects are rather stated as mere facts without displaying any overt emotions of grief, anger or despair that might be justified in light of the fact that the mother was crippled and the daughter was killed by their respective husbands.

These emotions linger in what is not articulated in the stanza – that is in the silence between the lines. It is thus what is not articulated in the poem that holds the reader in suspense and that triggers emotions in the readers' minds. Consequently, the effect of the statements is made stronger through what is left unsaid. The power of silence also surfaces in the fourth stanza. By "refus[ing]" to talk about "the manly pact", but by still describing it as a pact between Ugandan men from which they draw their right of power over women and by which women can be bought for "a bag of potatoes and pepper", the speaker condemns it indirectly. The comparison between the "manly pact" and the women as "a bag of potatoes and pepper" in stanza four creates a dichotomy between men and women, constructing the unequal power relationship between those objectifying and those objectified. Without stating it directly, the lyric persona reveals the way by which women in Ugandan society are reduced to objects such as "a bag of potatoes and pepper", which is voiceless and passive, yet ironically enough, as nutrition indispensable for the survival of mankind.

Throughout the poem, this effect of the delineation between men and women as two separate social groups is especially achieved by the usage of pronouns. The plural personal pronoun 'we' in stanza one and two is not used in the inclusive sense (you and I), but in the exclusive sense (someone else and I but not you) as most explicitly, for instance, in "*I* will tell *you* how *we* held *our* heads."[33] The juxtaposition of 'you' versus 'we' and the possessive determiner 'our' exclude the person talked to. Since the 'our' in the poem is linked to women as in "[o]ur mother" and "our daughter", it becomes clear that men are the persons talked to and hence excluded from the 'we' whom the lyric voice addresses. The identification with 'we' and 'our' moreover reveals the identity of the speaker as a woman.

The dichotomy between men and women, which the lyric persona constructs, is, however, dissolved at the same time. The power relations within the poem thus shift as the lyric persona moves from the description of the violence and pain in the first two stanzas to a very self-confident agenda of demands against men actively voiced in the stanzas three, four and five. The self-determination is constructed through the introductory verses of each stanza. Whereas the opening lines of the first two stanzas, "I will talk plainly" and "I will remind you", first and foremost only signal that the lyric persona wants to make a point, the introductory verses of the stanzas three, four and five demand not only a right to speak but already define what the speaker demands: "No, I will not use images/ I refuse to talk about [...]/ All I want".

The presence of 'I' and 'you' in the absence of 'we' and 'our' in the last three stanzas is noticeable and eventually leads to the dissolution of the dichotomy between the powerful and the powerless when the lyric persona states "stop denying Me/ My presence needs no metaphors,/ I am here/ Just as you are./ I am not a machine/ For you to dismantle whenever you whim/ I demand for my human dignity." Demanding her presence and equal place in society alongside the man, the speaker transcends the image of the victim-cum-object and emancipates herself. The emancipated 'I' emerges again through a pronoun, 'Me', indicating self-confidence through the capital letter. Acknowledging her presence in capital letters, the lyric 'I' shows that she is astutely aware of her physical presence and her rights as a human being. Equality between men and women is achieved when the lyric persona announces her presence on the same level as men in "I am here/ Just as you are", thus dissolving the dichotomy of men and women constructed earlier on.

Notwithstanding the fact that the lyric voice criticises patriarchy and highlights womanhood, it is interesting to note that she does not directly demand the replacement of patriarchy by matriarchy. "I do not fight to take your place", she points out, thus not attacking the supremacy of men. Her appeal in "I demand my human dignity" speaks of a strong person who in the light of the inequalities women experience within patriarchy has managed to sustain a sense of sanity and dignity. Despite all the pain, she accepts patriarchy as the ruling system after all. Her call for human dignity, it could therefore be argued, is not a call for the overcoming of male authority, but an appeal to men for their humanity.

Considering the fact her demand for "human dignity" is the only emotional statement in absence of the expression of any other emotions and direct accusations, makes the appeal of the speaker even stronger. Since the poem furthermore ends on this demand of "human dignity", the request by the lyric persona for gender equality and respect resonates with the reader in a powerful manner.

At the same time, however, this request can also be read differently. Although she accepts patriarchy after all, it could also be argued that her demands are anything but submissive. The lyric persona illustrates that men's power over women in the Ugandan context is expressed as well as exercised through non-verbal communication as in physical strength and violence. Unlike men, however, she just wants to communicate verbally to make her point. "I will talk plainly/ [...] I do not [...]/ [...] constantly wave my fist in your face", she points out. Showing that she is able to communicate effectively verbally and by refusing to take revenge through physical violence, the speaker actually attacks and dismantles male authority since her way of communicating does not result in mutilation and killings. If read in this way, it could therefore be argued that the lyric persona embarrasses men by illustrating that they, contrary to her as a woman, are either unwilling or unable to communicate verbally. She thereby criticises male arrogance and adds a tinge of irony to her appeal for human dignity by highlighting that she does not need to threaten anyone with violence because she is able to voice her concerns and desires. Bearing in mind the strength and pride in her womanhood as expressed in the poem, her actively articulated agenda for human rights could ultimately be read as a patronising, if not even slightly condescending ultimatum, not only criticising, but actually ridiculing male authority in view of her self-confidence.

Like Okurut and Kyomuhendo in their novels, Kiguli ultimately breaks with a taboo. Her taboo is not so much the depiction of male violence against women through language and detailed description, but much more through the self-confident announcement of "talk[ing] plainly". Sylvia Tamale, the author of *When Hens Begin to Crow. Gender and Parliamentary Politics in Uganda* (1999), points out that in Uganda as well as in other contexts of African societies, women's sexuality and emotional subordination through men "is usually mediated through metaphors and symbols".[34] In the poem above, the lyric persona breaks with this convention as she is "moved to abandon riddles" and "tired of using metaphors". The presence of the 'I' throughout the poem emphasises the direct communication of the lyric persona, thus underlining her personality and existence as a 'subject' and refusing her label as an 'object'. Her refusal of speaking in metaphors about her feelings appears as the breaking with a social convention and a taboo.

In Uganda, such explicit and continuously strong proclamation of gender issues as well as female self-confidence have not been welcomed by some male critics. They have disliked *Femrite*'s literature as it offers a rather uncomfortable picture of male behaviour that, according to these critics, had never been criticised previously in such a blunt way.[35] In *Secrets No More*, for instance, the protagonist Marina, as a grown-up, has an affair with Dee. In a private moment with Dee,

> a throbbing sensation was beginning to grow inside her and an animal-like sound escaped her. [...] Marina was aroused to the highest heights. [...] At first, she thought she was having a dream. Then she felt the damp, but warm sticky liquid trickling between her thighs and gingerly felt for its source; it was still hard.[36]

Apart from explicit descriptions of sexual abuse as well as the use of vulgar language, sex scenes highlighting the lust of a woman in detail through female authorship had never been depicted in Ugandan literature. Rather women's lust and grief have generally been communicated indirectly, as Kiguli's poem highlights. As for the public reaction to *Secrets No More* and *The Official Wife* in Uganda, Susan Kiguli remembers that such presentation of the material provoked a fierce debate, especially among the male audience.[37] Alongside a number of other *Femrite* writers, Kyomuhendo and Okurut were labeled as "the top honcho among the *Vaginalists*."[38] In view of such criticism, it also surfaces clearly that the problem of *Femrite* members has not only been the explicit content and language in their writing, but the primary question of authorship. What was much more disturbing to these male critics in the late 1990s was the fact that such writing was done through *female* authorship.

The criticism of *Femrite*'s feminist leanings in the Ugandan literary field, therefore, is not just a power struggle over content and language; what surfaces in this literature by *Femrite* is a power struggle over emancipation and authority between the sexes. Any change to the status quo, Kiguli sums up, always leads to resistances.[39] By 2006, at its tenth anniversary, *Femrite* had developed into an accepted player and an integral part of the Ugandan literary scene. The LINGO had managed to transform the Ugandan literary field to the extent that, as Kaiza notes in his review of *Femrite* in 2007, "young male writers in Kampala say wryly that they ought to write under women's names to get published."[40]

5. Kwani Trust *and* Femrite. *Portraying Life Realities through Survivor Narratives and Testimonials*

Through recent publications by *Femrite* and *Kwani Trust*, life-writing has become a cornerstone for recording trauma and memorialising suffering in Uganda and Kenya. In fact, contributors to *Femrite* have made it their "business to record" the stories of Ugandan women who have been "forced to endure terrible things".[41] To record and to publish true-life accounts "of marginalised women in different fields"[42] is presently one of *Femrite*'s major programmes. With this kind of writing the LINGO aims to "inspire the reader and listener to construct meaningful social and political opinions towards a collective responsibility for our societies, addressing both a Ugandan and non-Ugandan audience".[43] Between 2003 and July 2009, *Femrite* released five collections, which the LINGO promotes as "true life stories".[44] These collections revolve around the issues of women and law, women and HIV/AIDS, women in armed conflict situations in rural Uganda as well as women and female genital mutilation. *Tears of Hope* (2003) contains "the stories of eight different women in southwestern Uganda who endured shocking abuse of their [human] rights, but went on and fought to re-claim their lives".[45] *I Dare to Say* (2007) is about "five courageous women [from southwestern Uganda] with varying experiences in finding out their HIV+ status and living with HIV/AIDS".[46] *Today You Will Understand* (2008) presents sixteen stories of women from northern Uganda who narrowly escaped the violence by Lord's Resistance Army (LRA) rebels. Similarly to this, *Farming Ashes* (2009) is made up of nine stories "of women from northern Uganda who have survived the LRA conflict,"[47] whereas *Beyond the Dance* (2009) is a compilation of testimonies and poems about the humiliation of female genital mutilation. [...] It encompasses accounts [...] of the experience of this practice lived or witnessed, and the visceral responses to the practice.[48]

The women portrayed in these five collections have faced extreme human pain and massive psychic trauma. Above all, many of them have fought for their survival.

With its twin edition, *Kwani? 05*, *Kwani Trust* also focused on stories of survival. In the section "Revelation and Conversation", this volume contains interviews with inhabitants from regions of Kenya affected by riots during the post-election violence. The post-election violence occurred in Kenya in 2007/2008 following the presidential election. Kenya's population suspected the government to have manipulated the election result. Involved in the election campaign, these interviewees have either witnessed or actively participated in the riots. Within the pages of this edition, their individual accounts are enriched by the incorporation of SMS, flyers and emails circulated during the post-election violence. With their story collections as well as their interviews, *Femrite* and *Kwani Trust* showcase the genre of survivor narratives and testimonials.[49] By representing life stories, these survivor narratives and testimonials function as a tool by which African LINGOs contribute to the process of sociopolitical and sociocultural opinion-making inside their countries as well as to cultural outsiders.

When reading *Femrite*'s life-writing collections, it becomes clear that there is a common strand running through all the anthologies. Regardless of whether they have been suffering from HIV/AIDS, judicial injustice or domestic violence, the women portrayed in all of the collections are constructed as survivors. Joyce in *Today You Will Understand* survived an attack of the Lord's Resistance Army, whereas her niece was "axed to death" and her "husband's face had been sliced into four pieces with a machete";[50] Frieda in *Tears of Hope* has managed to successfully organise a life of her own after years of extreme domestic violence, in which her husband finally threatened to kill her "with a bright new *panga* [machete]".[51] As presented in the stories, their life experiences have eventually turned Joyce, Kyosha and Frieda into survivors. "All central figures have a strong survival instinct and none of the narratives leaves the reader in despair", Dominic Dipio, a senior lecturer of English literature and film at Makerere University, notes in her foreword to *Farming Ashes*.[52] This survival instinct, as the close-reading of Frieda's and Joyce's story will show later on, rings true for all survivor narrative publications by *Femrite*.

The second strand the narratives share is the fact that they are all based on true-life accounts, recorded by personal interviews between *Femrite* women writers and women of the lower social strata from south-western and northern Uganda. Many of the interviewed women are farmers who barely make ends meet. The stories are personal insights cutting across the multi-ethnic and multilinguistic continuum from these regions of Uganda. In the *Femrite* collections, these stories come together to form a greater picture, suggesting that the challenges and hardships these women endure are not unique, but rather typical of women across Uganda. Embedded in the greater context of an anthology, these *Femrite* texts thus form a more generalised statement about the situation of the rights and status of women in rural Uganda. Certainly, the references to the protagonists' ethnic and linguistic backgrounds render the stories in a local context, making it more difficult to comprehend every detail unless one is familiar with the multi-ethnic and social continuum of Ugandan society. Nevertheless, the translation of the stories into English through *Femrite* authors also makes these stories accessible to a non-Ugandan audience.

Despite these common aspects, the narratives vary significantly in terms of their format and style. Jackee Budesta Batanda, contributing to the anthology *Tears of Hope*, remembers: "We had guiding questions on what to look out for, but the entirety of the story depended on the writers. The main guideline was to look for unique untold stories."[53] Based on true life interviews often recorded in local languages, but translated into English and embedded in a fictionalised framework, the stories of *Femrite*'s life-story collections are creative non-fiction. The texts straddle the world of fiction and non-fiction to varying degrees as the individual authors decide to merge the comments of their narrators in the stories with personal comments by the interviewee, at times making it hard to distinguish who reports what.

In "Frieda's World" from *Tears of Hope*, Frieda is presented as a survivor of domestic violence against women, which as Michael König *et al.* point out in "Domestic Violence in Rural Uganda. Evidence from a Community-Based Study" is common practice and a serious problem seldom directly addressed in public.[54] At the beginning of the story, the female first-person narrator gives her impression of the protagonist, thereby entering immediately into Frieda's world.

> She does not look any different from thousands of Bafumbira peasant women. Frieda is only thirty-four years old, small and strong. Her rough hands grip mine firmly. The soil of the field she has been working on still clings up to her elbows like a thick coating. Her arms are thin and jut out from under her torn dress like sticks. [...] Her hair knows only the rough blue soap, expensive in the village for her, but for those with cars given free at the petrol stations in the city.[55]

According to the narrator, Frieda does not stand out as a woman. She does not look any different from thousands of Bafumbira peasant women, implying that her story is not unique but exemplary of many other similar stories of rural Bafumbira women. Frieda is presented as a woman living at the lower level of society and as someone of little social power. She is thin and her clothes are torn. She is poor and cannot afford better soap than the rough soap in the village that, as the narrator notes almost ironically in view of the social differences in Uganda, would even be given for free to her if she was richer and living in the city. The narrator interprets and judges Frieda by personal impressions as someone who is poor and lacks social authority. Reading the personal impression of the reporting narrator, one cannot help but look at Frieda through the narrator's eyes. Frieda's strength and hunger for life can only be guessed by means of the narrator's hint about Frieda being strong and gripping the narrator's hand firmly.

Throughout the first part of "Frieda's World", one comes to witness Frieda's fear and anxiety, disgrace and pain during this marriage as the narrator shares Frieda's experiences with her husband in greater detail.

> With ability she had not thought him capable of, he suddenly jumped forward with a thick stick in his hand. He hit her hard on the back. [...] She was beaten again and again, sometimes nearly to death. [...] [F]or the next fourteen years, the whole cycle kept repeating itself.[56]

Through the detailed depiction of her experience, Frieda is constructed as a victim of domestic violence, passively enduring the pain and helplessness in view of her husband's brutality for fourteen years.

In the course of the story, the re-construction of Frieda as a survivor is largely achieved by a shift in narration from third-person towards a focus on the witnessing first-person narrator and Frieda's own words:

> "I had nothing to lose by going there," Frieda says. "There was no harm in going to Kisoro and trying to find out whether that office could help me. [...] The man in the office [...] gave me a letter, one for my husband and another for the Local Council Chairman. He wrote that in all matters concerning the house[57] and the land [...] the Legal Aid Office in Kisoro had to be asked for advice. On top of that, each party, that is me and my husband, had to come with a witness to the office to discuss our case."
> "Whom did you go with?" I ask.
> "I went with the woman who used to give me and my children refuge."
> "And your husband, who did he go with?"
> "His brother." [...]
> "And your husband's brother, what did he say?" I ask.
> She laughs. "He said exactly the same thing – that my husband is terrible when he is drunk and harassed me and the children [...]. I was happy – I was so happy, because the man in the office gave my husband a letter and another one to the Chairman of the Local Council forbidding him to sell anything, land or the house without my consent."[58]

Not only do Frieda's supposedly original words give evidence of the fact that she survived the brutal attacks by her husband. The report about her courage to go and fight for her rights regarding the house that she had built with her own money and that her husband wanted to take away from her, suggests that she is also a winner and eventually a survivor of the local judicial system, which, as the narrator critically remarks, generally allows men like Frieda's husband to bribe "all the members of the council with beer to be on his side".[59]

The witnessing narrator concludes her account by turning Frieda's story into a general example of what women and children have to endure since there is "no law in Uganda that specifically addresses domestic violence".[60] The narrator's comment is extended to an appeal to the readers, hinting at the flaws in the Ugandan judicial system and expressing her hope.

> So the criminality of the offences that constitute what we refer to as domestic violence are pricked from various legislations, especially the Penal Code Act, Chapter 106, Laws of Uganda. Maybe in future, women

111

such as Frieda will be better protected not only by laws but also by communities that care more about the welfare of women and mothers.[61]

Thereby Frieda's personal story is projected onto a larger sociopolitical foil. It serves to criticise the lack of protection of women against domestic violence by men and calls for the need to publicly address this problem in the Ugandan judicial system. The witnessing narrator thus comes full circle by connecting Frieda, the woman who looks just like any other among thousands of Bafumbira women, to a more generalised group of Ugandan/African women and mothers. In doing so, the narrator underlines the women's crucial role as reproducers and nurturers for the development of any society. Since Frieda's experience is linked to a critique of Uganda's judicial system and the implicit demand for communities to care about mothers and women, "Frieda's World" can be read as sociopolitical commentary about the (rural) life of women in Uganda.

The survivor narratives in *Kwani?* are not in short story form but are rendered as non-fictional personal interviews. They are therefore of a more journalistic genre than the fictionalised stories by *Femrite*. Arno Kopecky, a *Kwani Trust* contributor at that time, remembers that "in March [2008], we [at *Kwani Trust*] armed a team of young writers with voice recorders and sent them across the country to hear what people had to say".[62] The twin issue of *Kwani? 05* includes 44 out of "almost 200"[63] interviews from low-income areas in Nairobi such as Mathare, Dandora and Kibera as well as interviews from more rural and small-town areas such as the Rift Valley, Eldoret, Nakuru, Kisumu, Kisii and Kakamega.

Reflecting on the post-election violence from different geographical locations as well as from various ethnic and social backgrounds within Kenya, these interviews – like flash-lights – throw light on the riots from unique personal perspectives, coming together to provide a greater picture of the country-wide uproar within the pages of the magazine. Thus, thirty-year-old Stephen Kioko from Ngei, Huruma estate, points out that when the violence broke out,

> I sneaked back to my house and fetched a bow and some arrows [...] – we managed to chase the ODM people [Orange Democratic Movement][64] away and they never attacked the area again. [...] Violence is not good. But then again, [...] I have no regrets [...]. It's called self-defence.[65]

The twenty-year-old Irene Muneni, a Kamba from Mathare, lived with her Luo boyfriend until the ethnic hostilities and her refusal to join the violence turned her life upside down:

> Before elections, my boyfriend and I had a good life and nobody imagined anything nasty would happen after we voted. […] On election day I voted for Kalonzo [i.e. the former Minister of Foreign Affairs and Vice-President to Kibaki] since I am a Kamba. That day my boyfriend came and said our relationship had ended because I had not supported Raila [i.e. the strongest political opponent to Kibaki] like he wanted me to. He even said he was to come and force me to join the Luo crowd who were throwing stones at rivals. […] That night my boyfriend came with my landlord. They said since I had refused everything they had told me, they had no option but to rape me. […] I wonder whether I will be married since I hear no man wants to marry a woman who has been raped.[66]

Yusuf Lumumba, a matatu tout from Kakamega, remarks plainly that this violence was also ignited by Members of Parliament. Before the elections, Lumumba reports, an "MP came and hired us with money to go and fight. But with my cowardice I refused to go. […] You are just bought by 100 shillings, and you may lose your life in the process."[67] In "Revelation and Conversation", all of these texts bear immediate testimony to the ferocity that broke loose across the country within minutes after the announcement of the election results, when houses were burnt down, friendships were reduced to the marker of ethnic belonging, and many people were left homeless, injured or killed. The texts also reveal the ways in which members of parliament were involved with corrupting fair campaigns on the ground and with instigating the violent clashes in favour of their own position within the government, thus confirming first-hand what international newspapers such as *The Washington Post* could only speculate about.[68] As personal statements from various regions, the interviews capture a great diversity of both social and individual circumstances, shedding light on the atrocities, anger, anxiety, racism and pain people experienced during this conflict. At the same time, these texts serve as valuable pieces of investigative journalism, unveiling first-hand information that government officials in Kenya supposedly have tried to keep back. Hence, Stephanie McCrummen, a journalist with the Foreign Service of

The Washington Post, points out that until 2009, the Kenyan "government has moved slowly on reforms, blocking any domestic judicial process for trying the perpetrators of the violence, who are widely believed to include Kenya's political elites."[69] The direct representation of the personal interview on page in *Kwani?* therefore provides unique information on a sociopolitical event otherwise neglected, bringing the information from the ground to world-wide recognition. On-site, the interviewee becomes the reporter of the events reporting to the interviewer who witnesses their stories and reports these events again in interview form for the magazine, where these stories ultimately are shared by the readers of *Kwani? 05*. Through the publication in the magazine this personal information eventually gains a public momentum as it can be accessed by a readership world-wide. With the genres of the survivor narrative and the testimonial, both LINGOs promote texts which clearly make a contribution to the ongoing debates about actual topics of the LINGOs' civil societies.

6. Conclusion

By shedding light on sensitive and silenced truths in conflict areas and by incorporating viewpoints from different social and economic backgrounds otherwise unnoticed by public media, *Femrite* and *Kwani Trust* contribute to democratising the literary canons as well as the sociocultural and sociopolitical knowledge of and about their civil societies. The discussion of selected texts in this article has illustrated that publications promoted by *Femrite* and *Kwani Trust* are highly reflective of their immediate Ugandan and Kenyan environments. These texts are not so much preoccupied with writing back to the (colonial) Empire – a notion which has previously been applied in postcolonial theory and thus has also been a recurring notion in the discussion of Anglophone writing from East Africa and the teaching of the very literature from this region. Rather the texts published and promoted by the contemporary LINGOs as well as their associated writers are occupied with writing back to the stereotypical African identity, place and self. African LINGOs like *Femrite* and *Kwani Trust* are institutions of literary creativity as well as platforms of social dialogue. With their creative writing, they are at a crossroads of literary innovation as well as sociopolitical commentary. It is exactly this interaction that renders LINGOs interesting as institutions for both the literary as well as the sociopolitical and sociocultural worlds. This is why in terms of topicality, diversity and accessibility, Anglophone publications by LINGOs like *Femrite* and *Kwani Trust* enrich the study and teaching of literature at secondary schools and universities.

Notes

1   For a detailed insight into this field, please also consult Marie Krüger's study *Women's Literature in Kenya and Uganda. The Trouble with Modernity* (2011).
2   *Kony 2012* is a short film created and distributed by Invisible Children, Inc. The American NGO is dedicated "to end the use of child soldiers in Joseph Kony's rebel war and restore LRA-affected communities in central Africa to peace and prosperity" (Invisible Children, Inc. 2012).
3   Wainaina (2012).
4   *Ibid.*
5   The weekly column "Whispers" was published between 1982 and 2003 in *The Daily Nation* and *The East African Standard* at different times. The column established creative writing successfully as a kind of journalism during Daniel arap Moi's oppressive political regime. Relying on narrative forms such as satire, rumour, gossip and fiction, the column "became a 'site of freedom' within a highly circumscribed and politically controlled platform, the newspaper" (Ogola 2006: 573).
6   From Nigeria, for example, Chinua Achebe engaged at the *Mbari Clubs* but later emerged most visibly as a university lecturer at Ibadan University, Nigeria, and in the USA. Achebe was also a driving force in the African Writers Series in the UK. Wole Soyinka was deeply involved with the *Mbari Clubs* and with Neogy's *Transition* but as a writer later drew his authority largely from the academic framework as a university lecturer at Ibadan and Ghana University. In Uganda and Kenya, Okot p'Bitek, Ngũgĩ wa Thiong'o or Taban lo Liyong at one point all contributed to the Ugandan LINGO *Transition*, yet gained their greatest authority as writers and university teachers associated with and writing from the literature departments at Makerere University and Nairobi University.
7   For an author's perspective on self-publishing, see Chukwumerije's contribution on writing and publishing in Nigeria.

8   *Femrite* and *Kwani Trust* serve as examples of how African LINGOs have been growing alongside technological advancement in terms of combining literary enterprise and online technology. The *Femrite* webpage can be accessed at www.femriteug.org. It offers a free download of publications previously printed and sold in Uganda, whereas the *Kwani Trust* website, which can be found at www.kwani.org, features podcasts, videos, audio commentaries, blog entries as well as links to *Kwani Trust*'s appearance on *Facebook* and *Twitter*. The Internet thus becomes a place where anyone interested in writing, reading and debating on literary, sociopolitical and sociocultural matters from Uganda and Kenya can find information on the events and literature of *Femrite* and *Kwani Trust* promptly.
9   Krüger (2011: 1).
10 All publications by *Femrite* and *Kwani Trust* have an ISB-number.
11 *Kwani?* is a Sheng word translating to "So what?".
12 In regard to the situation in East Africa, it is worthwhile to note that *Femart*, a women writers' organisation, has been operating as a LINGO in Kenya since 1997. Thus far, however, *Femart* has not achieved the level of impact that *Femrite* has.
13 Bourdieu (1990: 145).
14 Sheng and Engsh are age-marked urban dialects of Kenyan Kiswahili. Whereas Sheng is prominent in the low-income areas of Nairobi, Engsh thrives among the urban youth and adolescents of the wealthier areas of Nairobi. Therefore, Engsh functions as a social marker of higher socio-economic status. Unlike Sheng, Engsh contains Kiswahili elements, but largely follows the English grammar and borrows mostly from the local languages Gĩkũyũ, Dholuo, Luluhya and Kikamba.
15 Wainaina (2006).
16 *Kwani Trust* has also been offering courses on blogging for creative writing, such as at its literary festival in 2008.
17 Wainaina & Garland (2003: 103).
18 Ligaga (2005: 47).
19 *Ibid.* 48.
20 Wainaina & Garland (2003b: 103).
21 *Ibid.* 105.
22 Kaviti (2006: 7).
23 *Ibid.*
24 Ligaga (2005: 48).
25 *Ibid.*
26 *Ibid.*
27 *Ibid.* 49.

28 *Ibid.*
29 For a discussion on women playwrights from Ghana, Nigeria and South Africa, see Bartels's contribution to this volume.
30 Due to their explicit language, these works are more recommendable for university students. For teaching at high school level consider Glaydah Namukasa's novella *Voice of a Dream*.
31 Kiguli (1998: 4-5).
32 Kiguli (2005: 173).
33 My emphasis.
34 Tamale (2005: 9).
35 See Kigambo (2006).
36 Kyomuhendo (1996: 152).
37 Kiguli (2005: 183).
38 *Ibid.* 180, my emphasis.
39 Kiguli (2005: 264).
40 Kaiza (2007).
41 Twongyeirwe (2008: 3).
42 *Ibid.*
43 *Ibid.*
44 Femrite ("True Life Stories"). For an historian's perspective on life stories, see Rüther's contribution to this volume.
45 Twongyeirwe (2008: 3).
46 Wapakhabulo (2007: 1).
47 Dipio (2009: v).
48 *Ibid.*
49 In my understanding of the survivor narrative in this study, I follow Sidonie Smith and Julia Watson. The term 'survivor narrative', they note, "designates narratives by survivors of traumatic, abusive or genocidal experience" (Watson & Smith 2001: 205). As such, survivor narratives are also testimonials. In my understanding of the testimonial, I follow Paul Allatson, who notes that the "testimonial genre is a broad categorisation that may include, draw upon, or overlap with the concerns and conventions of many other genres, from the memoir and autobiography, to confession, oral history, and the nonfiction or 'factual' novel" (Allatson 2007: 226).
50 Twongyeirwe (2008: 22).
51 Ndagijimana (2003: 44), original emphasis.
52 Dipio (2009: v).
53 Strauhs (2010: 72).
54 König *et al.* (2003).
55 Ndagijimana (2003: 25).

56 *Ibid.*
57 Frieda built a house with the money she had made through the sale of vegetables. Her husband did not know about it.
58 Ndagijimana (2003: 47-48).
59 *Ibid.* 45.
60 *Ibid.* 50.
61 *Ibid.*
62 Kopecky (2008b: 48).
63 *Ibid.*
64 Orange Democratic Movement (ODM) is a political movement aiming to form a government that will build a democratic society.
65 Munene (2008: 54-55).
66 Kopecky (2008a: 49).
67 Were (2008: 274).
68 McCrummen (2009).
69 *Ibid.*

Bibliography

Allatson, Paul: *Key Terms in Latino/a Cultural and Literary Studies*, Malden, 2007.
Barungi, Violet & Susan Kiguli (Eds.): *I Dare to Say*, Kampala, 2007.
Barungi, Violet & Hilda Twongyeirwe (Eds.): *Beyond the Dance*, Kampala, 2009a.
--- (Eds.): *Farming Ashes. Tales of Agony and Resilience*, Kampala, 2009b.
Barungi, Violet & Ayeta Ann Wangusa (Eds.): *Tears of Hope*, Kampala, 2003.
Bourdieu, Pierre: "The Intellectual Field. A World Apart". – In P. B. (Ed.): *In Other Words. Essays Towards a Reflexive Sociology*, Stanford, 1990, pp. 140-149.
Dipio, Dominic: "Foreword". – In Violet Barungi & Hilda Twongyeirwe (Eds.): *Farming Ashes. Tales of Agony and Resilience*, Kampala, 2009, pp. vii-ix.
Femrite: "True Life Story", *List of Publications*, <http://www.femriteug.org/?view=5&type=True>, accessed 7 August 2012.
---: "Welcome to Femrite", <www.femriteug.org>, accessed 8 August 2012.
Invisible Children, Inc.: "Kony 2012", *Invisible Children*, <http://www.invisiblechildren.com.s3-website-us-east-1.amazonaws.com/>, accessed 15 August 2012.
Kahora, Billy (Ed.): *Kwani? 05 Part One*, Nairobi, 2008a.

--- (Ed.): *Kwani? 05 Part Two*, Nairobi, 2008b.

Kahora, Billy & Binyavanga Wainaina (Eds.): *Kwani? 04*, Nairobi, 2007.

Kaiza, David: "Women Writers Rule", *The East African*, 29 October - 4 November 2007, <http://www.theeastafrican.co.ke/magazine/-/434746/256502/-/1407uqn/-/index.html>, accessed 15 August 2012.

Kaviti, Lilian: "Rejoinder to Alina Rinkanya's Article", *The Nairobi Journal of Literature* 4, 2006, 1-12.

Kigambo, Gaaki: "Uganda. Femrite Turns 10", *The Monitor*, 6 July 2006.

Kiguli, Susan: *The African Saga*, Kampala, 1998.

---: "I Am Tired of Talking in Metaphors". – In S. K. (Ed.): *The African Saga*, Kampala, 1998, pp. 4-5.

---: "Femrite and the Woman's Writer's Position in Uganda. Personal Reflections". – In Susan Arndt & Katrin Berndt (Eds.): *Words and Worlds. African Writing, Literature and Society*, Trenton, 2005, pp. 170-183.

König, Michael A. *et al.*: "Domestic Violence in Rural Uganda. Evidence from a Community-Based Study", *Bulletin of the World Health Organization* 81, 2003, 53-60.

Kopecky, Arno: "Rift Valley". – In Billy Kahora (Ed.): *Kwani? 05 Part One*, Nairobi, 2008a, pp. 36-49.

---: "Some for the Record". – In Billy Kahora (Ed.): *Kwani? 05 Part Two*, Nairobi, 2008b, p. 48.

Krüger, Marie Luise: *Women's Literature in Kenya and Uganda. The Trouble with Modernity*, New York, 2011.

Kwani Trust: "Home", *Kwani?*, <www.kwani.org>, accessed 8 August 2012.

Kyomuhendo, Goretti: *Secrets No More*, Kampala, 1996.

Ligaga, Dinah: "Kwani? Exploring New Literary Spaces in Kenya", *Africa Insight* 35:2, 2005, 46-52.

McCrummen, Stephanie: "In Kenya, Ethnic Distrust Is as Deep as the Machete Scars", *The Washington Post*, 17 May 2009, <http://www.washingtonpost.com/wp-dyn/content/article/2009/12/21/AR2009122103382.html>, accessed 15 August 2012.

Mwangi, Evan Maina: *Africa Writes Back to Self. Metafiction, Gender, Sexuality*, Albany, 2009.

Munene, Samuel: "Mathare". – In Billy Kahora (Ed.): *Kwani? 05 Part Two*, Nairobi, 2008, pp. 49-57.

Ndagijimana, Waltraud: "Frieda's World". – In Violet Barungi & Ayeta Anne Wangusa (Eds.): *Tears of Hope*, Kampala, 2003, pp. 25-51.

Ocwinyo, Julius: Personal Communication with Doreen Strauhs, recorded in Kampala, 2008.

Ogola, George: "The Idiom of Age in a Popular Kenyan Newspaper Serial", *The Journal of the International African Institute* 76:4, 2006, 569-589.

Okurut, Mary Karooro: *The Official Wife*, Kampala, 2003.

Potash: "Ghetto Livity". – In Billy Kahora & Binyavanga Wainaina (Eds.): *Kwani? 03*, Nairobi, 2005, pp. 137-138.

Strauhs, Doreen: "'Guys, We Are Really Not Like This!' Jackee Budesta Batanda in Conversation", *Wasafiri* 25:1, 2010, 69-74.

Tamale, Sylvia: "Eroticism, Sensuality and 'Women's Secrets' among the Baganda. A Critical Analysis", *Feminist Africa* 5, 2005, 9-36.

Twongyeirwe, Hilda (Ed.): *Today You Will Understand*, Kampala, 2008.

Wainaina, Binyavanga (Ed.): *Kwani? 01*, Nairobi, 2003.

---: "How to Write About Africa", *Granta 92: The View from Africa*, 2005a, 92-95.

---: Personal Communication with Doreen Strauhs, recorded in Nairobi, 2005b.

---: "Viewpoint. Binyavanga on Why Africa's International Image is Unfair", *BBC News Africa*, 24 April 2012, <http://www.bbc.co.uk/news/world-africa-17814861>, accessed 13 August 2012.

Wainaina, Binyavanga & Muthoni Garland: "Fw.Fw.". – In Binyavanga Wainaina (Ed.): *Kwani? 01*, Nairobi, 2003, pp. 103-113.

Wainaina, Binyavanga & Billy Kahora (Eds.): *Kwani? 03*, Nairobi, 2006.

Wapakhabulo, Angelina: "Foreword". – In Violet Barungi & Susan Kiguli (Eds.): *I Dare to Say*, Kampala, 2007, pp. i-ii.

Watson, Sidonie & Julia Smith: *Reading Autobiography. A Guide for Interpreting Life Narratives*, Minneapolis, 2001.

Were, Brian Walumbe: "Kakamega". – In Billy Kahora (Ed.): *Kwani? 05 Part One*, Nairobi, 2008, pp. 270-274.

Claudia Böhme (Leipzig)

'Action, Cut and Roll!'
The Language Question in the Tanzanian Film Industry

> The choice of language and the use to which language is put is central to a people's definition of themselves in relation to their natural and social environment, indeed in relation to the entire universe. Hence language has always been at the heart of the two contending social forces in the Africa of the twentieth century.[1]

1. Introduction

During my fieldwork for research on the Tanzanian film industry in Dar es Salaam in October 2007, one of the staff members of the German embassy told me about the possibility of inviting a local film-maker to the Berlinale film festival in Germany and asked me to recommend someone. My choice was quickly made: Mussa Banzi, one of the initiators of the Tanzanian video and film industry who at that time had written, directed and photographed about 50 feature films spanning various genres and subjects. Together we compiled his curriculum vitae, sent it to the embassy, and he was finally invited to an interview on 31 January 2008.

On that very day a committee of the ambassador, the designated head of the Goethe Institute and two other members of the embassy were waiting for us at the embassy in the Umoja House. Banzi put the VCDs of some of his best films on the table, and we were asked to introduce ourselves. The ambassador then spoke directly to Banzi who had difficulties answering as he is not fluent in English. When I jumped in and asked if he could speak in Swahili, and I would translate, the ambassador said that if he is not able to master the English language, he cannot go to the festival. What followed was a rather uncomfortable interview as Banzi attempted to answer the questions put to him as fluently as possible. Two weeks later I received a call telling me that Banzi would not be invited to the Berlinale.

Should the inability to speak fluent English exclude a Tanzanian film-maker from participating in an international film festival? Other international film-makers who do not speak English do take part in the Berlinale and give interviews with the help of a translator. Even the director of the festival, Dieter Kosslick, makes fun of his own lack of fluency, speaking what is commonly called 'Denglisch'. The embassy's decision to deny someone participation because of possessing only basic knowledge of English is thus rendered absurd. Is it this lack, which hinders Tanzanian film-makers from participating in film festivals abroad? Or is it the films themselves, which do not correspond to the concept of film art in the eyes of diplomats?

In this article, which is based on long-term fieldwork and observation of agents in the Tanzanian film industry, I want to examine the roles both Swahili and English play in the development of this new cultural industry. The globalisation of media has not led to a homogenisation of media content as predicted but to a localisation and diversification of media cultures, as many studies have shown and as is exemplified by Swahili films. However, when these local media become more popular and expand into a global market, the question of language arises.

To understand the complex relationship between film and language in Tanzania, one has to shed light on the history of these two media, which have both been regulated and shaped under the control of ruling parties. The ongoing discussion of the question of language in the film industry reflects the history of language policies, language hierarchies and attitudes in Tanzania.[2] While Swahili represents the local, national unity and pride, English – as the language of former colonial power – is closely linked to the global, and knowledge of it is often the key to prosperity and success. In looking at these discourses, the relationship between the global and the local can be understood as an enduring negotiation of language, culture and identity.

To explain how the two media, language and film, were historically shaped, I will firstly give an overview of the language situation in Tanzania and the role of Swahili in foreign film production there. In tracing the history of Tanzanian film-making, I will discuss the importance of Swahili for local film production and its usage within the films' plots. As the language question is discussed by Tanzanian film-makers, the audience and in the movies, film has become a vehicle for negotiating the issue of language and identity in Tanzania.

2. What's my name? *The Role of English in Tanzania*

Walking through villages or city quarters in Tanzania, visitors often hear children shouting phrases such as *Good morning teacher!* They also pose confusing questions such as *What's my name?* To greet others with *Good morning* in the evening and *Good evening* in the morning are common mistakes children make in Tanzania. Waitresses are afraid of serving a *mzungu* ("white person") due to their inability to speak English. Many young people are simply not comfortable expressing themselves in English. Only privileged children whose parents send them to private English schools and later to university have a good command of the language. The discrepancy in language competence has its roots in the history of language and educational policies in Tanzania.

In a multi-ethnic country like Tanzania, with over 130 languages spoken there, multilingualism is the rule rather than the exception. However, in contrast to many other African countries, Tanzania has one advantage: a single lingua franca, Swahili, for communication between different ethnic groups. German colonisers and missionaries fostered the development of Swahili as a medium of education and colonial administration. For the missionaries it was a means to evangelise Tanzanians. The colonial government's decision to use Swahili and not German can be explained not only by the practical need to prepare Tanzanians to work in colonial administration but also by the political necessity to prevent Tanzanians from gaining equality with the colonisers.[3]

When the British took over the colony after the First World War, the Swahili-favouring language policy changed, and English replaced Swahili in many official areas.[4] During the 1950s, English was the language of the ruling class and a symbol of power. At the beginning of the struggle for independence, even the annual general meetings of the TANU – or Tanganyika (today mainland Tanzania) African Association

– were held in English until Swahili became the language of politics in 1947.[5] After independence in 1961, the first Tanzanian president, Julius K. Nyerere, declared his goal of implementing African socialism, *ujamaa* ("familyhood"), and the unification of the nation through the Swahili language. The Swahilification of Tanzania was one of his major aims.[6] In the 1990s, about 90% of all Tanzanians spoke Swahili and an additional local language.[7] Swahili, together with English, is the official language in Tanzania. Jan Blommaert, however, shows that "[…] while Swahili was spread to all corners of the country, and was used in almost every aspect of everyday life, post-primary education remained (and still is) a domain where English was hegemonic."[8] In other words: while Swahili is the language of instruction in primary school, at the secondary and university levels it is English. This would not be problematic if English would already be taught at primary school. Unfortunately, most pupils do not cope well with the sudden switch in language, which then leads to bad test scores and high dropout rates at secondary level. From the 1970s onward, linguists and education scholars declared that Tanzania had a language crisis, and members of the National Kiswahili Council proposed to use Swahili until the university level.[9] However, when the implementation of Swahili at secondary level was officially recommended by the Presidential Commission on Education in 1985, policymakers suddenly changed their minds. The possibility of an increasing demand for secondary education and the high costs of developing educational materials in Swahili caused this reticence.[10]

3. *Swahili in Film and Film in Tanzania in Colonial Times*

Swahili, which can be heard in Hollywood movies, Walt Disney productions and even in the TV series *Star Trek*, often stands for what is sometimes badly termed 'African', an imaginary single African language. In Tanzania the use of Swahili in film is closely connected to the history of film production in the country.

Film was in the hands of foreigners, who exploited the medium for their own aims and restricted Africans from appropriating it. For colonisers and missionaries it was a powerful tool for educating Africans, and thus the use of it in films became necessary. From the

1920s onward, foreign films produced in India, the United States and Europe were imported to the British East African Territory of Tanganyika. This was a valuable business for South African film distributors and Tanzanians of Asian origin, who had established several cinemas in Zanzibar as well as on the mainland.[11]

According to the African film scholar, Frank Nwachukwu Ukadike, the first movies produced in Tanganyika were the English language explorer films by Martin Johnson such as *On the Borderland* (1920), *Simba* (1924-28) and *Congorilla* (1929-33). Tanzanians were exploited and exoticised in these productions, as their only role was to appear in front of the camera, to agitate and to say a few words in Swahili. The postproduction took place abroad, and the African participants most likely never got to see the finished films.[12]

Between 1935 and 1937 the British Colonial Office initiated the Bantu Educational Kinema Experiment (BEKE), conceived by the International Missionary Council, to show Africans educational films as officials had "faith in the power of film as an agent for uplifting illiterate Africans".[13] Tanzania was the centre of production and the completed films toured through East and Central Africa via mini buses. Some of the BEKE films were conceptualised as narratives such as the film *Gumu* ("Hard"), a film aimed at educating the audience about the dangers of city life and attempting to deter young people from moving to the city.

In 1939 the English colonial administration under the Ministry of Information established a Colonial Film Unit (CFU) to produce and distribute war propaganda films with the aim of entertaining soldiers as well as disseminating propaganda to illiterate audiences.[14] The CFU also produced three comedies with Tanzanian actors, which centred on the character of Ali the Fool.[15]

After the Second World War, the CFU, together with departments in London, planned to train West and East Africans in the operation of the units and in film production with the aim of handing over the departments at a later date. This was only the case in West Africa where a CFU training school was conducted in Accra on the Gold Coast in 1948. In East Africa the Africans had been part of the departments, but they were barred from training by the Europeans who were too busy to follow through.[16]

The first attempt to establish local film production in Tanzania came about through the efforts of Sir Edward Twining, the governor of Tanganyika (1949-58), who brought the African Film Production Company from Johannesburg to Tanganyika after the Second World War and established a production base for Swahili films. By 1953 ten Swahili feature films had been produced with local actors and ideas for scripts developed by the African office and by development aid workers, among them *Chalo Amerudi* ("Chalo has Come Back"), *Wageni Wema* ("Good Guests"), *Ali Mjanja* ("Cunning Ali"), *Dawa ya Mapenzi* ("The Love Potion"), *Meli Inakwenda* ("The Boat is Leaving") and *Mhogo Mchungu* ("Bitter Maniok"). Despite this momentum, Twining's experiment failed in the end; there was growing uncertainty due to the struggle for independence at that time. In addition, the movies had low profitability on the local market as they were seen as too didactic.[17]

4. Film as a State Affair and Development Aid in Postcolonial Tanzania

Things changed with independence in 1961. In February 1967 the governing Tanganyika African National Union (TANU) assumed control over the renting of foreign films and the support for domestic film production in the Arusha Declaration,[18] TANU's policy on socialism and self reliance. The Tanzanian government recognised the potential of the film medium for cultural and economic development of the country and integrated the establishment of a "Film Processing Plant"[19] in its five-year development plan from 1969 to 1974.

Established in 1968 by the National Development Corporation (NDC) as part of the Tanzanian Tourist Corporation (TTC), the Tanzania Film Company Ltd (TFC) was officially founded in 1974/75 under the Ministry of Information and Broadcasting with the aim of fostering tourism. As a result, the import of foreign films and the production and distribution of locally produced films became a national affair.[20] In 1970 the Danish government, as part of their development efforts in Tanzania, offered support for the establishment of an Audio-Visual Aid Center (later the Audio Visual Institute or AVI) for the production of 16mm films, equipped with the latest technologies from all over Europe.[21] The aim of the Tanzanian government was to train their citizens in the art and techniques of film production and to produce educational films as well as documentaries and newsreels for national development.[22] In 1973 the AVI and TFC were able to produce ten educational films and documentaries, most of them being shot, edited and released in Tanzania. At the same time, the Ministry of National Education and the Adult Education Directorate sent mobile cinema wagons all over the country to educate the illiterate masses about health and agricultural issues.[23]

With the support of the Danish government and as part of a development aid project, the TFC produced their first feature length film in 1974/75, *Fimbo ya Mnyonge* ("The Poor Man's Stick"),[24] which was released in 1976 and starred Prime Minister Rashid Mfaume Kawawa himself. *Fimbo ya Mnyonge* is a socialist propaganda film promoting the government's Ujamaa Village Scheme to build up self-governed socialist villages all over the country for the resettlement of urban citizens. The title is part of the longer political slogan, *Fimbo ya Mnyonge ni kuishi pamoja, ujamaa ni kuishi pamoja* ("The poor man's stick means to live together, socialism means to live together"). With the aim of propagating socialism and the image of an ideal citizen, the storyline of the film reveals how this medium was used by the Tanzanian government to convey simple moralistic messages. Yombayomba[25] – an unsuccessful farmer – supports himself by begging from his friends. When he has accumulated enough money, he goes to Dar es Salaam and fails in setting up a business. He visits the main quarter of the TANU where he is advised to join an Ujamaa Village. After more difficulties in the city such as being attacked by a gang of robbers, he returns home and joins an Ujamaa Village together with his wife. The villagers educate Yombayomba on the meaning of socialism and he finally converts his home village into an Ujamaa Village.[26]

Despite good intentions, the TFC soon went bankrupt. The output of educational and documentary films sank from 45 in 1976 to only four films in 1983.[27] According to Rosaleen Smyth, the reason for the TFC's failure lay in its structure. While it was designated as a for-profit organization, it produced relatively unpopular movies, which could not make any profit.[28]

To come to terms with the financial crisis, the TFC started a programme of co-productions in which they only covered local costs. The co-productions were attractive for foreign film-makers. Due to the strict government regulations, this was the only way for foreigners to make movies in Tanzania.[29] The first collaboration was *Wimbo wa Mianzi* ("The Song of the Bamboo") together with One World Productions from the Netherlands in 1983. Like the production of the film itself, the story of the film revolves around the question of foreign development aid. It tells the story of a village whose inhabitants call on foreign experts to resolve a water problem. Before long, they realise that instead of installing an expensive pump they can solve the problem independently with local manpower and materials.[30]

Harusi ya Mariamu ("The Marriage of Mariamu")[31] was then co-produced by American film-maker Ron Mulvihill, receiving financial support from the Ethnographic Film Program at the University of California, Los Angeles (UCLA). In a documentary-style narrative, the film – just 36 minutes long – describes the interaction between an educated young woman, Mariamu, and a traditional healer, a *mganga*. Mariamu is sick, but modern doctors cannot determine the reason for her illness. When she finally puts her prejudices aside and consults the traditional healer, she discovers the cause: a childhood trauma triggered by the discovery of her father's body as well as her rejection of a traditional ritual at her wedding.[32]

The next film, produced with the help of the Norwegian Ministry of Development, was *Mama Tumaini* ("Mother Hope").[33] It tells the story of a broken marriage between two Norwegian development workers and the plight of Mama Tumaini and a group of women potters who fight a corrupt bureaucrat in order to organise a cooperative.[34]

The TFC's final co-production with Mulvihill and his company Gris-Gris Film was *Maangamizi* ("The Ancient One").[35] In this film, the African-American doctor, Asira, who comes to Tanzania to work for the National Institute of Psychiatric Medicine in Bagamoyo, meets Samehe, a patient who has not spoken for twenty years. When she becomes a confidant of Samehe, she learns about the world of her ancestors and meets Maangamizi, "[t]he grandmother of all grandmothers".[36]

When I asked the late author and film-maker, Hammie Rajab, about the Tanzanian Film Company, he recalled:

> Tanzanian Film Company was a film company as it sounds. It was a very nice company when it started. We made a few films, films actually, not videos. I think something went wrong somewhere along the line and the company trembled, you know, it just collapsed. I can't tell you

> exactly why, but the way I see it, it's the management. People not understanding, people not realizing how important a film industry is in a country. They didn't look at Tanzanian Film Company as something that would preserve our cultures and tell stories about our country. I think they looked at the company as some place where they can get money or something like that and then there was no money they needed, they let it go.[37]

Though the TFC collapsed and stood for the failure of a state to establish a state-run film industry, the company did have influence on the evolving film industry later, as TFC workers subsequently educated local artists. For one of the most popular comedy actors and forerunner of film-makers, Said Ngamba – also known as Mzee Small – the TFC stood for the idea and fascination of film-making.

> There was a white man he was the director of Film Tanzania his name was *Mzungu* Mr. Tok [sic]. He liked the plays we performed and the actors and he discovered me. […] When he met me he said to me 'Come, we will train you!' I visited the Tanzania Film Company and watched TV; there was a kind of tape running 'Te-te-te-te'. He said to me: 'Sit down and look at it!'[38]

After the closure of the TFC, Tanzanian artists like Mzee Small, who had neither the capital nor the education to produce their own movies, were left to work for local TV stations. Only privileged artists had the means to go into film production. Among them was Beatrix Mugishagwe, who had been trained by and had worked with Deutsche Welle in Germany for twenty years. After returning to Tanzania in 1994, she started her film and TV production company Abantu Visions. Specialising in documentaries and with the help of the Norwegian embassy, she released her first feature length film, *Tumaini* ("Hope") in 2005, a development film about HIV/AIDS.[39] Another example of this film-making elite is Imruh Bakari who had been working with the London-based film company Ceddo in the 1990s. In 2003, he founded his film company Savannah Films and released a set of five short films between 2005 and 2008 with the title *African Tales*. Although he distances himself from the video industry, most of the actors in his movies have actually become popular through these productions.

It was only after the introduction of the video technology that local artists were able to produce their own movies in their own language and independent of foreign sponsors.

5. The (R)Evolution of the Swahili Film Industry

The appropriation of the video medium in Tanzania started in the mid-1980s when the government loosened market restrictions. When they lifted the ban on the import of VHS recorders in 1985, large numbers of recorders and cassettes began flooding the country.[40] Indian businessmen started to pirate foreign films. This made films available for film-hungry audiences. While Tanzanians embraced action films made in the USA and Hong Kong, Bollywood classics and, later, Nigerian movies, there was one problem: the language gap. This gap was soon filled by film narrators who commented on the films live in the video halls[41] and evidentially dubbed their translation and commentaries into the films.[42] As Matthias Krings has shown in his work on Tanzanian film narrators, they do far more than a simple synchronisation. On the contrary, "their craft consists in the creation of new texts, texts that speak to both foreign film and its new and unforeseen local context."[43]

There was still a lively popular theatre scene in the Tanzania of the 1990s, with different art groups performing in local bars and social clubs, all in Swahili.[44] After the very late introduction of TV in 1993, theatre artists went to work for TV stations in order to reach a wider audience. But they soon felt exploited due to low wages, and the first pioneers recorded Swahili plays on video to gain independence and earn additional income.[45] Among them were two famous comedians, Mzee Small and King Majuto, who in subsequent years produced hundreds of Swahili video comedies.

However, it was not until 2003 that a distribution system developed with the release of the movie *Girlfriend*,[46] a film about a Bongo Flava[47] musician. Two companies, GMC[48] and Wananchi, led by a Tanzanian family of Indian origin who had started to distribute local music, made this development possible. Banzi became one of the initiators of this industry when he asked the director of Wananchi to finance and distribute his first film, *Nsyuka*. More and more artist groups were founded and started to work for the film market. Hundreds of young people joined these groups with the hope of becoming famous film stars. Small production units equipped with computers for editing the films were quickly made available. Today, with a release of five to seven movies a week and thousands of young people working in different areas of production, reception and sales, one can speak of a Tanzanian film industry.

Having been influenced by Nigerian horror movies early on, more diverse genres have since developed, among them comedies, love stories, martial arts, traditional and Christian movies. Across these genres, Tanzanian society's main problems and controversial issues are discussed such as generational conflicts, money and inheritance disputes, exploitation, power and corruption, Pentecostalism or the belief in witchcraft and occult powers as well as the clash of tradition and modernity along a rural-urban divide. By allowing viewers to watch a fictional rendering of their society played out on screen, these films have led to self-reflection. In presenting taboo themes such as alternative gender concepts, the films have an important role in shaping and transforming culture and attitudes in Tanzania.

Tanzanian films are mainly produced in Swahili. The use of other local languages is limited to particular scenes and certain characters in the films in order to accentuate 'traditional' village life or cultural authenticity. It is revealing that none of the other Tanzanian languages could compete with the lingua franca in this artistic field. This can be traced back to the language policy of Ujamaa and the implementation of Swahili as the national language, which has resulted in an exclusion of other languages in socio-cultural practices.[49]

Swahili is not only one of the main characteristics of the movies but also the medium of communication during production and in the film industry itself. However, as in other working areas of Tanzanian public life, code switching is very common during film production, and English remains dominant regarding certain technical terms. It is used for the common orders given by the director such as 'action', 'cut' and 'roll', while other orders like *rudia* ("do it again") or *endelea* ("carry on") are in Swahili. Technical terms like 'shot', 'take' and the different kinds of shots such as 'close up', 'mid-shot' or 'wide shot' remain in their original. Different job titles like *washiriki* ("cast"), *mwongozaji* ("director") and *mpiga picha* ("cameraman") have been translated into Swahili and are now used in either Swahili or English in the credits of a film.[50] Although sometimes phonologically adopted to Swahili or used as part of code switching, all technical vocabulary is in English in the cutting room. Editing vocabulary contains the terms 'capture', 'render', 'clips', 'special effects', 'fade-in', 'morphing' or 'voice-over'.

In the scripts and films, daily language use and different language attitudes are reflected. Characters are marked by their language use and their knowledge of English. Characters who speak English are educated, wealthy, foreigners and people who have been abroad, while the village idiot is marked by his local tongue and accent and would rarely use a word of English.[51] Characters in comedies in particular are made fun of in that they use incorrect English.

In the early films, characters rarely expressed themselves in English. Due to the influence of foreign media, however, the current positive attitude towards English, the will to learn it, the use of English phrases and code switching have increased in recent years. In contemporary movies, which exploit a modern urban setting, phrases like 'What?', 'Why?', 'I will kill you!', 'I love you', and 'Are you serious?' are very common. A film's title song might even be in English.

Through the use of Swahili, new terms and phrases are coined which are then integrated into daily language use, and I was able to witness the effect of film language on language use myself. After having acted in some films and TV series, I was approached by people in the streets who recognised me and quoted lines from my films. In the weekly running comedy series *Orijino Komedi*, a group of actors have become especially famous for inventing new terms, which are then actively appropriated by the audience. One example is the phrase *Umefulia!* ("You have failed!"), referring to any failure, loss or bad luck a person might encounter. Henceforth, this phrase has been used by the audience in appropriate situations.

More importantly, Swahili is an important identity marker of the movies, a local feature or flavour used by the film-makers and recognised by the audience. From the beginnings of the Tanzanian film industry, the level of Tanzanian influence on the movies was always defined first and foremost through its language, Kiswahili. As the industry grew and the numbers of newly-released films exploded, more and more film-makers began using English film titles as teasers for the audiences who very often do not understand their meanings. Despite this play of languages, most of the film-makers and actors as well as the audience members do not have sufficient competence in this language, and, therefore, movies are not shot in English. Although most of them have neither the time nor the means to do it, some actors and film-makers try to improve their English through formal training. Even the first Tanzanian-Nigerian film *Dar 2 Lagos-4 re-union*[52] was not shot exclusively in English. On the contrary, because the differences between the two countries were discussed in the movie, the Nigerian actors had to learn some Swahili for their parts.[53]

In the wake of the globalisation and transnationalisation of the film industry, the use of English subtitles became necessary in order to sell the films on the international market. Through diaspora networks, Swahili films are informally distributed in Europe, the United States and Arab countries and the Internet has become an important platform for promoting films. Since the establishment of the South African channel Africa Magic Plus and Swahili Magic, Tanzanian movies can be watched all over Africa.

6. Language and Identity

As the two African scholars and writers Alamin M. Mazrui and Ibrahim Noor Shariff have shown,

> [t]he concept of identity that defines 'the self' and 'the other', 'the we' and 'the they', is always rooted in the politics of its time and place. Identity is in fact a process by which power and status are negotiated, disinheritance and oppression legitimized, and liberation struggles waged.[54]

In Tanzania – as in many other parts of the world – language makes up one of the central parameters of how people define themselves and are defined by others. It is no wonder then that generic categorisations of films also follow linguistic lines. Like Swahili for Tanzanian films, the languages Igbo, Yoruba and Hausa stand for distinct genres of the Nigerian film industry, Nollywood. However, as the Nigerian sociolinguist Emmanuel Adedayo Adedun writes, even in Yoruba movies, English as part of the code switching in films is still dominant. According to him, the dominance of English in the films reflects the Nigerian language ideology.[55] While the use of Igbo and Yoruba in the movies has decreased in favour of English, Hausa as part of the North Nigerian Muslim culture has remained. According to the African literary scholar, Françoise Ugochukwu, Yoruba and Igbo are still crucial identity markers of the films and are enjoyed even among the Nigerian diaspora. In this way, the film industry plays an important part in the revival of language and cultural practices abroad.[56]

From the beginning of Swahili film production, the audience and Tanzanian public criticised film-makers for only translating Nigerian stories into Swahili. This opinion was even held by the film-makers themselves:

> For example people, young people of course, make a copy of what the Nigerians are doing, and they turn those films into Kiswahili to change the locations, the language, the characters, you know, and then you see, that's a Nigerian movie made in Kiswahili that's all. That's not a way to make a film.[57]

The extent to which the movies could be defined as Tanzanian was only through the language used, as the explanation by the film-maker Sultan Tamba reveals:

> I think we haven't reached that far. There is nothing except the language Swahili, which is the only Tanzanian marker of the films. Because the way it is spoken in Tanzania is not the way it is spoken elsewhere like in Kenya and other countries like Uganda, Malawi, Ruanda, Burundi and Congo. In Tanzania it's the same like in Bollywood, where they stage their own stories but speak Hindi as well. But in Indian movies it is more than one criterion for people to see that it's about India. But we have nothing but Swahili. The environment is the same like in Ruanda or Burundi; the places resemble each other. If you show a village, every country has villages. The only difference is maybe the Arabian influence but villages are everywhere. So I can say the Tanzanianess in the movies is only Kiswahili.[58]

While one of the first commercially successful movies, *Girlfriend – filamu ya maisha na muziki*, had an English title, all the other early film titles were predominantly in Swahili. Mussa Banzi's early movie titles began with the first few words of Swahili proverbs, as if prompting his audience to add the remaining ones. Among these proverbial titles are *Fungu la Kukosa*[59] – *ni kukosa tu* ("The Reason for Failing is Only

Failing") and *Sikio la Kufa*[60] – *hasikii dawa* ("A Deaf Ear Doesn't Listen to Medicine").

When more film-makers joined the business after the industry's boom in 2006 and 2007, the number of English titles rose as film-makers anticipated a global audience. However, even for the Swahili-speaking viewers, English titles act as teasers to make the films more attractive and sophisticated as well as to provoke curiosity. This sometimes results in strange titles such as *Yellow Banana-Expectation*,[61] which is not related to the movie's content. Other film-makers and viewers complain that English titles have a foreign air and that Tanzanians have difficulties deciphering what a film is about. Some film-makers even returned to Swahili titles to make their movies more distinctive, while others have bilingual titles beginning with English.

7. Lugha gongana *("Clashing Languages")*

The language question is also discussed in the movies themselves. The comedy *Lugha gongana* ("Clashing Languages")[62] centres on the language question. In the same way that Banzi's limited knowledge of English has restricted him from certain career opportunities, the main character, Mapembe, finds himself in trouble for possessing no English skills. Mapembe is the typical local caricature of a poor and simple-minded man looking for a job to support his small family. Naively, he enters a rich man's house to ask for a job, not knowing that the house owners are not from Tanzania. Before Mapembe enters, the viewer is introduced to the English-speaking couple while they look through a wildlife magazine on Tanzania. The following scene shows the absurd 'dialogue' between Mapembe, who addresses them in Swahili, and the house owners who do not understand and attempt to communicate in English. Luckily, a friend, Moses, arrives just in time and translates. Despite his awkward behaviour, Mapembe finally gets the job of the housekeeper and is to begin English lessons with Moses while on duty. As soon as he starts working, however, Mapembe provokes the anger of his employers because he does not understand their demands. Therefore, Moses is called upon to translate. Due to Moses's 'help', Mapembe answers his employers' requests with phrases like, "You cannot force yes to be no!" and "To hell!"[63] In the end, he is finally fired for stealing money.

His situation gets worse during his next job interview, when he meets a Massai in front of the office who refuses to speak Swahili and the office manager who speaks nothing but Arabic. While he is offered the job (again through the aid of a translator), in the end he is accused of stealing money and is fired in the presence of his family, who eventually leave him. Mapembe is left alone and concludes angrily:

> This all because I didn't go to school. At my first job it was because of English, and here in this office, it was Osama. My wife has left me claiming I am a thief. Now, what I am saying is that I will go to school, and when I have learned, I will see that these things can't happen to me again![64]

Lugha gongana can be read as a satirical reflection on the multilingual setting in Tanzania. Mapembe symbolises many people who are excluded from job opportunities because they do not speak English. Contrary to this film – whose characters cannot cross their languages' borders – in reality, Swahili would be used as the medium of communication. The final message of the comedy depicts one of the main concerns of the first president of Tanzania, Julius Nyerere: the education of the masses. However, the viewer also learns that it was not Mapembe's poor English but his thieving and dishonesty that resulted in his firing and abandonment.

8. 'Kanumba the Great' Becomes 'Kanumba the Bogas'

The language issue is not only re-enacted in the films, but actors themselves are also part of the discussion. I witnessed this in 2009 when a media debate about the English competence of one of the most famous actors arose. In September 2009, one of the most popular Tanzanian film stars, Steven Kanumba,[65] who called himself 'The Great', was invited to star in the premier of *Big Brother Africa – The Revolution* in South Africa. During this episode, viewers from all over Africa sent messages to the show commenting on Kanumba, his pink shirt and his poor knowledge of English. It was said that Kanumba's English was so bad that he could not speak or answer questions. The critics concluded that if

Kanumba as a film star could not speak proper English, he was an embarrassment to the whole nation.

The flourishing Swahili language tabloid press in Tanzania, soon jumped on the bandwagon, and the topic of Kanumba's inadequate knowledge of English filled the front pages of several local newspapers, which concluded that he had disgraced himself and, instead of 'The Great', he should be called 'The Bogas' (from the English term bogus) from then on.[66]

Additionally, the producers of the weekly comedy show *Orijino Komedi* used the story of Kanumba in their programme. The show is presented in a fake satirical news format with a news commentator, Masanja.[67] In one of these clips, the comedians acted out Kanumba's stay in the *Big Brother* house and presented him introducing himself to his African co-stars while stammering and making a fool of himself.[68]

The following week, the show continued to pursue the topic in a sketch in which not only Kanumba but all Tanzanian actors are characterised by poor English skills. They join an English course and Masanja's commentary sets the scene:

> The party of the Tanzanian actors, *wanawani*,[69] has said that they praised their actors who are thinking of their future and have had the faith to join an English course and, *wanawani*. I will bring you to the location where the actors are learning and on top of that I don't know if it's true or not![70]

In a very poorly equipped classroom with corrugated sheet metal and dirt floor, the Tanzanian actors sit on simple wooden benches. Their teacher, wearing a white doctor's coat – played by Masanja – cleans the black board. While the pupils are writing and reading, the teacher writes in bold letters "MOVIE STAR" and "FILMMAKER" on the board and turns to them:

> Teacher: O.k. good morning film stars!
> All: Good morning.
> Teacher: Say "Good morning, Sir." Good morning film stars!
> All: Good morning, Sir!
> Teacher: Ya, I know, I know, so what is your name?
> Pupils: My name is.
> Teacher: So, just say your name! What is your name?

> Pupil: My name, me.
> Teacher: Ah, jina lako nani? [What's your name?]
> Pupil: Na ni Moses.
> Teacher: Ya!
> All: My name is Moses!
> Teacher: No, just say your name! What is your name?
> All: My name is Moses!
> Teacher: You guys, wote mnaitwa Moses? [Are you all called Moses?]
> All: No!
> Teacher: Just say your name! What is your name?
> All: My name is (quiet and uncertainly) Moses.
> The teacher goes to the black board mumbling: This is a problem, ah! Anyway![71]

Masanja concludes the sketch in the studio:

> And that's the reason why we don't have development! And let me tell you something: This industry will not develop because they put all their strength lamenting on others instead of talking about the wealth which is taken away from us. The women in the films don't behave, the dealers go on our nerves, the business is not going well, I don't know what else is annoying. Other sellers have begun to sell our movies. But instead of taking care of the sales of the movies, you are sitting there and complaining 'Oh, why can't he speak English!' Are you kidding? Are you alright?[72]

Masanja's concluding comment reveals that the artists, despite having extensively exploited Kanumba's bad English, are criticising the scandal themselves and the ridiculous concern over an actor's weakness instead of addressing real problems in the film industry. In the film sector as well as in society, language has thus become a controversial topic, which distracts Tanzanians from their real problems including poverty and exploitation. Kanumba's television appearance has triggered a general discussion about language hierarchies, about the supposed 'superiority' of English and the alleged 'inferiority' of Swahili.

Orijino Komedi ends with a mock discussion of young Tanzanian actors and actresses being interviewed by a TV crew, who react to the accusations. They defend the use of their national language as the established medium of communication in the industry and protest against forcing artists to study English. As the crowd shouts in approval, one young man says angrily: "You can't go to Sweden and be forced to speak English. You have to talk Swedish, English later. So we will stay like that. Let us speak our Swahili! English comes later! Alright?"[73] The next guest, played by the show's presenter dressed in hip-hop style clothing, states that in going to South Africa as an ambassador for Tanzania, Kanumba's poor command of English has betrayed the nation. Finally, the last contributor, who looks like a film director, concludes: "And another important thing for us is to know three or four words: 'attention', 'action', 'cut' and 'roll' – that is enough!"[74]

9. Conclusion

Mussa Banzi was very disappointed when he learned that he would not be invited to the Berlinale. His hope was to broaden his horizons, increase networks and have the chance to be recognised by international film critics, which would lead to the opportunity of working abroad. However, he did not give up and continued producing Swahili films for the local audience. He was even able to sell some of his films to Africa Magic, which makes Swahili movies accessible to all Africans by adding English subtitles.

Tanzanian film-makers are caught in a double bind. On the one hand, they strive to break into the international market, the key to which is the English language. On the other hand, they risk losing their local audience to whom their own language symbolises identity and authenticity.

The result is a language predicament in the film industry as well as other areas of the Tanzanian public domain. While English was the language of the colonisers, Swahili was the key to independence and freedom. A poor knowledge of English hinders many young Tanzanians from taking advantage of opportunities. As the example of the comedy *Lugha gongana* demonstrates, film has become an important vehicle for discussing the language question. Film-making was introduced via colonialism; and the decolonisation of the screen would not have been possible without Swahili. Swahili thus became the engine of the growing independent film industry.

The global circulation of new media technologies such as video has fostered the development of new creative industries like Tanzanian film and hip-hop or Bongo Flava, their most important tool being the localising force of languages. As film-makers aim at achieving global recognition, the language question thus arises and was articulated and discussed through the figure of Steven Kanumba who, due to inadequate English knowledge, was said to have failed on the global stage. The scandal eventually dissipated, and it did not hurt Kanumba's reputation. Conversely, it has bolstered his popularity by showing a common insecurity among Tanzanians and the pride for Swahili as a national language.

As other examples have shown, it is not the use of local languages that hinders global popularity. In fact, it is this local flavour which makes these films distinct and therefore attractive for the world audience. What is essential to the expansion of the audience for Tanzanian film is having good promotion, (international) distribution networks and, lastly, translation.

Notes

1 Ngũgĩ wa Thiong'o (1986: 4).
2 For an overview of African varieties of English, see Schröder's contribution to this volume.
3 See Sa (2007: 3).
4 Rubagumya (1990: 7).
5 Roy-Campbell (1997: 116-117).
6 See also Blommaert (1999: 89 ff.).
7 Abdulaziz (1990: 9).
8 Blommaert (2005:399).
9 Roy-Campbell (1997), Rubagumya (1990).
10 Sa (2007: 5).
11 Smyth (1989: 391), Brennan (2005: 485).
12 Ukadike (1994: 33).
13 Smyth (1989: 389).
14 *Ibid.*
15 *Ibid.* 389-390.
16 *Ibid.* 390.
17 *Ibid.* 390-391.

18 The Arusha Declaration is the most important Tanzanian political initiative and statement proclaimed by Julius Nyerere in the city of Arusha on 5 February 1967.
19 Leveri (1983: 24).
20 *Ibid.* 28.
21 *Ibid.* 25-27.
22 *Ibid.* 26.
23 *Ibid.* 25.
24 Dir. Tørk Haxthausen, 1975.
25 From *kuombaomba* ("begging") (Brennan 2006: 401).
26 Brennan (2006: 401-403). The second part of the Back-to-the-village-classic, *Yombayomba*, has not been finalised until 1989 due to financial problems (Smyth 1989: 394).
27 Leveri (1983: 7).
28 Smyth (1989: 392).
29 Email communication with Martin Mhando, 8 June 2012.
30 Smyth (1989: 394).
31 Dir. Nangayoma Ng'oge, Ron Mulvihill, 1984.
32 See also Smyth (1989: 395), Bryce (2010: 173).
33 Dir. Martin Mhando, Sigve Endresen, 1986.
34 Smyth (1989: 39).
35 Dir. Martin Mhando, Ron Mulvihill, 2001.
36 Gris-Gris Films, Inc. (2005). *Maangamizi* was nominated for an Oscar (74th Academy Awards 2002) in the category Best Foreign Film. It received the Award for Best Film and the Award for Best Actress as well as the Golden Dhow Award for Best Feature at the Zanzibar Film Festival 1998, the Paul Robeson Award Best Feature Film at the Newark Black Film Festival and the Award for Best Actress on the Southern African Film Festival (*Ibid.*).
37 Interview with Hammie Rajab, former worker with TFC, in Dar es Salaam 10 September 2006.
38 Interview with Mzee Small in Dar es Salaam 26 September 2007.
39 See also Bryce (2010).
40 Smyth (1989: 396).
41 Video halls or *vibanda* ("huts") or video shows are simple rooms equipped with a TV and a VCR where videos are shown for a small entrance fee.
42 See also Krings (2009).
43 Krings (forthcoming).
44 See Lange (2002), Edmondson (2007).
45 Lange (2002: 152).
46 Dir. George Tyson, 2003.

47 Bongo Flava is a local form of rap and hip-hop. Today it is used as an umbrella term for several genres in Tanzanian music. For a detailed discussion of Bongo Flava, see Reuster-Jahn's contribution to this volume.
48 Global Sound, Mamu Stores and Congo Corridor.
49 Blommaert (1997: 1).
50 Further examples include *Msanii* ("Actor"), *Mtunzi* ("Author"), *Mtengenezaji* ("Producer"), *Mhariri* ("Cutter/Editor"), *Mavazi* ("Costumes"), *Muendelezo* ("Continuity"), *Mandhari* ("Setting"), *Mtaa* ("Light"), *Sauti* ("Sound"), *Sakafu* ("Floor Crew").
51 See also Böhme (2006).
52 Dir. Femi Ogedegbe, 2006.
53 See also Krings (2010).
54 Mazrui & Shariff (1994: 5).
55 Adedun (2010).
56 Ugochukwu (2011).
57 Interview with Hammie Rajab in Dar es Salaam, 10 September 2006.
58 Interview with Sultan Tamba in Dar es Salaam, 20 August 2006.
59 Dir. Mussa Banzi, Part 1 2004, Part II 2008.
60 Dir. Mussa Banzi, 2005.
61 Dir. Mtitu Game and Vincent Kigosi, 2008.
62 Dir. Khalfan Ahmed, 2007.
63 *Lugha gongana*, dir. Khalfan Ahmed, 2007.
64 *Ibid.*
65 Steven Kanumba died in April 2012.
66 See, for example, the newspapers *Kiu* (11 September 2009) and *Amani* (10 September 2009).
67 At the beginning of their careers the actors of *Orijino Komedi* were in the same actors' group as Kanumba, the Kaole Sanaa Group. They appeared in several videos before they became famous with their own show. The show, originally called *Ze Comedy*, which started with the privately owned East African TV (EATV), was such a huge success that the streets of Dar es Salaam were empty during the screening of the show. After a conflict with EATV, the show was broadcast by the state-run station Tanzania Broadcasting Corporation (TBC) under the new name *Orijino Komedi*.
68 *Orijino Komedi* (10 September 2009).
67 This ironical address to the viewers is probably a contracted form of *wapenzi watazamaji* ("dear viewers").
70 *Orijino Komedi* (10 September 2009).
71 *Ibid.*
72 *Ibid.*

73 *Orijino Komedi* (10 September 2009).
74 *Ibid.*

Bibliography

Abdulaziz, Mohamed H.: "Aspects of Lexical and Semantic Elaboration in the Process of Modernization of Swahili". – In Karsten Legère (Ed.): *The Role of Language in Literacy Programs with Special Reference to Kiswahili in Eastern Africa*, Bonn, 1990, pp. 439-458.

Adedun, Adedayo: "The Sociolinguistics of a Nollywood Movie", *Journal of Global Analysis* 1:2, 2010, 113-138.

Blommaert, Jan: "The Impact of State Ideology on Language. Ujamaa and Swahili Literature in Tanzania". – In Birgit Smieja & Meike Tasch (Eds.): *Human Contact Through Language and Linguistics*, Frankfurt, 1997, pp. 253-270.

---: *State Ideology and Language in Tanzania*, Köln, 1999.

---: "Situating Language Rights. English and Swahili in Tanzania Revisited", *Journal of Sociolinguistics* 9:3, 2005, 390-417.

Böhme, Claudia: "Der swahilisprachige Videofilm *Girlfriend*. Eine Sprachanalyse", *Arbeitspapiere des Instituts für Ethnologie und Afrikastudien der Johannes Gutenberg-Universität Mainz* 63, 2006, <www.ifeas.uni-mainz.de/workingpapers/Ap63.pdf>, accessed 27 February 2012.

Brennan, James: "Democratizing Cinema and Censorship in Tanzania, 1920-1980", *The International Journal of African Historical Studies* 38:3, 2005, 481-511.

---: "Blood Enemies. Exploitation and Urban Citizenship in the Nationalist Political Thought of Tanzania, 1958-75", *Journal of African History* 47, 2006, 389-413.

Bryce, Jane: "Outside the Machine? Donar Values and the Case of Film in Tanzania". – In Mahir Şaul & Ralph A. Austen (Eds.): *Viewing African Cinema in the Twenty-First Century. Art Films and the Nollywood Video Revolution*, Athens/Ohio, 2010, pp. 160-177.

Edmondson, Laura: *Performance and Politics in Tanzania. The Nation Stage*, Bloomington & Indianapolis, 2007.

Gris-Gris Films, Inc.: "Maangamizi", *Gris-Gris Films*, 2005, <http://www.grisgrisfilms.com/html/maangamizi.html>, accessed 8 October 2012.

Krings, Matthias: "Turning Rice into Pilau. The Art of Video Narration in Tanzania", *Intermédialités* 4, 2009, <http://cri.histart.umontreal.ca/cri/fr/

INTERMEDIALITES/interface/numeros.html>, accessed 16 September 2011. [Electronic issue of *Re-dire*, edited by Vincent Bouchard, Ute Fendler and Germain Lacasse]

---: "Nollywood Goes East. The Localization of Nigerian Video Films in Tanzania". – In Mahir Şaul & Ralph A. Austen (Eds.): *Viewing African Cinema in the Twenty-First Century. Art Films and the Nollywood Video Revolution*, Athens/Ohio, 2010, pp. 74-91.

---: "Karishika with Kiswahili Flavour. A Nigerian Film Retold by a Tanzanian Video Narrator". – In M. K. & Onookome Okome (Eds.): *Nollywood Beyond Nigeria. Transnational Dimensions of an African Video Film Industry*, Bloomington, forthcoming.

Lange, Siri: *Managing Modernity. Gender, State and Nation in the Popular Drama of Dar es Salaam, Tanzania*, Bergen, 2002.

Leveri, Mark Mbazi Elinaza: *Prospects in Developing a Viable National Film Industry. A "Close-Up" of a Decade's Performance of the Audio-Visual Institute of Dar es Salaam and the Tanzania Film Company Limited (1973-1983)*, Dar es Salaam, 1983. [unpublished dissertation, University of Dar es Salaam]

Lugha gongana, dir. Khalfan Ahmed, 2007.

Mazrui, Alamin M. & Ibrahin Noor Shariff: *The Swahili. Idiom and Identity of an African People*, Trenton, 1994.

Ngũgĩ wa Thiong'o: *Decolonising the Mind. The Politics of Language in African Literature*, Nairobi, 1986.

Orijino Komedi, Tanzania Broadcasting Corporation, 10 September 2009, 7 pm.

Roy-Campbell, Zaline M.: *Language Crisis in Tanzania. The Myth of English Versus Education*, Dar es Salaam, 1997.

Rubagumya, Casmir M.: *Language in Education in Africa. A Tanzanian Perspective*, Clevedon *et al.*, 1990.

Sa, Eleuthera: "Language Policy for Education and Development in Tanzania", *Swarthmore Department of Linguistics, Class of 2007 Theses*, 2007, <http://www.swarthmore.edu/SocSci/Linguistics/Papers/2007/sa_eleuthera.pdf>, accessed 27 February 2012.

Smyth, Rosaleen: "The Feature Film in Tanzania", *African Affairs* 88, 1989, 389-396.

Ukadike, Frank Nwachukwu: *Black African Cinema*, Berkeley & Los Angeles, 1994.

Ugochukwu, Françoise: "Language and Identity. The Impact of Nigerian Video Films on Diasporic Communities", paper presented at the conference *Language, Identity, and Intercultural Communication*, London, 9-10 June 2011. [the abstract can be found at <http://oro.open.ac.uk/32096/>, accessed 23 February 2012]

Uta Reuster-Jahn (Hamburg)

Am walking on the way kuiseti future yangu.[1] The Use of English in Bongo Flava Music in Tanzania

1. Introduction

Since the 1990s, the privatisation of media and new electronic production and distribution techniques have facilitated the emergence of a new music scene in Tanzania, popularly known as Bongo Flava or *muziki wa kizazi kipya* ("the music of the new generation"). This development began with the appropriation of African-American hip-hop and rhythm & blues (R&B) by Tanzanian urban youth. After an initial phase characterised by imitation of both the music and language of US-American songs, Swahilisation became central to youth's acceptance of the new music. Artists also started to mix musical styles such as Zouk, Reggae, Congolese Bolingo, Indian music and 'traditional' tunes and instrumentals, a combination which has made Bongo Flava a very heterogeneous variety of music. The term Bongo Flava was coined by radio DJs and was popularised through radio programmes. The name aptly conveys how Tanzanians conceive of this music: Bongo is a nickname for Dar es Salaam, being an augmentative form of the Swahili noun *ubongo* meaning "brain". The etymological motivation is that one has to use one's brains in order to survive in the city.[2] Bongo Flava is therefore understood as music of foreign, mostly African-American origin, which has become localised and infused with the flavour (*flava*) of Tanzania or Dar es Salaam, the country's cultural capital.[3] The musical styles and elements as well as the lyrical content were constantly debated by musicians and their audiences during the process of appropriation.

Despite a strong tendency to give the music a local flavour, the templates which Bongo Flava provide for youth identity transcend national and even African borders, connecting the young people to Jamaican and US American youth concepts. This is expressed in patterns of music, images of music videos as well as in language use in the lyrics.[4] Language choice is central to the expression and projection of identities. Most Bongo Flava lyrics are marked by the use of Tanzanian youth language based on Swahili, but including transfers of English words and expressions which have been assimilated into Swahili, often resulting in a semantic change.[5] English slang words belonging in the semantic domain of hip-hop culture and drug use form also part of this vocabulary. However, the attitude of Bongo Flava musicians towards language varies. It is the aim of this essay to explore this variation and to examine the functions of English elements in the lyrics. It will be shown that language choice depends to some extent on the social identity of musicians, but also on considerations regarding audiences and markets. I will first give a brief history of Bongo Flava, followed by a historical account of the use of English in Swahili poetry. A short outline of Tanzanian language policy will be given to trace the recent sociolinguistic relation between Swahili and English in the country.[6] Drawing from case studies, I will identify the various attitudes of musicians towards the use of English in Bongo Flava and discuss the functions of English in Bongo Flava lyrics.

2. The Localisation of Hip-hop and the Formation of Bongo Flava

Hip-hop reached Tanzania between 1984 and 1989, when, at the end of *ujamaa* socialism,[7] "the socialist practices that limited people's access to foreign music and culture began to break down",[8] and musicians resumed the pre-socialist practice of cultural borrowing from outside Africa. Music and video cassettes brought hip-hop sounds and images to Tanzania. Initially, they were only available if one had relatives or friends in Western countries. As a result, the first people to get to know them were youths from middle and upper class families. Through private exchange and copying of cassettes as well as through US American hip-hop films shown in cinemas hip-hop reached wider circles of secondary school students.[9] Local rap music took off slowly and the first stage was marked by imitation. Initially, a few youths performed original English rap versions with copied instrumentals played by DJs in discos and clubs. Through the process of imitation, the rappers learned to combine the music with rapid speech and developed a feeling for beats, rhyme, rhythm and flow. Over time, some artists became famous in these circles and first rap groups were formed. CDs with instrumentals of songs by US rap stars like Snoop Doggy Dogg, Dr. Dre or Naughty by Nature were sold on the streets, because the youth wanted to have something that "looks American", as Issah of the Dar es Salaam rap crew Big Dog Posse remembers.[10]

The rapper Saleh J's release of the Swahili version of "Ice Ice Baby" by Vanilla Ice in 1991 prompted Swahilisation and it soon became a powerful trend. Although the purist hip-hop pioneers tried to resist this development at first, they had no choice but to go along with it in order to stay in the game.[11] Saleh J's song, which was also the first hip-hop single on the Tanzanian music market, was about HIV/AIDS, a topic of great concern to many young Tanzanians. It pointed out the way for the further development of lyrical content. Facilitated by Swahilisation of the lyrics, hip-hop spread to more deprived youths who started using it to speak out about their lives, in a role perceived as a *kioo cha jamii* ("mirror of society").[12] For them, Bongo Flava became a means of drawing attention to their living conditions, of articulating their needs and desires and of making their voices heard in the public domain. Thus, they inform the public about the realities of poor people's lives especially in the urban environment. Often sung as a first-person narrative, the songs expose the hardships of the poor, warn against harmful behaviour, especially in the context of drugs and HIV/AIDS, and call on the audience to maintain moral values, even in difficult living conditions. In this respect, Tanzanian hip-hop differs significantly from the US hip-hop genre, since "much of Bongo Flava does not address the tangible category of 'youth', with corresponding subculture, but the whole of society, as a political leader would".[13] The Tanzanian rapper II Proud became a leading figure for socially conscious rap lyrics. In his album *Ndani ya Bongo* ("Inside Dar es Salaam"), he exposes inequality and injustice and challenges state authority with unprecedented directness.[14] For quite some time, this album set the standard for other musicians, both in terms of its lyrics and its musical style.[15] The artists see themselves as "educators of society", a role linked not only to trends in the socialist era but also to the long established tradition of song as social-political commentary.[16]

While many songs are socially critical, others celebrate enjoyment, parties and going to clubs with friends, initiating a discourse on values of the 'new generation' in the era of liberalism. In the early 2000s, a debate on appropriate lyrics brought issues in the localisation process out in the open. While all artists agreed on the importance of 'delivering a message', opinions diverged on hip-hop features such as battle and lifestyle,[17] classified pejoratively as "nothing but *flava*".[18] Battle and lifestyle-related lyrics are commonly perceived to collide with artists' roles as educators of society. I have suggested elsewhere that the "lifestyle lyrics" gain their meaning in the context of discourses on youth identity by claiming the right to enjoy life in the way one sees fit.[19] After hip-hop music had reached the poorer youth, part of this discourse centred on *msela*,[20] the Tanzanian version of the American *gangsta*. This model of the black male rapper has become a global pattern for identification.[21] However, in the Tanzanian context musicians and audiences rejected its violent component. To be an *msela* thus means having a hard life, sharing the love of rap music and a hip-hop dress style as well as greeting each other with certain gestures, using youth language and smoking marijuana.[22]

3. English in Swahili Poetry

Even if Swahilisation was crucial for shaping what is now known as Bongo Flava, this does not mean that the lyrics are free of English words and phrases. In fact, the incorporation of lexical elements from English was practised as early as the 19th century, in Swahili poetry.[23] As Saavedra Casco states,

> Swahili poetry has incorporated words of alien origin and, like the Swahili language itself, poetry enriched its vocabulary from an early stage with loans from Portuguese, Farsi and Hindi. Since the beginning of the nineteenth century it has also added loans from French, English, and German.[24]

The earliest known example of a poem incorporating English words is by Sheikh Swadi bin Ali from Lamu, from the early 19th century:

> Haifai, kutoyuwa yangu hali
> Nili hai, kwako siweki badali
> *Gudi bai,* yani*siki mai dali*
>
> You ought to know my condition:
> I am alive, I love no one but you;
> Good-bye, I am sick my darling.[25]

The last line consists mostly of English adapted to the phonetic, syllabic and syntactical structure of Swahili as well as to the requirements of rhyme and metre. Adaptation is a normal procedure for loan words, as "every foreign word that is adopted by Swahili speakers first undergoes a phonetic process of assimilation".[26] As Swahili is an agglutinative language, foreign words can be incorporated and treated as any other Swahili word stem. Thus, the English word "sick" in the example is interpreted as a verb stem meaning "to make sick". Prefixed to the stem is the subject marker *i-* ("it"), tense marker *a-* ("present") and the object marker *ni-* ("me"). The literal translation of the resulting *yanisiki* would be "it makes me sick".

According to Saavedra Casco, the incorporation of foreign loan words into Swahili poetry reflects linguistic and cultural contact on the East African coast. Poets created neologisms from foreign words lacking local equivalents "in order to be able to include them in the rhyme and metre of the verses",[27] especially as elaborated formal requirements are characteristic of Swahili poetry genres. The formal strictness of Swahili poetry is counterbalanced by the syllabic structure of Swahili with syllables consisting mainly of consonant-vowel or of a single vowel alone as well as the possibility of shortening sentences and phrases without losing the meaning.[28] The flexible nature of Swahili poetry has contributed to the incorporation of foreign loan words.[29]

In general, Swahili speakers have never had a problem with the assimilation of foreign loan words; over time these have been increasingly taken from English. This is reflected in an article published in 1962, in which the author F. A. Reynolds mocks the light-heartedness with which Swahili speakers adapted English lexemes to the rules of their language.[30] Reynolds had sifted through the vernacular press and found forms such as *hendikachifu* ("handkerchief"), *kuhepi* ("feel happy") and *kufotolewa* ("to be photographed").[31] The verb *kufotolewa* is another example of the creative strategies applied to foreign words. The word *foto* is preceded by the infinitive marker *ku-* and followed by derivational suffixes. While *kufotoa* means "to photograph", *kufotolewa* means "to be photographed".[32] However, this creative and playful attitude was soon to be curbed by the post-independence language policy, a policy which enforced the use of standard forms.

4. Language Policy in Tanzania

Swahili was initially standardised as a result of the efforts of the Inter-territorial (Swahili) Language Committee, founded in 1930.[33] Following Tanganyika's independence in 1961, Swahili was adopted as the national and official language together with English. The country's language policy emphasised "Swahili as an authentic symbol of the Tanzanian nation" while the National Swahili Council (BAKITA) was established to watch over the standard form.[34] Swahili manuscripts and even radio broadcasts had to be approved of by this institution before publication. This policy affected Swahili speakers' access to foreign linguistic elements as well as the attitude towards their use. As a result, the spontaneous assimilation of English words declined. However, Tanzania's language policy was not unambiguous. Swahili was implemented as the medium of instruction only in primary school, while English remained the medium of instruction in secondary and tertiary education.[35] This not only sharpened the gap between ordinary people and the educated elite, it also thwarted successful learning at secondary level as the students were badly prepared for the change in the medium of instruction, even if they had been taught English as a subject in the higher classes of primary school. Zaline Roy-Campbell and Martha Quorro have called the resulting unsatisfactory situation in the education sector a "language crisis".[36] In 1972, only some fifteen per cent of Tanzanians had any knowledge of English.[37]

A major economic and political shift took place at the end of the 1980s, when Tanzania had to abandon its socialist *ujamaa* model of society because the economy had collapsed. Democratisation and economic liberalisation led to the privatisation of the media in 1993. As a result, the country was more open to Western influence. And it was at about this time that Bongo Flava started to develop. Parallel to this, English terms were increasingly appropriated by youths to add to their urban slang or *Lugha ya Mitaani* ("language of the streets/town quarters"; *LyM*), as the young urban style of speech is called in Swahili.[38] In a study of *Lugha ya Mitaani* the authors state:

> While it is true that recent *LyM*-variants of Swahili are interspersed with mostly idiomatic English expressions, we reject the notion that English elements are constitutive for *Lugha ya Mitaani*. In older forms, and especially in areas distant from the urban centres and outside university and college campuses, *Lugha za Mitaani* [variants of *LyM*] until the 1990s were almost free of English.[39]

The primary characteristic of urban youth language in Tanzania is the deviation from Standard Swahili, especially in the lexicon, which is constantly changing as a result of deliberate manipulation of existing lexical items. This can be seen as a playful and provocative violation of linguistic norms, a characteristic of urban youth languages in general and of Africa in particular.[40] Only recently, it has become a "trend in colloquial speech practice in Tanzania to blend Swahili with English terms and expressions in order to demonstrate being up to date in a globalized world".[41] As Jan Blommaert puts it, "the use of English idiomatic expressions serves as a mark of worldliness, of being young and daring".[42] However, *LyM* should not be confused with "Campus Swahili", an older "form of mixed Swahili used by academic personnel of the University of Dar es Salaam", which is marked by code-switching between Swahili and English and which requires a high degree of competence in English.[43] Over the past few years, mushrooming private primary schools using English as medium of instruction have increased the prestige and use of English.[44]

The spirit of the *LyM* style of speech resides in its lexical creations and in the strategies it uses to create new items distinct from pre-existing ones. At first glance, one source of *LyM* items is the transfer from English, such as *muvi* "video" (from "movie"), *dili* "secret, affair, deal" (from "deal"), *sevu* "to run away" (from "save") or *kudedi* "to die" (from "dead").[45] However, as the examples show, in most cases the items are not simply transferred from English. They are instead altered phonologically, morphologically and semantically. Thus, to derive the meaning "youth's sleeping quarters" from English "ghetto" (*geto*) involves phonological adaptation and a metonymic shift in meaning. Swahili syllable structure may account for the epenthetic vowel in *dili*, but from the perspective of the donor language, it does not explain the semantic changes which produce what might be called pseudo-anglicisms.[46] In this respect it is important to remember that the creative strategies of urban youth languages combine artistic as well as competitive and provocative elements. Therefore, particular emphasis is placed on strategies of manipulation, which are applied to Swahili and foreign lexical items alike. The English language is denoted in *LyM* as *bibisii* (from "BBC"), as *ung'eng'e* (motivation unclear, probably *ung'eng'e* refers to the singing of the *chiriku* bird), as *kikristu* ("Christian") or as *kizungu* ("European"; "white man's language"). Speaking English is referred to as *kuingia external* ("switch to external"), *kutema ngeli* (spit the noun classes) or *kutema ung'eng'e* ("spit *ung'eng'e*", i.e. "English").[47]

5. Language Choice in Bongo Flava

The urban youth language, *Lugha ya Mitaani*, is a good analytic starting point for understanding Bongo Flava lyrics. Most agents involved in Bongo Flava – musicians, studio producers and DJs – are in fact urban male youths. Women play only a minor role in this music scene, even if there are a small number of female musicians and radio DJs. Thus, Bongo Flava musicians are a sub-group of the creators and users of the urban youth language. Moreover, Bongo Flava song lyrics are a vehicle for youth language and sometimes even introduce new terms. As one informant stated, Bongo Flava music has added vitality to the street language.[48] Some musicians have coined new words in their lyrics, words which were enthusiastically taken up by the urban youths; some Bongo Flava artists' names have even been used in onomastic synecdoche. The artist Feruzi, for example, had a popular song about HIV/AIDS, and thus his name became a euphemistic term to denote the disease. A journalist from the region once described Gangwe Mobb, a Dar es Salaam rap crew, as "major enforcers of street slanguistics".[49] However, as musicians try to reach larger audiences, they mix both musical and speech styles in their lyrics as a strategy for success.[50] Thus, their attitudes towards the use of youth language vary according to the image they want to project. Those who prefer to be linked with *msela* target an exclusively young audience and thus tend to use youth language. Others, who want to target youths and older people alike use proverbs and demonstrate their knowledge of 'indigenous' wisdom. Those who want to be associated with cosmopolitanism and international connections tend to use more English. The case studies below will give evidence of this. I will present some extracts from Bongo Flava lyrics, which show the amount of English words and their contexts in the songs, and I will discuss the function of code-switching and code-mixing in the songs.

Bongo Flava as a music scene also has its own linguistic register. The term Bongo Flava itself is made up of a Swahili (Bongo) and an English (Flavour) word. While it was initially written Bongo Flavour, it soon became written as Bongo Flava and is now increasingly written Bongo Fleva, which is a phonetic spelling. Since both the technological procedures and the original role models for Bongo Flava stem from the West, "the lexicon of the Bongo Flava scene draws on English terms".[51] As Table 1 shows, in many cases there is no Standard Swahili term corresponding to specific English terms used in the music scene, especially if the source is a slang term connected to the US hip-hop culture, such as *beef* and *swagger*. In the case of technical terms such a *kurekodi* (*ku-* is the infinitive marker in Swahili) and *mikrofoni* English transfers have already been incorporated into the standard lexicon. However, *mikrofoni* is not widely known and the young musicians and studio producers have instead adopted the informal *maiki* (from "mic"). The paraphrase *chumba cha kurekodia* ("room for recording") for "studio" probably is too clumsy and rather 'unworldly', hence the English term studio is used in the popular music scene. In other cases the standard terms are not specific enough. For instance, *kupiga muziki* means "play music", but this is not the same thing as "perform", especially as some artists often just pretend to sing or rap on stage while their track is being played back. *Geti persent* is a local creation and is a fusion of "gate" and "percent". The term refers to the payment procedure for musicians where they agree with the organiser of a show to get a certain percentage of the entrance fees.

Table 1: Some specific terms used in the Bongo Flava music scene

Slang/*LyM*	English	Standard Swahili equivalent[52]
kupafomu	to perform	*kupiga muziki*
steji	stage	*jukwaa*
maiki	mic (microphone)	*mikrofoni*
shoo	show	*tamasha*
promota	promoter	*mdhamini*

Slang/LyM	English	Standard Swahili equivalent
geti percent	gate percent	-------
studio	studio	*chumba cha kurekodia*
kurekodi	to record	*kurekodi*
traki	track	-------
kuediti	to edit	*kuhariri*
masta	master CD	-------
supastaa	superstar	-------
bifu	beef (quarrel)	-------
swagga	swagger (style, rhythm)	-------

Interestingly, expressions referring to the production process of a new song in the studio are metaphorical Swahili. A new song is called *jiwe* ("stone") or *ngoma* ("drum"), which is "cooked on the stove" (*ipo jikoni*) before it can be released.[53] This is by no means just a technical procedure. It is a creative process which involves different musical ingredients and collaboration with one or more studio producers and fellow musicians who sing the chorus or contribute a verse. This collaboration is the motivation for the cooking metaphor, while the stone metaphor alludes to the power and solidity of a song and the drum metaphor to traditional musical culture.[54]

6. Connections to Global Youth Culture

The first song to be examined here is "*Mikasi*" ("Sex"), released by Bongo Flava star Ngwair in 2004.[55] Starting in the first person, the singer boastfully describes the everyday lives of a group of young men from the Bongo Flava scene. They enjoy hanging around together, with the chorus making it clear that 'enjoying life' especially means smoking, drinking and having sex. It also stresses the need to have money in order to enjoy life. The song was very successful and was awarded the national Kilimanjaro Best Hip-hop Award in 2005.[56] With this song Ngwair coined the slang term *mikasi* – in Standard Swahili "scissors" – meaning sex. The chorus encapsulates the message of the song:

1	*Mitungi-i-iiii, blanti-i-iiii,*
	Alcohol, Marijuana
2	*Mikasi-i-iiiiii {oooh yeeeaaaaaaaah}*
	Sex
3	*Kama ukitaka kuvinjari nasi*
	If you want to enjoy yourself with us,
4	*Basi mfukoni mwako nawe uwe safi*
	Then you too gotta have something in your pocket

While *mitungi* and *mikasi* work by metonymy – *mitungi* literally means "clay pots for storage of liquids" –, *blanti* is a transfer of the English slang term "blunt" meaning marijuana.[57]

The first verse narrates what Ngwair does during the day (English transfers as well as their translations are underlined):

Verse 1

1	*Ni asubuhi naamka ninapiga mswaki*
	It's morning, I get up and brush my teeth
2	*Kisha naenda ku<u>bath</u> kuweka mwili safi*
	Then I go and <u>wash myself</u>, clean my body
3	*Narudi <u>ghetto</u> nafungua kabati*
	I go back to <u>my room</u>, I open my wardrobe
4	*Nachukua pamba, <u>blingbling,</u> kwa <u>chati</u>*
	I take stylish clothes, <u>jewelry</u>, only the <u>best</u>
5	*N'na <u>t-shirt black</u> n'na <u>jeanz</u> ya kaki*
	I've got a <u>black t-shirt</u> and <u>khaki jeans</u>
6	*Na chini nina <u>simple white</u>* [waiti] *<u>chapa Nike</u>* [naiki]
	And down there I'm wearing "<u>Simple White</u>", trademark <u>Nike</u>
7	*Kisha, mzee, najipulizia marashi*
	Then, dude, I spray myself with perfume
8	*Aahhh, nanukia safi*
	Aahhh, I'm smelling nicely now
9	*Niko na <u>machizi</u> wa <u>Chamber Squad</u> na <u>Dark</u>* [da:ki]
	I'm together with the <u>mates</u> from "<u>Chamber Squad</u>" and "<u>Dark</u>"
10	*Tunapiga simu <u>Rich Coast</u> wako wapi*
	We call "<u>Rich Coast</u>", asking where they are
11	*Tunakutana mitaa ya Chaga <u>Bite</u>* [baiti]
	We meet in the area around "Chaga <u>Bite</u>"
12	*Asubuhi tunapata zetu supu kwa chapati*
	In the morning we get our soup with *chapati*[58]

13	*Na mitungi ya kupotezea wakati*
	And alcohol, to waste some time
14	*Ukitaka <u>fegi</u> mezani kuna <u>pakti</u>*
	If you want <u>cigs</u>, there are <u>packets</u> on the table
15	*Iwe sports yaani SM au Embassy*
	Nevermind if you like "Sports", "SM" or "Embassy"
16	*Hapa utakula raha mpaka mwenyewe utasema basi*
	Here you can chill out until you have enough
17	*Tunakamua mpaka ile mida ya <u>lunch</u>* [lanchi]
	We're enjoying ourselves until it's time for <u>lunch</u>
18	*Tunaagiza ugali mkubwa na samaki*
	We order a huge meal of *ugali*[59] and fish
19	*Makamuzi yanaendelea mpaka <u>night</u>* [naiti]
	The chilling out continues, until it's <u>nighttime</u>
20	*Watu wanaingia <u>graveyard</u> kwanza kupata nyasi*
	People go at first to the <u>graveyard</u>[60] to buy weed
21	*Tunarudi kila mmoja anaji<u>sachi</u> {mmh}*
	We come back and everyone is searching
22	*Ni kiasi gani mfukoni kilichobaki {oouuhh}*
	How much is left in his pocket
23	*Kuji<u>cheki</u> mi n'na kama laki*
	<u>Checking</u> myself I realize I have got around hundred thousand
24	*Nikawaambia <u>machizi</u> kinachofuata MIKASI*[61]
	Then I tell my <u>dudes</u> what's coming up now is SEX

The English lexemes in "*Mikasi*" fall into three categories: firstly, English lexemes that have become part of youth or colloquial language (*LyM*) in Tanzania and, in some cases, even standard language found in dictionary entries; secondly, terms connected to Western and particularly hip-hop culture, including dress styles. These are particular markers of urban youth identity; thirdly, English lexemes used in code-mixing which have not or not yet become part of *LyM*, lacking distinct semantics. The use of lexemes from these three categories helps to express aspects of the musician's identity as a Tanzanian youth, as a member of the global hip-hop culture and as a modern, educated and cosmopolitan Tanzanian. English lexemes occur in the form of verbs, nouns and adjectives.

Category 1: Transfers from English used in *LyM*
1) line 4: *chati* "best". Transfer of English "chart". Commonly in use.
2) line 9: *machizi* (sg. *chizi*) "dudes, mates". The etymology is not quite clear; however, Reuster-Jahn & Kießling assume that it is a dysphemistic extension of Standard Swahili *chizi* "stupid person, crazy person".[62] In older Swahili slang it is attested as "white man, European", a dysphemistic extension of English "cheese", motivated by its white colour.[63] Part of *LyM* used by youth.
3) line 14: *fegi* "cigarette". Transfer of English slang "fag". Part of *LyM* used by youth.
4) line 14: *pakti* "packet". Transfer of English "packet" which has already become part of the standard lexicon.[64]
5) line 21: *kusachi* "check, search, look for". Could be replaced by Standard Swahili *kutafuta, kuangalia*. The verb is widely in use.
6) line 23: *kucheki*, transfer of English "check". In *LyM* it means "see, look at" and in some contexts, such as here, also "check". It could be replaced by Standard Swahili *kuona, kuangalia* or *kutazama*, depending on context. This verb is widely in use.

In the second and third verse, whose full text can be accessed elsewhere,[65] the word *kumaindi* is found, a transfer of English "mind", but with the meaning "like, want, demand, care", which could be replaced by Standard Swahili *kupenda, kutaka, kudai*. Again, *anti* and *braza* are used as terms of address. *Anti* is a transfer of English "aunt", used as a respectful and neutral address for a young woman. *Braza* is a transfer of English "brother" and is also a neutral term of address for a man of the speaker's age. The term *kitchen party* in verse three is used to denote a gathering of women. This meaning is derived from a certain ceremony before a wedding where only women are admitted. There is no direct Swahili equivalent, and the term is commonly used. The noun *skintaiti,* in the fourth verse, refers to a woman's skintight dress and has no direct Standard Swahili equivalent. *Nyasi* (line 20 in verse 1), "grass" is a calque from the English slang terms "grass" and "weed" for marijuana.

Category 2: Lexemes connected to youth or hip-hop culture
1) line 3: *ghetto*. In contrast to the original meaning in American hip-hop culture, where this term denotes poor black neighbourhoods, in Tanzanian youth language it has come to denote a room in which young people live together or meet regularly. Therefore, it denotes a room rather than a neighbourhood. In "*Mikasi*" it refers to the narrator's bedroom.
2) line 4: *blingbling*. As in American hip-hop culture, this term denotes jewelry, especially chains.
3) line 5: *T-shirt black*. While it translates as *fulana nyeusi*, this would not have the same meaning as *T-shirt black*, which is imagined as a Western style T-shirt. Dressing style is very important in hip-hop culture. The word order follows Swahili syntax and makes the phrase a hybrid form.
4) line 5: *Jeanz ya kaki* "khaki jeans". As elsewhere in the world, jeans are not just trousers, in Swahili *suruali*, but are an expression of lifestyle and youth identity.
5) line 6: *simple white*, short form for "simple white trainers" evoking good quality, trendy sneakers.
6) line 6: *Nike* trendy brand for trainers.
7) line 9: *Chamber Squad*. Name of Ngwair's first rap crew.
8) line 9: *Dark*. Name of a Tanzanian rapper.
9) line 10: *Rich Coast*. Name of a Tanzanian rap crew.
10) line 11: *Chaga Bite*. Name of a fashionable restaurant in Dar es Salaam.

In addition, in verses 2 and 3, the term "party" which has no direct Standard Swahili equivalent, is used recurrently.

Category 3: English lexemes used in code-mixing
1) line 2: *bath* "wash oneself, take a shower". Could be replaced by Standard Swahili *kuoga*.
2) line 5: *black*. Could be replaced by Standard Swahili *-eusi*.
3) line 17: *lunch*. Could be replaced by Standard Swahili *chakula cha mchana*.
4) line 19: *night*. Could be replaced by Standard Swahili *usiku*.
5) line 20: *graveyard*. Could be replaced by Standard Swahili *makaburini*.

Each of the three categories serves a specific purpose with regard to the identities Ngwair wants to project. English lexemes that have become part of *LyM* function as markers of Tanzanian youth identity. The English (slang) words and expressions which relate to drugs and hip-hop culture identify the musician as someone well versed in the particular conventions and habits. English lexemes of the third category have the highest degree of markedness, as they are not motivated by the lack of a Swahili equivalent. There is no obvious reason why Ngwair should say *kubath* instead of *kuoga*. It is rather a case of code-mixing functioning as a linguistic marker of the urban elite, even if, in the case of "lunch" and "night", the need for a fitting rhyme may also have played a role. In any case, Ngwair's use of lexemes from each of these categories authenticates him as a versatile hip-hopper, an urban youth and a member of the elite.

7. Aiming at Regional and International Markets through Code-Switching and Code-Mixing

As Swahili is increasingly becoming the African lingua franca for the whole East African region, it is quite common for songs in Swahili to become popular in neighbouring countries and it is no surprise that Tanzanian Bongo Flava is known across the whole region. The private TV station, East Africa Television, which covers the East African region, broadcasts popular music programmes in which Bongo Flava features quite prominently. Moreover, legal as well as pirated copies of copyrighted CDs are available in all East African countries. English words and phrases in Bongo Flava lyrics help people in Uganda and Kenya to understand the songs. It may therefore be argued that English code-switching and code-mixing in the basically Swahili lyrics may be a strategic choice aimed at increasing marketability. The examples given below will illustrate this point.

The first song is a collaboration of the Tanzanian artist A.Y. with Uganda's Maurice Kirya and Hamdee Kiwamba and was released in 2005.[66] "*Binadamu*" ("Humans")[67] was part of A.Y.'s second album in which he collaborated with various popular artists from Kenya and Uganda. This collaboration considerably increased his recognition in the region. Today, A.Y. is one of the few internationally successful Bongo

Flava artists, appreciated in many African countries.[68] In "*Binadamu*" he raps the verses while his Ugandan counterparts sing the chorus. Most of the song is in Swahili, but some English phrases are inserted. This may well be motivated by commercial considerations regarding the Ugandan and Kenyan music markets. In both countries, language policy has given English a higher priority than in Tanzania and, as a result, a higher percentage of the population speaks English. However, in recent years Swahili is increasingly taught in Ugandan and Kenyan schools, so that especially young people are now familiar with the language, even if they may have a limited command of it.

The song is about times of trouble, times when one feels abandoned by family and friends. Given the serious and melancholic character of the theme, the song is, appropriately, in Standard Swahili, with no elements of youth language. Its poetic style is marked by metaphors and by a careful handling of rhyme. English is used, but not by dropping a word here and there to demonstrate proficiency in the language, as in "*Mikasi*". Rather, the songwriters switch to English, using whole phrases to summarise the basic message, which is overtly Social-Darwinistic. Nevertheless, the English in the lyrics is not always standard. The phrase "survival of the fittest" is impressionistically rendered as "survive for fittest" in the text. As before, English elements in the original text are underlined.

Intro
> This is A.Y. from Tanzania, Maurice Kirya and Hamdee from Uganda.
> It's a dedication to all Africans living in poverty.

Verse 1
1 *Usiombee mambo yaharibike*
  Don't pray for getting into trouble
2 *Pesa usiishike, mfano wa mti upukutike*
  For not having money, like a tree without leaves
3 *Utaonekana si lolote si chochote*
  You will be considered absolutely meaningless
4 *Utaonekana karaha kwa watu siku zote*
  A nuisance for people, always
5 *Walimwengu hawatakupa mikono*
  People will not offer you a helping hand
6 *Magonjwa yatakuvuta ndani ya shimo*
  Diseases will drag you into the grave

7	*Utakata tamaa, utaandama na balaa*
	You will be hopeless, as if cursed
8	*Pumzi hutovuta kwa raha*
	You will not breathe with ease
9	*Kweli usiombee kuwahi*
	Really, don't pray for untimely problems
10	<u>Survive for fittest; never trust nobody in this world of weakness</u>
11	*Watakukana hata kama ndugu zako*
	Even your kin will disown you
12	*Watadiriki sema hawajui utokako*
	They will dare to say they don't know you
13	*Mama acha kulia*
	Mama, don't cry
14	*Hayo uliyo nayo ni majaribu tu ya dunia*
	These are the trials of the world
15	*Ipo siku mambo yako yatatulia*
	One day your affairs will be settled
16	*Utasahau hata mabaya ya zamani uliyopitia*
	You will forget the problems you have gone through
17	*Ooh hii dunia...*
	Ooh, this world...

The chorus switches between Uganda's major language, Luganda, and English, giving the song a particularly Ugandan flavour:

1	*Bagala alinaa, Genda okole,*
	They love people who have something, so go and work
2	<u>You should think about tomorrow</u>
3	<u>Not only today</u>
4	*Bagala alinaa, Genda okolee, uuh, Genda okoleee*

The second verse continues in Swahili and describes life without money, how even close kin will abandon you, until you wish you had never been born. Again, the last two lines summarise the message in English, so that an English speaking audience, with or without a limited knowledge of Swahili, gets a clear impression of the lyrical content: "Remain strong in this world, don't be jealous, dat's all...".

Another Bongo Flava song that illustrates the intermixing of English and Swahili with the aim of reaching a regional audience is *Pii pii* (an onomatopoetic title imitating the sound of a car horn) by Dar es Salaam based artist Marlaw. This song became a huge hit in the region in 2009.[69] In the song, a man is stuck in a traffic jam on a highway somewhere between Nairobi and Dar es Salaam. In contrast to "*Binadamu*", this song is marked by code-mixing, not by code-switching. Furthermore, the melody gives English words and phrases, such as "home", "time", "highway", "long time now" and "move out the way" [sic] a particular prominence.

Verse 1
1 *Ninataka niwahi kufika, njia ina jam sasa wapi nitapita*
 I want to be in time, but there is a traffic jam, where can I pass
2 *Nimekaa karibia saa sita, sasa kukaa nimechoka ooh baby*
 I'm stuck for almost six hours, I'm now tired, ohh baby
3 *Sijamwona long time now, nimerudi toka mwezi jana*
 I haven't seen her for a long time now, for one month
4 *Nimeshakwambia mama nimefika tangu mchana*
 I have told you, mama, that I would arrive at noon
5 *Anajua nimeshafika, ameshapika, amekasirika*
 She thinks that I have already arrived, she has cooked, and is angry
6 *Alipika tangu mchana, ila sasa, lunch imegeuka dinner*
 Food is ready since noon, now lunch has turned into dinner

Chorus
1 *Nimechoka kupiga honi now (pii pii) hatuelewani*
 I'm now tired of hooting (pii pii), we don't understand each other
2 *Pii pii, move out the way, nimechoka kupoteza time*
 Pii pii, move out of the way, I'm tired of wasting time
3 *Nina siku nyingu kwenda home, I'm missing my baby*
 I've been away from home for long, I'm missing my baby
4 *Pii pii, hello baby, natamani niwe nyumbani*
 Pii pii, hello baby, I wish I were at home
5 *Nimekwama hapa njiani kuna jam baby*
 I'm stuck here on the road, there is a jam, baby
6 *Aah aah, kuna jam baby*
 Aah ahh, there is a jam, baby

The second verse is entirely in Swahili. In it, Marlaw asks his wife to believe him and not to be angry when he comes home late. In the hook, a second chorus, Marlaw sings:

1 *Nimechoka kungoja <u>highway</u>, nitapita popote mradi wee*
 I'm tired of waiting on the <u>highway</u>, I will pass anywhere
2 *Ili kama ni kesi na iwe (hatuelewani)*
 Even if it comes to a court case, I don't care (we don't understand each other)

With the interspersed English words, an English speaking audience not well conversant in Swahili will be able to get the message of the song, especially if we take into account that most people in Kenya have at least some knowledge of Swahili and that even in Uganda a growing number of people learn and understand Swahili.

With regard to switching between languages in a song, the most consistent performer is the female Bongo Flava superstar, Lady Jay Dee, who enjoys widespread recognition in the region. In her song "Distance",[70] from 2005, she sings the chorus in Swahili, English, French, the regional languages Luganda, Kinyarwanda and Lingala as well as in South African Bantu languages. In fact, most of the song with a running time of more than five minutes consists of the chorus repeatedly sung in the different languages. Its Swahili and English versions are given below:

> *Nakupenda, nakutaka, nakuhitaji,*
> *moyo wangu wakuwaza*
> *mpenzi uko mbali nami*
>
> I love you, I want you, and I need you,
> my heart is thinking of you
> but you are far away from me

Indeed, this is one of Lady Jay Dee's most popular songs. The video on *YouTube* has had more than 250,000 views in six years and about 150 mostly enthusiastic comments, mainly from Africa and the African diaspora. In comparison, A.Y.'s song "*Binadamu*" got about 16,000 views over the same period.

Code-mixing between Swahili and English in Bongo Flava songs is also used as a linguistic marker of upper class speakers. It is used in this way in the very popular song "*Zali la mentali*" ("Poor guy's luck") by Bongo Flava star Prof. Jay.[71] It is about a poor youth who lives a hard life doing jobs as a porter. One day a rich young lady falls in love with him during a short encounter in the street. Eventually, they marry and the young man lives a happy and luxurious life ever after. To highlight the different social backgrounds of the protagonists, the poor youth speaks *LyM*, while the girl speaks smirkingly and mixes English with Swahili. During their first encounter the boy does a service for the girl who gives him money for this. But she refuses to take the change he wants to give her by saying, "<u>*Ohh no keep chenji* una mawazo mengi itakufariji <u>*week end*</u>" ("Ohh no, keep the change, you have many problems, it will help you over the weekend"). While the English loan words *chenji* ("change") and *wikiendi* ("weekend") are commonly used and have even been incorporated into the Swahili lexicon, the use of "no" instead of *hapana* and the verb "keep" instead of *-chukua* are clear examples of code-mixing. Another instance of this use is found when, at their second meeting, the girl says "I love you" to the youth, instead of the Swahili *nakupenda*. Again, this underlines her upper class background and has the advantage of being less direct than the Swahili, in case she is refused.

8. The 'Underground' Strategy of Mixing Style and Language

The final example illustrates the lack of uniformity regarding the use of English in Bongo Flava music. The following song is by Saidawg a.k.a. Ghetto King, a so-called *andagraundi* – a musician who has not yet become well-known, even if some of his songs have already been played on the radio and some music videos have been shown on TV. *Andagraundi* is a transfer of English "underground" that "refers to an economic category and does not carry the Western connotation of 'alternative' music styles".[72] In her study of topic and language choice of *maandagraundi* from outside Dar es Salaam, Birgit Englert has shown that performers intentionally avoid too much *LyM* in their lyrics so that large and diverse audiences, including older people, can understand them. Although *maandagraundi* from Dar es Salaam, such as Saidawg, often use *LyM* and also experiment with English – despite their often limited command of the language – they still employ the same strategy of mixing styles as their rural colleagues. The difference lies in their imagined audiences. Thus, Dar es Salaam musicians give their songs an urban and even cosmopolitan appeal in order to reach audiences in the

East African metropolises and beyond. Saidawg began to take his career seriously around 2007, but is still waiting for a breakthrough. As he explains, his biggest obstacle is the fact that he has to pay radio DJs and programme directors to get rotation. This form of "payola" is common practice in Tanzania.[73] In the song "My way" which he released in 2012,[74] he expresses his determination to finally make it, despite all odds. The song contains some English phrases and lexemes and is sung in the reggae style. Thus it exemplifies the diversity Bongo Flava musicians employ to reach different audiences, especially if they are *andagraundi*. In this case, the artist who usually raps has produced a reggae song. In addition, he employs English but sticks to Swahili in many of his other songs and is heavily biased toward *LyM*. As can be seen, the English phrases do not represent the standard form. The artist uses his phonetic command of English rather than sticking to standard grammar and vocabulary. As he says in the outro, "play with your rule, use your feeling". In the song text, English elements are underlined.

Chorus
1 *Am walking on the way,*
2 *Kuiseti future yangu*
  To set my future
3 *This is my life*
4 *Am walking in the way*
5 *Kufurahi na watu wangu*
  Be happy with my friends
6 *Jah, love*

Verse 1
1 *Siwezi kunywa sumu ndani ya hii dunia nguruwe heee*
  I will not take poison in this bad world, heee
2 *Kwani yeye ni muweza muumba wa yote hehee*
  Because He is almighty, the creator of everything
3 *Mojamoja mdogomdogo kileleni n'tafika*
  One by one, little by little, I will arrive
4 *Imani yangu kubwa jangwani mimi n'tavuka*
  It is my great belief that I will cross the desert

Verse 2
1 *Ndio maana mi napanda napanda daima sitoshuka*
  That's why I always climb up, never will I descend

2	*Deile mi nasonga nasonga nakonga milele ntasikika*
	Every day I push forward, I grow old, and I will always be heard
3	*Am on the way this is ma way*
4	*Am on the way, this is ma way*
5	*Let us be together to be there*
6	*To stand in harder to win this war*
7	*This is my life that's why I do*
8	*This is my life thats why I do, jah, love*

Bridge

I need love show me love
Jah, show me love
God, show me love
Rasta, show me love, one love

Outro

Yooh, it's Gheto King again, it's time to make the people know the truth.
You know what, play with your rule, use your feeling, this is feeling

Saidawg uses two English transfers, which have become part of Tanzanian urban youth language. *Deile* (verse 2, line 2) is a transfer of "daily" with the same meaning. The Swahili equivalent is *kila siku* "every day". With *kuiseti future yangu*, the expression "to set my future" is the basis. This expression has been Swahilised by firstly treating "set" as a Swahili verb stem *-seti*. It is preceded by the infinitive marker *ku-* and the object marker *-i-*. Secondly, the possessive "my" has been translated into its Swahili equivalent *yangu*. The result is not a full loan translation but a truly hybrid linguistic form.

9. Conclusion

As the examples have shown, English plays an important role in Bongo Flava lyrics, even if, in terms of quantity, English is not prominent. However, English finds its way into the lyrics mainly through the urban youth language, of which it has become a part, through transfer, assimilation and, often, semantic change. Bongo Flava as a music culture connects with global hip-hop and Jamaican reggae. In turn, Bongo Flava lyrics provide templates for youth identities, which connect with African-American youth concepts. Accordingly, many English terms are transfers of slang words (such as blingbling, fegi), or they relate to cultural domains such as dress style (T-shirt, jeanz, simple white). Moreover, technical terms relating to the music sector are often English loan words, such as *maiki*, *steji* and *kupafomu*. However, there is no general rule regarding the use of English in Bongo Flava. Rather the examples show that choice of language is a complex issue. If the artists want to emphasise their identities as young urbanites, they tend to use youth language with a suitable percentage of English words. If they want to project their hip-hop identity, they can mark this linguistically by the use of appropriate slang terms and expressions. Furthermore, they may use code-mixing and add assorted English words to demonstrate their cosmopolitanism or urbanity, as was done by Ngwair in "*Mikasi*". But code-mixing can also be used as a literary technique to mark a character in a song as having an upper class background, as in "*Zali la mentali*" by Prof. Jay. Again, the use of English as a linguistic marker of identity in Bongo Flava is complemented by commercial considerations which also play a role in the artists' choice of language. A.Y. and his fellow Ugandan musicians inserted English phrases into their song "*Binadamu*". Here, they targeted an East African audience which is more familiar with English than Swahili. Thus, both the imagined East African audiences and the music market motivate language choice. The same holds true for Lady Jay Dee's "Distance", which became popular well beyond East Africa, reaching a pan-African audience as well as the African diaspora. Commercial considerations may also have motivated Saidawg to try out a song with quite a high percentage of English; this is the Dar es Salaam variety of the distinctly *andagraundi* strategy of style-mixing, described by Englert for artists from the Tanzanian periphery.[75] In the cases studied by her, the artists preferred Swahili to *LyM* because they wanted to reach not only young but also older Tanzanians as their audience. From the Dar es Salaam perspective, an imagined wider audience is a regional or even a global audience, which requires a language choice that includes English.

A second look at the song "*Binadamu*" reveals that the Swahili section is remarkably free of youth language. Given the fact that the theme of the song is a philosophical problem, we may conclude that lyrical content also influences language choice. Thus we see that questions of identity, commercial considerations and lyrical content all play a role in determining the use of English in Bongo Flava.

Notes

1. "I am walking on the way to set my future", line from "My way" by Saidawg a.k.a. Ghetto King discussed in this article, incorporating the English verb "set" into the Swahili phrase.
2. Reuster-Jahn & Kießling (2006: 100). As a result of generalisation, this term has recently come to be used for the whole of Tanzania.
3. The delineation of Bongo Flava and hip-hop is somewhat problematic, as artists may blend rap music freely with song in one track or mix rapped tracks with reggae or R&B songs on their albums. They do so to cater to a broad spectrum of tastes, aiming at the highest possible number of consumers, as they ultimately want to make a living from their music (Englert 2008).
4. Hacke (forthcoming) discusses this trend with regard to the images of music videos, drawing on the concept of the Black Atlantic.
5. Reuster-Jahn & Kießling (2006).
6. For an overview of African varieties of English, see Schröder's contribution to this volume.
7. *Ujamaa* is derived from the Swahili word *jamaa* meaning family, society and assembly (Johnson 1939). *Ujamaa*, also called "African socialism", was introduced by the ruling party CCM (Chama cha Mapinduzi, "Party of the Revolution") and is associated with its leader and first president of Tanzania, Julius Kambarage Nyerere. The concept focused on self-reliance and collectivism.
8. Perullo (2007: 252).
9. *Ibid.* 255.
10. Hacke & Roch (2004).
11. Perullo (2007: 261).
12. Suriano (2007).
13. Stroeken (2005: 9).
14. Especially in the song "*Nimesimama*" ("I am standing upright").
15. Perullo (2007: 266-267).
16. Englert (2008: 48). It should be added that this role perception is not confined to music and poetry, but is found equally among writers and filmmakers.
17. "Battle" refers to the competition between groups and individuals involved which is a basic feature of hip-hop culture. Speech acts connected to "battle" are "boasting" and "dissing" (clipped form of "disrespecting").
18. Roch & Hacke (2006), Raab (2006).
19. Reuster-Jahn (2007).

20 Often translated as "urban sailor".
21 Klein & Friedrich (2003: 24).
22 Hacke (2007: 41).
23 Knappert (1979: 34-35), Saavedra Casco (2005).
24 Saavedra Casco (2005: 198).
25 Knappert (1979: 34), English elements emphasised by me.
26 *Ibid.* 33.
27 Saavedra Casco (2005: 194).
28 Shariff (1983: 88-9), cited in Saavedra Casco (2005: 198).
29 Saavedra Casco (2005: 195).
30 Reynolds (1962).
31 *Ibid.* 203.
32 This form is no longer in use. It has been replaced by *kupiga picha* "to take a photograph".
33 The Committee was formed by the British colonial administration and consisted of members from Kenya, Uganda, Tanganyika and Zanzibar. African membership dates from 1939 (Whiteley 1969: 81-82).
34 Legère (2006: 176).
35 Tanzania has a tripartite schooling system: 7 years (primary) – 4 years (secondary > O-level) – 2 years (secondary > A-level).
36 Roy-Campbell & Quorro (1997).
37 Abdulaziz-Mkilifi (1972) cited in Rubagumya (1990: 9).
38 Reuster-Jahn & Kießling (2006).
39 *Ibid.* 3.
40 For youth languages in general see Androutsopoulos & Scholz (1998), for African youth languages see Kießling & Mous (2004).
41 Reuster-Jahn & Kießling (2006: 3).
42 Blommaert (1990: 24).
43 *Ibid.*
44 English as medium of instruction is allowed in private primary schools, while in government schools Swahili is the compulsory medium of instruction.
45 Transfers from other languages, mainly English, accounted for seventeen per cent of Reuster-Jahn and Kießling's data of more than 1,100 words and phrases (Reuster-Jahn & Kießling 2006: 35).
46 *Ibid.* 34-35.
47 Swahili is characterised by a system of noun classes. All nouns belong to one of fifteen noun classes and are marked accordingly by nominal prefixes. The ng' in ung'eng'e is pronounced ŋ.
48 Reuster-Jahn & Kießling (2006: 63).

49 Khaemba (2002).
50 Englert (2008).
51 Reuster-Jahn & Kießling (2006: 33), see also Böhme (2004: 43).
52 According to the *English-Swahili Dictionary* (TUKI 1996).
53 This expression is also used for films.
54 The term *ngoma* not only denotes the instrument but also the whole performance of drumming, with particular beat patterns, dance, costumes and other contextual features.
55 It features the Bongo Flava artists Mchizi Mox, Ferooz and Rah P, one of the few female Bongo Flava artists. The music video can be viewed on <http://www.youtube.com/watch?v=ov_2L8MUEwI>. It was produced by Khalfan Majani, also known as P. Funk, in his "Bongo Records" studio, and was included in Ngwair's first album *a.k.a. mimi*.
56 Hip-hop is one category of the annual Kilimanjaro Music Award, see <http://www.kilitimetz.com/awards/2009/>.
57 A number of other terms from *Lugha ya Mitaani* in the song "*Mikasi*" is discussed in Reuster-Jahn (2007).
58 A pancake made of flour, salt and water.
59 A stiff maize porridge.
60 This refers to a graveyard near Ngwair's residence where one can buy marijuana.
61 Capital letters are used in the version on the website.
62 Reuster-Jahn & Kießling (2006: 107).
63 Ohly (1987: 28).
64 The entry in Johnson is "paketi" (1939: 362).
65 For the full text of the song, including my translation, see Reuster-Jahn (2007).
66 A.Y.'s civil name is Ambwene Yessaya.
67 Written by Ambwene Yessaya, Hamdee Kiwamba & Maurice Kirya; my translation. Music produced by Henry from No End Production, mixed by Master Jay from MJ Production, video by Paparazzi. The video can be accessed on *YouTube*: <http://www.youtube.com/watch?v=jzSolNRh BDM>.
68 A.Y. received the MTV African Music Award in 2009 in the Hip-hop category. He is one of the few internationally successful Bongo Flava artists. He has done a number of collaborations which boosted his career, for example with Jose Chameleone (Uganda), Wahuu (Kenya) and Ms Trinity (Trinidad/United Kingdom).
69 Text by Lawrence Malima. The video can be accessed on *YouTube*: <http://www.youtube.com/watch?v=E74ucVpG400>.

70 Song and text by Lady Jay Dee (Judith Mbibo Wambura). The video can be accessed on *YouTube*: <http://www.youtube.com/watch?v=ckFYKo SMHaY>.
71 Released in 2004. The video can be accessed on *YouTube*: <http://www.youtube.com/watch?v=mjT11idRcSc>.
72 Englert (2008: 46).
73 Reuster-Jahn & Hacke (2011: 14).
74 Lyrics written by Saidawg, my translation. The video of the song can be accessed on *YouTube*: <http://www.youtube.com/watch?v=8zJ2Q119OZs>. It was produced by Mubyzo at Bamba Records.
75 Englert (2008).

Bibliography

Abdulaziz-Mkilifi, M. H.: "Triglossia and Swahili. English Bilingualism in Tanzania", *Language in Society* 1:2, 1972, 197-213.

Androutsopoulos, Jannis K. & Arno Scholz (Eds.): *Jugendsprache = Langue des jeunes = Youth Language. Linguistische und Soziolinguistische Perspektiven*, Frankfurt am Main *et al.*, 1998.

Blommaert, Jan: "Standardization and Diversification in Kiswahili", *Kiswahili* 57, 1990, 22-32.

Böhme, Claudia: *Der swahilisprachige Videofilm* Girlfriend*: eine Sprachanalyse*, Hamburg, 2004. [unpublished MA-thesis]

Englert, Birgit: "Kuchanganyachanganya. Topic and Language Choices in Tanzanian Youth Culture", *Journal of African Cultural Studies* 20:1, 2008, 45-55.

Hacke, Gabriel: *Bongo Flava – Populäre Kultur in Tanzania. Eine Jugendkultur in den Auseinandersetzungen um 'nationale Kultur'*, Berlin, 2007. [unpublished MA thesis]

---: "Music, Business and Images of the 'Black Atlantic'. The Production, Distribution and Visual References of Bongo Flava Music Videos." – In Matthias Krings & Uta Reuster-Jahn (Eds.): *Bongo Media Worlds*, Cologne, forthcoming 2013.

Hacke, Gabriel & Anna Roch: *Bongo Flava. HipHop-Kultur in Tanzania*, 2004. [documentary video]

Johnson, Frederick: *A Standard Swahili-English Dictionary*, Oxford *et al.*, 1939.

Khaemba, Moses: "Bongo's New Ghetto Narrators", *Africanhiphop*, 2002, <http://www.africanhiphop.com/archive/index.php?module=subjects&func=viewpage&pageid=132>, accessed 14 June 2012.

Kießling, Roland & Maarten Mous: "Urban Youth Languages in Africa", *Anthropological Linguistics* 46, 2004, 303-341.

Klein, Gabriele & Malte Friedrich: *Is This Real? Die Kultur des HipHop*, Frankfurt am Main, 2003.

Knappert, Jan: *Four Centuries of Swahili Verse. A Literary History and Anthology*, London, 1979.

Legère, Karsten: "Formal and Informal Development of the Swahili Language. Focus on Tanzania". – In Olaoba F. Arasanyin & Michael A. Pemberton (Eds.): *Selected Proceedings of the 36th Annual Conference on African Linguistics*, Somerville, 2006, pp. 176-184.

Mangesho, Peter: *Global Cultural Trends. The Case of Hip-hop Music in Dar es Salaam*, Dar es Salaam, 2003. [unpublished MA-thesis]

Ohly, Rajmund: *Swahili-English Slang Pocket-Dictionary*, Vienna, 1987.

Perullo, Alex, "'Here's a Little Something Local'. An Early History of Hip Hop in Dar es Salaam, Tanzania, 1984-1997". – In Andrew Burton, James Brennan & Yusuf Lawi (Eds.): *Dar es Salaam. The History of an Emerging East African Metropolis*, London, 2007, pp. 250-272.

Raab, Klaus: *Rapping the Nation. Die Aneignung von HipHop in Tanzania*, Musikethnologie 6, Berlin, 2006.

Reuster-Jahn, Uta: "Let's Go Party! Discourse and Self-Portrayal in the Bongo Fleva Song Mikasi ("Sex", Ngwair 2004)", *Swahili Forum* 14, 2007, 225-254.

Reuster-Jahn, Uta & Gabriel Hacke: "The Bongo Flava Industry in Tanzania and Artists' Strategies for Success", *Mainzer Arbeitspapiere* 127, 2011.

Reuster-Jahn, Uta & Roland Kießling: "Lugha ya Mitaani in Tanzania. The Poetics and Sociology of a Young Urban Style of Speaking. With a Dictionary Comprising 1100 Words and Phrases", *Swahili Forum* 13, 2006, 1-196. [http://www.ifeas.unimainz.de/SwaFo/SF_13.pdf]

Roch, Anna & Gabriel Hacke: "Hip Hop in Tansania zwischen Message und Flava", *Sozialanthropologische Arbeitspapiere* 101, Berlin, 2006.

Reynolds, F. A.: "Lavu huzungusha dunia", *Tanganyika Notes and Records* 58/59, 1962, 203-204.

Roy-Campbell, Zaline M. & Martha A.S. Qorro: *Language Crisis in Tanzania. The Myth of English Versus Education*, Dar es Salaam, 1997.

Rubagumya, Casmir M.: "Language in Tanzania". – In C. M. R. (Ed.): *Language in Education in Africa. A Tanzanian Perspective*, Clevedon & Philadelphia, 1990, pp. 5-14.

Saavedra Casco, José Arturo: "Modernity or Adaptability? The Incorporation of Foreign Words into Swahili Poetry". – In Pat Caplan & Farouk Topan (Eds.): *Swahili Modernities. Culture, Politics, and Identity on the East Coast of Africa*, Trenton, 2005, pp. 193-211.

Shariff, Ibrahim Noor: *The Function of Dialogue Poetry in Swahili Society*, New Brunswick, 1983. [PhD thesis]

Stroeken, Koen: "This is Not a Haircut. Neoliberalism and Revolt in Kiswahili Rap", *Image & Narrative*, 2005, <http://www.imageandnarrative.be/inarchive/worldmusicb_advertising/koenstroeken.htm>, accessed 13 August 2012.

Suriano, Maria: "'Mimi ni msanii, kioo cha jamii'. Urban Youth Culture as Seen Through Bongo Fleva and Hip-Hop", *Swahili Forum* 14, 2007, 207-223. [http://www.ifeas.uni-mainz.de/SwaFo/SF_14_12%20Suriano.pdf]

TUKI (Taasisi ya Uchunguzi wa Kiswahili): *English-Swahili Dictionary*, Dar es Salaam, 1996.

Whiteley, Wilfred: *Swahili. The Rise of a National Language*, London, 1969.

Dike-Ogu Chukwumerije (Abuja)

Writing and Publishing in Nigeria.
An Author's Perspective

As counter-intuitive as it may sound, one of the popular ways of making money in Nigeria is by writing and publishing a book. It all depends on *what kind* of book you write; and *how* you expect it to make money for you. Non-fiction offers the better prospects. The safest bet of all is to write a textbook and get it on the appropriate compulsory reading list in the public school system. That would attract the biggest publishers in the country. A close second is to land a writing commission; find someone (preferably a high-profile political figure) willing to sponsor a flattering biography. Beyond these options, you have to venture into more uncertain territory. You could self-publish – motivational books, religious books, eyewitness accounts of political spectacles, as these are some of the more popular products.

Fiction offers slightly dimmer prospects. Trade publishers willing to publish fictional titles are not as big as their textbook-publishing counterparts; but they are just as risk averse. Conventional wisdom suggests that Nigerian readers are most likely to read those Nigerian authors that have achieved some foreign recognition. So, a major part of the Nigerian trade publishing industry is dedicated to publishing foreign-award-winning Nigerian authors. The chances of an unknown writer getting a trade publishing deal because of the quality of their writing alone is practically nil; and those lucky enough to get published in this way cannot expect the same marketing support for their works as their colleagues with foreign credentials. So, we come again to the option of self-publishing.

Having self-published in Nigeria as well as abroad, I can tell you that self-publishing in Nigeria is the more challenging experience. An author wishing to self-publish anywhere in the world will have two basic choices. You could manage the entire process of editing, designing, printing and marketing your book yourself; or you could pay a 'vanity publisher', as they are called, to handle it all for you. Regardless of where you self-publish, you are going to have to shoulder the costs and responsibilities. However, advancements in technology have slashed the up-front costs of self-publishing in many Western countries. The availability of online book sales channels and Print-On-Demand (POD) technology has given authors a way around the most significant singular cost element in self-publishing: printing books in bulk in advance of sales. In countries where these technologies are available, books can be bought online and are then printed for delivery.

But, alas, Nigeria is not yet one of such countries. So, self-publishing here still requires a significant amount of financial investment, up-front. However, without well-developed distribution channels, it is quite difficult to rely on book sales alone to recover that investment. Amazon does not deliver to Nigeria. Online retailing of anything in Nigeria is still in its infancy. Everything has to be done on foot. One option is to go from bookshop to bookshop placing your books. But the difficulties are rife. There is the hassle of dealing with so many bookshops on an individual basis. There are the ridiculous mark-ups bookshops place on your books (sometimes they can ask for as much as 100%). There is the slow pace of sales in brick-and-mortar bookshops. There is the, sometimes, shady record-keeping and accounting that could see your share of revenues, when sales do occur, staying put with the bookseller. But, at least, your books are on a shelf, somewhere. That *could* be some consolation.

If it is not, though, you *do* have another option. You could turn the trunk of your car into a mobile bookshop and sell your books yourself. The marketing tricks are the same as anywhere else in the world. You organise seminars, put together workshops, have readings, work the literary circuits, put your product out on the Internet, leverage on your social network; do the legwork. *Sell! Sell! Sell!* Methods like these actually account for a lot of the book sales in Nigeria.

Nevertheless, as I pointed out earlier, it is difficult to break even on book sales alone. That is why many authors resort to a unique Nigerian money-recouping-mechanism called the 'book launch'. Now, I know the term 'book launch' may sound familiar, but 'launching' a book in Nigeria is very different from anything that occurs anywhere else. It is not just about putting together a reading, having your book reviewed and selling a few copies of your book at the event. In Nigeria, the book launch is *the* primary means of recouping *all* the investments made in getting your book published, at once. A successful book launch actually relieves the author of any financial need to sell copies of his/her book, afterwards. Essentially, it is a fund-raising ceremony organised by, or on behalf, of the author. As a well established socio-cultural practice, people invited to a book launch know what is expected of them. They are supposed to donate *large* sums of money to the author in exchange for 'complimentary' copies of the book. It really does not matter what they do with the book afterwards; whether they read it or throw it in a bin; as long as the cost of publishing is, at the very least, recovered. An effective book launch should, however, yield a lot more money than that; the author should walk away with a substantial profit from the launch alone. In fact, in many instances, a failed book launch is a failed book; at least, as a business venture.

But to the obsessively creative, all this talk of profits can, sometimes, be depressing. For the writer at heart, money may always be an adequate reward, but it is never a sufficient one. You do not just want to be paid; you also want to be *read*. Being understood or misunderstood; critiqued or criticised; discussed, quoted, referred to, heard; these are all important (and greatly desired) rewards for a writer. Secretly, every writer wants to move the world (or, at least, somebody) with his/her words. So, even when the economics of writing do not make sense, people still *write*…on dog-eared pieces of paper and scrappy notebooks; on mobile phones and laptops; during their lunch breaks and after dull, uninspiring days at the office. It is an addiction, after all. Then they find each other in small, nondescript reading circles scattered all over the city and indulge in that most exotic of luxuries – *literature for literature's sake*.

In Abuja, where I live, there are many such circles. The Abuja Literary Society (ALS) meets every Friday; and the Abuja Writers' Forum (AWF) meets every Sunday. The local chapter of the Association of Nigerian Authors (ANA) meets on the odd Tuesday; and you have *Infusion*, an eclectic mix of music and readings, held on the last Thursday of the month. It all happens after the mind-numbing grind of day jobs. People loosen ties and take off jackets. They come with children and friends, but not to drink or watch movies or laugh over junk food. They come to read. They come to listen. They come to share. They come to exhale.

And this is not just the case in Abuja. There are similar groups all over the country; in cities like Lagos, Port-Harcourt and Kaduna. Here, you find the love for the word, written or spoken, alive and well. Authors pass through in steady droves. Rooms come alive with surreal discussions of style and content. New writers bring their tender scribblings into the soft light of positive criticism. Unknown maestros thrill delighted audiences with the beauty of their crafts. The world is seen and touched, felt and tasted through the mercurial senses of writers. It always makes me wonder: who says the reading culture in Nigeria is dead?

Just the other day, Chuma Nwokolo dropped in to read from *The Ghost of Sani Abacha*; and he had the whole room in stitches with his hilarious short stories. And, the other night, we argued about the characters and themes in Marilyn Heward Mill's *Cloth Girl*. And, before that, it was Lola Shoneyin's turn to hold us all spell-bound with tasteful excerpts from her book *The Secret Lives of Baba Segi's Wives*. And how can I forget the evening I looked up and saw Gabriel Okara, the legendary Nigerian poet, walking into our little reading? But we do not only come for glimpses of greatness. The streams that birthed the likes of Chinua Achebe, Wole Soyinka, Helon Habila and Chimamanda Ngozi Adichie have not yet dried up. There are new, exciting literary discoveries every week. And whether it is the cynical stories of an Elnathan John or the mild philosophies of a Samuel Anyaoha; the graphic tales of a Jide Attah or the earthy realism of a Spencer Okoroafor; it is always delightful to discover treasure in the most unlikely of places. Like in Adinoyi Onukaba's exquisite drama, *The Killing Swamp*, or Okechukwu Ofili's idiosyncratic masterpiece *How Stupidity Saved My Life*.

Even poetry, that most endangered of genres, is finding new life in this vibrant literary undergrowth. Once upon a time, in the eyes of Generation X, it was the embodiment of everything boring and opaque about classical literature. But not anymore – poetry is slowly becoming 'cool' again. Maybe, it is the similarities between rap and performance poetry; between hip-hop and spoken word. But Nigerians, especially *young* Nigerians, are taking to it in increasing numbers; and poetry slams are becoming a staple feature of the cultural life of many Nigerian cities. And the *forms* of expression are as diverse as the nation itself. They rhyme about love and its incomprehensible ways; standing up straight in a crooked world; the unpredictable patterns of a butterfly's flight; the indescribable depths of pain. It could be the measured rhythm of Ken Ike Okere's "The River Died"; the delicate introspection of Hajo Isa's "Shadow Fall"; the urban rhythms of Nwabundo Onyeabo's "Out Of Curiousity". It could be the highly talented Reward Enakerakpor with his innovative combination of music and poetry; or the silky smoothness of the serial slam sensation, Ifueko Ogbomo.

But, invariably, it is protest poetry – with its tortured stanzas weighed down by metaphors from our daily struggles – that resonates the loudest. On a quiet evening, you could find Simeon Abiodun immortalising the tragedy of the terrorist attack on the U.N. building in Abuja, or Razak Ivori painting the ills of crime and corruption in poignant verse; you could stumble on Edwin Oribhabor bringing his art even closer to his listeners with his ground-breaking use of Pidgin English, or Michael Ogah asking us difficult questions. Here you find anger and bitterness, bewilderment and frustration. But, here, you also find hope, nesting between one verse and the next, hanging on to the last line of a furious recital, gently woven into the fabric of that euphoria a skilled performance poet could wrap you up in. You find hope. And it warms your heart; knowing that, in the midst of all the roiling madness, there are still people who believe in the power of words. Not guns. Not bullets. Not bombs. Just words. You could spend days reading a book. But in a few seconds poetry could light a fire in your heart. To a generation accustomed to getting things at the click of a button, this may just be the greatest attraction of the genre.

It certainly was, and still is, for me. The *succinctness* of poetry: its ability to say a lot with a little. It enthralled me as a child; consoled me as a teenager; empowered me as an adult. I did not have to stay silent in the face of my world. I *had* a voice. And it was important that I did, because as I grew older, I began to see that Africa needed, not just a voice, but many, *many* voices. The pulse of life in a city like Lagos; the broken, beautiful mosaic that is poverty; the unexplored perspectives littering the streets of cities like Abuja, begging to be expressed; *begging to be told.*

Ironically, it was in London that I, first, felt…truly…African. Maybe, it was the distance. Maybe, it was the way certain identities I had grown up believing were sacrosanct suddenly became irrelevant. There were no tribes. Just people; people who were content knowing they shared the same homeland; and that *that* homeland was not a village, or a town, or a city, or country; but an entire continent. And I thought how beautiful it all looked, from that distance; how beautiful it could all be if people did not think their ethnic and religious differences were sufficient reason to maim and kill, to discriminate and exclude; especially when they were all standing on the same piece of earth. And, so, one night, sufficiently inspired by the stirrings in my own heart, I wrote a poem. And when I had finished, I titled it "The Revolution Has No Tribe".

But there was, still, no peace. I wanted to say more. So, I went in search of my Muse. At the time, I was doing a degree in Law and Development; and my lectures were littered with other people's opinions about who Africa was, where she was coming from, and what she needed to do to get to where she needed to be. But everyone must find his/her own truth. So, I went in search of mine. I walked up the Nile and across the Kalahari; peered over Mount Pati and lay beside the Cubango. I had never *really* studied *African* history before, but the past always yields the most fascinating stories. As I learned about civilisations and migrations, empires and peoples; the names began to make sense. *Kush, Nok, Songhay* and *Ghana*; *Tiharka, Nzingha, Samori* and *Madiba*. It all made sense to me. Information fed inspiration; and inspiration found expression in poetry. It ran like a river, for days, weeks, months. And when it finally stopped, I had a collection. I did not need to search for a title; I had one already. This collection would be named after the poem that inspired it – *The Revolution Has No Tribe*.

It was the end of a beautiful experience and the beginning of a difficult one. For now, I looked to *publish* my collection of poetry. And that was how I learned, firsthand, those publishing difficulties, which I described at the beginning of this article; all of which are infinitely multiplied when what you would like to publish is *poetry*. But when I had been rejected enough, like many others before me, I took my fate in my own hands and self-published. And you, certainly, would *not* be reading this article now if I had not done so. But that is just the way it works. Sometimes, the only way to get our stories out in the *exact* words that came to us when we were first inspired, is to tell them ourselves. Ultimately, that is why we write and, against all odds, publish.

Dike-Ogu Chukwumerije (Abuja)

The Revolution Has No Tribe

Do you not know that poverty is not Ghanaian?
He will not spare the rest of us and afflict only the Kenyan
He will step over the river and come across the border
So, when the drums sound, let everybody answer

Do you not know that corruption is not from Tripoli?
He will not hear that Islam has no dealings with Christianity
He will wake up all of our children at night with hunger
So, when the drums sound, let everybody answer

Do you not know that HIV/AIDS is not Tswana?
He will not select his victims and kill only the Nyanja
He will set the land ablaze from the Cape to the Sahara
So, when the drums sound, let everybody answer

Do you not know that our enemies have no face?
They are indigenes of no state, they come from no place
And, if this boat capsizes every one of us will go under
So, when the drums sound, let everybody answer

Do not say, "I am an iroko", when the forest is burning
Do not say, "I am an obeche", when the forest is burning
Our differences will not prevent us from perishing together
So, when the drums sound, let everybody answer

Dike-Ogu Chukwumerije has kindly allowed us to reprint this poem from his collection *The Revolution Has No Tribe. Contemporary Poetry on African History, Culture and Society*, London, 2008, p. 47.

Rainer Emig (Hanover)

Doing Business in West Africa.
The Case of Ghana

1. Introduction. How Africa is Seen in Terms of Business – and How It Sees Itself

In the narrow perception of the Western world, Africa is frequently seen as a land of natural catastrophes, of underdevelopment, hunger, political instabilities and cultural backwardness. Africa as a business location is not something that easily gains priority in Western thinking, yet this is exactly what it is, not only for Western companies, but increasingly for the new global players China and India. Simon Watkins, in an essay for the British tabloid *The Daily Mail*, pinpoints this ambivalence:

> The cliché of Africa is that it is indeed a source of untold mineral wealth hampered by corrupt governments and civil unrest, if not outright war. There is more than a little truth to this, but Africa is not homogeneous and has many economically and politically stable states. Botswana, for example, has one of the highest consistent growth rates in the world, albeit thanks to the mountain of diamonds on which it is sitting. To see Africa simply as a continent of resources would be simplistic, too. It is also one of consumers. Africa has a larger middle-class population than India. It is undergoing a rapid bout of urbanisation, not unlike that under way in China, bringing millions out of rural employment into service industries and manufacturing in cities. Renaissance estimates that growth in sub-Saharan Africa will be between four per cent and seven per cent this year, a figure at least double anything expected in Europe or America.
>
> Whether this will carry on is another matter. Despite its successes, Africa is still home to highly unstable or corrupt states where the risks to investors are huge.[1]

The present essay will introduce one West African country, Ghana, from the point of view of its economy. Ghana, the first sub-Saharan African nation to achieve independence (in 1957), has a medium-sized economy, some important natural resources, yet also an interesting economic development that provides in many respects a more realistic example of what goes on in many African countries than extreme cases of poverty or industrial exploitation.

Yet the present analysis wants to do more than merely present statistical data and factual information. In keeping with the theme of the present book, it aims at giving Africans in this region a voice and analyse how they view doing business with the West and the East. In doing so, new perspectives on Africa might emerge and perhaps, even more importantly, new perspectives on Western attitudes towards Africa.

2. Ghana. A 'Typical' Case

Ghana is a sub-Saharan country with a population of 24 million and a total size of 239,460 square kilometres.[2] (In comparison, Germany has a size of 357,022 square kilometres and more than 81 million inhabitants.) Ghana's GDP of 26.2 billion $ (1,098 $ per capita) is a far cry from Germany's 3,139 billion $ (and 38,400 $ per capita).[3] Ghana is an English-speaking country surrounded by mainly French-speaking ones.[4] This is due to its colonial history. Originally a series of independent kingdoms (of which those of the Ashanti and Fante are perhaps best known), what is now Ghana first became a – not always willing – trading partner of the Portuguese in the 15th century and the Dutch in the late 16th (the Danes also got a foot in the door), before the British turned parts of the country into their Gold Coast Crown Colony in 1874. Gold, besides slaves, had been Ghana's main attraction for foreign powers ever since the area was 'discovered' by them. Britain's colonial legacy is infrastructure (railways and hospitals) as well as education in the shape of a British-style school system. Ghana has a relatively high literacy rate (78.9 per cent among young women according to government statistics; 66.6 per cent overall according to Transparency International)[5] and a relatively low rate of HIV infections for a sub-Saharan country (an adult prevalence of 1.8 per cent, as established in 2009).[6]

Ghana is a country that should be doing well, but is not, at least not in all respects. The economists Todd Moss and Lauren Young provided the following assessment of its potential in 2009:

> Ghana can be considered a relative success story in Africa. We cite six variables – peace and stability, democracy and governance, control of corruption, macroeconomic management, poverty reduction, and signs of an emerging social contract – to suggest the country's admirable political and economic progress. The expected arrival of sizeable oil revenues beginning in 2011-13, however, threatens to undermine that progress. In fact, numerous studies have linked natural resources to negative outcomes such as conflict, authoritarianism, high corruption, economic instability, increased poverty, and the destruction of the social contract. The oil curse thus threatens the very outcomes that we consider signs of Ghana's success.[7]

A typical acknowledgement of its contradictory status is an article in the Ghanaian newspaper *The Chronicle* of 28 June 2012. Its title bodes badly indeed and seems to confirm the prejudices listed as typical of African countries in the introduction above: "Ghana among the world's 10 worst economies". In the article, we read:

> Ghana has the world's largest manmade lake and the 1-gigawatt Aksombo Hydroelectric Plant, built to supply electricity to Africa's largest aluminum smelter. But the smelter has been idle since 2009, a casualty of low aluminum prices and persistent electricity shortages that have forced the government to divert the power elsewhere.
>
> Ghana is a typical example of the world's worst-managed economies: It's a country that shouldn't be poor, but it is. The West African nation's gross domestic product per capita fell 9% last year to $621, ranking it 154th out of 184 countries tracked by the International Monetary Fund, below resource-impoverished Haiti.
>
> With a $3 billion trade deficit last year and $4.9 billion in external debt, Ghana is struggling to pay its bills even as it sits on some of the world's biggest reserves of gold and bauxite, as well as considerable amounts of offshore oil, which is being developed by Anadarko Petroleum […] and others.
>
> "Ghana's problems are mostly homegrown," said Peter Allum, the IMF's mission chief to Ghana, in February. Forbes ranks Ghana ninth on our list of the world's worst economies.[8]

The article once again focuses on Ghana's deposits of gold, oil and bauxite (the mineral used for the production of aluminium). In addition, Ghana is taken to possess the energy to process these materials. Yet this merely makes it very dependent on the world market, which is slow due to the ongoing financial crisis. Moreover, there are homemade problems in addition to global crises:

> Forbes screened IMF data for countries that have low and declining per-capita GDP, high trade deficits and high inflation, all indicators of bad economic management, regardless of the country's inherent wealth.
>
> All have at least one trait in common: Their governments discourage private investment – and economic growth – through policies of crony capitalism, expropriation or arbitrary enforcement of the laws. That makes it hard to generate hard currency to pay off government debt and discourages citizens from investing in education to improve their own economic lot.
>
> "Most of these vulnerably low-income countries are in a trap," said Otaviano Canuto, Vice President and head of the World Bank's Poverty Reduction and Economic Management Network. "The climate is not conducive to investments, not only in factories and agricultural improvements, but in education."[9]

What the article names are recurring issues in reports about business in Africa in general: mismanagement and corruption. Yet are these inherent in African politics, economy and culture, and if not, where do they originate? This question will be addressed below. That the picture is by no means all black is shown in an article by the same economics editor in the same newspaper only one day before the one quoted above, a news item entitled "Ghana leads FMCG investments in Africa":

> UBS AG, a financial services company with offices in more than 50 countries, has ranked Ghana among Nigeria, Zambia, Kenya and Tanzania, as the leading countries for Fast-Moving Consumer Goods (FMCG) investments in Sub-Saharan Africa.
>
> This means that these countries are identified as the most preferred destinations for FMCG investments on the African continent, according to a new UBS AG report.
>
> The report added that Sub-Saharan Africa boasts of some of the strongest economic growth in the world, and offers selective opportunities for consumer goods.

> Analyst Renier Swanepoel said the rankings were based on economic growth prospects, the size and future opportunity of available FMCG markets, and the overall ease of doing business. South Africa stood at the 18th position, because South African companies are looking outward to the North for better growth opportunities.[10]

Here, an optimistic note is struck that does mention investment, not only by Western and Eastern global players, but also by businesses from countries such as South Africa, and a belief in a rising consumer market based on growing incomes.

The *CIA World Factbook*, although of course produced for the United States of America, is generally seen as a good guide to economic and political facts that are regarded as relevant for the Western world. This is its current entry on Ghana's economy:

> Ghana's economy has been strengthened by a quarter century of relatively sound management, a competitive business environment, and sustained reductions in poverty levels. Ghana is well endowed with natural resources and agriculture accounts for roughly one-quarter of GDP and employs more than half of the workforce, mainly small landholders. The services sector accounts for 50% of GDP. Gold and cocoa production and individual remittances are major sources of foreign exchange. Oil production at Ghana's offshore Jubilee field began in mid-December, 2010, and is expected to boost economic growth. President Mills faces challenges in managing new oil revenue while maintaining fiscal discipline and resisting debt accumulation. Estimated oil reserves have jumped to almost 700 million barrels. Ghana signed a Millennium Challenge Corporation (MCC) Compact in 2006, which aims to assist in transforming Ghana's agricultural sector. Ghana opted for debt relief under the Heavily Indebted Poor Country (HIPC) program in 2002, and is also benefiting from the Multilateral Debt Relief Initiative that took effect in 2006. In 2009 Ghana signed a three-year Poverty Reduction and Growth Facility with the IMF to improve macroeconomic stability, private sector competitiveness, human resource development, and good governance and civic responsibility. Sound macro-economic management along with high prices for gold and cocoa helped sustain GDP growth in 2008-11.[11]

In what is typical of West African countries, Ghana's economy is a largely agricultural one – despite what has been said about its important mineral deposits. In what follows, the present essay will first have a look at Ghana's agriculture, then at the use of its natural resources, and finally combine the view on both in what will be an assessment of what kind of development the country is undergoing and how this is viewed by Ghana's inhabitants. As has been stated above, Ghanaian perspectives will provide the guide for the investigation, while selected Western views will be used as a contrast. Both angles will also be critically evaluated, which means that positions will be treated as exactly that, and not as 'truths' about Ghana's economy.

3. Agricultural Ghana. 'Improving' Tradition

The Ghanaian Ministry of Food and Agriculture provides the following statistical data for Ghana's agricultural output: livestock 6.1%, fisheries 7.3%, cocoa 8.2%, forestry 12.2% and crops 66.2%.[12] Cocoa and wood products make up a significant percentage of agricultural output, and these are the goods that are of particular prominence in foreign trade. Yet livestock and fisheries and general crop production are in fact much more dominant, although they matter most for domestic supply. The Ministry characterises the means of agricultural production as traditional and not (yet) industrial, but also as generally environmentally aware:

> Agriculture is predominantly on a smallholder basis in Ghana. About 90% of farm holdings are less than 2 hectares in size, although there are some large farms and plantations, particularly for rubber, oil palm and coconut and, to a lesser extent, rice, maize and pineapples. The main system of farming is traditional. The hoe and cutlass are the main farming tools. There is little mechanized farming, but bullock farming is practised in some places, especially in the North. Agricultural production varies with the amount and distribution of rainfall. Soil factors are also important. Most food crop farms are intercropped. Monocropping is mostly associated with larger-scale commercial farms.[13]

Contrary to what a Western perspective conditioned by the many media reports on multinational companies buying up and dominating crop production in African countries would expect, agriculture is still in the hands of many smallholders. For a country whose population grows by the relatively moderate figure of 2.4 per cent per annum, it is very well capable of feeding itself, since the growth rate in the production of major crops, such as rice and maize, display the impressive figures 18.92 and 10.88 per cent.[14]

The remainder of its agricultural output is varied and includes a number of fruits, such as pineapples, bananas, mangoes and oranges, but also the already mentioned cocoa and cashew nuts, the latter being of particular interest for Asian markets. Among fish, tuna provides significant revenue.[15] What do Ghanaian newspapers have to say about its agriculture, both for domestic use and for export?

Ghanaian papers as much as local politicians are exceedingly aware of the changes and multinational networks affecting agriculture. Thus, an article in *The Chronicle* from 6 December 2011 describes in some detail the effect of planned foreign investment and change in crop culture on the local population of the administrative region of Brong-Ahafo (shortened in local usage to 'BA'):

> "Foreign Agro-Investors Eye BA"
> The Brong Ahafo Regional Minster, Kwadwo Nyamekye-Marfo, has advised farmers and other stakeholders in the agricultural sector to strategically position themselves, to enable them to benefit from the imminent foreign investments in the sector in the region. He revealed that a number of foreign investors had expressed interest in investing in agriculture in the region, especially in the area of agro-processing.
>
> The Minister, who announced this at the regional celebration of National Farmers Day held in Wamfie in the Dormaa East District, was happy to note that the issue of post-harvest losses would soon be a thing of the past when the investors finally implement their decision to invest in the region. This, according to him, would not only enhance the income of farmers, but also offer more employment opportunities to the people, especially the youth. Some of the investors, he disclosed, were interested in the processing of cashew and tomatoes, while others, particularly the South African investors, had their eyes on the poultry industry in the Dormaa area.[16]

The article is interesting in many ways. First of all, intentionally or not, it manages to infuse a neutral piece of news with belligerent qualities when it not only shortens "agricultural investors" to "agro-" ones, thus implying potential aggression. That this is perhaps no coincidence is further proved by the reported choice of wording by the Regional

Minister who tells farmers to "strategically position themselves", a common enough military metaphor in politics and the economy, but here strangely mismatched with the small stakeholders that we have already encountered. More than that, the remainder of the article also indicates that not all is well in the world of Ghanaian farming:

> The Minister commended the farmers and the Ministry of Food and Agriculture (MoFA) for ensuring sufficient food supply in the country, and urged the unemployed youth to take advantage of the government's interventions in the agricultural sector to better their lots. On his part, the Regional MoFA Director, Mr. Emmanuel Osie Adade, entreated farmers to seek assistance from the agriculture extension officers on the application of agro-chemicals, to avoid misuse of those chemicals. He noted that as much as the country strives to ensure food security, there also was the need to regulate the use of the agro-chemicals to prevent health risks and other consequential effects of the misapplication of such chemicals.
> Congratulating farmers in the region, Mr. Adade mentioned that the hard work of farmers had paid so much that the region had not experienced famine for some years, disclosing that the region released about 3,000 bags of maize from the MoFA stores to support flood victims in other regions.
> Mr. I.K. Kyeremeh, District Chief Executive (DCE) of Dormaa East, observed that agriculture contributes largely to national development, but faces enormous challenges which must be addressed through research, to ensure sustainability. He entreated farmers in the area to put aside their political inclinations, and take advantage of the government's sensitive and pragmatic agricultural policies and programmes, expressing the worry that some people in the district, and the country at large, refuse to be beneficiaries of some government interventions, on the basis of partisan politics.[17]

Local unemployment, especially among the young, is still prevalent, and one wonders how its planned reduction squares with the modernisation efforts in agriculture that generally result in fewer rather than more jobs. That not all locals are supportive of government measures in this respect becomes evident in the closing section of the above quotation, which suddenly brings "political inclinations" into play, using a weak and imprecise term ("inclinations") that smacks of subjective prejudice to clash with the government's "sensitive and pragmatic" policies. This is, of course, what one would expect from a local politician such as the District Chief Executive of Dormaa East. But there are other convictions at stake, as the subsequent quotation, still from the same article, demonstrates:

> At Kwabenakumakrom, the Sunyani West District Director of MoFA, Madam Joyce Takyi-Kemevor, noted that the nation's quest to promote and ensure food security would be fruitless, if Ghanaians did not embrace and patronise the high yielding food crop species being introduced by the Ministry and other stakeholders in the sector. She observed that some people in the country still preferred the traditional food crop species to the improved ones. According to her, the traditional crop species have low yielding ability and are less resistant to diseases and unfavorable weather conditions, compared to the improved species, which have relatively shorter maturity periods.
>
> The public's taste preference, she noted, determines the need to commit more resources into researching and developing more hybrid crops and animals which have high yielding and reproduction abilities, to produce more food to feed the nation.[18]

Here we have a prototypical diatribe against traditionalism, which is apparently limited to "some people in the country" (a strange claim in a country in which half of the population live in the countryside), though resistance against the "high yielding food crop species" appears to be futile, as is coyly suggested by the adverb "still". Those behind the "improved species", i.e. the government and other unnamed "stakeholders" (which might mean national as well as multinational companies), merely follow the "public's taste preference", which is strange since local tastes seem to be diametrically opposed to them. Yet the article as such claims to speak for "the nation" and even its "quest".

The article, in short, is contradictory, but its contradictions very tellingly expose the ambivalence of Ghana's politicians and the people affected by their decisions towards the modernisation of one of the country's most important economic sectors, crop production. More efficiency and output are needed, as the reference to past famines makes more than clear. Yet it comes at a price: it involves not only the (often excessive and dangerous) use of fertilisers, whose producers we will re-encounter below, but also a change of crops towards "improved" ones, which can mean anything from new species to genetically modified ones, which often resist pests more easily, but sometimes require exactly the fertilisers for their survival whose excessive use is criticised in the same article.

That such ambivalences are hard to communicate is self-evident, and one must also take into consideration the still generally rather primitive methods of farming prevalent in the affected areas. This state of affairs becomes visible when the article mentions a prize awarded to the best local farmer:

> A 56-year old farmer, Mr. Stephen Kwadwo Adjei, a native of Nkoranza, emerged the 2011 Brong Ahafo Regional Best Farmer. He received as his prize a corn mill, wellington boots, radio set, sewing machine, cutlasses, and certificates among other items.[19]

As was mentioned in the introduction to the present essay, it is by no means only the West that is of importance for trade when it comes to Ghana. Especially in connection with agricultural products, but also with natural resources, countries like India have taken over in terms of dominance. Thus, the Ghanaian *Chronicle* reported on 16 August 2012:

> The Indian High Commissioner to Ghana, H.E Mr. Rajinder Bhagat, has revealed that trade turnover between Ghana and India increased from US$ 537.53 million in 2010 to US$ 818.10 million in 2011. This, he said, depicted an increase of 52% over the preceding year, with India's exports to Ghana at US$ 658.35 million, as against an import figure of US$ 159.75 million. [...] Mr. Bhagat noted that the trade volume favoured India, as that country's major exports to Ghana include pharmaceuticals, telecommunication, agricultural machinery, electrical equipment, plastics, steel, cement, while Ghana's major exports to India are gold, cocoa and timber products.
>
> The Indian diplomat observed that the exchanges of business delegations have led to an increase in investments by Indian companies in Ghana in sectors including construction, manufacturing, trading, services, cement, plastics, pharmaceuticals, ICT, agro-processing and agricultural machinery, electrical equipment, and pharmaceuticals [sic].[20]

Only in parts does this thriving trade with India follow the historical pattern of colonialism, where raw materials (here gold, cocoa and timber) were exported by the colonised region in exchange for industrial products (here pharmaceuticals, telecommunication equipment, agricultural machinery, electrical goods, plastics, steel and cement). Indian companies are also beginning to invest in companies manufacturing such products in Ghana. Since Ghana has oil and gas now, products that prove too expensive to manufacture in India can now be produced there, for both the Indian and the Ghanaian market. This becomes particularly poignant with respect to a product that has already featured critically in the above discussion of agriculture, namely fertiliser:

> Furthermore, Mr. Bhagat told the *Business Chronicle* that a draft joint venture agreement between Ghana and India for the setting up of a $1.2 billion fertiliser plant in the Western Region of Ghana where oil and gas are produced in commercial quantities was in an advanced stage of discussion. In this direction, the two countries have already signed the Memorandum of Understanding (MOU) for the setting up of the plant since 2010. Both governments – Ghana and India – are also working hard to conclude the deal very soon, according to the Indian High Commissioner to Ghana.
>
> The company, Rashtriya Chemicals & Fertilisers Limited, which is India's biggest state-run urea maker, indicated that the plant, when established, will have the capacity to produce one million metric tonnes of fertiliser.
>
> However reports said shortage of natural gas in India, the main feedstock for making urea, is forcing companies, including Indian Farmers Fertiliser Cooperative Limited, the nation's largest producer, to build plants overseas. India's cabinet, on May 19th, 2011, more than doubled the price of gas sold to makers of fertiliser, which is used to grow crops, including wheat, sugar, rice and edible oils.[21]

Although there is evidently an emerging manufacturing base in Ghana, even if it is partly owned or financed by foreign investment, there remain major infrastructural problems hampering Ghana's further economic development. One of the most serious ones is that of an insufficient energy supply. Thus, an article in *The Chronicle* of 13 August 2012 ominously declares:

> "Dark Clouds Hang over Ghana's Gas"
> One of the major problems hampering the rapid development of Ghana's economy is the lack of adequate energy to power industries. Currently,

the country produces a little over 2,000 megawatts of power, which is woefully inadequate to meet the ever-increasing demand of the market.[22]

This leads into the next section of the debate, which deals with Ghana's natural resources, their exploitation and its consequences.

4. *From Gold Coast to Oil Boom?*

When oil fields were discovered off the coast of Ghana in the early 2000s, the country was unexpectedly far from jubilant. This was how the US-American news company CNN reported on the find:

> So Ghana has joined the club of oil producing nations. The taps have been turned on at the offshore Jubilee field. So what does this mean for Ghana? How will ordinary Ghanaians benefit from this resource windfall? The first concern that should be addressed is the perception that suddenly the country will become flush with petrodollars. Importantly, expectations must be managed. As those citizens in Nigeria or Angola know, the oil money often doesn't trickle down to the people. Firstly, Ghanaians have to not think [sic] that oil will magically create more jobs, or make people richer. Secondly, civil society has to be tough on government and ensure they constantly monitor how proceeds are being spent. Also, Ghanaians need to quickly implement legislation to govern the administration of this new industry; hopefully these laws will be passed soon. An independent regulator is also needed to oversee the sector.
> Luckily, Ghana has a relatively diversified economy compared to other oil-rich African nations. The country earns foreign currency from gold and cocoa. This alone makes it more likely to avoid the mistakes of places like Nigeria, where oil revenue accounts for approximately 92% of the GDP, or Angola, which is just about entirely reliant on oil proceeds. However, the numbers are staggering. The Jubilee fields are some of the richest and largest oil deposits discovered in many years. In the long term, oil production is estimated to bring in $1 billion a year. This is a lot of responsibility, as well as a wonderful gift for Ghana.[23]

Voices in Ghana itself were just as aware and critical. The first news items about the discovery were still neutral, although already an article from *Ghana Web* dating from 21 February 2000 made it clear that foreign players would try to stake their claim in this.

> Oil discovered in Western Region: A British company, Dana Petroleum, is said to have struck oil in significant quantities close to the Tano fields in the Western Region, the Ghana Broadcasting Corporation (GBC) reported on Wednesday. The possible reserves are estimated at about 200 million barrels of oil and 300 billion cubic feet of gas, the radio report said. A test programme is being planned to resolve uncertainties about the find.[24]

More critical voices were quickly joining the chorus, as can be seen in the subsequent comment by Njei Moses Timah, a photographer and freelance writer on Africa and world affairs:[25]

> On Monday, the British firm Tullow Oil announced the discovery of the equivalent of 600 million barrels of oil off the coast of Ghana, one of the biggest oil discoveries in Africa in recent times. But is this discovery a good or bad omen? Even though the actual exploitation of the oil is still several years down the road, many in Ghana are already celebrating. An excited President John Kufuor told the BBC, "We're going to really zoom, accelerate, and if everything works, which I pray will happen positively, you come back in five years, and you'll see that Ghana truly is the African tiger, in economic terms, for development."
>
> This type of exhilaration could be accepted as normal if it were coming from ordinary innocent Ghanaians. Ordinary Nigerians, Cameroonians, Congolese, Chadians, Angolans, etc. manifested this type of elation when oil was discovered in their respective countries. Today, it is no secret that after years of oil exploitation, most of the petroleum revenue in these countries simply disappeared. It is my opinion that Kufuor's elation about this oil find is a little bit naive. As a seasoned politician and African Union (AU) chairman, he is better placed to know that oil and other minerals have contributed more to African backwardness than the want of resources.
>
> These resources have fanned civil wars in Nigeria, the Democratic Republic of the Congo, the Republic of Congo, Angola, Liberia, Sierra Leone and Chad. Coups and mercenary incursions have occurred in almost all resource-rich African countries. The corruption and graft that follows the discovery of these resources has destroyed the social fabric of many of these so-called oil or mineral producing African countries. Bad governance, weak and inefficient institutions, poor accountability,

> crime and parasitic state employees (now a hallmark of these countries) have all contributed to chase Africa's best brains out of the continent.[26]

That Timah hit a raw nerve can be seen in the fact that his article attracted the impressive number of 282 comments, many of which shared his scepticism – even to the extent of viewing the consequences of the oil find as part of an imperialist "New Scramble for Africa":

> If there is a New Great Game afoot in Asia there is also a "New Scramble for Africa" on the part of the great powers. The National Security Strategy of the United States of 2002 declared that "combating global terror" and ensuring U.S. energy security required that the United States increase its commitments to Africa and called upon "coalitions of the willing" to generate regional security arrangements on that continent. Soon after the U.S. European Command, based in Stuttgart, Germany – in charge of U.S. military operations in Sub-Saharan Africa – increased its activities in West Africa, centering on those states with substantial oil production and/or reserves in or around the Gulf of Guinea (stretching roughly from the Ivory Coast to Angola). The U.S. military's European Command now devotes 70 percent of its time to African affairs, up from almost nothing as recently as 2003.[27]

Irrespective of the plausibility of such claims, what has proved correct is that in the wake of the oil discovery the Ghanaian government has been subject to massive pressure by multinational companies to grant them access to the oil. On 15 March 2006, the Ghanaian Energy Minister made the following declaration:

> Professor Michael Oquaye, Energy Minister, on Wednesday said nine international oil companies have various commitments to operate in Ghana with three of these companies actively undertaking explorations in the basins. He said the three companies were an American company, Devon Energy Ghana Limited, operating in the deepwater Keta basin, Vanco Ghana Limited, operating in the deepwater Tano-Cape Three Points and Kosmos Energy and the E.O. Group, whose areas covers both the shallow and deepwater-Western Cape Three Points.[28]

The list of companies involved in the exploration and exploitation of Ghana's oil fields is long and names many global players.[29] While one would have expected Chevron and Shell, together with many other US-

American operations, it also contains the greatest Russian oil company Lukoil, the Japanese multinationals Itochu and Mitsui, the Italian oil company Eni and even the Austrian company Eternit. That things were not running smoothly from the beginning can be seen in news clippings such as the following one from 4 April 2003:

> The managements of Lushann-Eternit Energy Ghana Limited and its parent company in the US and Saltpond Offshore Company Limited have rendered their unqualified apology to the government and people of Ghana for the embarrassment caused them regarding the theft of crude oil from the Saltpond Oilfields.[30]

What appears to be happening is similar to Ghana's experience with its gold reserves. First an attraction to foreign traders and eventually colonialists, independent Ghana's use of its gold has also attracted controversial opinions. Here are the views of Chachu Daniel, a Ghanaian working for EITI, the Extractive Industries Transparency Initiative founded in 2002:[31]

> Generally, I agree with your analysis on the oil find in Ghana. However, a point worth commenting on is your assertion that Ghana has done a "pretty good job" in managing its gold revenues. Well, I am not sure that this is exactly the case. Indeed many concerns have been raised by many analysts and public officials about what Ghana has to show for around 100 years of mining. Large mining enclaves around Obuasi and Tarkwa, to mention a few, have very little to show for this mining record. Indeed as part of the EITI process, a Consultant was engaged to attempt reconciling payment of mining revenues by companies one side with receipt by the government revenue agencies on the other. Todd, you will have to read the Aggregator's report to see what I mean. For instance there was little evidence to show that government was receiving the 3% royalty it was actually entitled to. There were also issues about non-payment of other revenues streams due government, among others.[32]

While the jury is still out on the long-term effect of oil on Ghana's economy, the sceptics appear to have been right as far as the creation of jobs is concerned. An article in *The Chronicle* from 6 January 2012 paints a rather sobering picture, and one that is perfectly in line with the pessimistic predictions made by Timah above.

> About 840 Ghanaians have so far gained employment in the oil and gas sector since the country started producing 'black gold' in commercial quantities. The sector, since the discovery of oil in Ghana, has created about 1,500 jobs, out of which 660, representing 43%, have gone to expatriates.[33]

The environment, too, seems to suffer as a result of unchallenged exploitation by multinational corporations, as the following critical article demonstrates:

> A Senior Research Fellow of the Institute of Statistical, Social and Economic Research (ISSER), University of Ghana, Legon, Dr. George Botchie, has said that the Environmental Protection Agency (EPA) is weak in monitoring the activities of foreign investors, leading to environmental degradation in the country. According to him, activities of these multilateral organisations, especially in the fields of mining and forestry, have continued to cause environmental degradation of land without effective follow-up on their activities by the EPA.[34]

It is certainly no coincidence either that since the oil discovery Ghana has dropped to place 69 on Transparency International's Corruption Perceptions Index. (One should not feel too complacent about this as a European, as is demonstrated by the fact that Italy shares this place with Ghana.)[35]

China, which at a superficial glance appears to have been kept out of the Ghanaian oil boom, in fact provided the financial backing for most of it:

> Ghana is estimated to rake in one billion dollars of revenue a year from the gas industry, an amount that can make the country repay the three billion-dollar Chinese loan facility from the Chinese Development Bank. Vice President John Dramani Mahama made the disclosure at the weekend at the just-ended Third Ghana Policy Fair.[36]

In fact, China also controls some of the mining that goes on in Ghana. It not only provides the technology, but also imports cheap Chinese labourers, whose presence has recently led to some violent clashes with the local population, as documented in an article in *The Chronicle* of 8 August 2012:

[...] "the fact remains that many small scale mining companies owned by Ghanaians use Chinese equipment and technology. It is in this regard, coupled with the low cost of Chinese labour, that, even in the most remote and uninhabitable terrains in the country, Chinese workmen this time around, find themselves working for Ghanaian owners."

Over the years, the Ghana China Business Chamber of Commerce (GCBCC) have worked hard to promote the migration of Ghanaian skilled labour to very remote parts of this country to operate mining equipment (with Chinese technology) imported for use by small scale mining companies owned by Ghanaian businessmen. However, the union indicated that these efforts have been in futility as the locations of such industries are no longer attractive to identified Ghanaian skilled labour. In such difficult circumstances, the GCBCC has resolved to promote the use of cheaper alternatives such as employing low cost Chinese skilled labour by Ghanaian business men. This is especially so in the small scale mining sector, but a great cost to dear life. Thus, since 2005, over 87 Chinese men have been shot dead by armed robbers who attack them at their remote mining sites for gold. Hence, the resolution by such mining firms to arm their harmless Chinese nationals with licensed weapons used only for self-defence.[37]

5. *Between Multinational Business and Pan-Africanism. Balancing Ghana's Economic Prospects*

Ghana's economy, at least as far as its natural resources are concerned, is firmly tied up with the current multinational economy of massive loans, large-scale exploration and exploitation of resources as well as migrant workers. The local labour force only plays a minor role in this, as can be seen by the staggering number of expatriate experts that people Ghana's new oil industry. In keeping with this picture, Ghana's economy is also vulnerable when it comes to the recent exchange rate fluctuations or depression in food prices that minimise its revenue. None of this is colonial. Yet much of it is the long-term effect of a world order that, for centuries, has treated Africa as a storehouse of human labour, natural resources and agricultural goods. Since the end of colonies in the 20th century, African countries such as Ghana have tried to build on their remaining colonial legacy while at the same time maintaining traditional economies, especially in agriculture and to some extent in mining. Yet they have not managed to develop into industrialised nations or into service industries that are capable of competing realistically with the much longer-running models in Europe, the Americas and Australasia. The result is large-scale unemployment, also of the educated parts of the population.[38]

The sudden availability of crude materials such as oil, which are much sought after on the depleted world markets, instantly interferes with even such meagre measures and makes African economies susceptible to pressures from multinational companies, pressures that affect local allegiances all the way to national politics. These companies care or pretend to care for specific local conditions as little as financial investors such as China, and it would perhaps be unrealistic to expect this from them. It remains a curious fact, though, that it is frequently Europeans who worry about the impact of their economic investment in structures such as those of African nations and cultures. The present essay is evidence of this. What its investigation has shown, however, is that Ghana's perception of itself is remarkably self-critical.

Moreover, it does not do what a colonial – and also a post-colonial – perspective on the country would expect, namely look towards the so-called 'developed world' for approval and applause. Rather than that, many voices gathered in the "Opinion" pages of Ghanaian newspapers such as *The Chronicle* prefer to hark back to the anti-colonial and pan-African thinking of their still widely revered first president and proponent of Pan-Africanism, Kwame Nkrumah (1909-1972), and voice decidedly anti-Western, anti-American and anti-Asian sentiments. Thus, a reader's letter regards the sponsorship of the new African Union headquarters at Addis Ababa with a statue of Kwame Nkrumah in front, which has officially been labelled "China's gift to Africa", as "very disturbing" and calls it a case of "Neo-Colonization" (to be fair, a response by another reader calls Nkrumah a "cruel communist dictator who was a political bedfellow of Mao Tse Tung").[39] In a more sustained comment, which directly touches on the economic issues debated in the present essay, Peter N. Onumah states:

> Europe has been knocking at the door of Africa in the last decade for African leaders to sign the so called Economic Partnership Agreement. The partnership Europe has been touting means in essence perpetually subordinating raw-material producing Africa to the economic demands of hyper-industrialized Europe. This is consistent with the Euro-America design formulated and religiously pursued since the 16th century. […]

The growth and expansion of the industrial revolution ushered in the quest for and control of spheres of influence for markets and raw materials. The sequel was the scramble, partition and colonization of land by the Europeans suited to the primary purpose of their coming to Africa; that is to exploit the human and natural resources of the continent. The alien systems they set up have over the years been so pervasive in African societies that the beneficiaries, particularly the educated people, conceive of themselves as Lusophone, Anglophone or Francophone. In effect, they are saying they'd rather forget about their own culture. It is not surprising that a minister of state in the last administration proclaimed that Africa had no option other than to accept the EPA. A minister of trade and industry in the current administration is also advocating Ghana's acceptance of the EPA. Ghana's acceptance would irreversibly deepen her dependence on Europe to the stagnation of her economic development and attrition of her sovereignty.

Europe and America are very apprehensive of a truly independent Africa. They are now hyper-industrialized and they still need the raw materials: gold, manganese, cobalt, diamonds, timber, cocoa, ivory and many others. They still need the African market; so Africans should continue to remain hewers of wood and drawers of water. It must be clear to all Africans that the Euro-Americans are still hanging onto Africa where they are exploiting its human and natural resources.[40]

Such statements, which are, as has been stressed, anti-colonial in response to what they perceive as the neo-colonialism of multinational corporations and markets, may not suit Western readers. Yet they sit directly next to highly self-critical assessments that put the finger on developments that they often regard as home-made, even though they can also be seen in conjunction with the clash of traditional structures with modern economic and political pressures. Thus, the pseudonymous Paa Joe comments on Onumah's partisan statement:

> Without science, technology and radical innovation and creativity to accelerate economic growth, we will continue to fall behind, become underdeveloped and a country full of poor people. It is time for Ghanaians to realize that manipulation, bribery and corruption, stealing, embezzlement, falsification of accounts are intolerable evil. A country that breeds such a system only increases suffering, underdevelopment and extreme poverty.[41]

A naive post-colonial reading would accuse the anonymous writer of reproducing colonial positions from a subaltern perspective that has trained generations of oppressed people to interpret their enforced submission as 'natural'. Indeed the casual metaphoric use of the verb "breed" in the comment supports this reading, as does the theological view implied in the use of "evil". Nonetheless, such 'essentialist' views are common in African comments about their own situation and must be accepted as such. Moreover, any attempt at distilling a renewed (or perhaps still the old?) Western feeling of superiority out of such statements by a cultural Other can quickly be checked by a simple reminder that in terms of bribery and corruption Europeans have their own monopoly (and, like its civilization, it does not begin and end in Greece). When it comes to manipulation, Ghana can certainly learn much from the recent fiddling of the LIBOR, the London Interbank Offered Rate, by Barclays Bank and potentially several others.

It will be rewarding to watch the further development of a country like Ghana. It will be significant, too, since countries of its size and make-up will be important factors in a world economy whose effects will not merely reach Europe and Germany, but will affect both deeply. Looking at economic matters will have to be complemented by related investigations into the complexities of Ghanaian politics and into its equally complex and constantly changing cultural fabric. That there remains much to be done can be demonstrated by a simple test using one of Britain's leading newspapers, *The Guardian*, a publication that no one would accuse of being Eurocentric and unaware of matters colonial, post-colonial and neo-colonial. If one searches for mentions of Ghana in its computerised index, one comes across a large number of entries on football players and athletes (the latter undoubtedly the fallout of the 2012 London Olympics) and two meagre accounts of tourist trips to the country.[42] Africa deserves better than that. But so do Western readers and critics who wish to gain insights into African economies from the point of view of Africans.

Notes

1. Watkins (25 September 2010). Minor mistakes in the newspaper reports and readers' letters used in this essay have been silently corrected throughout.
2. Ghana Government Portal (2012). All data on Ghana in the subsequent paragraph derive from this official source. No dates are provided for the GDP figures.
3. Central Intelligence Agency (24 August 2012b). The GDP figures are estimates for 2011.
4. As is common in Africa, Ghana is home to around 100 ethnic groups, each with its own language. English is the official language; see GhanaWeb (2012).
5. Transparency International (2012a).
6. Central Intelligence Agency (24 August 2012a).
7. Moss & Young (2009).
8. Kunateh (28 June 2012). The IMF is the International Monetary Fund.
9. *Ibid.*
10. Kunateh (27 June 2012).
11. Central Intelligence Agency (24 August 2012a).
12. Ministry of Food and Agriculture, Republic of Ghana (2011).
13. *Ibid.*
14. These and many more detailed figures are listed in the Ministry of Food and Agriculture's Statistics, Research and Information Directorate (SRID)'s report *Agriculture in Ghana: Facts and Figures (2010)* (May 2011).
15. Once again, the detailed figures are in the already mentioned report *Agriculture in Ghana: Facts and Figures (2010)* (May 2011).
16. Boateng (6 December 2011).
17. *Ibid.*
18. *Ibid.*
19. *Ibid.*
20. Kunateh (16 August 2012).
21. *Ibid.*
22. Akli (12 August 2012).
23. Curnow (15 December 2010).
24. UN Integrated Regional Information Network (21 February 2000).
25. See http://www.njeitimah-outlook.com/google2133a7d8887d49e9.html (accessed 21 Agust 2012).
26. Timah (20 June 2007).
27. Anonymous (20 June 2007). The "Great Game" originally referred to the colonial competition between Russia and Great Britain for supremacy in

Central Asia. It became a popular term through Rudyard Kipling's colonial novel *Kim* (1901).
28 GNA (15 March 2006).
29 The full list reads: Afex Oil (Ghana) Ltd, Afren Plc, Aker ASA, Ati Petroleum ATIP, Atlas, British Borneo Oil and Gas Ltd, Challenger Minerals (Ghana) Ltd, Chemu Power Ltd, Chevron Nigeria Ltd, E.O. Group, Eni Ghana Exploration and Production Ltd, Eternit, Oranto Petroleum International Ltd, Gasop Oil Ghana Ltd, Saltpond Offshore Producing Company Ltd SOPCL, Ghana National Petroleum Corporation, GNPC, Hess Ghana Ltd, Kosmos Energy Ghana HC, Lukoil Overseas, Lushann, Mitsui E&P, Ghana Keta Ltd, Modec-Itochu, Nigerian National Petroleum Corporation NNPC, Oando, Sabre Oil & Gas Holdings Ltd, Anadarko WCTPC, Saipem, SBG, Shell SPDC, STG, Stone Energy, Tap Oil (Ghana) Ltd, Tullow Ghana Limited, Vanco Energy, Vitol Upstream (Ghana) Ltd, Volta River Authority Ghana, West African Gas Pipeline Company Ltd WAPGCO, Young Energy Prize YEP. See Cristeal (2006).
30 GNA (4 April 2003).
31 See http://eiti.org/eiti (accessed 30 August 2012).
32 Daniel (8 July 2009).
33 Odoi-Larbi (6 January 2012).
34 Osabutey (7 July 2011).
35 see Transparency International (2012a), (2012b).
36 Kunateh (23 April 2012).
37 Kunateh (8 August 2012). The article quotes an anonymous CNN report entitled "Attacks on Chinese. Too Sad!" of 2 August 2012, http://ireport.cnn.com/docs/DOC-823976 (accessed 30 August 2012).
38 See Anonymous (15 May 2012).
39 Akoto (31 January 2012).
40 Onumah (1 June 2012).
41 Pseudonymous response to Onumah (1 June 2012).
42 An example of the latter is Ensor (12 February 2000), which even sports the son of a former colonial administrator in Ghana as its author.

Bibliography

Akli, Emmanuel: "Dark Clouds Hang over Ghana's Gas", *The Chronicle*, 12 August 2012, <http://ghanaian-chronicle.com/?p=46838>, accessed 21 August 2012.

Akoto, Akwasi A. Afrifa: "Nkrumah Would Have Rejected 'China's Gift To Africa'", *The Chronicle*, 31 January 2012, <http://ghanaian-chronicle.com/?p=41401>, accessed 21 August 2012.

Anonymous: "Plundering Africa!!!", *GhanaWeb*, 20 June 2007, <http://www.ghanaweb.com/GhanaHomePage/NewsArchive/artikel.php?ID=125882&comment=2953112#com>, accessed 21 August 2012.

Anonymous: "When Graduates Cry for Jobs", *The Chronicle*, 15 May 2012, <http://ghanaian-chronicle.com/?p=44431>, accessed 21 August 2012.

Boateng, Clement: "Foreign Agro-Investors Eye BA", *The Chronicle*, 6 December 2011, <http://ghanaian-chronicle.com/?p=39041>, accessed 21 August 2012.

Central Intelligence Agency: "Africa. Ghana", *The World Factbook*, 24 August 2012a, <https://www.cia.gov/library/publications/the-world-factbook/geos/gh.html>, accessed 30 August 2012.

---: "Europe. Germany", *The World Factbook*, 24 August 2012b, <https://www.cia.gov/library/publications/the-world-factbook/geos/gm.html>, accessed 30 August 2012.

Curnow, Robyn: "Ghana's Oil Discovery. Blessing or Curse?", *CNN*, 15 December 2010, <http://business.blogs.cnn.com/2010/12/15/ghanas-oil-discovery-blessing-or-curse/>, accessed 21 August 2012.

Cristeal: "Ghana Oil and Gas Map Concessions Blocks. Soft Edition", *Africa Oil & Gas*, 2006, <http://www.africa-oil-gas.com/ghana_oil_and_gas_map_concessions_blocks_-_soft_edition-1444-1-2-c.html>, accessed 21 August 2012.

Daniel, Cachu: Untitled Post, *Center for Global Development*, 8 July 2009, <http://blogs.cgdev.org/globaldevelopment/2009/07/obama-right-to-highlight-ghana%E2%80%99s-success-but-will-oil-be-the-spoiler.php>, accessed 21 August 2012.

Ensor, Patrick: "Remains of the Day", *The Guardian*, 12 February 2000, <http://www.guardian.co.uk/travel/2000/feb/12/ghana?INTCMP=SRCH>, accessed 21 August 2012.

Ghana Government Portal: "Ghana at a Glance", *Government of Ghana*, 2012, <http://www.ghana.gov.gh/index.php/about-ghana/ghana-at-a-glance>, accessed 21 August 2012.

GhanaWeb: "The Country Ghana", *GhanaWeb*, 2012, <http://www.ghanaweb.com/GhanaHomePage/country_information/>, accessed 21 August 2012.

GNA: "Lushann-Eternit Apologises", *Modern Ghana*, 4 April 2003, <http://www.modernghana.com/news/33282/1/lushann-eternit-apologises.html>, accessed 21 August 2012.

---: "Nine Companies in Oil Business", *Modern Ghana*, 15 March 2006, <http://www.modernghana.com/news/96699/1/nine-companies-in-oil-business.html>, accessed 21 August 2012.

Kunateh, Masahudu Ankiilu: "Ghana to Rake in One Billion Dollars from Gas Annually", *The Chronicle*, 23 April 2012, <http://ghanaian-chronicle.com/?p=43911>, accessed 21 August 2012.

---: "Ghana Leads FMCG Investments in Africa", *The Chronicle*, 27 June 2012, <http://ghanaian-chronicle.com/ghana-leads-fmcg-investments-in-africa/>, accessed 21 August 2012.

---: "Ghana among World's 10 Worst Economies", *The Chronicle*, 28 June 2012, <http://ghanaian-chronicle.com/ghana-among-worlds-10-worst-economies/>, accessed 21 August 2012.

---: "China Friendship Union Worried over Attacks on Chinese", *The Chronicle*, 8 August 2012, <http://ghanaian-chronicle.com/?p=46695>, accessed 30 August 2012.

---: "Trade between Ghana and India Doubles", *The Chronicle*, 16 August 2012, <http://ghanaian-chronicle.com/?p=46971>, accessed 21 August 2012.

Ministry of Food and Agriculture, Republic of Ghana: "Agric Facts and Figures", *Publications*, 2011, <http://mofa.gov.gh/site/?page_id=6032>, accessed 21 August 2012.

Ministry of Food and Agriculture; Statistics, Research and Information Directorate: *Agriculture in Ghana. Facts and Figures (2010)*, May 2011, <http://mofa.gov.gh/site/wp-content/uploads/2011/10/AGRICULTURE-IN-GHANA-FF-2010.pdf>, accessed 21 August 2012.

Moss, Todd & Lauren Young: "Saving Ghana from Its Oil. The Case for Direct Cash Distribution", *Working Papers* 186, Center for Global Development, 2009, <http://EconPapers.repec.org/RePEc:cgd:wpaper:186>, accessed 21 August 2012.

Odoi-Larbi, Stephen: "840 Ghanaians Employed in Oil & Gas Sector", *The Chronicle*, 6 January 2012, <http://ghanaian-chronicle.com/?p=44976>, accessed 21 August 2012.

Onumah, Peter M.: "Don't Sell Africa Back into Slavery", *The Chronicle*, 1 June 2012, <http://ghanaian-chronicle.com/?p=44888>, accessed 21 August 2012.

Osabutey, Phyllis D.: "EPA is Weak in Monitoring Foreign Investors", *The Chronicle*, 7 July 2011, <http://ghanaian-chronicle.com/?p=28840>, accessed 21 August 2012.

Timah, Njei M.: "Discovery of Oil in Ghana. Is Kufuor Naive?", *GhanaWeb*, 20 June 2007, <http://www.ghanaweb.com/GhanaHomePage/NewsArchive/artikel.php?ID=125882>, accessed 21 August 2012.

Transparency International: "Ghana", *Corruption by Country / Territory*, 2012a, <http://transparency.org/country#GHA>, accessed 21 August 2012.

---: "Italy", *Corruption by Country / Territory*, 2012b, <http://transparency.org/country#ITA>, accessed 21 August 2012.

UN Integrated Regional Information Network: "Oil Discovered in Western Region", *GhanaWeb*, 21 February 2000, <http://www.ghanaweb.com/GhanaHomePage/NewsArchive/artikel.php?ID=9490>, accessed 21 August 2012.

Watkins, Simon: "Taking Stock. Bright Future for Africa's Dark Continent", *Mail Online*, 25 September 2010, <http://www.dailymail.co.uk/money/article-1315218/TAKING-STOCK-Bright-future-dark-continent-Africa.html>, accessed 21 August 2012.

Susanne Gehrmann (Berlin)

Re-Writing War in Contemporary Nigerian Fiction. From Biafra to Present Times

1. Introduction

The remembrance and representation of violence has been a dominant topic in African literature in English since its beginnings. Slavery, colonial violence, post-colonial dictatorship and wars as well as structural violence due to gender, class and ethnic issues have been on the forefront of writing. Authors from Nigeria, Africa's biggest nation,[1] have contributed substantially to all of these fields, be it the critique of colonialism's inherent violence against African cultures, beginning with such classics as Chinua Achebe's novel *Things Fall Apart* (1956) or Wole Soyinka's play *Death and the King's Horseman* (1975) or the genre of prison writing. This genre 'flourished' under the diverse Nigerian dictatorial regimes between the 1960s and the 1990s, ranging from such prominent examples as Wole Soyinka's *The Man Died: Prison Notes* (1972) to the recent *Prison Stories* by Helon Habila (2000) and his novel *Waiting for an Angel* (2003) up to Chris Abani's poems in *Kalakuta Republic* (2000).

The 20th century saw a large number of violent events in what was colonial Nigeria before 1960 and has been the Federal Republic of Nigeria since then. Yet, it is the Nigerian Civil War from 1967 to 1970, better known as the Biafra War, which has remained the most prominent topic of Nigerian literature until today. This dramatic event shook the young postcolonial state of Nigeria. Its traumata of a split nation, ethnic division, merciless battles and immense suffering of the civilian population in the East are still part of Nigeria's collective memory. An enormous body of literary and testimonial texts have dealt with the Nigerian Civil War since 1970. It is a "Harvest from Tragedy", as Chinyere Nwahunanya aptly entitled an essay collection on this war literature in 1996. In her recent study *Gender Palava. Nigerian Women Writing War*, Marion Pape now estimates the corpus to be "well over a hundred and fifty works encompassing almost every literary genre",[2] with roughly one third of the production contributed by women writers[3] and a clear domination of Igbo[4] authors.

Interestingly, after 2000, young Nigerian writers of the diaspora have been creating a new boom of the topic of war in literature. This generation, born in the 1960s and 1970s, knows about the Nigerian Civil War through family stories, historical accounts and literary narratives. The recent civil wars in Nigeria's neighbouring countries Liberia (1989-1996, 1999-2003), Sierra Leone (1991-2002) and Ivory Coast (2002-2007, since 2010) have also shaped their perception. Therefore, they refer to Biafra as well as to other theatres of war, both contemporary and historical. This essay focuses on the novels by the diasporic third-generation Nigerian authors Uzodinma Iweala, Chris Abani, Biyi Bandele, Chimamanda Ngozi Adichie and Helon Habila. I will consider in particular the perspective of children and young adolescents on the war, a narrator frequently used by the authors, as well as language and the contribution to the renegotiation of history through fiction. In this respect, Ken Saro-Wiwa's *Sozaboy* (1985) is an important founding text, to which the younger authors refer frequently by means of intertextual responses. Therefore, I will start with this novel before turning to the texts published after 2000. In terms of genre, I distinguish roughly between short novels in form of monologues, in which the character of a child soldier is used as a first-person narrator, and historical novels which employ a more complex set of characters and perspectives to rewrite history.

2. In Monologue. Small Soldiers' Voices

With regard to recent narrative reconstructions of the Nigerian Civil War as well as of the New Wars[5] in Africa, the child soldier has emerged as a major literary persona. It is a new archetypical figure in African writing which deals with trauma and recent history through individual stories.[6] This new archetype replaces, at least to some extent, the dictator whose career in literature started in the 1970s and went on through the 1980s and 1990s in different regions of the continent. In Nigeria, the dictator has especially been a prominent figure in poetry.[7]

Through the shift from the dictator to the child soldier, a shift from the embodied centre of power to its margins takes place. 'Small soldiers', as they are aptly termed in West African Englishes, are victims who become culprits; they are ambivalent, suspended between innocence and guilt. The novelists try to turn the unspeakable violence perpetrated on and by children into narration. Through the form of the monologue of an allegorical child soldier they symbolically give a voice to the otherwise often voiceless marginal figures of war. The naive, childish voices of small soldiers in literature allow for an especially effective uncovering of the absurdity of war. And yet, even as they unveil 'unspeakable things', the uncertainty and unreliability of those voices challenge the very possibility of representing violence and trauma through literary texts.

In Nigerian civil war literature, Ken Saro-Wiwa's *Sozaboy. A Novel in Rotten English* (1985) stands out as the seminal text which uses the monologue of a traumatised boy soldier, caught between childhood and adulthood, for the first time. As the subtitle of the novel suggests, it is a text, which develops a specific language; a text, indeed, which questions the possibilities of language to represent the reality of war through a marginalised young soldier. More recently Uzodinma Iweala and Chris Abani have rewritten this form with *Beasts of No Nation* (2005) and *Song for Night* (2007) respectively. All three texts point to the difficulties of human communication and interrogate the standard use of language. The specificity of the subgenre of the small soldier's monologue resides in this questioning of language in relation to power structures and the politics of representation through one subjective perspective: that of the lonely figure of the war child who is coming to voice.

2.1 Ken Saro-Wiwa's Sozaboy *as a Founding Text. Postcolonial Language and War*

Written and published fifteen years after the Nigerian Civil War and fifteen years before the boom of the New War literature, Ken Saro-Wiwa's protagonist Mene, nicknamed *Sozaboy* (soldier boy in Pidgin

English) is in fact the first small soldier narrator in Nigerian literature. Saro-Wiwa, himself a witness of the Nigerian Civil War,[8] chose a fictive setting for his novel, which as such becomes a more universal representation of war. *Sozaboy* undoubtedly offers a prominent example not only of the new literatures in English, but of a new English in literature: a perfect illustration of the postcolonial double process of language abrogation and appropriation.[9] Saro-Wiwa explains the specific language code which he even inscribes into the subtitle of his novel in his "Author's Note":

> Sozaboy's language is what I call 'rotten English', a mixture of Nigerian pidgin English, broken English and occasional flashes of good, even idiomatic English. This language is disordered and disorderly. Born of a mediocre education and severely limited opportunities, it borrows words, patterns and images freely from the mother-tongue and finds expression in a very limited English vocabulary. To its speakers, it has the advantage of having no rules and no syntax. It thrives on lawlessness, and is part of the dislocated and discordant society in which Sozaboy must live, move and have not his being.[10]

Drawing heavily on Pidgin structures and vocabulary (which is translated in a glossary at the end of the text) as well as on colloquial Nigerian English, the self-defined 'rotten English' is close to certain Nigerian language registers, but after all it is also a carefully constructed literary language,[11] as "no one in Nigeria actually speaks or writes like this".[12] This language reflects the complex sociolinguistic situation of diglossia in the multilingual setting of postcolonial societies, such as Nigeria. *Sozaboy* uses an interlanguage[13] that mediates between silenced local African languages and the unreachable British standard, called "big big English" with "fine fine grammar"[14] by the narrator. Diglossia is obviously linked to power structures. Standard English, as used by politicians, military leaders, media and the economic elite in the text, excludes the majority of the population from participation. The protagonist, who will join the army out of social pressure, never really understands what the war is about, because the ideological discourses on the war are in the official language, which remains out of his reach. Structural linguistic violence of a postcolonial society and the war's acts of violence thus come together in Mene's monologue.

Confronted with the terror of war, as both victim and perpetrator, Sozaboy tries to desert, but accidentally changes sides. This does not really matter because he lacks any identification with one or the other party of the war. Instead, he internalises the resigned catchphrase 'War is War', a recurrent leitmotif in the text: "the otherwise circular statement captures the foolishness and bestiality of war", as Chijoke Uwasomba put it.[15] Furthermore, Sozaboy's resigned acceptance of the war motto "To kill or to be killed. I will not forget that one at all",[16] stresses the vicious circle of violence. The effects of war on the body, psyche and mind of the young combatant drive him also to recognise the acceleration of his maturation: "I begin to know that after all I will not be small boy again."[17] But *Sozaboy* is not a bildungsroman, at least not in the classic sense of coming of age and acquiring an identity through education. If the experience of war slowly changes Sozaboy's naive, childish attitude, the situation does not allow him to grow into an adult person. On the contrary, at the end of the novel, his very humanity is being denied. When he comes back to his destroyed hometown where his family died, people believe that he is a ghost and chase him away. This pessimistic image drastically underlines the destructive effects of war.

2.2   Outspoken Violence in Recent Rewritings of War

Following the pattern established by Ken Saro-Wiwa, the link between language as a marker of social status and power in postcolonial societies and the role of the subaltern small soldier in warfare in a novel, that creates the effect of an unreliable confession, comes up again in the recent novels by Chris Abani and Uzodinma Iweala. The concern with language and the motif of the loss of humanity through war are major features of their texts as well although they chose different stylistic and narrative strategies.

It is remarkable that the monologic novels are relatively short: *Sozaboy* has 187 pages, *Song for Night* 158 pages and *Beasts of No Nation* 142 pages only. The monologue of one first-person narrator, constructed as the voice of a traumatised child with a limited educational background[18] is an effective narrative strategy. The suspense created by the perspective and language of Iweala's and Abani's protagonists is carefully built up through a series of intense actions and is oriented towards an ambivalent open ending before the reader can become wary of the style.

In how far do Iweala and Abani as Nigerian diasporic authors in the United States who write on child soldiers after 2000 refer to *Sozaboy*? In fact, both form and content of their texts show several intertextual links with Saro-Wiwa's novel. Beyond the already mentioned concern with language and the form of the monologue, there are several other motifs present in all three texts: the ambivalence of the child/young adult who is a victim and a perpetrator at the same time, the loss of innocence as well as of faith (in the sense of religious faith as well as of faith in humanity in general) and the important figure of a loving and caring mother.

In *Beasts of No Nation*, Iweala chooses an unnamed setting, which can stand in as a *mise en abyme* for any war situation, just as Ken Saro-Wiwa did in *Sozaboy*, whereas Abani's setting is explicitly the Nigerian Civil War from the perspective of a boy fighting for Biafra.[19] *Sozaboy* has always been read as referring to the Biafra War as seen by the ethnic minorities of the Nigerian middle belt because of the historical eye-witness position of Saro-Wiwa. Iweala, however, includes direct references to Igbo culture into his text which are more obviously reminiscent of Biafra.

As to the representation of violence, both Iweala and Abani go far beyond Saro-Wiwa's picturing of killings and physical harm. Nightmarish scenes of torture, dismembering, rape and hacking to death of civilians are prominent in the texts. Once caught in the spiral of violence, the children, often drugged, experience their power through violence as a form of ecstasy, an irrational folly that compensates their own trauma as abducted children and their powerlessness in the military hierarchy. However, scenes of violence, experienced as victims, seen as witnesses or perpetrated in their own role as war machines, haunt the memories of the protagonist-narrators. Furthermore, they are much younger than Mene in *Sozaboy* who was rather close to eighteen: Iweala's Agu is about ten, and Abani's My Luck narrates from the perspective of a now fifteen-year-old boy who started fighting at the age of twelve. Without doubt, both texts are impressive literary attempts to give a voice to child soldiers and to give a language to their war traumata. This does not mean that fiction can speak for 'real' child soldiers or even represent their experiences adequately. Rather, fiction attempts to contribute to a better understanding of situations of political and/or social crisis, moments of extreme violence and trauma through creative imaginations about what could be the inner landscape of war children, the latter being symbolic figures for the breakdown of human values in general. In so far, the link to the history of internal African wars is not that fiction can be considered as source material about wars, but rather that fiction can help to rework violence by means of symbolic narrations. Within these narrations, the trauma of individual characters represents a collective trauma, especially in the ambivalent figure of the small soldier who combines both the most vulnerable and the most aggressive parts of society.

2.2.1 The Language of Trauma in Iweala's Beasts of No Nation

Iweala's title *Beasts of No Nation* quotes a Fela Kuti song from 1989. Kuti himself took the line from Chinua Achebe's *No Longer at Ease* (1960) where it refers to the wandering protagonist, but in the song lyrics the beasts are explicit metaphors of postcolonial African dictators. While shifting from the bestiality of dictatorships to other forms of bestiality in war and especially those perpetuated by children as fighters, the title indicates the correlations between different levels of structural and physical violence in postcolonial Africa. If the 'new beasts' are of 'no nation', the title suggests at the same time that the project of postcolonial nation-building, so dear to the generation of Achebe, has failed because it generates wars that even bestialise children, those who are usually considered the future of each nation.[20]

On the time level, the narration in *Beasts of No Nation* is in the first place progressive and starts with the forced recruitment of the narrator, Agu, who then goes on to narrate his experiences during the war, crisscrossed by flashbacks into childhood memories. After an ellipsis, which can be associated with traumatic amnesia, in the last chapter the boy is in a refugee camp where both a catholic priest and an American psychologist try to make him speak out about the war. Whilst the communication with the priest fails completely and the dialogue with the white American woman remains superficial, it is the text as a whole which offers the expected confession to us as readers, and if not a psychoanalytic 'talking cure', it is at least a coming to voice of the narrator.

Iweala rewrites Saro-Wiwa's experiment with a new form of English by turning references to popular Nigerian English even more into fiction. The use of reduplications of adjectives and verbs and the use of onomatopoeia are prominent in both texts. However, the most outstanding rupture of Standard English grammar in Iweala is the overall use of the present progressive tense. This gives the text a touch of immediacy, even breathlessness. While the use of reduplications and the preference of the progressive tense reflect tendencies in Nigerian pidgin, the novel is a much easier read for an international audience than *Sozaboy* ever was. Strikingly, Iweala does not use lexical references to Pidgin or African languages.[21] Therefore, Nigerian reviewers have criticised Iweala as unauthentic and as a diasporic outsider to Nigerian realities. But can authenticity, if it exists at all, be measured in a literary text? Does it have to function as a mere mirroring of empirical – linguistic or historical – material in literary texts? Chimamanda Ngozi Adichie's expression "emotional truth",[22] which she uses for her own writing about Biafra, can very well be applied here. Iweala's literary language, especially the use of tense, obviously creates powerful effects such as speed, drama, emotional intimacy with the protagonist and a feeling of timeless absurdity, as "all actions seem to be continuously ongoing, interminable".[23] Despite all the dramatic outer action, the text focuses on the inner perspective of Agu. As an example of how this perspective and the language work together, I quote from the scene in which the boy will be forced to kill for the first time:

> KILL HIM NOW! I am starting to crying and I am starting to shaking. And in my head I am shouting NO! NO! NO! But my mouth is not moving and I am not saying anything. And I am thinking if I am killing killing then I am just going to hell so I am smelling fire and smoke and it is harding to breath, so I am just standing there crying crying, shaking shaking, looking looking.[24]

As in this quotation, the dialectics of silence and speaking are an important motif throughout the text. As forceful as its own language is, *Beasts of No Nation* is actually also a story about the loss of human language "as the author explores a child's ability to articulate or respond to the terror and trauma of war".[25] Several traumatised child soldiers lose their capacity of speech; in general the soldiers do not speak to each other, but rather yell orders and curses; whilst during the killings, their cynical laughter compensates for the horror of their actions.

Furthermore, beyond the title, there are many more animal metaphors as well as similes in the text which implement a menacing fauna as key element of the text. Mosquitoes, ants and other biting and stinging insects torture the protagonist throughout his journey through the war. They metaphorically represent the overwhelming presence of physical and psychological aggression and harm. Finally, Agu, who has not only been turned into a war machine, but has also been sexually abused by his commander, values the life of insects more than his own:

> When I am seeing all of this, all of this bombing bombing, killing killing, and dying dying, I am thinking to myself that now, as we are in the bush, only ant is still making and living. I am wishing I am ant.[26]

The protagonist's name Agu ("leopard") refers to an Igbo myth about twins: in this myth, the first twins on earth held magical powers and could change into any animal they wanted to. When one twin brother changed into an ox, the other twin brother who had changed into a leopard killed his brother. This myth, told by his grandfather, as well as the parallel Kain and Abel story from the bible, told by his mother, are part of Agu's early childhood memories. Both parables of fratricide prefigure Agu's role in the war, while the Igbo myth stresses the dehumanisation of murderers through its animal allegories. In the final lines of the novel, the protagonist realises that his environment perceives him as "some sort of beast or devil" or as "thing".[27] Like Sozaboy, he has lost his place as a respected human being. Given that it is unclear whether the rehabilitation process will succeed, the end of *Beasts of No Nation* is a depressingly open one: "Agu's continued ability to use language to negotiate what has happened to him is left ambivalent and ambiguous".[28]

2.2.2   From Muteness to Outspokenness. Chris Abani's Song for Night

In his short novel *Song for Night*, Chris Abani also dwells upon important questions of language and the dialectics of silencing and speaking out but he goes against the grain of Ken Saro-Wiwa's and Uzodinma Iweala's experimentation with new varieties of English. Although the text is written entirely in Standard English, the protagonist and first-person narrator My Luck refers to the language construction in literary texts as fiction per se when he explains:

> Of course if you are hearing any of this at all it's because you have gained access to my head. You would also know then that my inner-speech is not in English, because there is something atavistic about war that rejects all but the primal language of the genes to comprehend it, so you are in fact hearing my thoughts in Igbo. But we shan't waste time on trying to figure all that out because as I said before, time here is precious and not to be wasted on peculiarities, only on what is essential.[29]

Abani points out that the use of – whatever form of – English in African literatures always remains artificial to some extent, and especially so when it refers to an African environment where local languages are spoken as mother tongues. After all, African languages shape the thinking and communication of African communities. The irony of My Luck's statement when he says that we shall not waste time on language peculiarities surrenders to the postcolonial situation which imposed English as the national language of Nigeria – and after all as the international language of the book market. It also suggests that content is superior to formal language although language is an important subject in the text, albeit on a different level. As member of a special unit of children who were trained to detect landmines, the small soldier protagonist is literally mute. The dangerous job denies the children the right to speak or shout during the process, which is why their vocal cords have been cut. However, throughout the text, elements of the sign language the children of the special unit invent among themselves serve as headings of the many short chapters which considerably fragment the novel's structure. To give but some examples of the titles: "Mercy is Palm Turning Out from the Heart", "Love is a Backhanded Stroke to the Cheek" or "Dawn is Two Hands Parting Before the Face".[30] This sign language, put into written English (which the reader has in mind to be a fictional translation of thinking in Igbo) in form of verses, is poetic and even tender: it contrasts with the authoritarian language use of the warlords and with the overall atmosphere of violence, death, depression and guilt. As an alternative mode of communication, the sign language opens up spaces of friendship, hope, even love, during a merciless war.

Abani's title *Song for Night* can be read as a quotation of Friedrich Hölderlin's volume *Nachtgesänge* ("Night Songs") of 1805, a collection of melancholic poems on depression, the loss of faith and the longing for death. While *Song for Night* is less hermetic in content, an atmosphere of depression surrounds the protagonist My Luck who has been silenced during the war. The physical muteness is metonymic, given that it is the subordinate position of children in the military hierarchy that after all silences their expression of opinions, desires and emotions. On the other hand, My Luck's inner language – which constitutes the testimonial text we are offered as readers – is made up of both strong emotions and astonishingly mature, almost philosophical reflections. As in Agu's case, the soliloquising voice is subjugated to trauma which is reflected through the fragmented structure of the text. But instead of regression into an atavistic state (Agu's sentiment to become beastly), My Luck seems to become too wise for his age, bearing knowledge about cruelty and power into which a boy of his age should not yet have been initiated.

The basic plot in *Song for Night* is constructed around an odyssey of the autodiegetic narrator who lost his military unit during a battle and searches for his comrades while travelling down the river. The symbolic river which is crowded with dead bodies – the victims of war – is reminiscent of the Greek myth of Styx. My Luck's travel is a passage to death. Sometimes, when he is afraid to be discovered by the enemy, the boy also hides in the bush, a dense tropical rainforest. These spatial motifs establish an intertextual link with Joseph Conrad's *Heart of Darkness*: in both texts, the trip down the river and into the African rainforest leads to death and madness. Furthermore, Abani makes use of the metaphoric tension between light and darkness as well as between the dialectics of outward and inward 'darkness'. For example, in one passage the narrator is confronted with "an impenetrable darkness" of the landscape, which he immediately links to his 'darkest' anguishes: "There is something sinister about this particular darkness, as though every childhood fear I have is woven into its very fibre."[31]

Like Iweala's Agu, Abani's My Luck is a narrator who is haunted by the guilt he has accumulated through his war atrocities. During his lonely travel, memories of his own violent acts mix up with traumatic dreams. But in contrast to the ongoing childlike perspective in *Sozaboy* and *Beasts of No Nation*, Abani constructs a narrator who reaches a highly mature, almost metatextual consciousness about his own post-traumatic stress disorder. He comments on the pressure of his memories and how they intensify throughout the journey:

> This trek of mine is getting more and more ridiculous. I am mostly moving from one scene of past trauma to another, the distances between them, though vast, have collapsed to the span of a thought.[32]

However, the frontier between life and death, reason and madness becomes more and more permeable. At the end of the text, the boy, who finally climbs into the drastically metaphoric vehicle of a coffin for his trip down the river reunites with his beloved mother who was killed during the war. Madness and/or death through exhaustion become the only possibility for a tragic relief.

3. Recent 'Historical Novels'. From World War II to Biafra and into the 1990s

The Oxford Concise Dictionary of Literary Terms roughly defines the historical novel as

> a novel in which the action takes place during a specific historical period well before the time of writing (often one or two generations before, sometimes several centuries), and in which some attempt is made to depict accurately the customs and mentality of the period[33]

and Beckson/Ganz understand it as "a narrative which utilizes history to present an imaginative reconstruction of events, using either fictional or historical personages or both."[34] In my second group of texts, these classic definitions can be applied to Biyi Bandele's *Burma Boy* (2007) and Chimamanda Ngozi Adichie's *Half of a Yellow Sun* (2005). Both texts, although clearly fiction, tackle a specific historical period – World War II and the Nigerian Civil War respectively – referring in detail to historical settings, political facts and social circumstances. The third text, *Measuring Time* (2007) by Helon Habila, is a historical novel in a different sense. Habila mixes a fictional setting with historical references and foregrounds the metanarrative level of reflection on the possibilities and means of historical narration.

While Habila constructs his plot around the research of a young historian into his community's past, Bandele and Adichie have themselves done extensive research about the wars they are writing on. In his author's note at the end of the book, Bandele points out that he went to the archives in the Imperial War Museum, London, and he quotes some of the sources he used to nourish his writing: a series of English reports and memoirs on the World War II battles in Burma, in particular James Shaw's *The March Out* (1953) from whom he borrows the names and some of the manners of his characters Samanja Jamees Show and Farabiti Ali Banana. The other source, as important as the written texts from England, is the oral narrative of Bandele's father, who had fought in Burma for the British and told stories about this to his son at an early age. The novel is dedicated to the memory of the father and to the Royal West African Frontier Force. Chimamanda Ngozi Adichie did extensive historical and literary reading on the Nigerian Civil War. In the appendix to her novel she quotes no less than 31 titles: Nigerian novels and memoirs as well as historical and political analyses by African and Western scholars. While she puts this list at the end of her text, she inscribes her novel into the collective memory of her family through her opening dedication of the book.

> My grandfathers whom I never knew, Nwoye David Adichie and Aro-Nweke Felix Odigwe, did not survive the war. My grandmothers Nwabuodu Regina Odigwe and Nwamgbafor Agnes Adichie, remarkable women both, did.[35]

She strengthens this double bind further in her author's note when she quotes her father, her mother, her uncles and her cousin as the most inspiring narrators of Civil War stories as well as books by Chukwuemeka Ike, Flora Nwapa, Christopher Okigbo and Alexander Madiebo as sources for her middle-class Biafran setting and some secondary characters.[36]

3.1 Biyi Bandele's Rewriting of World War II from a Nigerian Perspective. Burma Boy

In the midst of a general boom of African literature on child soldiers and in a generation of Nigerian diasporic writers who turn again to the Civil War between the Nigerian central state and Biafra, the setting of Biyi Bandele's novel clearly stands out. He chooses the historical Burma of 1942/1943 and turns to the participation of West African colonial soldiers in World War II as a literary subject. His thirteen-year-old protagonist Ali Banana clearly shares the naive attitude towards war with Ken Saro-Wiwa's *Sozaboy* to whom the title *Burma Boy* of the English edition of the novel clearly alludes. Just like Mene, Ali Banana joins the army as a volunteer pretending to be older in order to be accepted. However, *Burma Boy* is composed as a third-person narration thus breaking with the monologue of the child soldier in favour of a historically much more detailed story and changing narrative perspectives through multiple focalisations.

In *Sozaboy* the war in Burma was present through the character of a veteran who bragged about his successful fight against "Hitla"[37] for which he was allegedly compensated. Although it later turns out that the heroic story was invented, Burma serves as a symbol of honour through warfare and motivates Mene to become a soldier. Through the focus on the real hardships of the battles in Burma, to some extent Bandele's novel fills in the elusive allusions to the war in *Sozaboy*.

Furthermore, Bandele reminds us that the phenomenon of child soldiers is of course not a recent African invention but that young men (and to a lesser extent women) under eighteen have been used widely in all kinds of wars all over the world, including the two World Wars. Whilst the Second World War is more often than not narrated as a scenario between the great powers of the time, Bandele foregrounds a Nigerian battalion which fights for "King Jiogi"[38] (the Pidgin form of King George) against the Japanese. The fact that the African soldiers do not understand the political and strategic reasons for the war reveals but one of the absurd dimensions of World War II and its entanglements with colonial policies. It becomes obvious that a postcolonial subversion of perspective takes place in the novel which also qualifies the text as a revisionist historical novel following the definition of Ansgar Nünning:

Revisionist historical novels are inspired by the wish to rewrite history, particularly from the point of view of those all too long ignored by traditional historiography, and to offer alternative histories. They often do so by relying heavily on multiple internal focalization, adopting the points of view of several character-focalizers whose limited perspectives project highly subjective views of history. These narrative strategies are not an end in themselves but rather serve as a means to challenge both hegemonic historiographic discourses and the generic conventions of the realist historical novel.[39]

While Africans are mentioned as brave combatants for the crown in the British sources used by Bandele, they obviously remain secondary characters, superficially painted colonial staff in the British-Japanese war. As Bandele reconstructs a neglected view on the events, his text functions as a corrective to British historical writing, a revisionist *and* postcolonial rewriting of history through fiction. The second campaign of the Burma War is re-narrated through the perspective of a small Nigerian unit, of which the formerly comic character of James Shaw's Ali Banana turns into the main focaliser and a rounded character. Strategically, the novelist chooses to privilege the perspective of the youngest and least experienced member of the unit, which allows him to enhance the dramatic aspect of the text and, for the amusement of the reader, to build in a series of linguistic as well as content-based misunderstandings between Ali Banana and his comrades.

Basically, the language in *Burma Boy* is Standard English, although Bandele introduces all the military denominations in Pidgin and uses extensive dialogues to point to the problem of language in a multilingual colonial setting. The members of the Nigerian battalion come from different regions of the crown colony and master English and Hausa (the lingua franca of the North which was also used in the army) to different degrees. They speak to each other in a mixture of Pidgin English and, according to their level of instruction, correct or imperfect English and Hausa (re-translated in the text). However, in spite of their differences, the troop members develop strong bounds of solidarity. The young men – most of them are between eighteen and twenty years old – care fatherly for the boy Ali Banana. In contrast to the novels on child soldiers analysed above, there is no place for violence or mistrust among the soldiers of the same side, and this extends even to the relations between the Nigerian and the white British troops.

Nevertheless, the structural violence of the military hierarchy becomes obvious when the colonial units are deliberately used for dangerous operations. At the end, the Nigerians fall victim to an ambush, and Ali Banana is the only survivor. The now fifteen-year-old boy kills one of his deadly injured friends with his rifle in order to shorten his suffering. The dead man, the first one Ali kills consciously and with regret, will haunt him as a ghost during his odyssey through the Burmese rainforest. Left all alone, he marches for several days through the forest before he gets back to the military camp. Ali Banana will finally lose his reason and his respect for death. Leeches attack his body: their parasitic sucking of the young body drastically symbolizes the effect of war. When he finally reaches the camp, Ali is physically and mentally altered to a degree that does not allow the soldiers to recognise him:

> He'd survived on a diet of leeches. The sentries took one look at the African singing loudly as he approached the wire and rushed to help him inside. His face was badly swollen and covered in leech bites. They couldn't make out who he was but they knew that any black man in Burma had to be one of them. All they could tell was that the man looked to be about fifty years old.[40]

The image of the mad man who eats the leeches that just sucked his blood stands as a pessimistic closure to the reproductive logic of violence and counter-violence inherent in all wars. Be it the insect metaphors as in *Beasts of No Nation* or the lonely travel through a hostile nature into madness and death as in *Song for Night*, several motifs of *Burma Boy* show its interconnection with other recent texts on small soldiers despite the different historical settings. Obviously, it is not only postcolonial and inner-African conflicts, which produce unspeakable experiences of children in war, but colonial wars and the two World Wars of the 20th century as well, which are dominated by the colonial powers. *Burma Boy* provokes a rethinking of the continuities between colonial violence, neocolonialism and violence in Africa today.

3.2 Twins in Times of War

Interestingly, two of the internationally most acclaimed young Nigerian writers, Chimamanda Ngozi Adichie and Helon Habila, chose a couple of twins as characters in their war novels with one of the siblings serving as protagonist and the other playing a decisive role for the structure and plot of the novel. In Adichie's *Half of a Yellow Sun* (2005), the story of the Biafran war unfolds around the twin sisters Olanna and Kainene. In Habila's *Measuring Time* (2007) the twin brothers Mamo and LaMamo are the protagonists in a novel which questions the possibility of writing history and addresses some of Africa's violent conflicts of the 1980s and 1990s.

Twins play a specific role in Nigerian cultures and especially in Igbo culture. The myth (for example employed in Iweala's novel) about their magical power that can turn into evil led to the practice of killing twin babies. In Chinua Achebe's classic *Things Fall Apart* (1956) this is one of the negative aspects of Igbo culture which eventually attracts parents of twins to the colonisers' religion and thus contributes to the breakdown of the pre-colonial cultural and political system.[41] Elleke Boehmer reads the featuring of twins in several contemporary Nigerian novels as a sign of Achebe's influence. While twins had to die in the world of Achebe's protagonist Okonkwo, in the world of his postcolonial offspring "these accursed twins crying in the bush, doomed to die, triumphantly if also ambiguously become the ebullient central characters of the novels".[42] But in both novels discussed here, one of the twins dies at the end (or at least disappears mysteriously). This may be read as a reference to the war context which "does not permit the twoness of the twins to last. One of the twins has, it seems, to be sacrificed to familial and national destiny".[43]

3.2.1 Entangled Lives and Voices. Chimamanda Ngozi Adichie's Rewriting of Biafra in Half of a Yellow Sun

Adichie, using smooth Standard English frequently enriched by expressive Igbo word and phrases,[44] re-narrates the early 1960s in Nigeria, the growing political and ethnic tension, and finally, in more detail, the war years 1967-1970. From chapter to chapter, the point of view changes through the subjective perspectives of three protagonists: Olanna, the second twin sister, her houseboy Ugwu and Richard, the British lover of the first twin sister Kainene. The twin sisters belong to the new Nigerian upper middle-class. While their parents got rich through business but lack formal education, the sisters studied for higher degrees in England. Olanna, the beautiful and romantically idealistic twin, becomes a lecturer in sociology at the University of Nsukka and lives with the politically active Odenigbo. When university and schools close down during the war, Olanna, moved by patriotic zeal, organises lessons for Biafran children. Kainene, presented as physically androgynous, is the more pragmatically orientated businesswoman, albeit cynical in her down-to-earth approach to life. Although she challenges their parents' lifestyle more openly than the harmony-seeking Olanna, she takes over the role of the male daughter[45] who expands the family's wealth. During the war, she will become the manager of a refugee camp before she disappears in an attempt to barter food supplies for the refugees across the frontier line. Although the twin sisters developed a certain distance since they grew up – which is painfully resented at least by Olanna – they are obviously tied together through a powerful link. Each of the characters has its qualities and shortcomings that the other one lacks but it is exactly through this opposition that the twins shine as "an allegorical pair"[46] of the possible attitudes to the fundamentally human questions of belonging, love and loyalty. Even the specific war traumata of both complement each other: while Olanna is haunted by her memory of a mother who carried the head of her killed daughter from northern to eastern Nigeria in a calabash, Kainene is equally traumatised by the image of her houseboy's body still running after a bomb had blown away his head. It is through sharing the pain that the otherwise estranged twins reunite again. But at the end of the novel, Kainene has not returned from her 'attack trade' and Olanna's efforts to retrieve her other half remain futile. On the one hand, this uncertain ending "force[s] the text to remain open and unsolvable, [as] questions of history, identity and community asked in the text remain in a constant state of negotiation".[47] On the other hand, it tragically reunites the twin motif with its roots in Achebe's early Igbo narrative: "regardless of her survival into adulthood, Kainene the twin has entered and been lost to the realm of ghosts, the Bad Bush or Forest populated with Deads that traditionally claim twins".[48] Adichie's didactic message that "war is evil"[49] manifests itself not least through the twin symbolism.

The two male focalisers of the narrative are closely linked to the twins and, as it turns out in the last third of the novel, through their common project to write a book about the atrocities of the Biafra war. In the early 1960s, Ugwu, an uneducated thirteen-year-old village boy, becomes the houseboy of Odenigbo, his unconventional master who integrates him fully into his household and cares for his schooling. When Olanna joins the house, Ugwu's admiration for her binds him even closer to Odenigbo. While the family manages to keep him during most of the war times, at one point Ugwe is caught by recruiters of the Biafran army and is made to serve as a soldier for some months before he is severely wounded. Not only does Ugwe's perspective allow the reader to see the often complicated love story between the protagonists Olanna and Odenigbo from a "most honest and clear-sighted view",[50] but Ugwe's strand of the story alone can count as a full-blown bildungsroman.[51] By the end of the novel, the formerly naive boy has turned into a serious, self-critical and politically conscious young man.

Richard, the gentle Briton who falls in love with Igbo art first and then with the twin Kainene, chooses Nigeria as his home and Biafra as his nation. The love between a white European and an Igbo woman in times of ethnic tension cuts across ideological borders of both Nigerians and expatriates. Richard is a journalist and an occasional researcher. Throughout the novel we see him struggle with his plan to write a book. Kainene burns his first manuscript on Igbo art, when Richard deceives her. The second manuscript is left behind and lost when Nigerian troops conquer Nsukka. During the war the book project develops into an eyewitness account of the Civil War, provisionally entitled *The World Was Silent When We Died* of which we can read several excerpts throughout the novel. However, in the last chapters, Ugwu equally starts to write about the war, and Richard, somewhat surprisingly, quits his project. It seems rather unconvincing[52] that Richard, who identified so thoroughly with the Biafran cause, suddenly surrenders to a position as an outsider declaring "[t]he war is not my story to tell, really".[53] However, as a postcolonial stance, it is symbolically important that the book project is handed over to Ugwu who is not only an 'authentic' Igbo but also a representative of the disadvantaged social classes finding a voice of their own. Similar to using the strong twin sisters to subvert

Achebe's twin motif, the final materiality of Ugwu's book can be read as a reversal of (fictional) colonial book projects. One example of such an endeavour is the colonial commissioner's plan at the end of *Things Fall Apart* to write a book about *The Pacification of the Primitive Tribes of the Lower Niger* including a chapter on Okonkwo, the defeated hero of the novel.[54] Throughout the text, it is Ugwu's narrative from the perspective of below, presenting a postcolonial, socially disadvantaged subject coming to voice, which endows this historical novel with a special revisionist dimension.

Interestingly, some critical notes have recently been added to the generally enthusiastic reception of *Half of a Yellow Sun* by Adichie, "one of the most talked about of world writers of today".[55] The author is praised by one critic for her ability to "reconcile or at least balance the competing demands of historicism and storytelling",[56] by others for her "Sense for History" and her aesthetic achievement.[57] The South African critic Brenda Cooper, however, blames Adichie for her extensive reference to violent action and her graphic description of war horrors.[58] It is true that all of *Half of a Yellow Sun*'s characters suffer from drastically horrid war traumata as those of Olanna and Kainene. Ugwu, during his time as a soldier, participates in a gang rape that is also represented in painful detail. This criticism suggests that texts which foreground war horrors participate in a discourse which stereotypically presents Africa as a continent of violence and Africans as the archaic, cruel Other. These charges could be easily brought against all the other novels analysed above, especially against those by Iweala and Abani. Interestingly, I have not come across any Nigerian critics who would criticise any of these texts for displaying exaggerated cruelty or for adding to the misrepresentation of Africa. In her remarkable article on "Human Rights, Child Soldier Narratives, and the Problem of Form" Maureen Moynagh clearly points to the dangerous complicity between the Western image of Africa as a place of evil and the popularity of child soldier's narratives, and yet she reads testimonial and fictional texts by African authors as an effective tool to promote human solidarity.[59] The positionality of who is speaking seems crucial here. Adichie herself has explained her urge to write on Biafra in several interviews. Of all arguments, her statement "because I grew up in the shadow of Biafra"[60] can count as representative for the whole generation of contemporary Nigerian writers, especially those with an Igbo family background

(Iweala, Abani, Bandele), which means that a vivid collective memory of the suffering during 1967-70 has been passed on to the then very young authors and to those not yet born.

3.2.2 *The Historian and the Soldier in Helon Habila's* Measuring Time

In Habila's *Measuring Time* war is but the background to a larger family story and a questioning of the narratives of history. In this novel, a double-voiced structure comes up with the twin brothers Mamo and LaMamo, born in 1965, who lose their mother early and grow up with their indifferent father in the fictive northern Nigerian village of Keti. In the late seventies, the Nigerian Civil War cuts into the consciousness of the boys through the return of their mentally disturbed uncle Haruna who fought against Biafra at the age of thirteen. Deeply traumatised, the uncle will finally commit suicide. But instead of comprehending this as a warning against the evils of war, the adolescent twins are deeply impressed by the respect that people pay to the ex-combatant and they plan to run away from home for the adventures of war.

> "We could be famous as soldiers", they told each other. And in their eager, fifteen year old minds they saw themselves on some distant battlefield, surrounded by dead bodies, some of which they had killed, and only themselves standing, masters of all they surveyed; and far away in the villages, which they had liberated from some evil tyrant, hidden by dusk and the smoke of battle, the women waited to welcome them with garlands. Then, after achieving fame and wealth, they'd return to Keti as living legends.[61]

This romanticised vision of war and the role of soldiers as heroes is reminiscent of *Sozaboy*: Mene's motivation to enrol for the war was the hope for fame, too, combined with the desire to impress women. Meanwhile, the dream of winning fame through war is quickly disrupted for Mamo, the older twin, who is ill with sickle-cell anaemia and fails to realise the flight. LaMamo succeeds to escape and, after having been refused by the Nigerian military because of his young age, becomes a mercenary in Chad. He enrols for military training in Libya where Mouammar Gaddafi and Charles Taylor personally encourage the young fighters. Consequently, LaMamo will fight in various West African conflicts of the 1980s and 1990s from Mali to Liberia. But the reader does not follow these 'adventures of war' closely. Rather, it is from the perspective of Mamo, who stays in Keti, that the novel's main story is narrated.

Often compelled to stay at home and even in bed because of his illness, Mamo develops into a voracious reader. Although his health does not allow him to finish his university studies in history properly he becomes a schoolteacher and a passionate chronicler of the local history of Keti. LaMamo sporadically sends letters from his various military missions which are entirely reprinted in the text. While Mamo's increasing knowledge turns him into an historian who will eventually start to publish articles in refereed journals,[62] the English used by LaMamo is affected by misspellings and grammatical errors which reveal his interrupted school career. However, these letters are an important structural element of the novel and link Mamo's research into African colonial history to the violent condition of present wars. The reflective, intellectual twin and the rude, combatant soldier twin show two opposite choices to live and act in contemporary (West) Africa. And yet, the allegory of the twins indicates that they incarnate just two sides of the same medal linked by a (meta)physical bond which cannot be broken. After all, to refer to the image of the allegorical Igbo myth once again, LaMamo does not turn into a leopard (perpetrator) and Mamo not into an ox (victim). Instead, both characters develop into mature, politically aware and critical personalities.

When the Mai (the local authority of Keti) asks Mamo to become his official biographer, Mamo first marvels at the project to rewrite the local history which had so far only been put to paper by an American missionary. In his *A Brief History of the Peoples of Keti*, the missionary depicts the community according to Hegel's master narrative on Africa as a formerly archaic, uncivilised entity without history and then concentrates on the Christian conversion he introduced. Habila, even more clearly than Adichie in her novel, alludes to Achebe's *Things Fall Apart*. Just as Achebe rewrote the history of a pre-colonial Igbo community and the arrival of colonialism through a Nigerian perspective, Mamo strives to rewrite the history of Keti through a (fictional) local perspective and to restore the dignity of his community. However, the 'writing back' project in Habila's plot does not function in the same way as for

Achebe's generation. The more Mamo researches into Keti's history, the more he learns about the corruption and collaboration of the local elite which used the British system of indirect rule to its own advantages. The corrupt system continues in the present: colonial structures are reproduced in postcolonial patterns. Indeed, as Vincent put it,

> Habila's counter-text uncovers how local authority masks and reiterates colonial assumptions of power, in effect re-enacting colonial stereotypes, even as he reduces colonial figures to the very sort of stereotypes their discourse constructed.[63]

Consequently, Mamo realises that he will not be able to write a glorious, dignified history of Keti as this would be a misleading idealisation. Instead of the planned authorial historical narrative he will write a book entitled *Lives and Times of Keti* which contains the biographies of many different inhabitants of the town: the powerful and the marginal, the rich and the poor, men and women. The Mai is no longer the focus of this history consisting of multiple stories. The novel thus suggests that an alternative rewriting of history must not only break with a colonial perspective on Africa but that it must also go beyond the perspective of the powerful political and economic elites. Therefore, following the revisionist model, Mamo inscribes the historical traces of common people and their different perspectives into his book. At the same time, he questions the very possibility of objective truth in historical narratives. He concludes that a participative, multi-voiced and orally based vision of the past through the genre of biography proves to be more important than a scholarly surveying and ordering of the past: "He'd talk with the people, go into their houses, into their hearts, to write about their secret desires and aspirations. [...] He didn't know if the result would be a true history; he didn't care."[64]

Measuring Time is by and large a novel which reflects on the possibilities to reconstruct the past and its connections with the present. In doing so, it questions the established model of historiography which tends to privilege the representatives of power. The metaphoric title suggests the protagonist's efforts to make sense of times gone by: the present continuous form of the verb underlines that this process of "measuring" is never finished. Through the importance of this strong metalevel of reflection the text stands out as a metahistorical novel for whose definition I will once again quote Nünning:

> Metahistorical novels represent significant innovations in the treatment of history as a literary theme because what they highlight is the process of historical reconstruction and the protagonists' consciousness of the past rather than a represented historical world as such. Instead of portraying a historical world on the diegetic level of the characters, metahistorical novels are generally set in the present but concerned with the appropriation, revision, and transmission of history. Largely focusing on the representation of consciousness and perception, [...] metahistorical novels typically explore how characters try to come to terms with the past.[65]

While LaMamo's war epistles help immensely to sharpen Mamo's political awareness, they also reveal the twin brother's development from a naive small soldier into a disillusioned veteran of wars. He learns to understand that as a mercenary he has never been a revolutionary but rather an abused element of absurd wars which serve the economic and political interests of a few African and Western profiteers. LaMamo becomes a mature adult who wants to fight against structural violence but, unlike his intellectual brother, his approach remains action-oriented. When LaMamo returns to Keti in 1994, there are riots which set Christians against Muslims in his home village. These religious outbursts are closely linked to the degrading social conditions of the people who live under the corrupt rule of the local elite. Spontaneously, LaMamo leads a revolt against the Mai, but is killed by the police who turn down the attack on the palace. Thus, tragically, the novel ends with a reference to one of Nigeria's latest bouts of violence: the conflicts between Christians and Muslims which are still acute in 2012. Ironically, it is the 'stronger' twin soldier who must die at the end of the novel and not the anaemic twin. As an historian in his own right, the latter works against amnesia and will also write down the story of his brother whose revolutionary heritage will not be lost thanks to his twin's act of narrative memory.

4. Conclusion

In the monological novels of *Sozaboy, Beasts of No Nation* and *Song for Night* the concern with language, although dealt with in a specific manner in each text, reflects the overall difficulty of finding an adequate form for expressing traumatic war experiences through literature as a space of negotiation. In these texts, varieties of linguistic, political and human disorder interact on the different levels of narration. At the same time, the concern with a literary rewriting of the immediate or recent history of wars through the voice of the symbolic figure of the child soldier points to the urgency to deal with violence and trauma in both local and global contexts. On the one hand, these figurative soliloquies are indeed striving to reach out to their readers, to move them emotionally and not least to show the essential fragility of moral values and human lives – not only in Africa. On the other hand, the more classically written historical novels *Burma Boy, Half of a Yellow Sun* and *Measuring Time* – 'classic' with respect to their language use, their fidelity to historical events and their dialogical third person narration – can count as didactic literary approaches to the themes of war. Each of them teaches a historical and moral lesson with regard to violent situations: World War II (Bandele), the Nigerian Civil War (Adichie) and contemporary West African conflicts (Habila). *Measuring Time* questions war, structural violence and the possibilities of historical narratives to come to terms with human experience which qualifies this text as a metahistorical novel. All three texts, rewrite war from a postcolonial perspective presenting an alternative point of view, i.e. African, local and/or 'from below'.

Notes

1   Its population is estimated to be 140,000 million.
2   Pape (2011: 2).
3   See Pape's "Nigerian Civil war Literature by Women – A Preliminary Checklist of Primary Sources" (2011: 158-161).
4   The Igbo are the dominant linguistic group in those eastern parts of Nigeria that split from the Federation as the state of Biafra in 1967; two successive

military coups in 1966 had led to ethnic violence against Igbo minorities in northern and western Nigeria. Nigeria counts over 250 ethnic groups, of which the Hausa/Fulani in the North, the Yoruba in the West and the Igbo in the East are the dominant ones.

5. In 1999, political theorist Mary Kaldor coined the term New Wars for those contemporary conflicts which can no longer be understood in terms of wars between nation states or civil wars with politically clearly distinguished groups. Rather, rebellion against an unsatisfying political and social situation, economic interests of various groups inside and outside the country (including Western agents), ethnic and/or religious conflicts intermingle and lead to complex wars which tend to last for many years. See also Münkler (2002).
6. After 2000, there has been a boom of testimonial texts as well as of fiction from both Anglophone and Francophone Africa and its diaspora which deal with child soldiers.
7. See the research of Sule Egya on the character of the dictator in political Nigerian poetry (2007, 2011).
8. See his memoir *On a darkling Plain: An Account of the Nigerian Civil War* (1989).
9. Ashcroft *et al.* (1989: 27-76).
10. Saro-Wiwa (2001: VII).
11. See Uwasomba (2010: 18-25).
12. Boyd (2001: III).
13. On the phenomenon of interlanguage in Europhone African writing see Zabus (2007).
14. Saro-Wiwa (2001: passim).
15. Uwasomba (2010: 22).
16. Saro-Wiwa (2001: 128).
17. *Ibid.* 164.
18. It must be mentioned that in Iweala's and Abani's texts the protagonists have a much more sophisticated educational background than Saro-Wiwa's Mene. The war interrupts their otherwise promising school careers and their religious education (Christian in the case of Agu, Muslim in the case of My Luck).
19. Abani already touched on the issue of Biafra in his first novel, *GraceLand* (2004) which is set in the 1970s. The novel's protagonist Elvis has a cousin who fought as a child soldier in the Civil War, is mentally disturbed and eventually becomes a professional killer.
20. Hawley offers the following reading: "The 'no nation' of the title [...] suggests that Iweala offers the best Biafran war novel to date by raising the

war above the specificities of the historical setting his family knows best, and implicitly comparing it to wars that have passed and that are ongoing, that share a common brutalization of the young" (2008: 22).

21 The only exception is his protagonist's name, Agu, which means leopard in Igbo.
22 Adichie: "In the Shadow of Biafra", appendix to *Half of a Yellow Sun* (2009b: 9).
23 Hron (2008: 41).
24 Iweala (2005: 23).
25 Hron (2008: 40).
26 Iweala (2005: 119).
27 *Ibid*. 142.
28 Krishnan (2010: 193).
29 Abani (2008: 11).
30 *Ibid*. 75, 49 and 35 respectively.
31 Abani (2008: 139).
32 *Ibid*.
33 Baldick (2004: 114).
34 Beckson & Ganz (1990: 110).
35 Adichie (2009a: 435).
36 *Ibid*. She quotes Chukwuemeka Ike's novel *Sunset at Dawn*, Flora Nwapa's novel *Never Again*, Christopher Okigbo's poetry in *Labyrinths* and Alexander Madiebo's memoir *The Nigerian Revolution and the Biafran War*.
37 Saro-Wiwa (2001: passim).
38 Bandele (2007: passim).
39 Nünning (2004: 7).
40 Bandele (2007: 216). The US-American edition of the novel was published as *The King's Rifle*.
41 For an extended reading of Achebe's novel, see Gohrisch's contribution to this volume.
42 Boehmer (2009: 145).
43 *Ibid*. 149.
44 Adichie's literary language with special reference to *Half of a Yellow Sun* was extensively analysed by Onuakaogu & Onyerionwu in chapter 8: "Adichie: The Igboness of Narrative" (2010: 261-302). Suffice it to say, that her use of Igbo enriches the text without putting its international readability into question.
45 Regarding the flexibility of gender roles in Igbo society, see Amadiume (1987).
46 Obumselu, Ben: "Introduction", in: Onukaogu & Onyerionwu (2010: 24).

47 Krishnan (2010: 190).
48 Boehmer (2009: 149).
49 Kehine (2009: 137).
50 Andrade (2011: 93).
51 Onukaogu & Onyerionwu (2010: 146-147, 161-173).
52 See also Brenda Cooper's criticism of the plot in her chapter "An Abnormal Ordinary" (2008: 146-147).
53 Adichie (2009a: 425).
54 Achebe (1985: 148).
55 Onukaogu & Onyerionwu (2010: 8).
56 Hodges (2009: 3).
57 See chapter one in Onukaogu & Onyerionwu (2010).
58 Cooper (2008: 139f.).
59 Moynagh (2011: 40-42, 54).
60 Interview quoted in Onukaogu & Onyerionwu (2010: 77).
61 Habila (2007: 55).
62 While an English journal, following the stereotypical colonial discourse on Africa, refuses his article, it is published by the historical journal of Makerere University in Uganda. Subsequently, Mamo starts a passionate intellectual correspondance with one of the professors there. See Vincent's comment on this postcolonial negotiation of scholarly discourse (2011: 43-44).
63 Vincent (2011: 42-43). In this article, Vincent convincingly reads Habila's novel through the lense of Homi Bhabha's concept of postcolonial mimicry and dwells upon intertexual links with Achebe.
64 Habila (2007: 358).
65 Nünning (2004: 8).

Bibliography

Abani, Chris: *Kalakuta Republic*, London, 2000.
---: *GraceLand*, New York, 2004.
---: *Song for Night*, New York, 2008. [first published in 2007]
Achebe, Chinua: *Things Fall Apart*; London, 1985. [first published in 1958]
Adichie, Chimamanda Ngozi: *For Love of Biafra*, Ibadan, 1998.
---: *Half of a Yellow Sun*, London, 2009a. [first published in 2006]
---: "In the Shadow of Biafra", appendix to *Half of a Yellow Sun*, London, 2009b, appendix, pp. 9-12. [first published in 2006]

Amadiume, Ifi: *Male Daughters, Female Husbands. Gender and Sex in an African Society*, London, 1987.

Andrade, Susan Z.: "Adichie's Genealogies. National and Feminine Novels", *Research in African Literatures* 42:2, 2011, 91-101.

Ashcroft, Bill, Gareth Griffiths & Helen Tiffin: *The Empire Writes Back*, London & New York, 1989.

Baldick, Chris: *Oxford Concise Dictionary of Literary Terms*, Oxford, 2004.

Bandele, Biyi: *Burma Boy*, London, 2007.

Beckson, Karl & Arthur Ganz: *Literary Terms. A Dictionary*, London, 1990.

Boehmer, Elleke: "Achebe and his Influence in some Contemporary African Writing", *Interventions* 11:2, 2009, 141-153.

Boyd, William: "Introduction". – In Ken Saro-Wiwa: *Sozaboy. A Novel in Rotten English*, New York, 2001, pp. I-V. [first published in 1994]

Cooper, Brenda: "An Abnormal Ordinary. Chimamanda Ngozi Adichie's *Half of a Yellow Sun*". – In B. C. (Ed.): *A New Generation of African Writers. Migration, Material Culture and Language*, Scottsville, 2008, pp. 133-150.

Egya, Sule E.: "'Every Poem Becomes Dangerous'. The Aesthetics of Resistance in Contemporary Nigerian Poetry". – In Jaydeep Sarangi (Ed.): *Presentations of Postcolonialism in English. New Orientations*, New Delhi, 2007, pp. 95-106.

---: "Art and Outrage. A Critical Survey of Recent Nigerian Poetry in English", *Research in African Literatures* 42:1, 2011, 49-67.

Habila, Helon: *Prison Stories*, Lagos, 2000.

---: *Waiting for an Angel*, London, 2003.

---: *Measuring Time*, London, 2007.

Hawley, John C.: "Biafra as Heritage and Symbol. Adichie, Mbachu, and Iweala", *Research in African Literatures* 39:2, 2008, 15-26.

Hodges, Hugh: "Writing Biafra. Adichie, Emecheta and the Dilemmas of Biafran War Fiction", *Postcolonial Text* 5:1, 2009, 1-13.

Hron, Madelaine: "Oran a-azu nwa. The Figure of the Child in Third-Generation Nigerian Novels", *Research in African Literatures* 39:2, 2008, 27-48.

Iweala, Uzodinma: *Beasts of No Nation*, London, 2005.

Kaldor, Mary: *New and Old Wars. Organized Violence in a Global Era*, Cambridge & Stanford, 1999.

Kehinde, Ayo: "The Muse as Peace-Maker. The Moral Burden of Conflict Management and Resolution in Nigerian Literature", *The African Symposium* 9:2, 2009, 126-142.

Krishnan, Madhu: "Biafra and the Aesthetics of Closure in the Third Generation Nigerian Novel", *Rupkhata Journal on Interdisciplinary Studies in Humanities* 2:2, 2010, 185-195.

Moynagh, Maureen: "Human Rights, Child Soldier Narratives, and the Problem of Form", *Research in African Literatures* 42:4, 2011, 39-59.

Münkler, Herfried: *Die neuen Kriege*, Reinbek bei Hamburg, 2002.

Nünning, Ansgar: "Where Historiographic Metafiction and Narratology Meet. Towards an Applied Cultural Methodology", *Style* 38:3, 2004, 352-375. [<http://findarticles.com/p/articles/mi_m2342/is_3_38/ai_n27846938/pg_15/?tag=content;col1>, accessed 25 June 2012]

Nwahunanya, Chinyere (Ed.): *A Harvest from Tragedy. Critical Perspectives on Nigerian Civil War Literature*, Owerri, 1996.

Onukaogu, Allwell Abalogu & Ezechi Onyerionwu: *Chimamanda Ngozi Adichie. The Aesthetics of Commitment and Narrative*, Ibadan, 2010.

Pape, Marion: *Gender Palava. Nigerian Women Writing War*, Trier, 2011.

Saro-Wiwa, Ken: *On a Darkling Plain. An Account of the Nigerian Civil War*, Port Hartcourt, 1989.

---: *Sozaboy. A Novel in Rotten English*, New York, 2001. [first published in 1985]

Soyinka, Wole: *The Man Died. Prison Notes*, London, 1972

---: *Death and the King's Horseman*, London, 1975.

Uwasomba, Chijioke: "War, Violence and Language in Ken Saro-Wiwa's *Sozaboy*", *African Journal of History and Culture* 2:2, 2010, 18-25.

Vincent, Kerry: "(Re)Forming Stereotypes. Modes of Mimicry in Helon Habila's *Measuring Time*", *Journal of Postcolonial Writing* 47:1, 2011, 42-51.

Zabus, Chantal: *The African Palimpsest. Indigenization of Language in the West African Europhone Novel*, Amsterdam & Atlanta, 2007.

Anke Bartels (Potsdam)

Remembering the Past, Changing the Present. Anglophone Women Playwrights from West and South Africa

1. Introduction

Theatre practitioners and critics have rightly claimed that theatre is the most political of all art forms. This holds especially true when plays are performed as part of community endeavours or as theatre-for-development because this may draw a considerable number of spectators who might otherwise not come into contact with theatre plays at all. But what is hardly ever mentioned in this context is the fact that theatre is also the most male-dominated of all art forms.

While male African playwrights like Nobel Laureate Wole Soyinka are at least discussed comparatively often in the context of postcolonial drama, African female playwrights have for the most part remained invisible. This is partly due to the special challenges they face, i.e. the sometimes unwelcome public attention connected to the medium as well as the time-consuming work during rehearsals, but also to publishing houses which are not very receptive where creative women's writing is concerned. Women were not always relegated to the margins in the performing arts, though, because, as Jane Plastow states, their exclusion seems to be a post-contact phenomenon induced by the effects of colonialism:

> Women have struggled to be heard in the world of modern African theatre. Traditionally, they had secure roles as dancers, singers and story-tellers within a community context. However, as theatre and performance became professionalised and commercialised, and as control often came to lie in the hands of literate elites, women all too often lost their equal standing with men in the realm of performance.[1]

Nonetheless, African women playwrights have produced a considerable number of plays and continue to do so. These plays are not produced in a vacuum and respond not only to male texts but also envisage new roles for women while constituting a distinctive voice within their local communities as well as when performed to wider audiences. Before approaching these texts, it is necessary to explore briefly how African theatre developed. Of course, this cannot be satisfactorily done for a whole continent populated by numerous peoples with widely differing languages and cultures. Yet, one fact that is shared across most parts of sub-Saharan Africa is the paucity of sources where pre-contact theatre is concerned as there are simply no written texts. Nonetheless, some form of theatre definitely played a role in most sub-Saharan cultures as the

> roots of theatre in Africa are ancient and complex and lie in areas of community festival, seasonal rhythm and religious ritual as well as in the work of court jesters, travelling professional entertainers and storytellers.[2]

This theatre was, of course, performed in indigenous languages for specific audiences in specific localities but almost always included women.

The advent of Western-style theatre is closely connected to colonialism and the accompanying role of missionaries as well as British theatre clubs because the British regarded theatre as "an effective tool to promote the 'enlightening' virtues of Western civilization".[3] While at first, only re-enactments of Bible stories and plays by English (male) writers were performed, Africans soon took up some of the new forms of theatre as well. The early indigenous theatre movements performing plays in the first half of the 20th century, like Concert Party theatre in Ghana, the Yoruba Opera in Nigeria or the vaudeville presentations in southern Africa,[4] fused indigenous aesthetics with Western forms introduced by the colonial culture to respond to social and political developments through satire.

With the fight for liberation after the Second World War, Western models were further subverted by African theatre practitioners to write back to the centre and, even more important, theatre was employed to forge national identities after independence was acquired. As a result, a literary art theatre developed alongside more communal forms of theatre (even if some playwrights tried to overcome the divisions and merge various forms). The literary critic Tejumola Olaniyan distinguishes in this context between festival, popular, development and art theatre with the latter being closely intertwined with European aesthetics and written in a European language. Despite being only accessible to a limited elite audience in Africa, literary art theatre is the most prestigious because "it is the tradition by which Africa is known globally, and the primary bridge by which nationals of different African countries come into contact with one another's dramatic traditions".[5]

The Anglophone literary theatre written by African playwrights is generally characterised by a mix of indigenous African and Western elements, though these might be used and juxtaposed in diverse ways. This is probably where similarities end and generalisations for sub-Saharan Africa are no longer permissible. For a better understanding of the evolution of Anglophone literary theatres and women's contributions to them, an analysis of theatre history has to focus on smaller entities.

To introduce the oeuvre of Anglophone African women playwrights, I will discuss four plays representing different topical concerns in more detail. Additionally, some information about the theatre landscape with a special focus on the role of female playwrights in Ghana, Nigeria and South Africa will be provided. The selected countries have all produced a number of Anglophone female playwrights from the second half of the 20th century onwards and boast a rich theatrical tradition which has allowed for a transformation of local to (inter)national forms.[6]

In Ghana, women were involved in the development of Anglophone theatre and a questioning of gender roles even before independence. Efua Sutherland, Ghana's first female playwright, has rightly been credited with being a role model for generations of future women dramatists, including Ama Ata Aidoo, whose play *Anowa* will be discussed in more detail. In Nigeria, on the other hand, the first female playwright 'Zulu Sofola asserted the importance of traditional role models for women before a new generation of female playwrights started to create strong women characters interested in new gender roles, even if this implied breaking with traditions which had always been deemed important by the majority of the (male) members of local cultures. Julie Okoh's *Edewede* will serve as an example to show how female playwrights use Anglophone theatre to educate women about ways and means to counter their oppression. In the context of South

African drama, playwrights have not only been active during and after apartheid but here we also find Indic[7] theatre, plays produced by South Africans of Indian descent. The plays briefly discussed here are Sindiwe Magona's *Vukani!*, a didactic drama concerned with the HIV/AIDS epidemic, and Muthal Naidoo's *Flight from the Mahabarath*, a feminist play about women's oppression and the possibilities to transform patriarchal society.

Female playwrights have, of course, responded to all kinds of issues but I will focus on the interconnection of the individual and the community and the struggles women have fought to alter gender discourses. I will only briefly touch on ideas of African feminism as this would definitely merit a paper of its own.[8] A second emphasis will be placed on the theatre techniques employed by African women playwrights to demonstrate the juxtaposition of African and Western elements.

2. Female Playwrights in Ghana

In Ghana, Western-influenced theatre became prominent as so-called Concert Party theatre which was based on a Ghanaian performance aesthetic but influenced by European elements. Concert Party troupes enjoyed a huge popularity from the early 20th century onwards because they responded directly to contemporary social and political affairs. At the outset, women did not play a part in this kind of theatre, though, because in colonial times, it was an all-male affair with female roles played by men in disguise. Kwame Nkrumah, leader of the anti-colonial resistance and Ghana's first president after the country's independence in 1957, was aware of the political potential of drama and its possible contribution to forming a national and cultural identity. He encouraged female actors to become involved in Concert Party theatre as well as supporting Efua Sutherland in her endeavours to establish a national Ghanaian theatre.[9]

Efua Sutherland founded the Ghana Experimental Theatre Company in 1958. She is still appreciated as an important influence on women's theatre in Ghana and on the development of a national Ghanaian theatre as such. While she was interested in literary artistic drama, she also believed in the potential of popular theatre to bring political plays to a wider audience and was concerned with finding a way of successfully combining both. While this implied that she incorporated elements of Concert Party and Western theatre, she also used indigenous forms like the *Ananse* tales,[10] music and dance. Her most popular play to result from these endeavours is the *anansegoro* or 'spider play' *The Marriage of Anansenwa* (1975), which uses the spider/trickster figure, a central element in Akan folk tales.[11]

For Sutherland the question of language had always been a contested issue. In 1968 she set up the Kuisum Agoromba Players to tour plays in Ghanaian languages as a counterpoint to the elitist Anglophone theatre connected to an urban environment. She also started the journal *Okyeame*, initiated the School of Performing Arts at the University of Ghana at Legon and established the Drama Research Institute at the Institute of African Studies. Sutherland put an emphasis on the research in and teaching of drama as well as on the material side by becoming involved in the construction of actual theatre buildings.

The Drama Studio in Accra, which was modelled on Ghanaian courtyard theatres and encouraged audience response, became intricately connected to her way of performing and scripting drama. It was razed in the early 1990s to be replaced by a new National Theatre (a gift from the Chinese government[12]), which separates audience and performers. This new theatre also marks a new phase in the development of theatre in Ghana as such. With its huge proscenium stage it calls for a different kind of theatre than the one envisaged by Sutherland. As a consequence it was rejected by Sutherland as well as by her most successful student, Ama Ata Aidoo, who worked with Sutherland at the Drama Studio in the early 1960s.

2.1   *The New Woman? Ama Ata Aidoo's* Anowa

Ama Ata Aidoo is one of the most prolific and versatile writers in Ghana and one of the best-known African writers outside the continent. Apart from two highly influential plays, *The Dilemma of a Ghost* (1964) and *Anowa* (1970),[13] she published poems and novels[14] and participated in discussions about African feminism.

While *The Dilemma of a Ghost* is one of the rare plays to feature the troubles of an African-American woman who moves to Ghana with her

Ghanaian husband, the canonical *Anowa* is a postcolonial play that looks to the past in order to better understand the present. Like Sutherlands *Foriwa,* the play has its origins in the traditional dilemma tale[15] of the disobedient daughter which is used here to deconstruct notions of normative femininity. Aidoo emphasises the role of female storytellers by recounting how she got to know the tale: "My mother 'talks' stories and sings songs. *Anowa* [...] directly grows out of a story she told me although as the play has come out, she cannot even recognize the story she told".[16] In the play, Aidoo employs not only the oral African format of the dilemma tale but also African musical instruments, which symbolise the characters, juxtaposed with a version of English which uses verse, prose, proverbs, mime and song to achieve the overall effect of an Akan rhythm.

Set some 30 years after the Bond Treaty,[17] which signalled the permanent presence of the British at the Gold Coast, *Anowa* represents the decisive moment in history when the local Fanti people signed a contract that ultimately led to the colonisation of their territory. While the Fanti are granted agency instead of being portrayed as hapless victims, it becomes clear that they ultimately played a decisive role in submitting their own territories to colonial rule.

While the loss of self-determination concerns the whole community and represents part of a deliberately 'forgotten' history, which also includes internal slavery, on a second level the play is concerned with individual choices and their repercussions within the community. These topics come together in Anowa, the central character. In the play, which consists of a prologue and three phases, Anowa, like the disobedient daughter in the dilemma tale, chooses her own husband, Kofi. Their relationship deteriorates when Kofi becomes involved in trading with the British and buys slaves to increase his profits. The corrective voice of the village is represented in the character of the choric storytellers[18] 'The-Mouth-that-Eats-Salt-and-Pepper', an old man and an old woman who appear in the prologue and at the end of each phase. They comment on the events and provide the conflicting views within Fanti society.

In the first phase, "In Yebi",[19] the audience is introduced to the workings of Fanti culture and their interpretation of gender roles. While marriage and motherhood are the ultimate aims for rural women, it becomes clear that the associated female gender role is far from passive. While matrilineal structures ensure that women (like Anowa's mother

Badua) play a part in all relevant decisions, there is also an alternative for women unwilling or not capable of fulfilling this role model as they may become priestesses. Anowa, though, decides not to adhere to any tradition but to rely on her own ideas where the choice of her future husband is concerned. Eventually, she severs all ties with her mother and the whole village.

Phase Two, "On the Highway", which at first shows Kofi and Anowa working side by side in a partnership based on equality and trust, represents a transitory moment, a phase of in-betweenness, which might allow for new definitions of male and female identities to emerge. Anowa experiences the freedom to be different and appears at her most happy and spirited in this phase, while Kofi is increasingly drawn to trading with the British, even if this means becoming actively involved in slavery. Kofi soon declares that "I shall be the new husband and you the new wife".[20] This statement signifies that he is gradually accepting the gender roles favoured by the British as "the new wife" for Kofi has to subscribe to the domestic ideal.

The third phase, "In the Big House", represents these new, hybrid identities at play. Space becomes an important element of representation in this context because Kofi's opulent new house, which is in Oguaa (Cape Coast), the centre of colonial trading operations, combines African and Western elements with the most telling being the portrait of Queen Victoria next to one of Kofi and one of a crow, "the totem bird of the Nsona clan".[21] But all the newly acquired wealth comes at a price: Kofi has presumably lost his masculinity and virility, an impotence, which can be read as a symbol for the damaging effects of British colonialism on the African male, and exchanged it for a limited local power. Anowa rejects everything he stands for and is slowly but surely going mad, if madness means that her actions are unintelligible to the people around her. She identifies herself as somebody who does not belong, a wayfarer.[22] Feminist critic Carol Boyce Davies rightly claims that Anowa thus "activates in a pre-colonial context what would now be called postmodernist notions of displacement, deterritorialization or homelessness".[23]

Anowa's dream at the beginning of Phase Three, which Africanist Thérèse Migraine George has called a "painful embodiment of her continent's history"[24] and which deserves to be quoted at some length, links the individual and the collective. It provides a reason for Anowa's barrenness as well as stressing the link between global exploitation and corruption:

> I dreamt that I was a big, big woman. And from my insides were huge holes out of which poured men, women and children. And the sea was boiling hot and steaming. And as it boiled, it threw out many, many giant lobsters, boiled lobsters, each of whom as it fell turned into a man or woman, but keeping its lobster head and claws. And they rushed to where I sat and seized the men and women as they poured out of me, and they tore them apart, and dashed them to the ground and stamped upon them.[25]

With Anowa being depicted as a 'Mother Africa' figure, her dream refers directly back to the past of the Atlantic slave trade when Africans were sold from the forts at the coast. While the triangular trade is slowly dwindling out in the present of the play, internal slavery is still going strong and Anowa feels connected to and responsible for the slaves whose misery she wants to end. Thus, she refuses to give birth to children who will only end up in captivity. Aidoo cleverly connects a gender analysis with one of class and the corruption of power in an emerging capitalist society which is at the same time subject to colonial oppression. Of course, the dream also serves as a moment of foreshadowing with regard to the ending when both, Kofi and Anowa commit suicide.

While this might look at first glance to be a mere repetition of the ending of the dilemma tale, *Anowa* shows that it is not only the individual choice of the heroine that leads to unhappiness but that the whole community is implicated. The Old Man has realised that Anowa might not be the only one at fault: "Who knows if Anowa would have been a better woman, a better person if we had not been what we are?"[26] Ultimately, Anowa's suicide does not make her a failed feminist heroine but underlines her role as an in-between wayfarer whose progressive ideas cannot yet be appreciated, as the literary critic Omofolabo Ajayi-Soyinka also concludes:

> A compassionate visionary, Anowa is a woman too early for her time. She is the truth that reveals the secrets hidden deep in the recesses of the mind, of a people's conscience. She stands poised between the past and the future, but unable to fit into the present.[27]

3. Female Playwrights in Nigeria

Nigeria is the most populous African country and has a rich and varied theatre tradition which goes back to traditional masks and rituals. Despite the continuing influence of Western theatre practices (which is similar to that in Ghana), even before independence the extremely popular Yoruba Opera restored pre-contact elements like Yoruba dance and music, but above all Yoruba language, to colonial forms like satire. While women played an important role as performers in these Travelling Theatres, they mostly acted in subordinate parts as wives or mothers. The leadership of these large hierarchical companies was generally reserved for men like Hubert Ogunde or Duro Lapido.

Anglophone literary theatre, on the other hand, was very much centred on the universities, the most influential being the University of Ibadan. Next to Wole Soyinka, a number of other male playwrights developed new forms of syncretic drama but the women characters in these early plays by men, which came to prominence in the time around independence, followed a very limited number of stereotypes.[28] They were either portrayed as virgins, benevolent mother figures or as prostitutes, a phenomenon also visible in early Anglophone West African novels.[29]

Nearly a decade later than in Ghana, women playwrights started to intervene and writers like 'Zulu Sofola, the first published female playwright in Nigeria,[30] became vital in establishing a different gender discourse in dramatic art. While she is biased towards promoting traditional ways for women, in plays like *The Sweet Trap* (1977) she also shows that tensions between men and women are not least caused by the alienation of the Nigerian urban middle class from their rural origins. Sofola, who was part of a Western-educated elite, definitely acted as a role model for further female playwrights coming to prominence after the first heydays of independence as well as the Biafran war were over.

Two of the most prominent writers of this generation are Stella Oyedepo, who has taken up all kinds of issues but mostly satirises greed and corruption in political plays like *Worshippers of the Naira* (1994), and Tess Onwueme who writes feminist/womanist drama like *The Broken Calabash* (1984), *Tell It to Women* (1992) or *What Mama Said*

(2003). Onwueme is especially concerned with the disempowerment of rural women and explores women's

> disenfranchisement by tyrannical cultural practices and traditions, class, gender, postcolonial national and international politics. In an attempt to give women voice and to imbue their lives with meaning, Onwueme creates combatant female characters who confront the structures that seek to subordinate them.[31]

Meanwhile, next to older female dramatists still active, there is a successful second generation of playwrights which includes Irene Salami whose *More Than Dancing* (2003) is about women and politics, and Tracie Chima Utoh-Ezeajugh. Her play *Cauldron of Death* (2001) deals with HIV/AIDS, while *Nneora, an African Doll's House* (2005) is a reworking of Ibsen's play. Nevertheless, Nollywood, the Nigerian film industry, represents a severe challenge to (women's) theatre in Nigeria. Playwrights like Tess Onwueme consider scripting Nollywood films in order to capture an audience because "theatre as we know it is really an endangered space today".[32]

3.1 Bottom Power. Julie Okoh's Edewede

Julie Okoh, who started writing plays in the 1980s, is still active and has written more than a dozen plays[33] which all feature women who are engaged in social transformations. She teaches theatre history and playwriting at the University of Port Harcourt. One of the reasons she turned to playwriting is her desire to promote vital discussions in largely illiterate communities:

> The majority of Nigerians are illiterate. Even many of those who are literate do not […] read. Thus theatre performance […] is the more appropriate and more effective medium for reaching my target audience.[34]

While it remains debatable whether illiterate audiences are captivated by Anglophone plays performed at a university, Okoh definitely has a point because she makes contentious issues known to a larger number of people.

Her play *Edewede*, first performed on 25 August, 1998 at the University of Port Harcourt Arts Theatre, deals with female circumcision, a practice which not only threatens female corporeal integrity but actually claims women's lives. Divided into nine dramas (instead of acts), Okoh places three generations of village women at the heart of the play who have widely differing attitudes towards this practice.

Edewede, the title character whose name translates as "The Dawn of a New Day", has already lost one daughter to the detrimental after-effects of circumcision and refuses to let her last remaining daughter take part in the initiation ceremony, while her mother-in-law as an advocate of the practice insists on her granddaughter going through with it. Edewede, with the help of Eriala or Mama-Nurse, a midwife, and Ebun, her friend, manages to get her age-group on her side in the fight against circumcision. After all the younger women have left the village to go on a sex strike reminiscent of that in Aristophanes' *Lysistrata*, the men and the king finally vote for circumcision to be abolished in their village. The women return and the villagers are reconciled. It is important for the outcome of the play that the collective is able to change without forsaking their cultural identity as their traditions prove to be flexible. In the future, there will still be an initiation ceremony, albeit without the blade.

It becomes apparent from this short summary that the play advocates cultural transformations if they are for the good of society. The play is accordingly dedicated "to all the EDEWEDES in Africa.// Cultural practices are resistant to change.// But culture is never static but dynamic".[35] In order to bring about the necessary changes regarding circumcision, Okoh employs the health approach by having various characters recounting deaths they have witnessed or illnesses caused by the practice while the whole procedure is explained to the audience. The literary critic Chantal Zabus maintains that this approach promises to be the most effective because it "has been deemed the most politically correct one, the human rights approach invariably conjuring up the Western bugaboo of imperialistic intervention and feminisms of Euro-American manufacture".[36]

Apart from the health issues, circumcision is shown as a practice that is part of creating a docile female body which serves as a prerequisite to subservience and a resulting oppression of women by men. Still, it is important to stress that it is mainly women who keep this tradition going, be it as the ones wielding the blade or as mothers who willingly send their daughters to the ceremonies even if they have doubts about the benefits and are afraid of the possibility of being confronted with a lethal outcome.

In the play, the dead girls resulting from former circumcision 'accidents' are visualised as a repeatedly appearing chorus of Maiden Ghosts who dance and repeat the phrase: "Why did you do that to us?"[37] This underlines that the whole village was implicated in their premature deaths. The Maiden Ghosts are not the only element of popular theatre employed by Okoh. There is also a masquerade,[38] dance, and a theme song in Esan, which invites the audience to sing along. Audience response is vital for this play, as it is definitely on Okoh's agenda to influence real-life decisions regarding circumcision.

The positive ending of the play highlights two basic effects of the women's rebellion. They have learned to use female solidarity as a weapon and brought about a lasting effect for the whole community because the men had to rethink stereotypes about women as well as the use of the debilitating practice of circumcision. It is evident, though, that the community is far more important than the individual. While Edewede may decide on her own to boycott circumcision, it is important that the whole village sanctions and practises a change in cultural traditions to achieve a lasting alteration to the benefit of all women and, ultimately, men.

4. Female Playwrights in South Africa

In South Africa, the development of an Anglophone black theatre is quite different from that in West Africa due to the long presence of the racist apartheid regime. What has not changed, though, is the fact that theatre has always been an effective political tool. In the early days of apartheid, black and white performers were actually working together in various theatre projects. But the strict enforcement of apartheid legislation in the 1960s made this form of collaboration impossible, a development that ultimately led to an invigoration of Black theatre. Township musicals, which were mainly written in English but also in isiZulu, isiXhosa and other languages, focused on social tensions and represented "a form of resistance to the government's insistence on separate development, while simultaneously enabling performers to communicate their experience beyond themselves to international audiences".[39]

Alongside township theatre, the experimental workers' theatre also provided an important outlet for suppressed voices. Phyllis Klotz collaborated with Nomvula Qosha, Thobeka Maqhutyana, Poppy Tsira and others to produce plays like *You Strike the Women, You Strike the Rock* (1986) to give a voice to women's perspectives on migrant labour and their specific role in the struggle against apartheid. In the decidedly political theatre inspired by the Black Consciousness Movement female playwrights sadly lacked a voice.

Another form of syncretic theatre, which came to prominence with a gradual desegregation of the theatre landscape after 1976, was the collaborative theatre. Collaborative theatres used workshops and incorporated African and Western forms "while challenging politics through the individual stories of silenced, marginalised people. They also signalled the more multi-lingual nature of the emergent South African theatre".[40] Two of the most important spaces connected to collaborative theatre and especially the advancement of female voices were the Space Theatre in Cape Town and the Market Theatre in Johannesburg.

It was in this context that female playwrights like Fatima Dike started to emerge. Her play *Sacrifice of Kreli* (1976), the first play of a black South African woman playwright to be published, was produced at the Space Theatre. It is a history play which makes use of a traditional tale to connect the past and the present. First written in isiXhosa, the translation sought to keep intact the rhythm of the indigenous language. Another important voice in South African women's theatre is that of Gcina Mhlophe. Her autobiographical *Have You Seen Zendile?* (1986) continuously moves between English, isiXhosa and isiZulu. Mhlophe made her mark via the Market Theatre which still is an important venue for new writing by women.

The development of South African theatre after the end of apartheid is characterised by vast changes and necessary redefinitions as marginalised forms of theatre have now become 'the centre'. Additionally, the struggle against apartheid as the dominant topic has to be replaced by new concerns with one pressing issue definitely being the fight against HIV/AIDS as in Sindiwe Magona's play which will be discussed next. It is evident, though, that the voices of women playwrights play an important role in the new South Africa.[41]

4.1 A New ABC. Sindiwe Magona's Vukani!

Born in Gungululu, Sindiwe Magona is an internationally acclaimed playwright, poet and novelist. In her writings she focuses on the empowerment of women and a synthesis between the community and the individual, an endeavour prevalent in all the theatre plays discussed so far. Her play *Vukani!*,[42] which means "Wake up!" in isiXhosa, is set in Guguletu township a couple of years after the end of apartheid and deals with the misconceptions surrounding HIV/AIDS as well as the repercussions the virus has on the population. Sindiwe Magona's take on the topic is gendered because she does not only fight against the stigma of HIV/AIDS but at the heart of the play is the myth that sleeping with a virgin will cure the disease – a fateful idea that also found support in high government circles. Additionally, Thabo Mbeki's health minister Manto Tshabalala-Msimang recommended the use of garlic, African potatoes and beetroot as cures for AIDS.[43]

Magona would ideally have performed her play, which is deliberately didactic in tone, on a nation-wide basis:

> My dream, when writing the play, was that troops of amateur actors would be trained and unleashed on the entire country to go perform it – in different languages, as the occasion demanded – accompanied by trained personnel who would then field questions. Yes, there would be a Q&A at the end of each performance.[44]

The community in *Vukani!* resembles a microcosm of South African townships with the cast consisting of eight individually named characters, the Lonzi family, Vuyo and his mother and the next-door neighbours. 14-year-old Zama Lonzi is raped by 17-year-old Vuyo in her own bedroom because he wants to cure his HIV-infection. In the aftermath of the assault, the whole community is shaken by the event as it dawns on all of them that even their children "who will not see thirty, the children who will never grow old"[45] are no longer safe and that the whole township literally has to 'wake up'.

Magona shows that it is also the attitudes towards sexuality and morality which are responsible for the wide-spread phenomenon of virgin rapes and the seemingly unstoppable dissemination of the HI-virus. Thus, Mfundo Lonzi, Zama's father and a school principal, at the beginning of the play does not condone that his children are provided with sexual education in the form of a new ABC, "Abstain. Be Loyal. Condomize",[46] in the Youth Centre. For him, it is of vital importance to keep his good reputation intact. His change of attitude in the course of the play represents the transformative potential of the older generation.

The play can also be seen as part of an urgently needed health education for the audience because it takes care to explain the spread of HIV/AIDS, the disease shrouded in silence. It is called *gulawayo*, "the merciless, ruthless chopper",[47] though usually not acknowledged for what it is but only treated in secondary symptoms like pneumonia or the flu. In the play, this is made evident by not even Fina knowing that her son Vuyo has tested positive for the illness.

The discussions in the township after Zama's rape mark a new beginning for the whole community. First of all, the affected parties decide that they do not want to resort to forms of justice which are deemed 'white', like a prison sentence, but establish a neighbourhood council meting out restorative justice instead. At this point, the audience becomes involved in the play because they become part of the meeting. Vuyo receives the following sentence from the council: he will be shunned by the community, has to give half of his wages to the Lonzis and do community work by educating people that raping virgins does not cure AIDS. As a long-term prospect, he will regain his former rights. As a second result, the community and especially the younger male members as exemplified by Jongi Lonzi, Zama's brother, endeavour to revise and correct their image of women and girls to secure them some measure of equality in the future. Like in *Edewede*, it is interesting to note that the individual is only important as an integral part of the community that comes up with the final decision.

4.2 Showing an Alternative World. Muthal Naidoo's Flight from the Mahabarath

Last but by no means least, I will briefly introduce a play by a South African Indian. In histories of South African theatre, (women) playwrights of Indian descent tend to be neglected although they have developed a distinctive voice. Director and actress Krijay Govender claims that they are not least motivated by writing back to male South African Indian playwrights and thereby develop a specific cultural identity:

> South African Indian women playwrights like Nadine Naidoo (*Nadia*), Devi Sarinjeive (*Acts of God*) and myself (*Women in Brown*) produced their own work as a response to the often demeaning ways in which South African Indian men playwrights have represented women in their plays.[48]

One of the playwrights, who has been intricately connected to Indic theatre from its very beginnings, is Muthal Naidoo. She was part of the Shah Theatre Academy in Durban which was established to honour director Krishna Shah in 1963 and which directly challenged apartheid. The term Indic theatre highlights the search for an identity for people of Indian decent in South Africa. Naidoo states:

> In my own attempt to reconcile the diversity of factors that influence the way I behave, I have rejected the term 'Indian' for myself. I was born and raised in South Africa and my life has been influenced by material conditions here and not India. I have a residual culture that originated in India but that is where my 'Indianness' begins and ends. I am a South African. I fall somewhere between extremes. I am proud of my origins, but what I try to express in my work is my South African heritage, which is a mixture of Western, African and Indian influences, and I hope that my artistic creativity reflects the uniqueness of my background.[49]

Her play *Flight from the Mahabarath*, which, written in the early 1990s, was unfortunately never performed[50] is an example of a decidedly feminist play.[51] Taking the Indian epic as her point of departure, Naidoo shows how looking at the *Mahabarath* from a different point of view might be useful for all women, not just for South Africans of Indian descent. Thus, she prescribes for the cast that

> the characters should represent the rainbow nation of South Africa and any tendency towards ethnic stereotyping should be scrupulously avoided. [...] Traditions, customs, rituals should also come from the diversity of the South African cultural context.[52]

The play features the women of the *Mahabarath* who have left the epic because they are no longer content with being just submissive wives and mothers of heroes. Instead, they want to create their own world which is characterised by non-violence and recognition of their own talents. The situation is complicated by the arrival of two men, Brihannala, the female disguise of the warrior hero Arjun, and Sikandi, who is the male representation of Amba.

In the course of the play, the women deconstruct and recreate the *Mahabarath* by telling their stories from a feminist point of view and thus endowing them with new meaning. They insist on choosing their own husbands (as in the stories of Amba and Draupadi), condemn accusations of witchcraft (like in Hidimba's story), show Ganga not killing her children but remaining unmarried and independent instead or, finally, Draupadi coming to terms with the fact that Arjun is gay which goes together with a recognition that the gender roles ascribed to men may be equally restrictive. The moments of female suppression raised in the play cannot only be deemed almost universal, but are also problematic in post-apartheid South Africa. Naidoo regards her play as a plea to promote women's equality because she believes that the situation has not really changed as "a lot of lip service is being paid to gender issues. We have a long way to go".[53]

5. Conclusion

Since the second half of the 20th century, sub-Saharan African women playwrights have dramatised issues as diverse as women's roles in history, the divide between rural and urban women, corruption, virgin rapes and the dangers inherent in the wide spread of HIV/AIDS. What unites them in their diversity is that they challenge hegemonic discourses and address the multiple roles of women in ever-changing postcolonial contexts. In all three countries discussed here, women playwrights have also started to transform the landscape of theatre and performance in their respective countries by creating powerful female characters who invite change and point out social and political problems on local as well as global levels.

6. Recommended Reading

6.1 Primary Sources

Playtexts by Anglophone sub-Saharan women playwrights are notoriously expensive as they have to be ordered from African publishers and/or hard to come by because many plays have not been published at all. A couple of plays by Efua Sutherland and Ama Ata Aidoo have been published by Longman. Tess Onwueme, who now resides in the US, got most of her plays published by African Heritage Press and Wayne State University Press. Recommended are the following anthologies:

Gilbert, Helen (Ed.): *Postcolonial Plays. An Anthology*, London, 2001.
    Includes Ama Ata Aidoo's *Anowa* as well as plays by renowned male playwrights like Wole Soyinka, Femi Osofisan and Maishe Maponya.

Jeyifo, Biodun (Ed.): *Modern African Drama*, New York & London, 2002.
    Includes not only *Dilemma of a Ghost* by Ama Ata Aidoo but also introductory material on African drama in general as well as plays by influential male playwrights like Ngũgĩ wa Thiong'o, Femi Osofisan or Wole Soyinka.

Perkins, Kathy A. (Ed.): *Black South African Women. An Anthology of Plays*, London, 1998.
    Includes plays by Gcina Mhlophe, Fatima Dike, Sindiwe Magona, Muthal Naidoo and others as well as a number of plays by South African male playwrights with a special focus on women.

Perkins, Kathy A. (Ed.): *African Women Playwrights*, Urbana & Chicago, 2009.
Includes plays by Ama Ata Aidoo, Julie Okoh, Sindiwe Magona, Violet Barungi and Tsitsi Dangarembga, among others.

6.2 Secondary Sources

As general introductions to African theatre the following are recommended:

Banham, Martin *et al.* (Eds.): *The Cambridge Guide to African and Caribbean Theatre*, Cambridge, 1994.
The authors are all specialists in their chosen field and the short but comprehensive entries for all African countries provide a general overview, name the most important theatre practitioners and end with a helpful bibliography. Longer essays can be found in

Banham, Martin (Ed.): *A History of Theatre in Africa,* Cambridge, 2004.
This book covers the history of theatre in Africa in detail and is divided into subsections about each country.

With regard to book-length studies about African women's theatre, the following are definitely worth reading:

Esser, Sibylle: *Dramen in englischer Sprache von Frauen aus Nigeria*, Frankfurt/M., 1993.
Esser introduces plays by Catherine Achonolu, Tess Onwueme, Grace Osifo, Stella Oyedepo and 'Zulu Sofola with an emphasis on gender discourses and identity as well as dramatic form.

Migraine-George, Thérèse: *African Women and Representation. From Performance to Politics*, Trenton & Asmara, 2008.
Migraine-George engages in a cross-cultural discussion of Anglophone and Francophone female playwrights with a focus on women's cultural, social and political representation.

Plastow, Jane (Ed.): *African Theatre. Women*, Oxford, 2002.
This special issue of the series *African Theatre* contains not only various contributions on women's theatre in Africa but also a playscript by Fatima Dike.

For discussions of individual plays by women, there are a number of articles in journals like *Research in African Literatures, African Literature Today, The Journal of Commonwealth Literature, Theatre Research International, South African Theatre Journal* or the fairly new Nigerian journal *Creative Artist. A Journal of Theatre and Media Studies*.

Notes

1 Plastow (2002: xi).
2 Banham (1994: 3).
3 Migraine-George (2008: 95).
4 For a comprehensive discussion of Concert Party, Yoruba Opera and other forms of popular theatre, see Kerr (1995).
5 Olaniyan (2007: 361).
6 For a discussion of South African theatre, see Oppelt; for an insight into East African women writing, see Strauhs, both in this volume.
7 The term 'Indic' stands for South African Indian Intercultural Practice (see Hutchison 2004: 366).
8 For various positions on African feminism/womanism the anthology by Obioma Nnaemeka (1998) can be highly recommended. It also includes essays by Ama Ata Aidoo and 'Zulu Sofola.
9 In Ghana, the connection between the theatre and politics is quite remarkable. Not only has the theatre been employed to assist in nation building but playwrights have also become involved in politics at government level. Ama Ata Aidoo, for example, served as the Provisional National Defence Council's Secretary for Education under J.J. Rawlings in 1982/83. She resigned when she realised that she would not be able to fulfill her aim of providing free access to education for all Ghanaians.
10 The *Ananse* tales revolve around the trickster figure of Ananse, the spider. Originally told by the Akan, they were taken up by local Akan and non-

Akan dramatists to become part of a national Ghanaian theatre tradition. For more information, see Gibbs (2004: 160).

11 Other plays by Efua Sutherland include *Foriwa* (1967), which was first performed in Akan in 1962, and *Edufa* (1969), a re-interpretation of Euripides' *Alkestis*.
12 The National Theatre was built as part of a technical cooperation agreement between Ghana and China and demonstrates the People's Republic increasing engagement in Africa.
13 The play was published before it was actually produced. James Gibbs states that it was probably only first performed in 1991 at the Gate Theatre in London (see Gibbs 2012: 433). Nonetheless, it has become one of the plays most widely discussed in the contexts of postcolonial theatre and African women writers.
14 *Our Sister Killjoy* (1977), which is partly set in Germany, became famous as one of the very few African novels featuring a lesbian relationship.
15 Dilemma tales are used by the Akan to debate socially relevant topics. Usually, they do not provide unequivocal answers but ask the questions that need to be discussed.
16 James (1990: 19).
17 The Bond Treaty was signed in 1844 because the Fanti hoped to secure protection against the Ashanti, another Akan people.
18 The character of 'The-Mouth-That-Eats-Salt-and-Pepper' is similar to the narrator figure in the dilemma tale who also interprets events. In *Anowa* the old man talks mostly in verse, while the old woman uses colloquial English. It is also interesting to note that the old man shows sympathy with Anowa's plight, while the old woman is immediately ready to condemn her for defying traditions.
19 The titles of the three phases reflect Aidoo's interest in the deconstruction of the symbolic meaning of spatial configurations where notions of belonging are concerned.
20 Aidoo (2001: 111).
21 *Ibid.* 117.
22 See *Ibid.* 115.
23 Davies (1994: 65).
24 Migraine-George (2008: 186).
25 Aidoo (2001: 119).
26 *Ibid.* 127.
27 Ajayi-Soyinka (2012: 356).
28 See Davies (1986).

29 See, for example, Cyprian Ekwensi's *Jagua Nana* (1961) or Elechi Amadi's *The Concubine* (1966).
30 Allegedly, Sofola's *The Deer Hunter and the Hunter's Pearl* (1969) was the first play by a Nigerian female playwright.
31 Eke (2003: 8).
32 Migraine-George (2008: 278).
33 Okoh's first play was *Masks* (1988). Unfortunately, nearly all of her plays (except for *Edewede*) have only been published in Nigeria and are not easily available.
34 Okoh (2009: 245).
35 *Ibid.* 252.
36 Zabus (2007: 256).
37 Okoh (2009: 304).
38 A masquerade is a character usually serving as a form of social control but it is deconstructed here. Despite humiliating and exiling Edewede for her endeavours to change traditional practices, she emerges victorious and reveals the masquerade's obvious bias.
39 Hutchison (2004: 353).
40 *Ibid.* 354.
41 For venues encouraging the work of women playwrights and important festivals like the Grahamstown Festival, see Perkins 1998: 4.
42 The play was first performed on 26 September 2003 in the Theatre of the Riverside Church in New York City where Magona was residing at the time. It has meanwhile also been performed at various theatres in South Africa.
43 See Attree (2010: 7).
44 Stark (2010).
45 Magona (2009: 175).
46 *Ibid.* 176.
47 *Ibid.* 178.
48 Govender (2001: 38).
49 Naidoo (1992).
50 See Naidoo (2009).
51 Naidoo read all the works by feminist Mary Daly before writing the play and was impressed with Daly's brand of feminism which is characterised by the search for a new symbolic order (see Naidoo 1998: 114).
52 Naidoo (1998: 116).
53 *Ibid.* 115.

Bibliography

Aidoo, Ama Ata: "Anowa". – In Helen Gilbert (Ed.): *Postcolonial Plays. An Anthology*, London, 2001, pp. 97-128.

Ajayi-Soyinka, Omofolabo: "Disobedient Subversions. *Anowa*'s Unending Quest". – In Anne V. Adams (Ed.): *Essays in Honour of Ama Ata Aidoo at 70. A Reader in African Cultural Studies*, Banbury, 2012, pp. 347-362.

Attree, Lizzy: *Blood on the Page. Interviews with African Authors Writing about HIV/AIDS*, Newcastle upon Tyne, 2010.

Banham, Martin *et al.* (Eds.): *The Cambridge Guide to African and Caribbean Theatre*, Cambridge, 1994.

Davies, Carol Boyce: "Maidens, Mistresses and Matrons. Feminine Images in Selected Soyinka Works". – In C. B. D. & Anne Adams Graves (Eds.): *Ngambika. Studies of Women in African Literature*, Trenton & Asmara, 1986, pp. 75-89.

---: *Black Women, Writing and Identity. Migrations of the Subject*, London, 1994.

Eke, Maureen N.: "Introduction". – In Tess Onwueme: *What Mama Said. An Epic Drama*, Detroit, 2003, pp. 7-13.

Gibbs, James: "Ghana". – In Martin Benham (Ed.): *A History of Theatre in Africa*, Cambridge, 2004, pp. 159-170.

---: "A Bibliography of Writing by and about Ama Ata Aidoo. A Compilation in Progress". – In Anne V. Adams (Ed.): *Essays in Honour of Ama Ata Aidoo at 70. A Reader in African Cultural Studies*, Banbury, 2012, pp. 430-470.

Govender, Krijay: "Subverting Identity after 1994. The South African Indian Woman as Playwright", *Agenda* 49, 2001, 33-43.

Hutchison, Yvette: "South African Theatre". – In Martin Benham (Ed.): *A History of Theatre in Africa*, Cambridge, 2004, pp. 312-380.

James, Adeola: *In Their Own Voices. African Women Writers Talk*, London, 1990.

Kerr, David: *African Popular Theatre*, Oxford, 1995.

Magona, Sindiwe: "Vukani! (Wake Up!)". – In Kathy A. Perkins (Ed.): *African Women Playwrights*, Urbana & Chicago, 2009, pp. 170-222.

Migraine-George, Thérèse: *African Women and Representation. From Performance to Politics*, Trenton & Asmara, 2008.

Naidoo, Muthal: "'Indian' Theatre in Durban", *Muthal Naidoo*, 1992, <http://www.muthalnaidoo.co.za/theatre-othermenu-120/60-indian-theatre-in-durban>, accessed 13 September 2012.

---: "Flight from the Mahabarath". – In Kathy A. Perkins (Ed.): *Black South African Women. An Anthology of Plays*, London 1998, pp. 113-142.

---: "Wip Theatre Plays", *Muthal Naidoo*, 2009, <http://www.muthalnaidoo.co.za/wip-theatre-plays-othermenu-113/162-flight-from-the-mahabharath>, accessed 13 September 2012.

Nnaemeka, Obioma (Ed.): *Sisterhood, Feminisms and Power. From Africa to the Diaspora*, Trenton, 1998.

Okoh, Julie: "Edewede (The Dawn of a New Day)". – In Kathy A. Perkins (Ed.): *African Women Playwrights*, Urbana & Chicago, 2009, pp. 248-318.

Olaniyan, Tejumola: "Festivals, Ritual and Drama in Africa". – In Ato Quayson (Ed.): *African Literature. An Anthology of Criticism and Theory*, Oxford, 2007, pp. 353-363.

Plastow, Jane: "Introduction". – In J. P. (Ed.): *African Theatre. Women*, Oxford, 2002, pp. xi-xiii.

Stark, Astrid: "Interview with Dr Sindiwe Magona. For the Love of Literature", *Astrid Stark*, 17 March 2010, <http://astridstark1.wordpress.com/2010/03/17/interview-with-dr-sindiwe-magona-for-the-love-of-literature/>, accessed 13 September 2012.

Zabus, Chantal J.: *Between Rites and Rights. Excision in Women's Experiential Texts and Human Contexts*, Palo Alto, 2007.

Henning Marquardt (Hanover)

Literary History and the Publishers.
South African Mission Presses and Secular Publishing from the 1920s to the 1940s

1. Introduction. Literary History and Publishing

When reviewing histories of South African literature, it is striking that most authors concentrate their efforts on the period from 1948 to 1994, the apartheid years. Except for some scholars, such as Michael Chapman and Christopher Heywood, most basically skip the time before 1948, naming only a few outstanding writers. To understand this, one has to consider the context of these scholarly publications: the majority of them were published in the 1980s, 1990s and 2000s, when the impact of apartheid was clearly visible and when coming to terms with the (cultural) history of the regime was of utmost importance. Still, this leaves a gap, which needs to be filled, since the period before 1948 shaped South Africa's political and cultural landscapes. To understand the country's development until today it is necessary to approach this early phase. When engaging with pre-apartheid literature in South Africa, the impact of Christian missionaries becomes obvious – the mission stations were among the first to set up printing presses in South Africa.[1] The missions therefore played an active role in the literary scene in South Africa before 1948, operating alongside some local secular publishers and a number of British and US-American publishing houses. However, publishing processes are – at best – briefly commented on in the few accounts of South African literature before 1948.[2]

In the following, this paper will give an overview of the development of South African literature in English between the 1920s and 1948. With special attention to publishing, I will contrast Christian and secular publications to show that similarities and differences can be traced back to the modes of publication. I furthermore want to point out that segregation legislation, which was the precursor of the apartheid system and which massively increased in the 1920s, caused considerable resonance in the literature of the times and that a relevant tradition of protest writing developed already before 1948.

In doing so, I consider fictional texts within what Pierre Bourdieu labelled the literary field. According to this theory, literature is produced in a framework of institutions and interests that is determined by the opposition between literature's artistic autonomy and its dependence on market principles.[3] This allows for including publishers into the analysis of literature since they are crucial constituents of the literary field.

Contrasting missionary publishing in English and secular publishing creates chances and restrictions for literary history. The chances are that, firstly, this approach helps to analyse the influence of different publishing systems on South African literature. Secondly, this combination establishes a point of connection to the history of African literatures in African languages. Since the majority of African language publishing was done by the missions, the analysis of English language mission-published literature is one step towards an integrated history of South African literatures. Thirdly, I will be able to compare two different target audiences. According to Tim White's article on the largest South African mission press Lovedale that was operated by the Glasgow Missionary Society, target audiences of religious and secular publishing houses differed decisively. White points out that as a result of segregation legislation Lovedale almost exclusively provided black South Africans with literature, while commercial publishing houses produced literature for people of European descent.[4]

The major restriction of contrasting mission and secular publications is that English language mission publishing is limited to very few literary publications because the mission presses were mainly dedicated to literature in African languages and to religious texts. Therefore, a comparative analysis of these texts and their secular counterparts is restricted to a rather narrow frame of time; the first English language mission publication originates from 1926. I will nonetheless concentrate on literature in English because of the overall focus of this publication as well as my personal expertise and the importance of English for South African literature. I will use Lovedale Press as an example because this press was most active and a number of its publications are still available.

The essay follows thematic categories to show how the texts construct ethnic oppositions by using different themes and motifs. Thereby, content-related coherences between different texts and modes of publishing can be foregrounded. The little critical attention that pre-apartheid literature has received results in the fact that many primary texts have not been reissued (regularly) and are difficult to obtain. I will comment on the texts' availability in my endnotes to provide necessary information for teaching and research.

2. Urban and Rural Life

A key feature of South African literature is geographical space and the way it influences writing. South Africa is a country of open spaces and its people have a long history of using these spaces for making a living. The indigenous people lived off hunting and farming and so did the Dutch settlers who were the first Europeans to colonise what is now the Republic of South Africa. The struggles over land that resulted from the movements of African peoples as well as of the Trek Boers in the 19th century appear in various literary texts. I will get back to these issues in the following chapter on war fiction. This chapter will focus on urbanisation, which largely changed South African geography in the first half of the 20th century. Urbanisation ties in with the development of segregation legislation and industrialisation. The Natives Land Act of 1913, the basis of what would become apartheid legislation after 1948, restricted black land owning and resulted in labour migration to the cities. The surplus of workforce was in fact needed by the expanding mining industry on the Witwatersrand. This resulted in the massive growth of the cities, especially Johannesburg, which again led to large-scale social transformations. In this chapter I will argue that the literary city takes on a double function; it represents both the ongoing industrialisation and increasing segregation.

The intertwined processes described above are most often represented using the Jim-comes-to-Jo'burg motif, which was named after Donald Swanson's 1949 film *African Jim* that became popular under the name *Jim comes to Jo'burg*. The motif usually describes a young man's journey from his rural home to Johannesburg, where he wants to quickly earn money in the mines. Once there, he gives in to alcohol, gambling and prostitution. This is the case in Rolfes Dhlomo's *An African Tragedy*, which was published in 1928 by Lovedale Press.[5] Dhlomo was an author and journalist who published his texts in the polyglot daily newspaper *Bantu World* and the weekly magazine *Sjambok*. In *An African Tragedy*, the protagonist Robert Zulu leaves behind his family and job as a teacher in the small town of Siam to go to Johannesburg to earn the money that he is required to pay to marry his fiancée Jane. There, a dubious new friend draws him into drinking, affairs with women and gambling until one night Robert is associated with a fatal stabbing. He flees from Johannesburg and returns to his home town, where he marries his fiancée. Shortly afterwards, Robert is murdered. Just before he dies by his wife's side, he confesses to a priest who absolves him.

The central theme of *An African Tragedy* is religion. When Robert Zulu comes to Johannesburg, he settles in a township, a place of loose morals, according to the text. The text presents Christianity as the key to overcome these issues. The narrative's distinctly realist mode emphasises the publication's religious implications; the heterodiegetic, overt narrator sets him- or herself up as a moral authority. I want to contrast Dhlomo's realist writing with another Jim-comes-to-Jo'burg text, namely William Plomer's short novel "Ula Masondo" (1927).[6] Plomer is best known for his debut novel *Turbott Wolfe*, to which I will return later. He furthermore edited the English and Afrikaans monthly journal *Voorslag* (Afrikaans for "whiplash") together with Roy Campbell and Laurence van der Post. The latter also took up the theme of rural spaces in his debut novel *In a Province* (1934).

In "Ula Masondo", published by Virginia and Leonard Woolf's Hogarth Press, a young, black, male protagonist goes to Goldenville, a fictional city that metaphorically refers to Johannesburg, to earn money in the mines where his new friends introduce him to drugs, alcohol, affairs with women and crime. When his colleagues save Ula only last-minute after a mining accident, he returns to his home region. But instead of returning to his family, he settles with the pregnant prostitute Emma, who left Goldenville with him. Ula's mother hangs herself in response.

Through its character constellation and plot design, Plomer's text chiefly attributes Ula's misdemeanour to the bad influence of an older friend and the gang Ula joins. He enters a vicious circle of gambling, drinking, debts and crime from which he can only escape after his traumatic accident. The text supports the alteration in Ula's attitude with a change of genre, from prose to verse, when Ula hallucinates after his accident. This rupture in the narrative allows for abstract comments on industrialisation, mechanisation, environmental issues and colonialism. Also, "Ula Masondo" is not as conservative in its ending as *An African Tragedy* is: Ula permanently parts with his family. He is not reintegrated into the old structures, as Robert Zulu is, but he leaves his past behind. His mother's suicide can be read as her being unable to cope with this change. Similar to the problems Ula faced in the city, his mother's death critically assesses the process of urbanisation that Ula represents. Just as its modernist elements distinguish "Ula Masondo" from *An African Tragedy* on a structural level, on the content level Plomer's text is also much less concerned with religious aspects. Christianity is presented as a cult-like phenomenon practised by one of the gang members and does not set moral standards by which the plot is evaluated. Another difference to Dhlomo's text is the inclusion of skin colour as an explicit theme. *An African Tragedy* briefly comments on different ethnicities among Robert Zulu's companions and on the pass laws but does not go into detail on the difference in status of black and white South Africans. In "Ula Masondo" the relation of blacks and whites is addressed, especially in terms of economic differences. This is a topic that Plomer takes up frequently, for example, also linked to a mining accident, in his poem "A Fall of Rock" or, most famously, in *Turbott Wolfe*. Plomer thereby shows an awareness of the connection between skin colour and living conditions that *An African Tragedy* does not display to this extent.

Roughly twenty years later, the two probably best known Jim-comes-to-Jo'burg stories were published. These are Peter Abrahams's *Mine Boy* (1946) and Alan Paton's *Cry, the Beloved Country* (1948).[7] While they are less experimental than "Ula Masondo" in terms of their form, both texts are rather explicit in their social criticism. Also, the ongoing segregation becomes quite obvious; race relations and the economic and social effects of segregation are central. *Mine Boy*, published by Faber & Faber in London, illustrates the impact of the criminalisation of blacks. The story circles around Leah's shebeen, where she and others illegally sell beer to the inhabitants of Malay Camp, a slum district of Johannesburg. The protagonist Xuma works in the mines and is good friends with Leah and her fellows. They frequently come into conflict with the police and even though Leah pays an informer, she is finally arrested. This suggests that a system cannot be overcome by adjusting to it, but that it requires reform for everybody to make a living in it. The case of Xuma himself takes this insight to another level by offering a solution for the problems. After an accident in the mine, he refuses to go back to work instantly. Even though he is supported by his white boss Paddy, the mining company calls his refusal a strike and has both arrested. Xuma escapes at first but turns himself in later to support his colleague: "He is not a black man but he is going to jail for our people, how can I not go?"[8] Xuma makes clear that it requires joint efforts by whites and blacks to change the system. However, ultimately the reader does not know whether Paddy is still under arrest at that time or if he has been released in the meantime. This open ending comments on the racist unequal treatment and, in more general terms, on the country heading towards apartheid.

Paton's *Cry, the Beloved Country*, published by Scribner in New York and Jonathan Cape in London, differs from the previous examples in that the protagonist is not a young, black man but the father of a young black man who came to Johannesburg. The protagonist Stephen Kumalo is a parson who tries to save his sister as well as his son from poverty, crime and prostitution in the city. The novel suggests rural development as a solution for the challenges of urbanisation. Kumalo returns from Johannesburg without his son, who was convicted for murder which could as well have been manslaughter, and without his sister, who has fled. The city permanently separates the family. However, he brings with him his pregnant daughter-in-law and his nephew. With this new generation he tries to organise life apart from the big city. Receiving little help from the Chief, the black Christian parson turns to a white man who helps him to build a dam and to improve agriculture in his home village. Ironically, Kumalo has to rely on South Africa's colonial legacy for his project of rural development. The legal system that enables the severe judgement on Kumalo's son, however, draws on this legacy, too.

The related themes of industrialisation and segregation are not restricted to the city, especially to Johannesburg, but they also appear in rural settings, for example in Pauline Smith's "The Pain". The short story was published in the collection *The Little Karoo* by the American George H. Doran Company in 1926.[9] Smith, who is also known for her novels *The Beadle* (1926) and *Platkops Children* (1935), does not tell the story of a young man who travels to the big city, but of the elderly couple Juriaan and Deltje van Royen who travel from the Aangenaam Valley (*aangenaam* is Afrikans for "pleasant") to Platkops Dorp, two fictional places in the Little Karoo. They do so because Deltje has got an inexplicable pain in her side, which they hope she will be cured of in the newly-built hospital in Platkops Dorp. Once there, they learn that they have to part – Juriaan has to leave her in the hospital. They do so for a while until they realise that Deltje cannot be cured and Juriaan finally decides to take her away. The element that represents urbanisation and even industrialisation is the hospital, where health care facilities are concentrated and made more efficient. To benefit from that, the van Royens have to travel there from their remote farm. Like the mines in Johannesburg separate the families, so does the hospital. This separation represents the challenges that urbanisation poses for South Africa's rural population, since the people have to cope with changes that profoundly affect their ways of life.

Against the background of the political development of the 1920s, I interpret "The Pain" as a comment on the escalating segregation. As opposed to all previously analysed texts, the van Royens embody not a young man but an old couple that is, nonetheless, separated by an institution. This institution then starts to regulate every aspect of their life, which goes as far as the nurse actually deciding whether Deltje is better or not: "It is for me to say when you have no pain in the side."[10] The couple can only withdraw by physically fleeing by night. The text points out that segregation, that is represented here by the separation that the couple experience just like Ula Masondo or Robert Zulu do, is not only a problem of young, black South Africans, but that it affects the entire society.

The pain can be read as a metaphor for segregation and urbanisation; it drives the old couple into the city where they are separated. To avoid problems arising from these developments, the story suggests withdrawal from the centre. "The Pain" therefore shares certain aspects with Dhlomo's Lovedale-text. Opposed to that, *Mine Boy*, *Cry, the Beloved Country* and "Ula Masondo" rather suggest to face up to the situation and to actively intervene in South Africa's political and social processes.

Further texts using the contrast of rural and urban settings as a literary means to negotiate modernisation, industrialisation and segregation can only be named. These include, for example, John Charlton's[11] *Broken Earth* (1940), where rural life is constructed as a retreat, and Es'kia Mphahlele's *Man Must Live, and Other Stories* (1946), a collection of five short stories set in a Pretoria slum.

3. War Fiction

As mentioned in the previous sub-chapter, space and the change of spaces in literature do not only translate into the motif of urbanisation, but are also closely related to warfare. War scenarios usually include opposing groups of people fighting for land or resources. In this sub-chapter I will show that South African texts use war to construct clearly defined, oppositional groups divided along ethnic lines. War writing therefore negotiates a key issue of both colonialism and segregation. It fictionally constructs oppositions in an historical setting which parallels the oppositions that segregation legislation enforced. In the following, I will demonstrate how South African war fiction of the early 20th century addresses segregation and apartheid and how it relates the then current socio-political situation to colonialism.

In 1937, Stuart Cloete's *The Turning Wheels* was published by Houghton Mifflin in the USA.[12] The text represents the Great Trek, the northwards movement of the Boers who left the Cape Colony due to the British claim to supremacy, and is therefore in line with other South African texts of the early 20th century, such as Francis Carey Slater's poem "The Trek" (1938).

Even though *The Turning Wheels* calls the Trek "[t]he logical outcome of the freeing of the slaves by the English in the middle of harvest",[13] Britain as an enemy is quickly replaced by the different native peoples the Boers encounter on their trek. It is them, the 'common enemy' in different wars, who unite the Trekboers: the different treks of Hendrik van der Berg and Paul Pieters only come together when they plan a joint attack. As soon as this situation is over, they part again. The character Zwart Piete, who kidnaps Hendrik's young wife, can be read to crosscheck this argument. By taking Hendrik's wife, he expels himself from Boer society. Directly before doing so, he begins to question the open racism that he and the other Afrikaners have espoused: "I sometimes wonder if there is as much difference as we think between black and white."[14] He parts with his community and at the same time gives up their 'common enemy'. However, in the end Zwart Piete returns and reunites with his people just prior to another battle against the Zulu and Xhosa, who have joined forces in order to finally defeat the Boers.

The Turning Wheels constructs groups along ethnic lines through the depiction of warfare. The text thereby identifies war as a key element in the formation of Afrikaner nationalism and at the same time comments on segregation legislation and colonialism by relating inter-ethnic conflicts to warfare.

A similar situation can be found in Herman Charles Bosman's "Mafeking Road", published in the eponymous collection of short stories in 1947 by the Central News Agency, a Cape Town publishing house and retailer.[15] However, the short story deals with a different historical setting as it focuses on the South African War. The South African War, fought by British and Afrikaner troops from 1899 to 1902, resulting in the British annexation of the Transvaal and the Orange Free State, is probably the most popular war setting in early 20th century South Africa. It features in many texts, such as Sol Plaatje's *Boer War Diary* (around 1900) as well as two out of three of Deneys Reitz's autobiographical texts, *Commando* (1929) and *Trekking On* (1933), which are completed by the final episode *No Outspan* (1943). This focus is due to the time of the South African War – most writers active in the early 20th century experienced the war themselves.

As was the case with *The Turning Wheels*, Bosman's "Mafeking Road" also constructs oppositions. Framed by a discourse about story telling and competing perspectives, Bosman's frequently featuring narrator Oom Schalk tells the story of father and son in a Boer regiment. After being ordered to Mafeking, they are beaten there by the British but they manage to escape. When they are attacked after they have re-trooped, the son loses his nerves and tries to surrender to the British. His father prevents this by killing him before he can reach the enemy lines. The father represents a nationalist attitude; he stands for the tight cohesion of the Boers. "Mafeking Road" constructs a violent victory of a nationalist Boer union over individual freedom, for which the son had yearned. If he could, he would "draw up a peace treaty between Stephanus van Barnevelt [the son] and England".[16] Bosman's text allows for a number of related interpretations. Firstly, it suggests that the war against the British contributed decisively to the formation of a nationalist Afrikaner group. Secondly, the community is more important than individual families and, thirdly, it is the older generation, in this case the father, who pushes through their ideals against the young ones. I therefore read the story as a comment on existing segregation and looming apartheid that draws on outdated ideals instead of following visionary individuals.

It is striking that Cloete's and Bosman's texts use different 'opponents' to construct the Boers as a fixed unit. This change in the representation of Afrikaner nationalism indicates that South Africa's multi-ethnic conflict is being more and more politicised throughout the decades prior to apartheid. While in 1937 the Xhosa are constructed as the Boers' enemies, which represents the conflict as an allegedly real one that is related to natural resources, in 1947 the British are constructed as the enemies, which adds an institutionalised political dimension to the conflict, since the British were the opponents to the Boers in (the exclusively white) parliament.

Sol Plaatje's novel *Mhudi*[17] is a war related text that takes a different perspective on war settings, namely from a black African point of view. Similar to *The Turning Wheels*, the novel is set in southern Africa in the 1830s. However, it focuses on the Mfecane, a period of conflicts and mass migration caused by the Zulu expansion, and not so much on the Great Trek. It describes the conflict between the Tswana people Barolong and the Zulu people Matabele, which, in the text, is solved militarily in favour of the Barolong with the help of the Boers. Parallel to this conflict, the plot features the partnership of the protagonist Mhudi and her husband Ra-Thaga.

An interesting debate has been going on about the originality of *Mhudi*'s script. Plaatje already wrote his novel around the year 1917, but was only able to publish it in 1930 with Lovedale, after a number of publishers had turned it down.[18] Long after Lovedale had published the text, Stephen Gray discovered Plaatje's manuscript in the nineteen-seventies and had it published by Quagga Press in 1975 and in Heinemann's acclaimed *African Writers* series in 1978.[19] The versions at hand differ in a number of details. I will show that the different publishers influence the text's representation of colonial history and therefore also its interpretation as a text that criticises colonialism.

The major difference between the two editions is that in the Heinemann edition the narrator is explicitly referred to as the son of the protagonists. The text connects past and present by suggesting a continuity between the fictional time and the time of publication, the narrator becomes an element of the text's constructed reliability. In the Lovedale edition, the respective reference is left out, so that the narrator does not become visible to the readers. Furthermore, allusions to the imperial aspirations of the Matabele are omitted in the Lovedale edition. Much more so than the Lovedale version, the Heinemann text therefore creates the image of indigenous people fighting against unjust imperialists, which equally alludes to the British and the Boers. Finally, in the very end, the Lovedale edition contains a reference to tribal structures, which is not included in the Heinemann text.[20] Throughout colonial history, these allegedly tribal structures were enforced by colonial rulers to uphold power.[21] Hence, the Heinemann edition constructs an indigenous past that does not rely on colonial structures as much as the Lovedale edition suggests.

The most important question then is how these changes came about. On the one hand, Tim Couzens and Stephen Gray conclude that it was the influence of Lovedale Press that led to the changes in the manuscript from their assumption that Plaatje's manuscript was the 'original' version.[22] On the other hand, according to Michael Chapman and A. E. Voss, no proof exists that Plaatje had to change his text. Voss suggests that the text should not be viewed as static but as developing, which makes it difficult to speak of an original text.[23] I suggest to turn to Plaatje's political ideology to find possible answers to this question – he was the first secretary of the South African Native National Congress (SANNC), the precursor of the African National Congress (ANC), and he is the author of *Native Life in South Africa* (1916), in which he indicts the Natives Land Act of 1913. It remains unclear whether Plaatje was actually forced to change the manuscript or if it was preemptive obedience that caused the adjustments. In any case, it turns out that Lovedale published a text that had obviously been conceptualised in a far less colonial manner. Hence, I attribute the changes in *Mhudi* to the direct or indirect Lovedale influence since mitigating his critique of colonialism does not meet Plaatje's political activism.

4. Indigenous Communities

In addition to war, a second popular means of constructing groups along ethnic lines is the representation of indigenous communities – that is black South African communities that relate back to a pre-colonial era and that are usually portrayed in opposition to missionaries. Just as the city, the depiction of indigenous groups has different functions. On the one hand, it constructs communities in their own right that exclude European or Christian elements and therefore rejects missionaries and colonialism in general. On the other hand, the texts include Christian elements into their representations of these communities and partly abandon indigenous elements completely to create a point of connection between the indigenous past and Christian missionaries.

Mary W. Waters's *Cameos from the Kraal*, published by Lovedale in 1926,[24] uses indigenous settings for Christian purposes. Little is known about the author herself or her origins, except that she received a European education. *Cameos from the Kraal* is a collection of short folk tales, which are framed by narratives in which European people come together with Africans in a native village to tell and hear stories. South African oral literature is therefore appropriated by Europeans on the level of publication, the stories are published as a book, and on the plot level since the stories are embedded in frame narratives featuring European characters. In some episodes white characters narrate the stories themselves. This can be read as a colonial attitude, especially when considering the introductory remarks that precede the stories: "The illustrations in this book are remarkable in that they have been drawn by an untrained Native who had never received a lesson in drawing."[25] Since missionaries have institutionalised education they can hardly believe that anyone can cope without them.

To illustrate the impact the missionaries' ideas must have had on the text, I want to comment on one of the stories in the book, namely "The Winter's Tale". Here, the first-person narrator Maria, "the White Girl", asks Makulu, the grandmother, why people must die.[26] As an answer Makulu retells a creation myth that combines Christian and Zulu beliefs. While the act of creation is closely modelled on Genesis, the reason for mortality lies in a Zulu belief. This episode shows how Christianity is mediated through allegedly 'native' folk tales – this fits Lovedale's general orientation towards religious education.[27]

The poet Roy Campbell, author of *The Flamming Terrapin* (1924) and *The Wayzgoose* (1928) among others, displays an alternative to Waters's missionary attitude. In his poem "The Zulu Girl", published in the collection *Adamastor* by Faber & Faber in London in 1930, he describes a young mother who interrupts her work in the field to feed her baby.[28] Campbell uses an animal simile to describe the baby being fed: "Tugs like a puppy, grunting as he feeds."[29] Even though this might sound derogative, it also integrates the scene into the following description of the natural surroundings.[30] This account then leads to the speaker admiring the pride of those who have been colonised.

> Yet in that drowsy stream his flesh imbibes
> An old unquenched unsmotherable heat–
> The curbed ferocity of beaten tribes,
> The sullen dignity of their defeat.[31]

I therefore read the poem as a critique of the colonisers' interfering with indigenous people; colonialisation is depicted as an unreasonable affair. However, the Zulu girl does not change her way of life. She seems to carry on with her habits and traditions – only in "curbed ferocity."[32] The description of the baby being suckled implies that it takes in specific characteristics and memories. These include temperament and dignity but also the colonisers' defeat of the colonised South Africans. I therefore interpret the poem as a warning to the former coloniseres that colonialism will not be forgotten but that the memories are passed on to future generations.

I want to complete this chapter by analysing two texts by Herbert Dhlomo,[33] who is Rolfes Dhlomo's younger brother. Herbert Dhlomo's work is especially relevant for this essay because he published fiction both with Lovedale and with the secular presses. These texts do not merely illustrate a personal development, but also the possibilities that came with leaving the mission press behind. In 1936, Lovedale published Dhlomo's play *The Girl who Killed to Save*.[34] The play deals with the Xhosa cattle-killing of 1856,[35] when, following a young woman's prophecy, Xhosa people killed their cattle and destroyed their crop because they believed that this would bring back their dead ancestors who would then drive the colonisers out of South Africa. Dhlomo provides a historiographical sketch as a background to which the fictional text can be related. Just as was the case whith *Mhudi*, the text seems quite plausible because it is rooted in allegedly historical facts. In the play, the cattle-killing at first appears to be something between superstition and fraud. The killing is then exploited by the missionary, who interprets the incident as God's way of leading the 'natives' to a 'better', a Christian life, which he generously offers. By providing for the starving victims, who have destroyed their harvest and killed their cattle in hope for a better future, the Christian church becomes a rescuer and beneficiary at the same time. The character Daba, a convert, sums up his newly found belief: "[H]unger and destitution drove them into the paths of life, led them to the missionary and his divine message."[36] Dhlomo reconstructs an episode of South African, especially of Xhosa history as a sign of God and therefore integrates Christian religion into Xhosa history. Hence, *The Girl who Killed to Save* is an even clearer constituent of mission policy than Waters's *Cameos from the Kraal* was. Dhlomo presents the mission both as a God-given institution and as Africa's future.

Only five years after *The Girl who Killed to Save*, in 1941, the Durban-based publishing house Knox published Dhlomo's epic poem *Valley of a Thousand Hills*. Not only does it differ in genre and publisher, it also differs decisively in terms of content. The speaker yearns for the past, praising indigenous life, the South African landscapes as well as Zulu gods and heroes. At the same time, the poem displays an anti-colonial attitude:

> Man-made steel monsters crush all flesh,
> And flashing darts and words kill joy!
> Greed-storms tear down the groves of Hope!
> Man fights 'gainst beasts of his own form
> Who claw and nail him to the Cross[37]

Here, both the colonisers' armed forces and politics, metonymically referred to as "darts and words", are blamed for interfering with African people. This dissatisfaction with white politics, even of the liberal kind, also becomes obvious in Dhlomo's further works. The subtitle of his poem "Fired!", for example, reads "Lines on an African intellectual being sacked by White Liberals for his independent ideas". Another play's title is telling, when considering the pass laws of the 1920s that enforced segregation by regulating residence and movements of non-whites: *The Pass (Arrested and Discharged)* (1943).[38]

The quote from *Valley of a Thousand Hills* also underlines the role Christian missionaries play, who are referred to as a significant part of the colonial machinery. *Valley of a Thousand Hills* criticises the very Christian influence on South African peoples that *The Girl who Killed to Save* advocated. It is certain that Lovedale would never have published a text like *Valley of a Thousand Hills* because of its critical attitude towards the missions. Consequently, Dhlomo chose a secular publishing house instead. Even though this does not necessarily indicate the mission press's Christian influence, this case illustrates the narrow thematic focus that was set by the mission press. This is also suggested by a text that resembles *The Girl who Killed to Save* in its content structure. In his epic poem *Thuthula*, J. J. R. Jolobe narrates the story of an abduction of one of Chief Ndlambe's wives. Through this event, the text discusses mono- and polygamy on a meta-level. David Attwell ironically claims that "[t]he implication is also that only when the currently imperfect historical adjustment to Christianity is complete […] will the unhappy Thuthulas of the world be relieved."[39] Just as it was with all the mission case studies, Lovedale always kept an eye on the mission's didactic-religious purpose.

5. Miscegenation

I have demonstrated so far that race relations and segregation had been key issues in South African writing already before apartheid. In my last section, I want to discuss literary representations of relationships between partners of different skin colour, to show how race relations are represented within the family, the most private sphere.

In all previous sections I considered Lovedale texts and compared them to other publications. This will not be possible for this chapter, since miscegenation does not feature in the mission texts – it is a purely secular theme. However, also in non-mission texts there are different attitudes towards miscegenation, which I want to outline in the following.

A prominent example of this theme is Sarah Gertrude Millin's *God's Step-Children*, published by Constable & Co., London, in 1924.[40] In her episodic bildungsroman, Millin focuses on miscegenation by outlining the lives of Reverend Andrew Flood, who comes to a small Khoi village as a missionary in the 1820s, and his descendants. Flood marries a 'Hottentot', as the text refers to the south-western African Khoi, to demonstrate that, before God, all people are equal – no matter the colour of their skin. The text presents four generations whose members are shown to marry and have children with white partners. The last in this line is Barry, whose skin is virtually white. Around 1910, he marries an English woman and has a baby with her. However, he is so afraid that his child might have a darker skin than himself that he leaves his pregnant wife and goes to a small Khoi village as a missionary, just as his ancestor Andrew Flood had done. Barry's fear shows how important skin colour in the (fictional) newly founded Union of South Africa is and that being recognised by white society is not possible as long as prejudices and social barriers still exist. The text uses Barry's double return to his roots, both Khoi and missionary, to comment on the ongoing racism that reproduces an 1820s situation around 1910.

Reading this text in the context of my section on urbanisation helps putting Barry's fate into perspective. Parallel to the protagonists turning 'whiter' from generation to generation, they also move closer to the city until Barry finally lives in Cape Town. *God's Step-Children* suggests whiteness as a necessary prerequisite for successfully coping with the then current social and political developments, ongoing urbanisation and segregation. Being white has always been the aim throughout the generations of Flood's descendants. Barry is, however, still not able to be part of society – instead the novel removes him to the 'Hottentot' village and therefore to the 1820s.

William Plomer, in contrast, approaches miscegenation differently in his debut novel *Turbott Wolfe* that was published in 1926 by Hogarth Press.[41] Along with the English missionary Friston, the Dutch-born Mabel, the black priest Zachary and his black shop assistant Caleb, the protagonist Turbott Wolfe founds the organisation Young Africa. They believe "[t]hat Africa is not the white man's country" and propagate miscegenation, which here means 'mixing' of ethnicities rather than attempting to become white, as the key to a unified South Africa.[42] Although Wolfe commits himself to these principles and openly socialises with black South Africans, he does not actually live miscegenation, as Mabel and Zachary do, who get married. I therefore read Wolfe as a critical representation of a British liberalism that only pays lip services to pro-African movements.[43] However, the novel

Turbott Wolfe gives miscegenation a chance. This is also the main difference to *God's Step-Children*. Millin's text accounts for miscegenation as a failed attempt on the part of the natives at becoming white, Plomer's text suggests it as a means of bringing the different ethnicities, i.e. people of different skin colour in this context, together.

Roy Campbell's 1928 poem "The Wayzgoose, Part I" comments on the political impact of *Turbott Wolfe*: "Plomer, 'twas you who, though a boy in age, / Awoke a sleepy continent to rage".[44] This "rage" does not only refer to resistance against racism but also to the reaction of Plomer's political opponents – *Turbott Wolfe* was received very critically in South Africa.[45] This shows that miscegenation was a controversial topic in South Africa. It was so controversial that mission presses seem to have avoided it completely. Of course, a valid statement on such non-existence is difficult. This blank space, nevertheless, is quite telling.

6. Conclusion

My overview of South African writing between the 1920s and 1948 has shown that critical writing is not a phenomenon restricted to apartheid literature, but that a culture of political writing was established much earlier. The texts use urbanisation, war, indigenous communities and miscegenation to criticise colonialism, racism and especially the segregation legislation that was passed during this period. However, religious and secular publications approach these themes differently. It turns out that Lovedale texts are far less critical than their secular counterparts. Mission texts suggest Christianity to cope with all issues the texts raise. Secular publications also include Christian religion, but they represent it far more critically. Accordingly, Lovedale texts tend to support colonialism. Even if the texts reject segregation and racism, they approve of the general idea of colonialism since Christian missions and colonial activities go hand in hand.

As especially the case of *Mhudi* has shown, it is difficult to find out whether and how far mission presses have actually exerted pressure, demanded changes or maybe exclusively accepted material suitable to their aims. However, a clear policy is visible when comparing missionary with secular literary publications. Considering the fact that mission publications aimed at black readers and secular publishing houses almost exclusively addressed a white readership, it can be concluded that black South African readers were largely confronted with rather uncritical literature. With their distinct and unquestionable principles, the mission presses thus continued a colonial tradition well into 20th century South Africa.

Notes

1 Oliphant (2000: 111-112).
2 There are a number of studies and overviews on publishing in South Africa without a special focus on literature, such as Nicholas Evans's and Monica Seeber's *The Politics of Publishing in South Africa*. The volume includes contributions by Nhlanhla Maake and Andries Oliphant that consider the period before apartheid but that do not prominently address the publishing of fictional texts.
3 See Bourdieu (1995); for a German summary of Bourdieu's theory see Jurt (1995: 69-107).
4 See White (1992: 74-77).
5 *An African Tragedy* is available online at "Empire Online" which can be accessed via German university libraries under <http://www.empire.amdigital.co.uk/contents/document-detail.aspx?sectionid=210>.
6 Plomer's collection *I Speak of Africa* that contains "Ula Masondo" is out of print and it is hardly ever available in libraries or second-hand book shops.
7 New editions of *Mine Boy* and *Cry, the Beloved Country* are available in Germany, the UK and the USA. For further comments on *Mine Boy* and labour migration see also Kirsten Rüther's article in this volume.
8 Abrahams (1989: 183).
9 *The Little Karoo* has been reprinted and it is available in Germany, the UK and the USA.
10 P. Smith (1952: 35).
11 The author later adopted the praise name Tatamkulu Afrika under which he started to publish poetry and prose again in the 1990s.
12 *The Turning Wheels* is out of print but it is available second-hand.
13 Cloete (1946: 2).
14 *Ibid.* 233.
15 *Mafeking Road* has been reprinted by Archipelago Books in 1998 and it is available in Germany, the UK and the USA.
16 Bosman (1998: 62).

17 Stephen Gray's edition of *Mhudi* has been reissued by Penguin in 2006 and it is available in Germany, the UK and the USA.
18 See Couzens (1994: 7).
19 See Voss (1989: 20); Since the Heinemann version is the best known edition, I will refer to it in the course of this chapter when referring to the 'original' script.
20 *Ibid.* 21.
21 Bley (1986: 6).
22 Chapman (1996: 210).
23 Voss (1989: 21).
24 *Cameos from the Kraal* has been made accessible by the non-profit organisation *Internet Archive* under <http://www.archive.org/details/cameosfromkraalw00wateiala>.
25 Waters (1926: 13).
26 *Ibid.* 37.
27 See White (1992: 70).
28 *Adamastor* has not been reissued but single poems can easily be found on the internet.
29 Campbell (1971: 43).
30 See R. Smith (1970: 7).
31 Campbell (1971: 43).
32 *Ibid.*
33 For further information on Herbert Dhlomo, see Riaan Oppelt's article in this volume.
34 It is very difficult to obtain any of Herbert Dhlomo's works. All his texts are out of print. His *Collected Works*, edited by Nick Visser and Tim Couzens in 1985, have not been reissued and his texts are hardly ever available second-hand and if so, they are quite expensive. Only very few libraries hold copies of Dhlomo's texts.
35 The Xhosa cattle-killing is a popular element of South African Literature that still features in recent South African texts such as, most prominently, in Zakes Mda's novel *Heart of Redness* (2000).
36 H. Dhlomo (1985b: 29).
37 H. Dhlomo (1962: 36).
38 See Visser & Couzens (1985: XI).
39 Attwell (1999: 277).
40 *God's Step-Children* is out of print but it is available second-hand.
41 *Turbott Wolfe* has been reissued in 2003 but it is scarcely obtainable anymore. There are, however, a number of copies available second-hand.
42 Plomer (1993: 70).
43 See for example Davis (2007: 98).

44 Campbell (1989: 142), see also Davis (2007: 97).
45 See Davis (2007: 97).

Bibliography

Abrahams, Peter: *Mine Boy*, Oxford, 1989. [first published in 1946]
Attwell, David: "Reprisals of Modernity in Black South African 'Mission' Writing", *Journal of Southern African Studies* 25:2, 1999, 267-285.
Bley, Helmut: "Tribalismus oder die Verzerrung der afrikanischen Geschichte", *SOWI* 15, 1986, 5-10.
Bosman, Herman Charles: "Mafeking Road". – In H. C. B.: *Mafeking Road*, New York, 1998, pp. 57-64. [first published in 1947]
Bourdieu, Pierre: *The Rules of Art. Genesis and Structure of the Literary Field*, Stanford, 1995.
Campbell, Roy: "The Zulu Girl". – In R. C.: *Adamastor*, Westport, 1971, p. 43. [first published in 1930]
---: "The Wayzgoose, Part I". – In Stephen Gray (Ed.): *The Penguin Book of Southern African Verse*, London et al., 1989, pp. 130-143.
Chapman, Michael: *Southern African Literatures*, London & New York, 1996.
Charlton, John: *Broken Earth*, London & Melbourne, 1940.
Cloete, Stuart: *The Turning Wheels*, New York, 1946.
Couzens, Tim: "Introduction". – In Solomon T. Plaatje: *Mhudi*. Ed. Stephen Gray, Oxford, 1994, pp. 1-20.
Davis, Geoffrey: "South Africa". – In Lars Eckstein (Ed.): *English Literatures Across the Globe*, Paderborn, 2007, pp. 86-107.
Dhlomo, Herbert I. E.: *Valley of a Thousand Hills*, Durban, 1962. [first published in 1941]
---: "Fired". – In H. D.: *Collected Works*. Eds. Nick Visser & Tim Couzens, Johannesburg, 1985a, pp. 373-374.
---: "The Girl Who Killed to Save". – In H. D.: *Collected Works*. Eds. Nick Visser & Tim Couzens, Johannesburg, 1985b, pp. 3-29.
---: "The Pass (Arrested and Discharged)". – In H. D.: *Collected Works*. Eds. Nick Visser & Tim Couzens, Johannesburg, 1985c, pp. 189-209.
Dhlomo, Rolfes R. R.: *An African Tragedy*, Alice, 1928.
Heywood, Christopher: *A History of South African Literature*, Cambridge, 2004.
Jolobe, James J. R.: *Thuthula*, London, 1938.
Jurt, Joseph: *Das Literarische Feld. Das Konzept Pierre Bourdieus in Theorie und Praxis*, Darmstadt, 1995.

Maake, Nhlanhla: "Publishing and Perishing. Books, People and Reading in African Languages in South Africa". – In Nicholas Evans & Monica Seeber (Eds.): *The Politics of Publishing in South Africa*, London & Scottsville, 2000, pp. 127-159.

Millin, Sarah Gertrude: *God's Step-Children*, Johannesburg *et al.*, 1951. [first published in 1924]

Mphahlele, Es'kia: *Man Must Live, and Other Stories*, Cape Town, 1946.

Oliphant, Andries: "From Colonialism to Democracy. Writers and Publishing in South Africa". – In Nicholas Evans & Monica Seeber (Eds.): *The Politics of Publishing in South Africa*, London & Scottsville, 2000, pp. 107-126.

Paton, Alan: *Cry, the Beloved Country*, London, 1984. [first published in 1948]

Plaatje, Solomon T.: *Mhudi*. Ed. A. E. Voss, Jeppestown, 1989. [first published by Lovedale in 1930]

---: *Mhudi*. Ed. Stephen Gray, Oxford, 1994. ['original' typescript, first published in 1975]

Plomer, William: "Ula Masondo". – In W. P.: *I speak of Africa*, London, 1938, pp. 83-150. [first published in 1927]

---: "A Fall of Rock". – In Stephen Gray (Ed.): *The Penguin Book of Southern African Verse*, London *et al.*, 1989, pp. 156-157.

---: *Turbott Wolfe*, Jeppestown, 1993. [first published in 1926]

Smith, Pauline: "The Pain". – In P. S.: *The Little Karoo*, New York, 1952, pp. 1-19. [first published in 1926]

Smith, Rowland: "Roy Campbell and His French Sources", *Comparative Literature* 22:1, 1970, 1-18.

Visser, Nick & Tim Couzens: "Introduction". – In Herbert I. E. Dhlomo: *Collected Works*. Eds. N. V. & T. C., Johannesburg, 1985, pp. IX-XV.

Voss, A. E.: "Introduction". – In Solomon T. Plaatje: *Mhudi*. Ed. A. E. V., Jeppestown, 1989, pp. 13-22.

Waters, Mary W.: *Cameos from the Kraal*, Alice, 1926.

White, Tim: "The Lovedale Press during the Directorship of R.H.W. Shepherd", *English in Africa* 19:2, 1992, 69-84.

Riaan Oppelt (*Stellenbosch*)

Dialogues between 'Old' and 'New' in Contemporary South African Theatre

1. Introduction

After the first democratic elections in South Africa in 1994, the country forged a unique international identity for itself by emphasising the concept of the 'New South Africa', symbolised by a multi-coloured national flag, a reworked constitution and eleven languages officially registered. These steps pointed to the country's multi-cultural make-up, so long distanced by apartheid policies, and in the arts the changes followed suit. What was formerly split between a theatre of rebellion and a theatre of the establishment began to merge as a fragmented, commercial theatre, combining the underground force of anti-establishment theatre with the larger audience of mainstream local theatre. This paper aims to explore the voices apparent in contemporary South African theatre,[1] addressing immediate national concerns while engaging with the voices of pre-1994 South African theatre.

Key media events in South Africa since 1994 had an element of performance to them, as if the country's new-found democracy was being presented as live theatre. After a storied struggle and victory against universally-condemned forces of injustice, South Africa held a media spotlight few countries could aspire to, and three media events in the mid-to-late 1990s emphasised exactly why the real-life drama of South Africa was playing to packed houses: the presidential inauguration of Nelson Mandela in 1994, the country's hosting of the 1995 Rugby World Cup and the televised amnesty hearings of the Truth and Reconciliation Commission (TRC) in 1996-99. Mandela's inauguration was the moment of both the fairy-tale ending and the new beginning in this dramatic presentation of the new South Africa. The Rugby World Cup, with Mandela again in a starring role, showed the consummative harmony of a country with itself. The televised amnesty hearings of the TRC declared that the country's new beginning was realistic and that the country was aware of itself, aware of the hardships of reconciliation and moving forward, and not simply awash in romance and denial. The Shakespearian adage that "all the world's a stage" may certainly ring true if one's own country is the star performer on a stage with the rest of the world as its audience. It is proposed later in this paper that in contemporary South African theatre there is reflexivity, a self-awareness that the play is not the only thing anymore, that with the rich, complex socio-cultural history of South Africa, no play post-1994 can even hope to deny, or pretend to deny, the epoch it is a part of. Of course, South African theatre before 1994 could say exactly the same thing, as the most important plays and musical productions were the ones that carried messages against apartheid, that drew attention to their resistance, their commentary, their protest and their largely mutual goals of seeing, inspiring or actively bringing about change. The dialogue between the old and the new must consider the dynamic between performer and spectator, character and audience. In the 21st century, perhaps more so than in the 20th (or even 19th) century, but for entirely different reasons, the audience knows it is a part of the theatre experience of South Africa: it is as much a part of any production as it is in the day-to-day life of the country, and it knows its part in the success or failure of any venture. To identify South African theatre post-1994 is very much also an exercise in identifying South African theatre audiences post-1994.

It is here where we may insert an idea of 'cultural performance' as theatre to discuss "'particular instances of cultural festivals, recitations, plays, dances, musical concepts' and the like [...as] a culture articulates its self-image through such performances and thus represents and exhibits itself to its own members as well as to outsiders".[2] Yet, to further explore this idea in the context of 21st-century South African theatre, Gino Fransman[3] discusses a liminal co-habitation between the communion of performers and audience and mainstream society, quoting Carlson:

> The sense of occasion and focus, as well as the overarching social envelope [...] combine with the physicality of theatrical performance to make it one of the most powerful and efficacious procedures that human

society has developed for the endlessly fascinating process of cultural and personal self-reflection and experimentation.[4]

Fransman notes that "highlighted by Carlson is the way that participants can be reflected upon within the performance space",[5] indicating ways in which, on the part of both performers and audience, there is an actual act. The performers could 'break frame' and step out of character to address the audience as themselves, the actors, and still construct this as part of the performance, and the effect of this on the audience would doubtless be monitored by the audience itself. A well-aimed joke or barb, for instance, or a cast member 'breaking frame' to interact with members of the audience, may result in the unity of the audience fragmenting as certain members of the audience scrutinise other members. Those audience members being scrutinised suddenly become aware that they are being watched, that the show has now transferred to them, and they could start 'acting' differently, or 'playing' their part.

While far from being unique, this tendency to get the audience involved with itself as well as the play/musical is a regular feature of South African theatre post-1994, and merits further study of "the performance space that enables the identity negotiation" and, on another level, "expressing national culture".[6] A section of national culture expressed through comedy, especially plays or stand-up comedy routines, finds the performer often surprising (or perhaps not) the audience with a moment in which it gasps and looks at itself, and not the stage.

In this paper, I attempt to pursue a concept of performance and performativity that suggests a very close relationship between South African theatre and a notion of enacting nationhood that sees theatre on the streets as much as on a stage. The vague idea of a dialogue between 'old' and 'new' South African theatre is more a suggestion of instances in which a play from before 1994 (particularly between the 1960s and 1990s) looked ahead to a new South Africa, and a play from after 1994 looked back to, or referred to, theatre from before 1994. There are far too many relevant plays and other theatre works, as well as epochs and theatre forms to mention and discuss in any agreeable capacity in a paper such as this, so only selected examples are cited and very briefly discussed. Too often, essays on South African theatre end up as being essays on Athol Fugard, which is a tendency this paper hopes to avoid, while still giving Fugard the necessary respect and mention he deserves as one of the most important writers in South African literary history. Temple Hauptfleisch's *Theatre & Society in South Africa* (1997) and Loren Kruger's *The Drama of South Africa* (1999) are perhaps the two most dynamic, must-read texts that are recommended to gain a fuller appreciation of discussions on South African theatre. Very minor surveys of South African drama in the 20th century are offered before the paper returns to looking at the present and at questions of cultural performativity that are invited by a comedy show that has endured for over a decade on the South African stage.

2. *21st-Century South African Theatre*

According to Temple Hauptfleisch in an unpublished lecture, in the last five years of the previous millennium South African theatre could almost be said to have been present in the social fabric of everyday South African life post-1994. This was a time when the well-vaunted and seductive 'Madiba Magic'—the effervescent influence of Nelson Mandela on South Africa's people as well as the impression he made abroad—was at its peak. Apart from the almost theatrical events of Mandela's inauguration and the Rugby World Cup final in 1995 (the basis for the book *Playing the Enemy*, by John Carlin, and the film *Invictus*, directed by Clint Eastwood), the gruelling 'performances' of the televised amnesty hearings in this period became major talking points internationally. It would be a telling component in much of the local theatrical output up to 2011, the most famous example being an early one: Jane Taylor's *Ubu and the Truth Commission* (1997), a multi-media venture that combined actors with puppetry and documentary footage, with the inclusion of actual witness testimonies from TRC hearings.

With the 21st century came increased urgency in socio-economic and socio-cultural concerns that had been obvious but not vociferously addressed before the end of the Mandela presidential term: escalating rates of violent crime, rape, child abuse, housing, poverty, critically high rises in HIV/AIDS afflictions, obvious in-fighting among the highest leaders of the ANC and xenophobia. These concerns were noted by both community and mainstream theatre outlets, with serious productions like Lara Foot Newton's *Tshepang* (2003), based on the real-life rape of a nine-month old baby in 2001, and Mpumelo Paul Grootboom's *Relativity* (2005), which dramatised violence against women in townships through its plot of a serial killer hunting and slaying young women at night. Theatre celebrating the new South Africa may still have been active, but certainly a sense of cynicism and interrogation became more apparent in the first ten years of the new millennium.

However, there could be no denying that South African theatre had also lost some of the manic energy cultivated by its own partaking in the fight against apartheid, and lavish imported musicals and stand-up comedy dominated the box-office (www.realreview.co.za) as a sign that global trends had taken firm hold. This marked an odd return to the 19th century and much of the 20th century, when English-language (and often Afrikaans) theatre in the country was mostly made up of famous European productions that local theatre historians describe as light entertainment. The 'straight' play format became increasingly outmuscled by revues, skits and one-man theatre. Veteran playwrights like Athol Fugard, the best-known South African theatre practitioner globally, especially due to his seminal works between the 1960s and 1990s, seemingly had less relevance for contemporary audiences, even if critics still lauded his later works like *Exits and Entrances* (2004) and *Victory* (2007). His older works are still unanimously revered: two revivals of Fugard plays, *Hello and Goodbye* (1966) and *Sizwe Banzi Is Dead* (1972, with the Serpent Players), were major successes mid-decade (www.realreview.co.za). Comedy, more often than not infused with satire, was arguably more successful in delivering commentary on the state of the nation in the 21st century. A veteran like Pieter Dirk-Uys delivered on the biting satire and suspicion mixed with humour that made him famous in the 1980s with the provocative one-man show *Elections and Erections* (2003), while a multi-lingual performer like Nik Rabinowitz earned praise for his comic skit, *One Man, One Goat* (2006).

Regular arts critic for the *Mail and Guardian* weekly, Brent Meersman, lamented in a 2011 overview of the last decade of South African theatre that the 'straight' play, the play-as-entertainment-but-still-relevant form, was dying out.[7] However, productions like Fiona Coyne's *The Shadrack Affair* (2004) and Ian Bruce's *Groundswell* (2005) were promising signs that conventionally structured plays (or plays in the Western tradition) were ploughing the humanitarian trepidations the country provided on a daily basis. While the former is a flawed but sensitive melodrama that deals with the theme of forgiveness and makes a nod to Paul Slabolepsky's *Saturday Night at the Palace* (1982, briefly discussed later), *Groundswell* is a gripping thriller that hinges around the contested issue of white guilt in post-apartheid South Africa.

Festivals like the annual Grahamstown Arts Festival, the InniBos, Volksblad-Kunstefees and the Klein Karoo National Arts Festival ensure the continued prominence of theatre in South Africa. This does not mean, though, that the government itself has been overwhelmingly supportive in providing structures for the growth of theatre in black communities. Mainstream theatre is still not much closer to these communities than it was pre-1994:

> The real culprit is government's poor implementation of a flawed arts and culture policy and gross under funding for the first decade after democracy. The highly subsidised state theatres under commercial pressure favour the already empowered rich producers. Theatre doesn't exist outside of its audience, and black theatre will see its heyday once audiences transform themselves, as is happening with coloured theatre in the Cape. If plays have to engage with audiences at many of our festivals and theatres that remain stubbornly white, well then, educating the elite is also a worthy pursuit.[8]

It is apt to call South African theatre vibrant, but that may come at the risk of assuming the vibrancy is necessarily associated with a spirit of celebration, when the vibrancy really includes works that question before they think of celebrating, or reflect on what they are supposed to be celebrating. The eminent Afrikaans novelist, Marlene van Niekerk, attacked the performativity of South Africa, especially around the 2010 Soccer World Cup hosted by the country, from a conflicted white perspective in her controversial play, *Die Kortstondige Raklewe van Anastasia W* (2011, "The Short-lived Shelf Life of Anastasia W", my translation), a play written and only available in Afrikaans. Her lament was similar to that of a local, controversial journalist, who in 2010 declared that it was her duty to puncture the aura of performativity during the World Cup whenever she could to report on news that mattered, such as the killing of a baby girl in a township. It is this form of anti-performance that is ironically burlesqued almost to the point of the grotesque in Van Niekerk's sensationalist but defective play, as her argument is intensely one-sided. While there are many acknowledgements of this one-sidedness in the dialogue of the play, it comes off as rather apologetic and hardly progressive.

3. Indigenous South African Theatre

In *Theatre & Society in South Africa* (1997), Temple Hauptfleisch identifies and outlines two distinct theatre traditions in South African history: African and European. The former, according to Hauptfleisch, is not easily traced historically, with the earliest written entries alluding to African performance going back to 17th-century travel writing,[9] although in some instances bushman rock art dating back 25,000 years depicts the shamanistic dances of the San in the Kalahari Desert. These and other elements of African performativity could also be identified in the later heritages of the Zulu, Xhosa and other cultures through wedding ceremonies, initiation ceremonies, harvest festivals and the like, which despite not existing in the preferred Western form of writing, nevertheless seemed to be arranged mimetically and based on the oral tradition. This predates the arrival of the European tradition in South Africa, and the mimetic tradition is still evident in contemporary South African theatre.[10] Hauptfleisch identifies five components that are useful in discussing indigenous theatre in South Africa: the presence of ritual and symbolism, the emphasis on public performance and audience participation, a musical base, the tradition of oral narrative and distinctive dance forms.[11]

The studies dedicated to the importance of oral tradition in indigenous theatre and South African cultures in general have, in fact, gained much academic momentum since 1994.[12] The influence definitely shows in post-1994 theatre, especially as part of the hybrid, new theatre of the country, prevalent in a production like Brett Bailey's *i-Mumbo Jumbo* (1998). This work contains depictions of indigenous rituals while implying, through re-enacting historical events, "the constructedness of cultural and historical memory" in a complex, controversial manner,[13] in effect putting ritualistic African performance on a Westernised stage. However, as this could still not be described as a large part of mainstream theatre in South Africa, Mzo Sirayi's argument that there remains a neglect of indigenous theatre may yet remain resonant. In fact, one of the concerns of Hauptfleisch's lifelong research is that Western culture undeniably affects African tradition, so much so that a synthesis of the two is more present now in the arts. In theatre, this would very much be a case of a new tradition being forged even if the origins of this new tradition are hard to trace.

For Western knowledge of South African indigenous theatre to have come about, contact between missionaries and Africans, as well as English settlers and Africans, Hauptfleisch briefly mentions, would have been of importance.[14] With the missionary influence in the 19th century came literacy, which owed much to the missionary's background and classical education and training in Europe. As this cultural exchange took place the English theatre tradition, following on from the Second British Occupation of the Cape (1806-1910), was beginning to operate in South Africa, and subsequently African theatre found itself pulled closer to European theatre through the English influence. A speculative assessment could be made that despite the work of missionaries to bring native South Africans closer to European religion, enlightenment and respectability, indigenous theatre would be ignored owing to the racist, colonial Western typecasting of native Africans as primitive and backward.[15]

Sirayi cites some examples of African indigenous theatre: oral narratives, an indigenous African wedding celebration, and an African indigenous doctors' celebration.[16] When he studies oral narratives, Sirayi points to the research of Green, who deconstructs oral narratives as "various types of narratives, such as myths, legends, tales, riddles and proverbs".[17]

Stephen Gray speaks of the authority assumed by the story-teller operating in the oral tradition, recasting original tales and sending them to the future based on the supposed authentication of his/her interpretation of history.[18] A history that is not written down, "cannot be wholly scientifically researched",[19] yet it strongly encourages the study of the culture it belongs to, which suggests a fluidity that is in itself theatrical because it demands witnesses, an audience that engages and participates. Sirayi offers an extensive description of how this kind of oral theatre functions:

> The story-teller does not have at his or her disposal some of the theatrical devices employed in other theatre forms. Characters are played by the story-teller although he or she does not use particular costumes, a special stage and settings to actualize the story. The narration is dramatized by the use of various other theatrical devices – for example, a deep voice demonstrates a wicked or frightening character such as a monster, chattering characterizes the liar, and mumbling is implied for stupid characters. Whispers or low voices indicate danger.... The occasion also determines a tale's theatricality. Occasions such as pleasure nights, hunting, herding and courtyard discussion dictate the types of stories performed.[20]

Often, such performances are both pedagogical and entertaining, providing a life lesson through symbolism and poetic representation that must be constantly exciting for the audience, or else the story-teller must relinquish his/her turn and vacate the performance area for someone else.[21] Keyan Tomaselli shows links to indigenous theatre in his overall definition of black theatre by describing it as a form of communication "which is oral in tradition, oral in construction and oral in rendition" and overtly makes the connection when he claims that "in indigenous black theatre the audience supplies the social and semiotic context which makes the play's message meaningful".[22]

The conflicts of the period (the early 1980s) that Tomaselli writes from are manifest in his assertions that black South African playwrights were, in the early Greek sense, using theatre to explore and communicate, and that black South African theatre avoided the "elitist activity" of the very act of going to the theatre and the routines that went with it, from dressing up to having "hushed conversation" during a performance.[23] Instead, he argues, black South African theatre is "the product of black social experience",[24] and this theatre operates much like indigenous theatre does: with the audience as much as for them. This is a type of "committed theatre", which forces consideration of the relationship between conflicting elements of society. This relationship also draws attention to the relationship between society and history in a sort of mechanism which interrogates history from the outside even as it takes part in it.

Of course, Tomaselli's critique dates back to 1981, and he was speaking from the perspective of the very troubled 1980s. However, Sirayi's concerns over the neglect of indigenous theatre twenty years later indicate that the 'new' theatre Hauptfleisch speaks of post-1994 may not yet be giving full mind to incorporating indigenous theatre in some of the forms Sirayi described. However, it is my argument that some of the views of indigenous theatre, not least its accent on the impact of community, are indeed apparent in certain forms of comedy in more recent South African theatre.

4. Theatre in English and Black Consciousness Theatre

English-language theatre in South Africa, through the 19th and early 20th century, was for the most part merely a re-staging of famous European or American works, and the earliest amateur theatre activities may have been started by British garrisons at the Cape in the early 19th century. Of the amateur theatre produced in Cape Town, the English emphasis was largely on light entertainment, Shakespeare productions and vaudeville fare. European touring companies and stagings of famous European plays would typify much of the 19th century theatre output in English, a trend that continued into the 20th century.

Through their education at the hands of the cultural missionaries,[25] some black English writers were visible by the 1920s, the most prominent being Herbert Dhlomo (1903-56).[26] Dhlomo was a playwright, poet and critic, vice president of the Bantu Dramatic Society, journalist and, later, African Nationalist.[27] Dhlomo tried to bring African performances and Western drama closer together. Only one of his plays was published before a resurgence of critical interest in his work saw belated publications appear in the 1980s; this was also the case with Stephen Black.[28] It was Dhlomo who "grappled in an exemplary way with the oppositions between elite and popular, imported and indigenous, literate and oral practises".[29] He is seen, especially in critical reconstruction from the 1980s onwards, as a pioneer of African literature,[30] drawing on urban settings and oral tradition as "materials for drama".[31] More common in recent re-readings of Dhlomo is a notion of him having tried to establish the idea of a national theatre that combines African and European forms.[32]

Increased racial oppression after the official implementation of apartheid in 1948 led to greater political resistance in the 1950s when an obvious protest theatre was emerging.[33] Athol Fugard's *No Good Friday*

(1959) was an indictment of the police force serving an oppressive state, while Lewis Sowden's *The Kimberley Train* (1958) took peculiar dramatic turns in representing the absurdity of race segregation. The play showed oppressed people turning on one another in ways that suggested they were enforcing apartheid practises against each other.

The vibrant Sophiatown suburb in Johannesburg provided a nucleus for black and coloured artistic culture in the 1940s and 1950s, a meeting place and place of origin for jazz musicians, writers and performers (and criminals, ranging from rogue gangsters to crime lords); comparisons are often made to New York's Harlem Renaissance. Black intellectuals were drawn to Sophiatown and, according to Kruger, may have been partly responsible for its enduring but embellished legacy in South African memory:

> Sophiatown was an actual but thoroughly imagined place that came, despite the violence perpetuated by the police as well as tsotsis [gangsters], to symbolize a utopia of racial tolerance and cultural diversity.[34]

While not disputing the memory of Sophiatown and its undeniable history as a hub for black artists and a refreshing centre of cosmopolitanism that stood up against the state, Kruger argues that "performance in and of Sophiatown formed a crucial part of urban African efforts to claim the city and with it, the attributes of urbanity, civitas, and citizenship".[35] In this context, the belief in Sophiatown and the cosmopolitanism enacted therein can be seen as a driving force in black artistic rebellion against the state, championed by political crusaders like Nelson Mandela and Ruth First. Although the police began the forced removals of Sophiatown inhabitants in 1955 and had systematically destroyed Sophiatown as a black living area (restructured as a white suburb, it was renamed Triomf) by 1957, just as it would destroy District Six in Cape Town a decade later, the area was immortalised as being the spirit behind the most famous black theatrical production of the decade, *King Kong* (1958), based on the life of boxer Ezekiel "King Kong" Dlamini, and billed as a "township musical". *King Kong* would have an enormous influence on the history of South African theatre and become the country's first major box office success abroad, touring the London West End in 1961-63. The vivacious musical (scored by Todd Matshikiza) "literally created the archetype of a new genre" and would spawn imitators like *Ipi Tombi* (1974).[36] For a while, Sophiatown's legacy rested on *King Kong* being considered as a great example of 'people's theatre' for those shut out by the apartheid system.

With increased international attention on South Africa and the fight for equal rights by those opposed to apartheid, Fugard's *The Blood Knot* (1961) found an international audience that quickly seized on the play's depiction of two coloured brothers psychologically distanced by the colour barrier the state had foisted on them. The play's disturbing suggestion of violence about to erupt at any point between the brothers, Morrie and Zach, along with its Absurd Theatre-like tone, inferred from the ridiculous role-playing games they play with each other, heralded the international arrival of Fugard as a compelling playwright.

Gibson Kente also emerged as a force in black South African theatre in the 1960s, creating dramas around performance numbers in *Manana, the Jazz Prophet* (1963) or around "stellar performers" like Kenny Majozi in *Sikhalo* (1966).[37] In the context of cultural struggle and the government's demands for segregated theatres, Kente became associated with black theatre that "turned to [its] own community for support and inspiration, adapting urban performance forms to a popular, new entertainment form which literally created its own audience and its own infrastructures".[38] Consolidating the 'people's theatre' that *King Kong* seemed an illustrious example of, *Sikhalo* and *Zwi* (1970) indicated how black theatre in the 1960s operated in the apartheid state through a shaky relationship with state-funded Performing Arts Councils (PACs); later the influence of Paulo Freire's Marxist text, *Pedagogy of the Oppressed* (1968) was evident. By the 1970s, Kente operated independently and was "one of the most successful theatre producers of popular entertainment in the country", largely on the back of his "township musicals".[39] Kente's brand of popular theatre was a statement in itself, a celebration of performing independently of the government – yet it was also defined by this very fact.

With more revolutionary content, black theatre plays of the 1970s were regarded as works of the anti-apartheid Black Consciousness Movement (BCM) which Robert Kavanagh, drawing on the work of BCM leader Steve Biko, estimates to have originated in the late 1950s but entered discourse in 1970.[40] Hauptfleisch carefully offers his definition of Black Consciousness Theatre by describing it as "[p]lays written in English by black authors, dealing with issues pertinent to the black experience".[41] Black Consciousness theatre expressed identification with sets of values and with the lives of black reality under apartheid, making it more of a proletarian theatre.[42] Matsemela Manaka's *Egoli – City of Gold* (1979), a play about a male workers' compound at a Witwatersrand gold mine represents the experience of the black man under apartheid, suffering economic exploitation. Mtuli Shenzi's *Shanti* (1972) is about a student activist who leaves his Asian girlfriend to join Mozambique guerrillas planning to overthrow South Africa's apartheid government. Kavanagh finds the student world and lifestyle represented in the play to be appropriate to the BCM, which had its origins at institutions of higher learning. It is worth noting that Shenzi was himself a student activist who subscribed to the principles of the BCM. Resistance and promises of the revolution abound in Black Consciousness Theatre.

Athol Fugard and two of the Serpent Players (a group he co-founded), John Kani and Winston Ntshona, delivered three famous contributions to the charged atmosphere of the 1970s. The problem of identity in a country, where black citizens were forced to carry pass books by law, is closely examined in *Sizwe Banzi is Dead* (1972), a play "devised" rather than written (to escape apartheid censure) by Fugard, Kani and Ntshona.[43] Although the play's timeline goes from the present to the past through a flashback structure (a letter being written), in the basic plot a man named Sizwe Banzi (played by Ntshona) arrives in Port Elizabeth looking for employment. He is unsuccessful and is told by the authorities that, as he cannot find work, he must leave the city within 72 hours. After drinking at a *shebeen*, Sizwe and an acquaintance, Buntu (played by Kani), stumble upon the dead body of a man whose pass book identifies him as Robert Zwelinzima. Buntu convinces Sizwe to take the dead man's identity, which would enable him to find work in Port Elizabeth, and their identities become switched, with Sizwe Banzi being 'killed off' for Robert Zwelinzima. The play ends where it started, with Sizwe/Robert in a photographic studio run by a man named Styles (also played by Kani) who takes the picture that will officially identify Sizwe as Robert.

Sizwe Banzi is Dead quickly became one of the most prominent plays in South African theatrical history. It had limited running opportunities in South Africa due to apartheid laws, but abroad the play was a critical and commercial smash hit that brought even greater attention to South Africa. No doubt its status as a 'banned' play contributed to its international success. The same international response also greeted the next Fugard-Kani-Ntshona production, *The Island* (1973); this play dealt with two prisoners on an unnamed island preparing to stage *Antigone* for their fellow inmates while enduring merciless hard labour on the island. The relationship between the two prisoners is strained by the news that one of them will be released shortly while the other has to serve out his life sentence. The two men also take on the antagonistic roles of Creon and Antigone in Sophocles's play. Although the production never once makes mention of it, it was common knowledge that the play referred to the notorious Robben Island, where political prisoners, of which Nelson Mandela is the best-known example, were kept by the state.[44] Apart from drawing massive international attention to South Africa and the work of Fugard and the Serpent Players, both *Sizwe Banzi is Dead* and *The Island* won numerous accolades for Kani and Ntshona.

Fugard's *Statements after an Arrest under the Immorality Act* (1972) deals with the arrest of an interracial couple, a white woman and a coloured man, after they have been caught in the act of sexual intimacy by the police. While not as overt and political as *Sizwe Banzi is Dead* and *The Island*, the play explores similar themes as these two plays; it offers resistance in ways that are more personal than political. The political sub-themes in plays like *Sizwe Banzi is Dead* and *The Island* were strong components of 1970s theatre. Black Consciousness plays emphasised their political overtones more overtly than plays Fugard was involved in, because black playwrights usually wrote with a sense of immediacy and urgency. That urgency derived from their own reality as oppressed South Africans.

Although Mtuli Shenzi's *Shanti,* mentioned above, is generally remembered as a high point of Black Consciousness Theatre, it is Zakes Mda's *We Shall Sing for the Fatherland* (1978) that is perhaps the most startling example, pointing what many critics could describe as a prophetic finger at what post-apartheid South Africa may eventually turn out to be, even though Mda sets his play in a nameless city in a nameless African country. The play, remembered for its Absurdist touches, features two tramps, former soldiers of a war for liberation in an African country, bargaining with a corrupt policeman in order to keep a city park as their habitat while they plan and manoeuvre military-style "operations" of thievery around the city. One tramp is a one-legged former sergeant who maintains rigid but humorous codes of military discipline and patriotism while the other is younger and increasingly cynical, the 'foot soldier' who acts out the sergeant's plans of theft for income and food. The interaction between the two is comedic to the point of burlesque but there is also an undeniable tragedy to their situation. They watch high-flying corporates walk by daily, men who occupy powerful positions as a result of the efforts of the soldiers, represented by the two tramps, but who give the tramps no acknowledgment. The liberated state that was fought for by two former soldiers/freedom fighters does little to hide how beaurocratised and elitist it has become, yet the performance of nationhood here emanates from the tramps who still wish to "sing for the fatherland" that has long since forgotten them, and by the end of the play there still has been no singing for the fatherland. The warning that "struggles" would continue and that a liberated African country would sooner or later fall into the hands of big business and leave the poor stranded as they were before is uncomfortable, but the play struck an adroit note. It may not overtly be about South Africa, but it is prescient enough to leave the mental image of South Africa behind, and viewed from a 21st-century perspective some elements of the play ring prophetically true.

Woza Albert!, written and developed by Percy Mtwa, Mbongeni Ngema and Barney Simon became the most successful international South African play after its 1981 premiere at the Market Theatre in Johannesburg. It found universal acclaim and recognition for its theme of an imagined Second Coming of Christ melding with the form of rebellion theatre as well as with suggestions of nuclear paranoia that link apartheid to the Cold War. Athol Fugard's very personal *Master Harold and the Boys* (1982) also drew international acclaim for its depiction of the effect of apartheid policies on a teenager, and on his friendship with two black men in his parents' employ. Paul Slabolepsky's *Saturday Night at the Palace* (1982) was a huge local success, depicting an urban, low-class realism in the setting and characterisation of two friends arguing at a roadhouse with fatal consequences. The roadhouse waiter, a black man, will unfairly be given the blame for the violence that ensues between the two white friends. Black theatre in the 1980s was dominated by playwright, actor, director and composer Mbongeni

Ngema, whose most famous work was arguably the musical *Sarafina!* (1987), about the involvement of children in the struggle for liberation.

5. *Afrikaner Nationalism as Theatre*

For most of the 20th century the National Party (NP), by promoting its own history as one associated with mobility and struggle (The Great Trek and the South African War), could appeal to the imagination of its followers: like the Trekkers almost a century before them, they could convince themselves that they were following a Biblical narrative of being a 'Chosen People'.

Afrikaans theatre in the first half of the 20th century was generally little more than another channel for the heartbeat of Afrikaner nationalism.[45] Afrikaans arts and media, rigorously structured by the political aims of group identity, nurtured a theatre that was steeped in the European tradition and enjoyed state subsidies that were not available to black theatre, leading to the only substantial body of locally written, performed and published plays in South Africa by the 1970s. While there would be rebellion against nationalism from within the Afrikaner theatre from the 1950s and 1960s onwards, not many well-known playwrights before then had produced works that openly attacked the system, although the following example was an exception.

C. Louis Leipoldt's play *Afgode* ("Idols", my own translation), written in 1928 and staged at a university performance in 1929 before being published in 1931, is generally underwhelming, yet it may count as an early example of an Afrikaans play dealing overtly with social issues. The NP's election slogan in 1929 was built around 'othering' black South Africans as *die swart gevaar* ("the black peril"), implying a doctrine of racial paranoia regarding any exposure, social, sexual or otherwise, to black South Africans – nineteen years before the implementation of apartheid. This fraught social nationalism is attacked by Leipoldt in *Afgode*'s depiction of a white Afrikaner family scandalised by miscegenation on the part of a husband and father who proclaims himself to be a fervent Nationalist.

The play is set in the 1920s in a time of polarisation and secularisation. Guys Van Staal is a retired attorney who has great wealth and power; he swears by the National Party and its promotion of

Afrikaner group identity. His wife Aletta is frail and sickly, and seemingly in awe of her husband, as is their daughter, Santa, newly returned from the UK where she qualified as a doctor; Santa has hopes of establishing a practice in the town in which her family resides. There is tension between Guys, Aletta and the head servant of their household, Aya Minah, whose daughter is dying of consumption in the nearby settlement for non-white peoples. Santa, who idolises her father and like him is a staunch believer in the National Party, and is zealously opposed to English culture, gradually discovers a secret that Guys had been hiding for years: unbeknown to Aletta, he is the father of Aya Minah's daughter, Hester. After Santa and other relatives confront Guys with the truth, he counters their threats with his knowledge that they would not reveal his secret to Aletta, who dotes on him too much and who is considered too frail to receive such shocking news. Aletta, however, reveals that she had known his secret all along, and this suggests that she is the powerful one in the relationship.

Characters like Guys van Staal, even in such early 'social' plays, hint at the playwright's resistance to segregationist policies. Guys is a 'performer', and in the context of the heritage discourses surrounding the Union of South Africa in 1910 and the Great Trek Centenary of 1938, he comes across as someone more involved with pageantry, with mimicry, than with real life.

On both the English and Afrikaner sides of white South African culture, pageantry was crucial in reinforcing group identity and heritage. With the founding of the Union of South Africa in 1910 and with the South African Party (SAP) unchallenged as the dominant political party in the country, pageants were held to emphasise the English side of Union – the promotion of English ideals and traditions.

The Afrikaner contribution to performances of heritage is shown by history to be memorable, perhaps even outrageous. The ambition Afrikaner Nationalists had to use pageantry to celebrate their history had already been suggested by the ardour with which Afrikaner group identity had been proposed during the 1920s; its strong emphasis on the history of the Great Trek and the Biblical parallels were deeply rooted in Afrikaner thinking.[46] The "Festival of the Ox-wagon trek" formed part of the 1938 Great Trek Centenary, during which ox wagons, symbolic of the Trekkers (and therefore of Afrikaner heritage), travelled and were displayed throughout South Africa, with Pretoria and Cape Town as the polar points. The Festival of the Ox-wagon trek was easily the most popular element of the Great Trek Centenary, which occurred exactly ten years before the official implementation of apartheid by the National Party in 1948, and fourteen years before an even larger festival celebrating white South African nationhood: the tercentennial celebrations in 1952 of Jan Van Riebeeck's landing in the Cape in 1652.

Even while Afrikaans theatre was very much stuck in the European mould,[47] following a blueprint of conventional three-part structure with suitable amounts of melodrama, this familiarity was also a vital tool for speaking against the norms of Afrikaner nationalism on the part of dissident artists. Rebelling against the exclusivist ideals being forced onto art and adding to the stigmatisation of the Afrikaans language, writers like Bartho Smit, Adam Small (*Kanna Hy Kô Hystoe*, 1965, "Kanna's Coming Home", my translation) and Andre P. Brink (*Pavane*) emerged in the 1950s and 1960s to produce a more vibrant, less predictable theatre. W.A. van Nierkerk's *Die Jaar van die Vuuros* (1952, "The Year of the Fire-Ox", my translation) was a vague but sustained intellectual critique of apartheid and Smit's *Die Verminktes* (1960, "The Maimed", my translation) was banned by the government for its open anti-apartheid stance. Introspective, realist theatre that focused on poor white Afrikaners was prominent in the 1960s and 1970s, with P. G. du Plessis's *Siener in Die Suburbs* (1972, "Seer in the Suburbs", my translation). Reza de Wet became a prominent female Afrikaner playwright whose works explored the moral consequences of "dubious philosophy" on generations of Afrikaners with important plays like *Mis* ("Mist", my translation), *Mirakel* ("Miracle", my translation) and *Drif* ("Ford", my translation), part of a trilogy published in 1993 called *Trits* for which she won the Hertzog literary award in 1994.[48]

6. Comedy and 'Coloured' Theatre in the 21st Century

The first ten years of the new millennium have seen some profound theatrical works in South Africa, excelling in gripping, realist drama, in particular comedies, and stand-up comedians have definitely found their niche with South African audiences. More so than before, interest in stand-up comedians, especially, has been significant. The internet popularity of international comedians in the 21st century and the availability of their shows on DVD are, judging by sales and word-of-mouth, quite notable in South Africa, particularly with young audiences. The profiles of South Africa's own stand-up comedians have been boosted by local tours and the DVD versions of their performances. One particularly well-known young comedian, Trevor Noah, became the first South African comic to appear on American television when he was a guest on the Jay Leno show in January 2012. The stand-up comedian Marc Lottering could even be compared to the traditional oral story-tellers of indigenous theatre, described earlier in this paper: he plays the part of a variety of characters in a number of his stand-up routines. The success of his portrayals depends on the audience identification.

Strongly associated with this comedic culture is 'coloured' culture: a significant number of the more popular stand-up comedians, especially in the Western Cape, could be described as 'coloured' – a problematic and contested term, yet one that features in countless human resources documents for employment equity purposes (alongside the classifications of 'white', 'black' and 'Indian'). However, with South Africa's history of "struggle" focussed primarily on the colours 'black' and 'white', 'coloured' culture is less easily defined. Wallerstein finds that the very category of being coloured is "nettlesome", and also states that in other parts of the world coloured people would have been called "mulattos" because of their mixed heritage.[49]

'Mixed race' and 'half-caste' are some of the other, pejorative terms that have been applied to this group. Fransman discusses the after-effects of such negative terms and the questions they raise in coloured people after 1994 when he claims that there is pronounced group dissatisfaction at being a perceived a 'middle' race.[50] Fransman also describes a "fluid uncertainty" that keeps coloured people from seeing themselves in a changed environment.[51]

Fransman goes on to quote Desiree Lewis:

> From the perspective of nineteenth century racial discourse, the term 'Coloured' has been linked to a fixation with maintaining racial boundaries… the coloured as debased in-betweener or 'racial mixture', perceived product of the transgression of a sacrosanct boundary, has connoted lack, deficiency, moral and cultural degeneration.[52]

Adam Small's *Kanna Hy Kô Hystoe* (1965, "Kanna's Coming Home") made for a well-structured and carefully crafted production in which a "coloured" play earned a state subsidy, even though the play's remounting in the 1970s featured an all-white cast.[53] The play is an intense psychological study of a household "held together, sociologically as well as dramaturgically", by a woman, thereby going against the grain of most Afrikaans theatre that studied male protagonists.[54] It includes themes of memory and trauma and the disturbing juxtaposition of music and violence, as well as an ingenious use of code-switching between 'high' Afrikaans and Kaaps, the dialect of Afrikaans mostly spoken by Cape-based coloured people. There is historical conjecture about this dialect of Afrikaans. Afrikaans is claimed to be a language creolised as a result of African and Asian influences,[55] with its written origin in Arabic text in the first half of the 19th century, pointing to the Cape as the birthplace of Afrikaans, among mostly coloured people. This point was, in various forms, denied by the Afrikaner Nationalist ideologies of the 20th century, when Kaaps was dismissed as quaint and derivative, and coloureds were, for the most part, regarded as degenerate. In contemporary mainstream theatre depicting coloured culture, Kaaps more often than not is presented as comedic, not a far cry from Dawid Kramer and Taliep Petersen's *District Six: The Musical* in 1986. Although it concentrated on the forced removals of coloured peoples from their living area – District Six – in Cape Town in the 1960s, and aimed for the jugular of sentiment, it has been routinely criticised for its saccharine tendencies and for representations of coloured people that are "fragmented and derivative".[56] The coloured-as-comedy propensity continued through the 'sequel' to *District Six*, *Fairlyland* (1991) and, arguably, in the very successful Kramer-Petersen musical *Kat and the Kings* (1998), which gained great acclaim abroad. Richard Rive's spirited novel, *Buckingham Palace* (1986), also about District Six, was brought to the stage in a respectful production in 2001, albeit one that still emphasised the comedic elements of the play/novel. In 2005 another Kramer-Petersen production, *Ghoema*, took the same populist route in concentrating on coloured history in the Western Cape, with Kaaps being played for effect rather than form. Ashraf Johaardien contributed a view of Muslim culture in the Cape with his very successful *Salaam Stories* (2002) but could also not escape accentuating the laughs at the expense of dramatic continuity. A similar criticism could be levelled against the Abduragman Adams-Lionel Newton collaboration, *It's Just Not Fez* (2008), which does very well to show cultural harmony between members of different racial groups and religions, but then resorts to a standard list of stereotypes played for laughs that become increasingly forced. In fact, there may well have been a danger that, even in conventional plays perceived as more 'serious', coloured and, sometimes, black characters were lurking somewhere as token comic relief. A question may be asked that relates to a certain idea of performativity within the coloured culture: in the New South Africa, how much do South Africans 'play' at their different identities (to rephrase a question posed at other points in this paper)? Do especially coloured stereotypes exist because they are in one way or another being performed, or is the performance almost expected? In the next two plays that I will briefly discuss, there may perhaps be something of a response to such questions, if indeed they are appropriate questions, which considers self-awareness as a theatrical device in a manner different to the pre-1994 theatre. Later in this section of the paper I discuss the importance of communal familiarity in securing laughs for some of these comedies, but I will first examine the self-awareness displayed by what I describe as 'coloured theatre'.

Strangely enough, a saving grace for the coloured-as-comedy paradigm came from its most popular exponents in the 21st century, the team behind the phenomenally successful interactive comedy *Joe Barber* (1999-2010). The comedy's success led to a series that extended as far as *Joe Barber 5* (in 2010), although the basic premise stayed the same: life as experienced in a Cape Town barber shop, where the patrons, Joe and Gamat, often talk about their past while regularly interacting with the audience. Only two actors are present in the show, but they also perform a number of other roles, thereby taking on multiple roles. When the actors break character to play themselves, as coloured actors, they are 'breaking frame' – redefining the role associated with this group,[57] and drawing attention to "constant repetition of acts or the re-presentation of specific type of performances".[58]

The "cultural hybridity that is integrally entrenched in Coloured society" can be found in the *Joe Barber* shows,[59] perhaps a communalised version of the 'new' theatre Hauptfleisch predicted in 1997, theatre that may even be teased out as a "new hybrid". Even if this particular comedy seems implicitly about and for coloured people, it opens itself up to wider study, especially when one notes that it merges indigenous story-telling techniques (derived from the oral narrative tradition) with self-reflexive awareness of its own performativity. In other words, at crucial moments, the actors break character to play themselves and enter a kind of meta-theatre, while still engaging with the audience, albeit on a different level. Added to this is the fact that most of *Joe Barber*'s audiences have been coloured, so when one character breaks frame and announces his displeasure at the coloured stereotype he is portraying, this is in keeping with other moments in the play where these very stereotypes are knowingly played up for laughs – but also presented for introspection. Both African and European theatre traditions are present here, but if one emphasises the extent to which the *Joe Barber* material is actually dependent on the coloured community to make it work, it may be concluded that basic African beliefs of community and community interaction are, on some level, being performed in *Joe Barber*. Conventional theatre often centres on the journey of a specific character and can explore the character's interiority, a practice Augusto Boal cautions against.[60] *Joe Barber*'s 'community' of characters all visit the barber shop, and the audience members also partake as barber shop 'regulars'. In each show, an audience member is asked to sit in the barber's chair or to sweep the floor, thereby becoming part of the performance. In *Joe Barber*, comedy is a device to enhance recognition of identity that is fluid (coloured identification between performers and audience) and broad (awareness between audience and performers that the play is actually also speaking to all members of South African society). In this, then, there is a knowingness, an element of performativity in the very act of watching the play. Those outside of coloured culture would doubtless miss most of the humour and the grace notes, but it is implied that the characters and most of the audience on the inside of that culture already knew that, as non-coloureds are directly addressed at numerous points in the performance. This kind of theatre operates outside of national pageantry but within the intimacy of the theatre it underscores the presence of the new in everything that it does, without necessarily having to do so through an enormous gesture that incessantly reminds of the past.

The success of the interactive element of the *Joe Barber* performance may be based on the willing conscription of a coloured audience, but that would be to assume that a coloured audience member is always selected to sit in the barber's chair or sweep the stage, and that would also be to disregard the fact that the play's script, along with the calculated deviations from the script, are aimed at an integrated audience. The performance itself, which is consistently light-hearted, earns its laughs from audience familiarity with jokes and themes in the script. The success of the show, in terms of its popularity, is that by the end of it, more than just coloured audiences are laughing and, more to the point, more than just coloured audiences are laughing at themselves. Like African indigenous theatre, the audience is an integral part of the story being told and if the story-teller lags, it is almost as if the audience could demand that he be replaced – a risk the *Joe Barber* performers almost invite every time they select an audience member to take part in the show on-stage. In a strange manner, there is an element of trust in this process, rather than an arrogant assumption that an audience member will 'play along', and the trust speaks more to a positive idea of community.

Two members of the *Joe Barber* team, Oscar Petersen and Heinrich Reinoffer, went on to create *Suip!* (2005, "Drink/Drunk", my translation), a dark instance of looking back from the present, from the perspective of a group of homeless people, to the influence of alcohol in Cape Coloured history. Unlike *District Six*, which sentimentalised and was rather dated (the youth of the 21st century would not have the connection to District Six their parents had), *Suip!* looks at the timelessness of social and economic impoverishment. The harsh stereotype that "Coloured people […] drink" is described by Fransman, following Judith Butler, as derivative—the lessening of a group to a few distinguishing characteristics.[61] In *Suip!*, these derivatives are almost brutally questioned, as the provocative text of the play reveals an interrogation of the audience by the homeless characters. The play selectively uses humour and harsh dialogue in an uncompromising manner that defies audience expectations even as it engages with the audience in almost the way that *Joe Barber* did. The homeless characters in *Suip!* are not as blindly forgiving as the tramps in *We Shall Sing for the Fatherland*, as they furiously blame the government for leaving them behind. It is beyond the scope of this paper to discuss *Suip!* in much detail, although it may possibly be considered among the more controversial, successful 'coloured theatre' productions and something of a benchmark for a new kind of protest theatre, where the protest is against the performativity of the nation, the New South Africa itself.

7. Conclusion

In 2012 South African theatre finds itself with plenty of material to draw from. Whereas events in the country prior to 1994 have informed many theatrical works, events post-1994 are becoming more evident in contemporary South African theatre. To summarise: the past has offered plenty to write about, but the present is finally letting go of its preoccupation with the past. This is indeed happening in theatre, but only because of a stasis in the political context of 2012 South Africa. I wish to end this argument on an anecdotal note that perhaps illustrates my point.

This paper was in development during the celebrations of the African National Congress (ANC) Centenary Festival in January 2012, marking one hundred years since the formation of the ANC. The party was celebrating its history as perhaps the most recognisable revolutionary movement on the African continent, and without doubt the most famous political agent of change due to its role in what will forever be known as the 'struggle' for democracy in South Africa. South Africa had caught the world's imagination and the ANC could lay claim to one of the most inspiring political victories any country could be proud of.

That 1994 victory, the stuff dreams are made of, would be the greatest prize in both the history of the ANC and the country itself and, deservedly so, it quickly became part of national folklore. Yet, by January 2012, the heroic visage and the fairy-tale glitter had, perhaps predictably, worn off somewhat and the ANC was openly troubled by internal conflicts and its moves to anact a Protection of Information Bill that would effectively deny the country's media access to any documentary material labelled 'secret' by the ruling party, thereby preventing any unwanted media exposure, curtailing transparency and undermining some of the very tenets of press freedom proposed by the ANC itself in its Media Charter of 1992. This bill was the focus of much of the country's media in 2012. However, President Zuma's first, eagerly-awaited centenary address, delivered to a capacity crowd at a soccer stadium, chose only to focus on the glorious history of the party and said little, defensively or otherwise, about the current state of the ANC. Many spectators began leaving the stadium during their president's speech, which was criticised as bland and evasive by television commentators. In 1994, the party promulgated a 'looking forward' stance in media events; in 2012, it was only looking back. After Zuma's 90-minute speech, rain fell hard on the soccer stadium where the event took place. A group of dancers, dressed in traditional tribal clothes, was scheduled to perform after the presidential address but as they took the stage, the stadium started emptying. Nevertheless, in pouring rain, they were still instructed to go ahead with their routine. Even to an empty house, the show had to go on.

Notes

1   For a discussion of women playwrights from South Africa (as well as from Ghana and Nigeria), see Bartels's contribution to this volume.
2   Sirayi (2001: 15).
3   Fransman (2005: 12).
4   Carlson (1996: 198-199).
5   Fransman (2005: 12-13).
6   *Ibid.* 14, 37.
7   Meersman (2010).
8   *Ibid.*
9   Hauptfleisch (1997: 31).
10 *Ibid.* 51.
11 *Ibid.* 33.
12 *Ibid.* 51.
13 Flockeman (2001: 25).
14 Hauptfleisch (1997: 52).
15 Sirayi (2001: 16).
16 *Ibid.* 15.
17 Green (1981: 71).
18 Gray (1979: 6-9).
19 *Ibid.* 1.
20 Sirayi (2001: 17).
21 Mlama (1983: 287), Sirayi (2001: 20).
22 Tomaselli (1981: 51).
23 *Ibid.* 54.
24 *Ibid.*
25 Hauptfleisch (1997: 4).

26 For a discussion of Dhlomo's play *The Girl who Killed to Save* and his epic poem *Valley of a Thousand Hills*, see Marquardt's contribution to this volume.
27 Kruger (1999: 48-49).
28 Heywood (2004: 81).
29 Kruger (1999: 48).
30 Heywood (2004: 83).
31 *Ibid.*
32 Kruger (1999: 47).
33 Kruger (1997: 569).
34 *Ibid.* 576.
35 *Ibid.*
36 Hauptfleisch (1997: 41).
37 Kruger (1999: 139).
38 Hauptfleisch (1997: 41).
39 *Ibid.* 29
40 Kavanagh (1985: 146).
41 Hauptfleisch (1997: 128).
42 Tomaselli (1981: 54).
43 Walder (1984: 77).
44 *Ibid.* 88.
45 Hauptfleisch (1997: 67).
46 Merrington (2003: 35).
47 Hauptfleisch (1997: 41).
48 *Ibid.* 123.
49 Wallerstein (1987: 374).
50 Fransman (2005: 22-24).
51 *Ibid.* 24.
52 Desiree Lewis, in Fransman (2005: 22).
53 Kruger (1999: 119).
54 *Ibid.* 120.
55 *Ibid.*
56 Fransman (2005: 39).
57 *Ibid.* 76.
58 *Ibid.* 57.
59 *Ibid.* 25.
60 Boal (1985: 86).
61 Fransman (2005: 52-53).

Bibliography

Boal, Augusto: *Theatre of the Oppressed*, New York, 1985.
Carlson, Marvin: *Performance. A Critical Introduction*, New York, 1996.
Flockeman, Miki: "The Aesthetics of Transformation. Reading Strategies for South African Theatre Entering the New Millennium", *South African Theatre Journal* 15:1, 2001, 25-39.
Fransman, Gino: *Negotiating Coloured Identity through Encounters with Performance,* Cape Town, 2005.
Gray, Stephen: *South African Literature. An Introduction*, Cape Town, 1979.
Green, Linda Lee: *A Description of Makonde Oral Narratives as Theatre*, Bowling Green, 1981.
Hauptfleisch, Temple: *The Theatre & Society in South Africa*, Pretoria, 1997.
Heywood, Christopher: *A History of South African Literature*, Cambridge, 2004.
Kavanagh, Robert: *Theatre and Cultural Struggle in South Africa*, London, 1985.
Kruger, Loren: "The Drama of Country and City. Tribalization, Urbanization and Theatre under Apartheid", *Journal of South African Studies* 23:4, 1997, 565-584.
---: *The Drama of South Africa. Plays, Pageants and Publics since 1910*, New York, 1999.
Mda, Zakes: *The Plays of Zakes Mda*, Johannesburg, 1990.
Meersman, Brent: "SA Theatre. The Decade", *The Real Review*, 2010, <http://realreview.co.za/category/articles-on-sa-theatre>, accessed 26 January 2012.
Merrington, Peter: "C. Louis Leipoldt's Valley Trilogy and Contested South African Nationalisms in the Twentieth Century", *Current Writing* 15:3, 2003, 32-44.
Mlama, Penina: *Traditional Theatre as a Pedagogical Institution. The Kaguru Theatre as Case Study*, Dar es Salaam, 1983.
Mtwa, Percy, Mbongeni Ngema & Barney Simon: *Woza Albert!*, London, 1983.
Sirayi, Mzo: "Indigenous African Theatre in South Africa". – In Lokangaka Losambe & Devi Sarinjeive (Eds): *Pre-Colonial and Post-Colonial Drama and Theatre in Africa*, Claremont, 2001, pp.14-29.
Tomaselli, Keyan: "Black South African Theatre", *English in Africa* 8:1, 1981, 51-58.
Walder, Dennis: *Athol Fugard*, London, 1984.
Wallerstein, Immanuel: "The Construction of Peoplehood. Racism, Nationalism, Ethnicity", *Sociological Forum* 2:2, 1987, 373-388.

Internet Resources
(accessed 30 October 2012)

http://myfundi.co.za/e/South_African_playwrights_of_the_apartheid_era
http://www.iol.co.za/capetimes/comment-anc-centenary-celebrations-1.1209685
http://mg.co.za/specialreport/anc-centenary-celebrations
http://mg.co.za/article/2012-01-08-anc-centenary-celebration-the-scene-of-pomp-and-ceremony
http://www.timeslive.co.za/local/2011/10/04/anc-worse-than-apartheid-govt-tutu
http://mg.co.za/article/2007-12-23-umshini-wami-echoes-through-sa

Russell Harold Kaschula (Grahamstown)

Teaching Oral Literature in the 21st Century

1. Introducing Technauriture in the Context of Teaching Oral Poetry

Literature has been dramatically transformed by the spread of digital media over the last two or three decades. There are new ways in which contemporary orality can be captured, stored, disseminated and aesthetically appreciated. This paper takes the view that contemporary African oral poetry forms part of the concept of technauriture.[1] Technauriture encompasses the fluid movement of oral poetry from auriture, to the written literary word via technology such as websites. It is the aim of this paper to show that the teaching of African oral poetry can be further enhanced when one takes the view that this literary form is now inter-disciplinary and cross-fertilised; the world-view and background of the poet, the capture and dissemination of the poetry, the poetry itself, are often facilitated by modern technology such as the book as well as the Internet. The teaching of oral literature in the 21st century thus needs to encapsulate this new, emerging, and constantly changing dialectic between orality/auriture, literacy and technology. The poem should be taught holistically, taking into account not only the poem, its literary worthiness, but also the context of the performance, the capturing and dissemination of the poem through various technologies, as well as the life and background of the poet.

David Coplan is of the opinion that, "[m]any authors […] pay lip service to the expressive inseparability of verbal, sonic, and visual media in constituting meaning in African genres, but do not address this unity in their analysis".[2] Coplan thus makes use of the term auriture "for these performances as a caution against the application of Western categories of literary analysis to African performance".[3] In other words what is heard, and the accompanying performance context is equally important to the actual words, which form the basis of a Western model of critique. Coplan's term implies the use of a range of senses in one's appreciation of the oral word: hearing, speaking and the more abstract aesthetic analysis of the word. It is important to consider these points prior to analysing any oral poetic performance, or attempting to teach about this discipline.

It is then the combination of technology and auriture, which offers a fresh perspective to the debate on oral literature, orality, auriture or "oraural".[4] The latter, a rather clumsy term, is used by Kishani in his insightful paper linking the effective study of "African philosophy" with the necessary use of indigenous languages. For the purposes of this paper, and in previous research,[5] I have chosen to use the term 'technauriture', as it captures the essence of the thesis of my research, namely, the re-emergence of performance poetry within what Walter Ong refers to as a "secondary orality",[6] in other words a society or culture influenced by literacy and technology, as opposed to a primary oral culture. A further challenge is how to develop contemporary teaching strategies for what is commonly known as African oral poetry.

The term 'technauriture' provides a theoretical paradigm and presents a methodology which may allow for researchers to find new ways of interpreting and analysing the changing oral literary scenario. This was explored in a Rhodes University MA thesis by my student, Andre Mostert, where he analysed the term in relation to finding suitable models for capturing, preserving and disseminating oral literature. What may be required now (more so than ever before) is a cross-disciplinary approach to the teaching of oral poetry and literature, which includes the arena of Information and Communication Technology (ICT) and contemporary communication forums such as websites, blogs, *Facebook, MySpace, MXit* and *YouTube*. This provides a voice to those who were previously voiceless. Many young people belong to writers' groups, whilst at the same time they take part in performance poetry and even script-writing and film production through the use of cheap contemporary digital media. Questions which need to be researched in relation to the above are: how is this 'new' genre-mixed literature produced; how is it circulated and received, and how do scholars propose to disseminate, document and analyse this literature without violating the copyright of artists? All of these issues and questions now need to come together into a single theoretical paradigm which is influenced by various disciplines, including ICT, ethnography, literary analysis, literary anthropology, forms of critical theory, eco-literature, narratology, structuralism, post-colonialism and so on. They can no longer be seen as separate entities. By having the oral material digitised and made available in the mother tongue as well as in English, allowing one to go to the source language, it is possible that counter-narratives may emerge which will challenge the Western paradigms mentioned above and that even new approaches may be provided in order to understand and re-interpret African history and literature. Interpreting African history and literature through the eyes of English monolinguals (in translation) does not necessarily provide an accurate interpretation.[7]

Modern technology, for example the Internet, requires the use of various sensory perceptions such as sight and hearing, including the oral word – hence the choice of the loose term 'technauriture'. It is the emergence of this technologised auriture, which forms the main focus of this paper. The emergence of technauriture in the form of contemporary poetry such as performance poetry, including rap, dub-poetry, slam and *izibongo* (Xhosa oral poetry) should form part of the poetic corpus when teaching African oral poetry in the 21st century.

Two particular poems will be traced here from the oral performance/conception, to the appearance of these poems in isiXhosa and English written forms. Further mention will be made of how this poetry is infused with technology to form part of technauriture and how this entire process can be used to enhance the teaching of oral poetry as part of technauriture as a discipline.

2. *The Xhosa Oral Poet. A Case Study*

This article provides a case study of the late Bongani Sitole in order to show how the tradition of oral poetry has adapted into a technologised, globalised world where orality, literacy and technology now constantly interact. The rapid emergence of new technologies has had an effect on the tradition. David Coplan's research which analyses changes in performance creativity and culture over the years in South Africa provides concrete evidence of the adaptability of tradition. Coplan states that, "the production and reproduction of performances must be located within the set of political, economic, social and cultural, relations between performers and the total context in which they perform".[8]

In accordance with Coplan's methodology, it is the purpose of this paper to contextualise Sitole's performances. This will provide a more holistic impression of the *imbongi*, or oral poet, as well as the factors which have contributed to change in the tradition within the reality of globalisation and increasing reliance on technologised literacy or technauriture. It is these factors which must also form part of the pedagogic strategies used when it comes to the teaching of African oral poetry.

Bongani Sitole's book *Qhiwu-u-u-ula!! Return to the Fold!!*[9] has been re-released in a second edition. This article discusses the accompanying technologising and digitising of this South African poetry, whilst a contextual analysis of selected poetry is provided in order to contribute to a more effective teaching strategy of this poetry in the 21st century. The essay presents an opportunity to trace the contemporary development of the oral word as part of a process: firstly, capturing the oral word through technology and transcribing the oral word into written isiXhosa; secondly, translating the written isiXhosa into English; thirdly, the publication of both the isiXhosa and the English translation in book form; fourthly, the digitising of some of the material and making it available on a website for downloading by interested parties; fifthly, the oral and live performance of some of the poetry by new and innovative youth groups.

It is important to note that parts of Sitole's book are now available online together with an accompanying teacher/student guide. This completes the orality-literacy-techno continuum and brings it full-circle. Exercises accompany each of the poems in the book and this study guide can be downloaded from the site www.oralliterature.co.za together with the oral poems (both the isiXhosa and English versions).

Sitole's poetry was fuelled by present-day events immediately prior to the first South African democratic elections in 1994, the audience's response and so on. It also contains historical perspectives regarding, for example, the origins of the armed struggle against apartheid led primarily by the African National Congress's (ANC) armed wing, Umkhonto Wesizwe (MK). Again the adaptation of themes in this oral poetry reflects change in "textual elements", those features which, according to Jeff Opland, are reflected in a transcribed text.[10] The themes changed because the political and social environment of which the poetry is a commentary also changed. Changes in themes are also linked directly to changes in what Opland terms "contextual elements".[11] The context in which the poetry is performed is no longer limited to the chief. The use of, for example, political rallies and meetings as well as contemporary open mike sessions as a platform in order to perform *izibongo* also encouraged a change in the thematic repertoire of poets such as Sitole and the more recently acknowledged 'President's Poet', Zolani Mkiva who has performed in honour of erstwhile Presidents Nelson Mandela and Thabo Mbeki.[12] The repertoire now often reflects the new power bases which were legitimised with the emergence of a democratic South African society.

In terms of what Opland refers to as those features which an audience can see and hear, but which are not reflected in a transcribed text,[13] some changes have taken place. Individual poets such as Sitole adapted dress in order to suit their particular power bases. Individual poets have therefore reacted differently over time to these "textual, contextual and textural elements".[14]

The poetry in Sitole's book[15] was initially recorded on tape and video, with more than one hundred recordings made, which reflect the volatile pre-election period from 1990-1994. The poetry was then transcribed into isiXhosa by the performer. Together with the book's co-author Mandla Matyumza all three of us then worked together to translate the material into English. The book *Qhiwu-u-u-la!! Return to the Fold!!* – containing fifteen selected poems in both languages, was then published by Nasou-Via Afrika in 1996 and re-issued in 2006. Nasou-Via Afrika is primarily an educational publisher, publishing textbooks for the school market, including material in all eleven official languages. Some of the abovementioned Sitole poems also appear in my book *The Bones of the Ancestors are Shaking: Xhosa Oral Poetry in Context,* which was published in 2002.

Sitole's poems provide valuable insights into the socio-political issues facing South Africans immediately prior to the first democratic elections. They represent a window, a 'slice of life' at a time when South Africa as a nation found itself at a turning point in its history. It is important that this history is infused into the teaching of these poems as illustrated below. Sitole's poetry was diverse and dynamic. Take the following extract produced at the re-burial of Chief Sabata Dalindyebo, an ANC supporter and opponent of the independent homeland system. This apartheid policy was part of the divide-and-rule strategy where homelands were created for Black people based on the languages that they spoke. A number of these homelands even gained so-called 'independence' under apartheid rule. Dalindyebo was Paramount Chief of the Thembu clan. He was deposed by K. D. Matanzima who eventually became the first Prime Minister of the primarily isiXhosa-speaking 'independent' homeland of the Republic of Transkei in 1976, in terms of the apartheid government's divide and rule apartheid policy. Chief Sabata died in exile in 1986 in Zambia, during the Matanzima era in Transkei. When the Paramount Chief's body was brought back to the capitol city of Mthatha, it was forcefully removed from the funeral parlour by Matanzima's bodyguards and buried in a women's graveyard as a final insult to the King. This angered many people. Matanzima was then ousted in a coup in 1989 by military leader Bantu Holomisa (now a parliamentarian and leader of the United Democratic Movement in the new South African democracy). With the blessing of Major-General Bantu Holomisa, who had by then become the new military leader and was pro-ANC at that time, the immediate exhumation of Chief Sabata's remains was allowed, and the King was buried at his rightful burial place at Bumbane Great Place. It was the first time that the revolutionary movements operated openly in the homeland. Also present was regional ANC representative for Transkei and councillor to the royal Dalindyebo family, A. S. Xobololo. The full version of this poem performed in his honour appears on pages 64 and 65 of *Qhiwu-u-u-la!! Return to the Fold!!* (2006)[16].

> *Amandla!*
> *Uza kuphakam' umzukulwana kaXobololo,*
> *UXobololo uza kuxobul' ixolow' emthini kuvel' intlaka,*
> *UXobololo uyaxoboloza,*
> *UXobolol' unesifo sombefu,*
> *Uxweb' impundu ngokuhlal' estoksini ngenxa kaDaliwonga*

> Power!
> The grandchild of Xobololo is going to stand up,
> Xobololo's going to peel the tree bark until gum appears,
> Xobololo's trying,
> Xobololo's suffering from asthma,
> His buttocks are chaffed due to being jailed because of Daliwonga (Matanzima).

The *imbongi* introduces the poem by making use of the power salute *Amandla!* This was common in the performance of *iimbongi* (plural) within the struggle for freedom in South Africa. In this poem it creates a sense of unity and power within the organisation and the people who support it. This is so because the audience would normally respond to this power salute with a suitable reply. This serves to integrate the audience with the occasion, the performer and the subject of the performance. Sitole is also critical of Chief K. D. Matanzima who is blamed for much hardship experienced by the ANC and its members in this region during earlier days under apartheid. By condemning the action of Matanzima, the *imbongi* is emphasising the power base of the ANC. This is especially true if one bears in mind that Matanzima was never an ANC supporter and that he always aligned himself with the previous apartheid regimes. Further analysis of Sitole's socio-political poetry has appeared in the *Journal of African Cultural Studies*.[17]

The tradition described above, together with the poet's stylistic techniques have now been transported into the realm of technology in order to enhance the teaching of this poetry. This represents another leap in the revitalisation of oral tradition. The tradition was initially set free in the 1990s, with political liberation, and it is now being allowed to re-invent itself within the realms of technology such as the Internet, and the World Wide Web.

3. The Technologising of Sitole's Work. Towards Technauriture

In late 2004 with a project team from elearning4Africa, a company based in the United Kingdom which was working in the educational sector, a vision to collect, collate and digitise oral literature and tradition, beginning with Sitole's oral poetry, was espoused by myself together with Andre Mostert. Through local, national and international linkages, an open source platform was established to make the Sitole material accessible for the widest possible audience: from learners in schools across South Africa using the material as learning resources, through to graduate students collecting oral traditions and writing teaching resources for postgraduate certificates and degrees, through to tourists learning about the 'real' history of the places they aim to visit.

Through this open source structure it was hoped that contributions would be made by both scholars and postgraduate students in the following areas: cultural identity; indigenous knowledge systems; development of African language and history for postgraduate study routes; creation of a platform to support cultural tourism (initially in the Eastern Cape province); expansion of open source digitisation options across partner organisations; creation of robust community-based initiatives to promote the ongoing development and sustainability of the platform, collaborating with international models for harnessing indigenous knowledge systems for the classroom and distributing learning material. One of the first development areas was supported by the Foundation for Human Rights, namely the technologising and digitisation of the Sitole material (this material is available online at www.technauriture.com).

Arguably, it is access to technology that creates and encourages a global culture of immediate access to information. From the above we can see that orality, literacy and technology are developing a special relationship. It may be argued that the whole idea of computers as machines is being replaced by computers as companions, facilitating the ability to speak, interact and even translate from one language to another, thereby enabling communication to take place, and, in many cases, community development. It is conceivable that in the not too distant future, oral poetry produced in African languages will instantly be made available visually and in other languages via technology.

The interaction between orality and literacy is now more complex than one would expect, as it now also involves various technologies, from video cameras, digital cameras, ipods, MP3 players, kindle as well as the Internet. It would seem to be dependent on the individual performer and where they find themselves on the oral-literacy-techno continuum, as well as the extent to which they choose to allow orality, or auriture and literacy to interact with modern technology. Isabel Hofmeyr rightly points out that there is an "appropriation" of the oral into the literate, and the extent of this process depends on the individual performer.[18] This "appropriation" is now often taken one step further, namely, into the arena of technology. In fact, those extralinguistic elements, which are often lost in the transmission of orality into literacy, can be re-captured through technology where sound-bites or video-clips are uploaded onto websites. The reaction of the audience, the performer's intonation, voice quality and emphasis, the effects of rhythm, context and speed of performance are lost in the written version, but can once again come alive through the technologised version. This renders a performance of differing impact and intensity, a performance based in technauriture.

The differences between individual poets and performers further complicate the debate surrounding appropriate literary criticism of transcribed oral texts.[19] Added to this would now be a literary criticism which incorporates aspects of technology. The dialectic between print, popular performance, technology and primary orality differs both in terms of individual performers, as well as the culture-specific community of, for example, Bongani Sitole's world as described in this paper.

Through a grant from the Foundation for Human Rights the first project for the Oral Literature Project (OLP) team has been the development of resources to support the oral poems of Bongani Sitole. The project aimed to deliver the following: development of learning materials; uploading of resources to the OLP platform; donation of books to pilot schools (Qunu, Port St Johns and Grahamstown); creation of a download option for accessing the poetry book; international dissemination of the project; establishment of a network to support phase 2 of the project. The project team identified a basic lesson plan outline for each poem, produced in both isiXhosa and English, to ensure that the material was made accessible to the widest possible audience. For example, the oral poem produced by Sitole in honour of Xobololo, already discussed above, which is Poem 11 in the book *Qhiwu-u-u-la!! Return to the Fold!!*

As indicated earlier, where a short extract from the poem was analysed, this poem deals with the life of Mr Xobololo who was an advisor to the late Paramount Chief Sabata Dalindyebo, King of the Xhosa Thembu group. He was an ANC supporter and rejected the homeland system. His relationship with Chief K. D. Matanzima, Transkei homeland leader who eventually forced the Paramount Chief into exile in Zambia, is explored in this poem. It is imperative to include this political and historical background when teaching this poem as it not only adds to the context of the performance, but it also adds to an understanding of the socio-political setting which influenced this performance. Again the poem has been translated into English and uploaded onto the website together with a lesson plan.

A further example of how technauriture has influenced the development, capturing, dissemination and teaching of Sitole's poetry is his famous poem, "Hail, Dalibhunga!" a poem in honour of Nelson Mandela. The poem follows together with a contextual analysis of how the poem was transported into the international arena, thereby providing some idea of how the poem can be taught and analysed. Again, any teaching of such a poem would need to emphasise technauriture as the basis for the movement of the poem from its original isiXhosa, as well as take into account the historical aspects surrounding the poem. The version that follows was published as the leading poem in a book entitled *The Heart in Exile. South African Poetry in English, 1990-1995*.[20] The significance of a translated isiXhosa oral poem placed as a leading poem in a selection of the best English poetry will be discussed below.

Hail, Dalibunga!

Hail, Dalibunga! It's Bongani Sitole.
Words of truth have been exposed.
A bull, kicking up dust, displacing stones.
Dust rises, ant heaps are broken.
A man, staring at the sky till the stars tumble down.
I say to you, Dalibunga, I say to you, Madiba,
I've done nothing, people of my home.
I remember you as a man I met at Mfulo in '57.
I say that you and Slovo played hide and seek,
Disguising yourselves to conceal your identity,
So you wouldn't be recognized.
You're the light-skinned Paramount of the Thembu,
The son of the Khonjwayo princess,
A king born of the nation's princess,
A bright man of the nation's woman,
Someone who stamped his feet on Umtata Mountain
And the whites took fright,
Someone who drank once from the waters of the sea
Till the water dried up and revealed the stones,
A king who did wonders among various nations,
So the Thembu house was shocked:

Saying, 'What manner of king is this?'
I've done nothing, Thembu, I've done nothing.
One day the Boers set down two bags,
A bag of soil and a bag of cash,
Saying the king should pick the one he liked.
King Sampu's son did a wondrous thing:
Good Lord! He picked the bag of soil, and other chiefs took the bag of cash!
I've done nothing people of my home.
One day I spoke, shocking the Boers with confusion.
They said, 'Who's this hounding us?
What battle's he hounding us to?'
So the whites harassed me,
Made me harassed, just like them,
In my very own land.
Alas, Dalibunga, you're a chief to be nurtured,
Alas, Dalibunga, you're a chief to be guarded,
You surprised me, tall son of Mandela,
You surprised me, lash that whipped certain nations:
In consultations with whites overseas
You terrified whites who never talk to blacks.
I say to you, old man,
I say to you, Madiba of Zondwa,
I've spoken, I'll not speak again,
I say to you, be strong, Dalibunga,
Be strong, Madiba, our ancestors watch you,
Our grandmothers promised you'd not die in jail.
Bring change, Madiba, things aren't right.
You were raised, Dalibunga, on Dalindyebo's cows' milk
So you would grow to stand tall
Like the river reeds of this country.
The men of our home shuffled their feet:
Cowards! Your cowardice will be bared!
So says the poet of tradition.
Long live Dalibunga!
Long live this old man!
Long live Sophitshi's Madiba!

Translated by Russell Kaschula

This poem was first performed in 1991 in honour of Nelson Mandela when he visited the University of Transkei.

From a pedagogic or didactic point of view the poem clearly contains historical references to Mandela's release from prison, his genealogy, his relationship with the leader of the South African Communist party, Joe Slovo, and so on. The poet cleverly uses the metaphor of a bag of soil and a bag of cash between which Mandela had to choose, the cash representing greed. Many of the chiefs under apartheid were bought over by the regime, for example the homeland leaders. However, Mandela chose to remain with the bag of soil, rooting him to his land and his convictions. It is easy to undertake a structural analysis of the poem, but the socio-political elements of the poem remain just as important. Furthermore, it is suggested that the literary and technological process that the poem has undergone may be of equal pedagogic significance.

In terms of content and form the poet shows innovation, not only in relation to the metaphor concerning the bag of soil, but also in the comparison of Nelson Mandela with a bull, a powerful animal that is extremely important in amaXhosa society, which was traditionally underpinned by a cattle-based economy. The reference to Mandela as a river-reed is also important as this is a very hardy, tall plant which can survive under difficult circumstances, always bending with the wind. The power of Mandela is also represented in the image of his ability to drain the oceans to reveal the stones, in other words the truth that is hidden beneath the surface. The poet cleverly uses Mandela's praise name as an opening formulae to the poem, *Dalibhunga*, meaning the 'creator of parliament'. Furthermore, the poet makes frequent use of parallelisms and repetition to emphasise his point, for example where he refers to Mandela as a chief to be nurtured and guarded.

There is "a note on the text" by the editors at the beginning of *The Heart in Exile* which reads as follows: "The poets in this book are arranged alphabetically by name, with the exception of the opening two writers, Bongani Sitole and Denis Hirson, whose works we felt aptly inaugurates the theme of the collection as a whole."[21] On reading this note one begins to forget that Sitole's poem originated as a spontaneously produced isiXhosa *isibongo* or oral poem, at a function to honour Mandela's release from prison, held in the Great Hall of the then University of Transkei. One fails to see the thousands of chanting comrades present, the animal skins that Sitole wore, the ANC colours carefully braided into the skins, his presence is forever lost to the performance in this text. He never wrote the poem in English, but transcribed it into isiXhosa from the video recorded version – does that qualify him as an English poet or writer as suggested, alongside other famous South African English poets such as Lionel Abrahams, Dennis Brutus, Patrick Cullinan, Gus Ferguson, Stephen Gray and others, whose poetry is contained in this anthology? Further to this, the process of translating and publishing Sitole's poem is completely lost. Initially Sitole transcribed and reworked the poem into written isiXhosa. Thereafter Matyumza and I attempted to translate the poem into English. These versions of written poetry were published in the collection *Qhiwu-u-u-la!! Return to the Fold!!* Finally the poem was again reworked by myself into the best English possible and this translated version, published in *The Heart in Exile,* went on to receive second place in the English FNB-Vita poetry awards in South Africa. These awards are for poetry translated from any one of South Africa's eleven official languages into English. Since then both the isiXhosa and English versions of the poems together with lesson plans have been uploaded onto the Sitole website.

Arguably the process of bringing the poem into the paradigm of technauriture began when the poem was recorded with a video camera. Thereafter was the transcription and translation process, followed by editing and publishing of the poems in various book/manuscript formats. Finally, a snippet of the initial isiXhosa oral poem was even purchased directly by Microsoft for use on a website. Finally, the point must again be stressed that in engaging with this poem from a teaching perspective, it is important to consider not only the poet, but the poem, the context of performance, the stylistic techniques used, as well as the process of the technologising of the poem from the oral isiXhosa version through to the poem finding its way onto the World Wide Web.

4. *International Examples of Technauriture*

Further to what has been pointed out above, intellectual or academic sites that set about discussing, analysing and preserving material electronically are also emerging internationally, the most recent being www.oralliterature.org, a site which is based in the United Kingdom. There is also the www.poetryinternationalweb.org, a professional website. The oralliterature.org website is run by Dr Mark Turin, under the auspices of The World Oral Literature Project and it was established at the University of Cambridge in 2009. This project aims to publish a library of oral texts and occasional papers, and to make any collections available through new media platforms. These websites are contributing to a new critical discourse and language awareness which, in my opinion, falls within the ambit of technauriture.[22] This 2011 publication contains an analysis of the work of Bongani Sitole published by the University of Cambridge Oral Literature Project. This is essentially a position paper which outlines technauriture in relation to Sitole's work, thereby transporting the poet and his work into the international arena. The publication is available online at the above website address.

Further examples of ground-breaking work in terms of technauriture would be the *Verba Africana* series which has been developed at the University of Leiden (Netherlands) as part of the project *Verba Africana; E-learning of African languages and Oral Literatures: DVDs and Internet Materials*. The aim of this project is to document African oral genres (poems, narratives, songs and so on) for both teaching and research purposes. An example of material is that of a DVD and website which include Ewe stories and storytelling. There are also *Taarab* and *Ngoma* performances, as well as a DVD and digital material on Ewe stories and storytellers from Ghana. This initiative is a collaborative one between various universities in Europe. There is also the project Encyclopedia of Literatures and Languages of Africa (ELLAf) supported by various organisations and coordinated by French scholars. This project provides an online encyclopedia devoted to the dissemination, archiving and study of African oral literature.[23]

The technauriture being developed at Leiden therefore goes beyond the work of an individual performer and begs the question as to what the future holds for technauriture. It would be most likely that various centralised sites should be set up in various parts of the world, at selected institutions, which specialise in documenting, preserving, teaching and disseminating various aspects of technauriture. This will facilitate further interaction between local and global literatures within a coordinated system.

In terms of the work that is being done at the University of Leiden[24] it is pointed out that "[n]owadays, the study of African Oral Literatures faces new research challenges due to expanding technologies of audio-video recording and their increasing popularisation and mass-diffusion".[25] It is also pointed out that there are only a small number of experimental projects where new technological documentation and research methodologies are being explored.[26] A further example of this type of research would be the comparative case study on creativity and the adaptation of new media in southern and eastern Africa that is currently being undertaken by Veit-Wild (Humboldt University) as well as Fendler and Wendl (University of Bayreuth). In essence they are looking at artistic, cinematic and literary practices in the digital age.

The important point that this digitisation makes is that for the contemporary classification of oral literature one is required not only to capture the textual content, but also the visual performance in order to classify, describe and comprehend the full aesthetic qualities of the performance. The next step in terms of the Sitole material would be to possibly upload video clips onto the existing website.

5. *Commercialisation and Globalisation of Oral Poetry*

Examples of poets who have attained financial gain and who are able to work closely with technology are Zolani Mkiva and spoken word artist, Lebo Mashile. Both Zolani Mkiva and Lebo Mashile performed at the World Cup Soccer draw in Cape Town (4 December, 2009 – SABC 1). These artists can be booked for functions. The traditional payment of a cow and a bag of maize by the Chief to the poet have now been replaced by contractual agreements and agents who represent these performers.

This commercialisation of oral art is clearly depicted on performer's websites where one can explore online performance bookings, purchase of books and related published material as well as hire performers as master of ceremonies and compères in order to coordinate events and functions – see for example www.lebomashile.co.za and www.poetofafrica.com. This "genre-crossing" and what Veit-Wild refers to as "transciplinary and inter-/transmedial" is encapsulated in the introduction to Lebo Mashile where she is referred to as: "The poet, performer, actress, presenter and producer".[27] This forms part of what Veit-Wild refers to as new global transmediatic culture.[28] These websites all contain an interesting cross-disciplinary approach and technological innovation, from podcasts, visual performances, examples of poetry, information about publications and performances and so on.

The website is literally the 'window' through which we now view the poets, their lives, history, performances and publications. It is again through the technological page that the poets come to life and offer themselves for critique through the medium of technauriture, whilst at the same time allowing for their commercial viability.

The global nature of Zolani Mkiva is represented in the awards that he has won and what he lists, on his website, as milestones in his poetic career. These range from performances and awards in Germany, Libya, Ireland, Brazil, Turkey, France to Uzbekistan. In the same way that great Xhosa poet, S. E. K. Mqhayi became known as *imbongi yesizwe jikelele* "the poet of the whole nation" in South Africa in the early 1900s, Mkiva now refers to himself continentally and perhaps ambitiously as the 'poet of Africa'. This title is also reflected on his website: www.poetofafrica.com. One wonders when he will take on the title 'poet of the world' and by what criteria these poets are judged when taking on these titles. Digital performers now have access to a world-wide audience perhaps through a new code-switched language idiom, 'globalese', as represented in some of Mkiva's poetry where up to seven languages are used in a single poem in order to attract and appeal to a global as well as a local audience.

Another group which has done particularly well in South Africa are the spoken-word poetry collective the Botsotso Jesters (http://botsotso.bookslive.co.za/about/). Performers include the well-known Lesego Rampolokeng, Siphiwe ka Ngewenya, Ike Muila and Alan Horwitz. The 'transciplinary' and 'transmedial' nature of their work as well as their cutting-edge societal commentary is encapsulated in the introduction to their website where they refer to speaking the

> art that is of and about the varied cultures and life experiences of people in South Africa as expressed in the many languages spoken [...]. Botsotso is committed to a proliferation of styles and a multiplicity of themes [...]. Multidisciplinary art forms and performances are similarly embraced.[29]

They conclude by pointing out that the lesson of apartheid must still be spoken of whilst the "challenges of the current period throws up [...] difficulties [and] complexities".[30]

6. Conclusion

The need to develop and harness indigenous knowledge systems across the developing world is a central aspect for the maintenance of cultural identity, while widening the exposure to the traditions and customs of indigenous societies through technauriture will ensure that the momentum of globalisation is of benefit to all the world's communities. The Sitole project has allowed the model to embark down the avenue that will see the creation of a vibrant and effective open source structure to support the collection, collation, teaching and utilisation of historical treasures. Not only does this project honour the name of a great, yet relatively unknown, South African poet, the late Bongani Sitole, it also helps to bring back to life and to preserve, via technology as well as the written word, the poetry of this great poet.

In this paper the term 'technauriture' has been used in order to highlight the complex nature of oral literature in the contemporary global reality, as indicated, for example, in the *Verba Africana* series. No poet or oral performer remains untouched by the influence of radio, television, the Internet and the constant interaction between the oral and written word. In Africa, television and particularly radio remain the driving technological influences promoting the oral word. Increasingly the Internet is also playing a pivotal role. This will follow on the emergence of technauriture as an established discipline in the rest of the world. There is no longer any society which is not affected by Walter Ong's notion of secondary orality.[31] The influence of technology on both the oral and written word has reached a point where both are inextricably linked, where both feed off each other in a symbiotic fashion – hence the term technauriture to encapsulate a discipline worthy of analysis, study and critique.

This article has shown how performers are, through the use of technology, positioning and repositioning themselves as not only continental performers, but also global performers. This is clearly illustrated through Zolani Mkiva, the fact that he has won international awards, including the *Die Woche* Award from Germany and through the use of his title: 'poet of Africa'. This implies both continental and global poetic interplay. It is argued that this is largely facilitated through technauriture and the embracing of contemporary technology. The challenge is now to find appropriate means and methods of teaching what were localised forms of oral poetry, which have been mediated through translation and technology, and thereby transported onto a global platform.

This paper argues that a holistic approach to the analysis of this poetry is needed. In other words any pedagogic approach needs to take into account historical-biographical details of the poet, where the poet and the poem are considered, alongside a structural approach where the language usage and literary worthiness itself is analysed. Furthermore, integrated into such a pedagogic approach would be the place of technology in the production, capturing and dissemination of the poetry as well as issues related to translation of culture-specific terminology. The power of the poem now rests with an analysis of the entirety of the process as to how the poem has come about. There is therefore no poem, poet, translation, website and stand-alone element – the entire poetic process should be seen as intertwined.

Notes

1 See Kaschula (2004), Kaschula & Mostert (2011).
2 Coplan (1994: 9).
3 *Ibid.* 8.
4 Kishani (2001: 27).
5 See Kaschula (2004, 2009, 2011), Kashula &Mostert (2009).
6 Ong (1982: 68).
7 See Opland (2009).
8 Coplan (1994: 242).
9 Kaschula, Matyumza & Sitole (1996/2006).
10 Opland (1983: 241).
11 *Ibid.* 253.
12 Kaschula (1999: 64-65).
13 Opland (1983: 248-250).
14 *Ibid.*
15 Kaschula, Matyumza & Sitole (1996/2006).
16 There are three basic clicks in isiXhosa: 'c' (front click where the tip of the tongue is placed against the upper front teeth and the tongue drops quickly) as in *icici* "an earring", 'q' (top click where the tongue is placed further back

in the mouth) as in *iqaqa* "skunk" and 'x' (side click where the air escapes on both sides of the tongue) as in *umXhosa* "a Xhosa person".
17 Kaschula & Mostert (2009).
18 See Hofmeyr (1993: 176).
19 Yai (1989: 62-63).
20 De Kock & Tromp (1996: 1-3), hereafter referred to as *The Heart in Exile*.
21 *Ibid.* xxiii.
22 See Kaschula & Mostert (2011).
23 For further information, see <www.ellaf.fr>, accessed 03 October 2012.
24 See Merolla (2009).
25 See Beck & Wittmann (2004), Ricard & Veit-Wild (2005).
26 See Furniss (2006), Merolla (2009).
27 Veit-Wild (2009: 4).
28 *Ibid.*
29 Botsotso.
30 *Ibid.*
31 See Ong (1982).

Bibliography

Beck, Rose Marie & Frank Wittman (Eds.): *African Media Cultures. Transdisciplinary Perspectives*, Köln, 2004.
Botsotso: "About Botsotso", *Books Live*, <http://botsotso.bookslive.co.za/about/>, accessed 19 September 2012.
Coplan, David: *In the Time of Cannibals. The Word Music of South Africa's Basotho Migrants*, Johannesburg, 1994.
Cronin, Jeremy: "Even Under the Rine of Terror... Insurgent South African Poetry", *Straffrider* 8:2, 1989, 22-25.
Finnegan, Ruth: *Orality and Literacy*, Oxford, 1988.
Furniss, Graham: *Research Database on Hausa Popular Literature and Video Film*, London, 2006, <http://hausa.soas.ac.uk/>, accessed 26 July 2012.
Hofmeyr, Isabel: *We Spend Our Lives as a Tale that is Told. Oral Historical Narrative in a South African Chiefdom*, Johannesburg, 1993.
Kaschula, Russell: "Imbongi and Griot. Toward a Comparative Analysis of Oral Poetics in Southern and West Africa", *Journal of African Cultural Studies* 12:1, 1999, 55-76.
---: *The Bones of the Ancestors are Shaking. Xhosa Oral Poetry in Context*, Cape Town, 2002.

---: "Imbongi to Slam. The Emergence of a Technologised Auriture", *Southern African Journal of Folklore Studies* 14:2, 2004, 45-58.

---: "Technauriture. Multimedia Research and Documentation of African Oral Performance", Keynote Address Delivered at the *Multimedia Research and Documentation of Oral Genres in Africa – the Step Forward Conference*, University of Leiden, 2009. [Unpublished manuscript]

Kaschula, Russell, Mandla Matyumza & Bongani Sitole: *Qhiwu-u-u-la!! Return to the fold!!*, Cape Town & Tshwane, 1996/2006.

Kaschula, Russell & Andre Mostert: "Analyzing, Digitizing and Technologizing the Oral Word. The Case of Bongani Sitole", *Journal of African Cultural Studies* 21:2, 2009, 159-176.

---: *From Oral Literature to Technauriture. What's in a Name?*, World Oral Literature Project. Voices of Vanishing Worlds, Occasional Paper 4, Cambridge, 2011.

Kishani, Bongasu: "On the Interface between Philosophy and Language in Africa. Some Practical and Theoretical Considerations", *African Studies Review* 44:3, 2001, 27-45.

De Kock, Leon & Ian Tromp (Eds.): *The Heart in Exile. South African Poetry in English, 1990-1995*, Johannesburg, 1996.

Merolla, Daniela: *Verba Africana. African Languages and Oral Literatures. DVD Documentation and Digital Materials*, Leiden, 2006 onwards, <http://www.let.leidenuniv.nl/verba-africana/swahili/>, accessed 10 May 2009.

Mostert, Andre: *Developing a Systematic Model for the Capturing and Use of African Oral Poetry. The Bongani Sitole Experience*, Grahamstown, 2011. [Unpublished MA thesis, Rhodes University]

Ong, Walter: *Orality and Literacy. The Technologizing of the Word*, London & New York, 1982.

Opland, Jeff: *Xhosa Oral Poetry. Aspects of a Black South African Tradition*, Johannesburg, 1983.

---: *Abantu Besizwe. Historical and Biographical Writings, 1902-1944. S. E. K. Mqhayi*, Johannesburg, 2009.

Ricard, Alain & Flora Veit-Wild (Eds.): *Interfaces between the Oral and the Written / Interfaces entre l'ecrit et l'oral*, Matatu Series, Amsterdam, 2005.

Veit-Wild, Flora: "Artistic, Cinematic and Literary Practices in the Digital Age", Berlin, 2009. [Unpublished Working Document]

Yai, Olayibi: "Issues in Oral Poetry. Criticism, Teaching and Translation". – In Karin Barber & Paulo de Moraes Farias (Eds.): *Discourse and its Disguises. The Interpretation of African Oral Texts,* Birmingham University African Studies Series 1, Birmingham, 1989, pp. 59-69.

Internet Resources
(accessed 3 October 2012)

http://www.ellaf.fr
http://www.Indigenousknowledgesystems.com
http://www.lebomashile.co.za
http://www.let.leidenuniv.nl/verba-africana/swahili
http://www.let.leidenuniv.nl/verba-africana/ewe
http://www.oralliterature.org
http://poetofafrica.com
http://www.technauriture.com

Ellen Grünkemeier (Hanover)

Teaching South Africa.
Histories, Literatures, Cultures

1. Introduction

"Always historicize!"[1] As Frederic Jameson emphasises in his famous statement, history should play a central role in the analysis of literature and culture. He argues that texts are not independent from but interrelated with the contexts in which they are produced, circulated and received. Jameson continues:

> [W]e never really confront a text immediately, in all its freshness as a thing-in-itself. Rather, texts come before us as the always-already-read; we apprehend them through sedimented layers of previous interpretations, or – if the text is brand-new – through the sedimented reading habits and categories developed by those interpretative traditions.[2]

Literary studies scholars with an inclination towards cultural studies put Jameson's argument to practice in research and teaching by using text- and context-oriented approaches to literature. In addition to close readings that serve to explore the aesthetic construction of literature, we also study the interrelations between the texts and their cultural, social, political and historical conditions.

As the cultural historian Joe Moran explains in his introductory guide, interdisciplinarity is a vague term that can denote

> forging connections across the different disciplines; but it can also mean establishing a kind of undisciplined space in the interstices between the disciplines, or even attempting to transcend disciplinary boundaries altogether.[3]

Focussing especially on the intersections of history and literary and cultural studies, this paper will discuss both the benefits and the challenges of combining the disciplines. The methodological reflections will set the ground for the second part of this paper which consists of two concrete examples of interdisciplinary seminars on South Africa that draw on the expertise of lecturers and students from the English and the History departments of Leibniz University of Hanover.[4]

2. Literary and Cultural Studies. Engaging with History

Generally speaking, it is one of the merits of interdisciplinary teamwork in research and teaching that scholars can draw on each other's expertise. By means of such cooperation, academics from different disciplinary backgrounds are introduced to perspectives that are new to them and that add to their understanding of the subject-matter. Following Joe Moran's definition, interdisciplinarity is not a "simple juxtaposition of two or more disciplines" but "always transformative in some way, producing new forms of knowledge in its engagement with discrete disciplines".[5] These new insights make it worthwhile to consider other (neighbouring) disciplines and their approaches to (similar) study objects.

For literary and cultural studies scholars it can be particularly rewarding to cooperate with historians because a context-related approach to literature requires not only a thorough understanding of the primary material but also of the circumstances. Since meaning is produced differently in different cultures and at different historical moments it is necessary to locate literary texts and other cultural products in their specific contexts. Drawing attention to the complexity and contingency of meaning, the US-American scholar Lawrence Grossberg explains that "the practice of cultural studies is radically contextualist, and cultural studies might be described as a discipline of contextuality".[6] The circumstances are highly relevant for the analysis because an "event or practice (even a text) does not exist apart from the forces of the context that constitute it as what it is. Obviously, context is not merely background but the very conditions of possibility of something."[7] The context is not, as Grossberg goes on, "empirically given beforehand; it has to be defined by the project, by the political question that is at stake".[8] It becomes evident that history does not provide mere 'facts', 'data' or 'background information'. History is rather, as E.P. Thompson explains, "the discipline of context; each fact can only be given meaning within an ensemble of other meanings".[9] In their introduction to cultural studies, Judy Giles and Tim Middleton describe history along similar lines as

> a key practice in the processes of culture. [...] Thinking about how the past is represented, and how ideas about it are communicated, in the present can offer insights into the process by which meaning is produced and circulated.[10]

History is a central feature of culture, which is why historical awareness is an important part of the analysis of (contemporary) cultural products and practices. In his contribution to *Research Methods in Cultural Studies* (2008), Michael Pickering shows in what ways scholars can benefit from straddling cultural studies and history. They gain a more profound historical awareness, i.e. an awareness of the (dis)continuities between past and present. As a result of such dialogue,

> we may better understand how things have changed and how we have arrived historically within the present, how people in the past have responded to the historical processes in their own time, how historical difference can inform the sense we have of our own historicity, and also how despite changed conditions and circumstances certain continuities endure across time.[11]

Yet, engaging with history is a complex part of doing cultural studies because the contexts are not fixed but have to be defined. Historical research is based on "contestation and debate, the advancement of alternative sources and alternative interpretations, or critical assessment of the grounds on which it is based in any particular case."[12] Historians have to study, question, evaluate, select and arrange sources in order to gain insight into the regionally specific social actors, power relations, events and circumstances that are subject to their investigation. Outlining how historians pursue their research, Pickering focuses on what he calls "moments of insight".[13]

> It seems that you have at last intensively recognised something you were searching for. These moments are unpredictable, and they depend on the

> long hours when you are studiously acquiring evidence and knowledge of your particular research topic. They are the basis for the moment when you reach a newly experienced depth of engagement with the evidence [...]. Such moments are not possible without the platform of knowledge you have laboriously assembled, whether through secondary or primary sources [...].[14]

As Pickering's choice of words such as "intensively", "long hours", "studiously" and "laboriously" suggests, historical research is time-consuming.[15] Still, the effort is worthwhile because the ensuing insight is one of the defining and rewarding aspects of historical research.

Working together with historians, academics from other disciplines can benefit from this expertise as they are introduced to the latest research debates, questions and findings. Otherwise, they could work with overview articles in history books and journals, which provide a general outline but which can hardly – by nature of the genre – present the most recent developments or particular details. In fact, even finding suitable overviews and other material for research and/or teaching is difficult for non-historians as they are not familiar with the publications, the authors or the different schools within the discipline.

It thus becomes apparent that academics who use each other's skills and knowledge can approach the study objects in their complexity through different disciplinary and methodological lenses. Interdisciplinary work encourages them to rethink the characteristics of their own field and methodology. These critical reflections require a strong disciplinary footing; otherwise, one would easily be lost in the broad variety of possible approaches. Therefore the courses presented here are targeted at advanced students who can both contribute to and benefit from the interdisciplinary encounters and the resulting innovative forms of knowledge.

3. Exemplary Courses

The reflections on forging connections between history and literary studies shall inform the following section that outlines exemplary courses on South African literature and history. Jointly taught by Ellen Grünkemeier and the Africa historian Kirsten Rüther, the seminars were targeted at students from both the English and the History Departments of Leibniz University of Hanover.[16] Although two lecturers share the responsibility for one course, interdisciplinary co-teaching is by no means an easy solution with only half the work of a regular class. Ideally, both lecturers participate actively in that they jointly design, prepare and teach the course and evaluate the students' performance. Analysing fictional texts, historical sources, historiographical and other secondary material, it was one of our key concerns to study how the texts and sources compare to each other and how they are interrelated with their contexts. Exploring the subject-matter from different disciplinary and methodological angles, the seminar participants were meant to gain insight into perspectives with which they were not familiar and to question and reflect more critically on their own approaches. In keeping with Moran's understanding of interdisciplinary work, the courses should thus not only add a historical dimension to the analysis of literature but promote new ways of engaging with (South) Africa.

3.1   Apartheid's Legacies

South Africa stands out from other former (British) colonies and other African countries, not least because of its history of institutionalised racism. Especially since the 1920s, colonial powers introduced policies of racial segregation, whereby they could oppress the African majority and secure their own privileges. This kind of racial discrimination was practised not only in South Africa, but across the continent. Not until 1948 did South Africa begin to stand out from other African countries for its drastically rigidified racial divisions. After its victory in the national election, the Afrikaner Nationalist Party came to power and introduced a state policy of separateness, or 'apartheid' as it is called in Afrikaans, which was designed to separate South Africans in virtually all spheres of social life on the basis of race classifications. Today, racism is no longer the basis of South Africa's state policy. White minority rule was abolished when political opposition organisations such as the African National Congress (ANC) were unbanned in 1990 and the first democratic elections were held in 1994. The end of the apartheid regime brought about high hopes for the future. As the seminar title suggests, it was our aim to look into the (dis)continuities of the apartheid period.

As part of their thorough preparation and active participation, the students had to give short oral presentations in groups. The topics ranged from methodological concerns such as interdisciplinary research, the distinction between 'text' (a term commonly used in literary and cultural studies) and 'source' (used in historical research) to context-related information that should trigger further debates about, for example, the Afrikaner Weerstandsbeweging, violence in the townships with a special focus on Amy Biehl, the Truth and Reconciliation Commission or the ANC and Jacob Zuma. As the seminar outline below will show, the assignments were closely connected to the set texts. In view of these broad topics, the students had both the opportunity and the responsibility to narrow down the subject-matter. They themselves decided on which aspects they would like to focus in order to make their presentations most productive for the course. Moreover, they were to find appropriate material on their own. In the short presentations in class, which should last no longer than twenty minutes, the students were to present the results of their research (no longer than fifteen minutes) and to reflect on their methodological approach (approximately five minutes). How did they tackle the assignment? What challenges did they face? What are possible reasons for the problems and how did they cope with them? By selecting specific issues and putting them up for discussion, the students could actively influence the seminar.

Setting the ground for the seminar, we started with an overview, namely "South Africa since 1976: An Historical Perspective" by Shula Marks and Stanley Trapido.[17] As revisionist historians, Marks and Trapido rewrite South African history: they try to move away from dominant historical perspectives towards diverse viewpoints that centre, for example, on women, blacks or trade unions. As the title suggests, the article discusses the ways in which "the consciousness of South Africa's black population has been radically transformed"[18] since the Soweto uprising in 1976. However, the authors do not study recent developments in political activism exclusively; instead they "analyse both the essential continuities with the past which constrain the present and the critical transformations which have taken place [...] as the state has responded to structural changes and increasing black militancy."[19] In keeping with this agenda, they locate recent events in the broader contexts of capitalism, racial segregation and the Black Consciousness movement. To ensure that students do not simply reproduce the information and ideas presented in the text, they were asked to reflect upon the ways in which Marks and Trapido construct their arguments and thus produce meaning. Since the article was published in 1988, i.e. before the end of apartheid, the publication date triggers some analytical and methodological questions. What significance does the publication date have for what is (not) being said in the article? What effects does the publication date have on how the arguments are presented? When does 'history' begin? How can scholars provide an historical view on recent events? How can students and scholars outside of South Africa get access to local perspectives on (contemporary) South Africa?

We used the engagement with this text as a starting point for our analysis of two novels, Gordimer's *None to Accompany Me* (1994) and Magona's *Mother to Mother* (1998), as well as two films, the feature film *Promised Land* (2002) and the documentary *Memories of Rain* (2004).[20]

Promised Land depicts a secluded Afrikaner community in post-apartheid South Africa that holds on to its land, regardless of droughts, the political transition and land claims of black Africans. As the title implies, the characters are convinced that they have a divine right to the land. The protagonist George Neethling, who grew up in Great Britain and has only vague memories of his early childhood in South Africa, returns to the farm in order to bury his late mother's ashes. Serving as an outsider, he questions the attitudes of the other characters and struggles with his own roles as an Afrikaner, as a South African, as an emigrant, as a returnee, as a young and educated man. George's unease is a central component of the film's sense of rising tension which finally erupts in violence. The expressionist aesthetics of the film, especially the use of camera movement, colours and lighting as well as the recurring motifs such as a defunct wind turbine and a graveyard, underscore the psychological dynamics of the plot. Since the film presents a fictional and aesthetically mediated account of post-apartheid South Africa, one might get the impression that the film provides much food for thought for film studies but less so for a historical approach. Yet, the film can also be made productive for debates about socio-political and historical issues. Although it centres on a small and supposedly homogenous group of Afrikaners, an analysis of the character conception and constellation makes apparent the power relations that are at work in this community.

To explore contexts and ideologies that are of relevance to *Promised Land*, we combined film analysis with further reading. In "Transformations in Boer Society", Timothy Keegan traces the slow and gradual changes that the Boers witnessed at the end of the 19th and the beginning of the 20th century. Highlighting the social and economic stratification within Boer society, he shows in what ways land became a central factor in determining an Afrikaner's status. Although Keegan does not refer to post-apartheid South Africa, in which *Promised Land* is set, the processes that he outlines are still useful for studying the film. After all, the fictional Afrikaner community considers land and other resources (such as water) as defining features of their power. Even if they can hardly live from farming, their understanding of Afrikaner identity and nationalism is strongly interrelated with (owning) land. We read Keegan's historical perspective in conjunction with Aletta Norval's theoretical analysis of constitutional concerns in contemporary South Africa. In "Reinventing the Politics of Cultural Recognition. The Freedom Front and the Demand for a *Volkstaat*", she uses conceptual debates about identity, cultural recognition and democracy to problematise the demands of the reactionary Freedom Front party for Afrikaner self-determination. Like Keegan's historical account, Norval's political theories can be applied to *Promised Land* as they provide further categories to analyse the ideologies that shape the film's Afrikaner community.

We then turned to Sindiwe Magona's novel *Mother to Mother*. Like *Promised Land*, this novel is concerned with a specific community, in this case the black township Guguletu near Cape Town. The novel is a fictionalised account of a murder case: the American scholar Amy Biehl, who helped to prepare the first democratic national elections, was killed by a group of black youth in Guguletu in August 1993.[21] Mandisa, the novel's first-person narrator and the mother of the murderer Mxolisi, addresses the mother of the killed daughter. She establishes a connection from 'mother to mother' as both of them lament the 'loss' of a child. Questions of belonging that surfaced in the investigation of the film are also of relevance here. In *Promised Land*, George returns to South Africa and feels caught between his different roles. *Mother to Mother*, by comparison, raises the question why the white student Amy Biehl went to the black township Guguletu. "What was she doing here, your daughter? What made her come to this of all places? Not an army of mad elephants would drag me here if I were her."[22] As *Mother to Mother* draws on an actual murder case, it was a central task for our interdisciplinary seminar to discuss the way in which the text spans literature and history. We therefore discussed the plot, setting, characters and major themes of the novel. Although the novel is strongly focussed on Guguletu in August 1993, the murder of Amy Biehl is not presented as an isolated case or as independent from South African history. Describing her own experiences and memories, Mandisa draws attention to the crimes that have shaped township life ever since the Afrikaner government implemented the Group Areas Act, created townships and removed black families by force. Yet Amy Biehl's murder seems to stand out from this general level of violence because of her skin colour. "For years... many, many years, we have lived with violence. This was nothing new to us. What was new was that this time, the victim was white. A white person killed in Guguletu, a black township."[23] However, Mandisa directly qualifies her own evaluation of the murder. "But then again, even that was not totally new, was it?"[24] Again, she does not present Amy Biehl's case as exceptional but compares it to similar crimes in East London and Langa. The murder is thus not presented as an isolated crime in which an individual perpetrator kills a particular victim. Instead, the novel stresses that the characters are interrelated with their surroundings and shaped by society, by politics and history.

Mother to Mother is a complex novel. Reading it in terms of Amy Biehl's murder is arguably the most central and obvious aspect but there are further issues that also lend themselves to investigation; one of them is the representation of family structures. Approaching this issue from a context-related perspective, the students were asked to reflect upon the family in South Africa. To further their research skills, we did not provide them with material but asked them to explore (in groups) relevant publications, e.g. *Journal of Southern African Studies*, *Journal of African History*, *Journal of Family History* or *Informationsdienst Südliches Afrika*. In class, the students were then to reflect on their research strategies and to discuss the results of their search. On this basis we proceeded to investigate how family relations in South African society compare to the literary appropriations in *Mother to Mother*.

We moved on to Nadine Gordimer's novel *None to Accompany Me*. Set at a similar time as *Mother to Mother*, it also tackles the turbulent times after the release of political prisoners and before the democratic election. Working as a civil rights lawyer for a legal foundation, the protagonist Vera Stark is concerned with black Africans' land claims. The novel thus attends to subjects such as forced removals, severe housing shortages and to questions of ownership – issues that are of relevance to the seminar and that come up in the discussions about the other texts as well. Because of her political commitment, Vera is nominated to serve on the Constitutional Committee and plays an active role in shaping South Africa's transition to majority rule. Moreover, the novel explores Vera's role as wife, lover and mother and traces changes in her private life. The narrator comments on the domestic developments by comparing them to the political makeover. "Perhaps the passing away of the old regime makes the abandonment of an old personal life also possible."[25] As in the case of *Mother to Mother*, family roles and constellations are a productive category for investigating *None to Accompany Me*.

The story of Vera Stark and her family is paralleled with the Maquomas, who – like many other South Africans – return from political exile. In keeping with this movement, the novel's sections are tellingly entitled "Baggage", "Transit" and "Arrivals". The section "Transit" is by far the longest one, which suggests that 'homecoming' is a lengthy and difficult endeavour. After all, the exiles have lived abroad for many years and are faced with an altered South Africa. Didymus and Sibongile Maquoma come to realise what consequences the political transition has for their own lives when they find their positions reversed: Didymus who used to be a prominent leader of the black resistance movement is no longer at the centre of public attention; suddenly it is Sibongile who rises to political prominence.

As an analysis of the plot design and character conceptions makes evident, the novel explores in what ways political and personal issues intersect. In both their private and their public lives, the characters have to adjust to new positions in the transforming South Africa. The title *None to Accompany Me* implies that each of them has to cope with the changes by him-/herself. The narration, however, cuts back and forth between the different threads so that the characters are not isolated from each other but incorporated into a complex portrayal of South Africa in the early 1990s.

The final part of our seminar was dedicated to the documentary *Memories of Rain. Szenen aus dem Untergrund*,[26] in which two South African political activists, Jenny Cargill and Kevin Quobasheane, reflect upon their lives as members of the ANC intelligence service. The film investigates how they grew up on different sides of the racial divide, how they became involved in the fight against apartheid and how they coped with going underground and living in exile. Placing the documentary in the context of *None to Accompany Me*, it is also worthwhile to examine how Didymus Maquoma's fictional experiences as a freedom fighter compare to this documentary. In addition to Cargill's and Quobasheane's perspectives, the film also contains interviews with various other South Africans who supported the resistance movement, including the lawyer Phyllis Naidoo, the Afrikaner clergyman Beyers Naudé and Jacob Zuma, then leader of the ANC intelligence. Zuma's different positions – in the armed struggle against apartheid and today as South Africa's president – underscore that an understanding of South Africa's history is essential in order to make sense of current political and social issues.

In terms of its form, the film invites a discussion of the generic characteristics of a documentary. With its frequent use of close-ups and its focus on interviews, the documentary puts emphasis on faces, on individuals and their stories. Still, by bringing together different groups and positions of power, namely men and women, blacks, whites and coloureds, members of the underground and of trade unions, clergymen, lawyers, journalists and family members, the film provides varied viewpoints and experiences. It thus draws attention to the complex and diverse forms resistance can take.

The directors Gisela Albrecht and Angela Mai worked on the film between 1994 and 2004 so that the interviewees look at apartheid in retrospective which allows for a critical and reflective distance. Due to its set-up, the film examines apartheid *and* considers present-day South Africa. By encouraging its audience to think about the traces of apartheid, the documentary provided an apt conclusion to this seminar. Working on the selected material and addressing issues such as race and power relations, violence, land rights, exile, home and belonging, we discussed in what ways the legacy of apartheid persists. It was highly productive to combine literary and historical approaches in order to examine in what ways South Africa's society, politics, culture and literature are strongly interrelated with the country's history.

3.2 Life Writing

Life writing has been of special significance in postcolonial literatures because of its potential to provide insight into diverse and hitherto socially and culturally unrecognised perspectives.[27] Life narratives have been common to present the lives and times of Africans. As Kirsten Rüther states in her contribution to this volume, the texts often work through mediation: an African tells his/her life, and another – often white – person converts this oral account into a written one. The narratives therefore do not fit neatly into the established genre categories of (auto)biographies, which is why scholars have preferred the more inclusive term life writing. While the literary history of (auto)biographies has long centred on dominant, white and male, history,[28] life writing also comprises literary (self-)representations of marginalised subjects; it provides alternative views and can thus challenge widespread perspectives.

To familiarise the students with the theoretical issues relevant to the study of life narratives, we started with a genre discussion. On the basis of selected material,[29] we addressed questions such as the following: what is life writing? How does it compare to (auto)biography? What issues are negotiated? Whose voices are included? Why is life writing of special interest to postcolonial studies? In a corresponding session on historical research, we considered oral history, its methodological concerns, its analytical categories and its relevance for African history.[30] Throughout the seminar we kept coming back to this theoretical input and discussed in what ways it can be made productive for studying the life narrative in question.

The seminar had an unusual focus in that we addressed exclusively one life story, namely *Zulu Woman*, in which the US-American journalist Rebecca Hourwich Reyher records the narrative of Christina Sibiya, the first of sixty-five wives of the Zulu king Solomon. In 1915, at the age of fifteen, Christina Sibiya, a mission-educated daughter of Christian peasants, married Solomon, despite the objections of her mother and the missionary. She lived in the royal household until 1931, when she left Solomon because he had increasingly abused her psychically and physically. From then on she struggled to make a living until she died in 1946. The book was originally published in 1948 by Columbia University Press and republished in 1999 by the Feminist Press of the City University of New York. The second edition includes a historical introduction by Marcia Wright, a literary afterword by Liz Gunner and an appendix that provides further contextual material. This edition therefore lends itself to an interdisciplinary investigation of *Zulu Woman* by students of literature and history.

To ensure that the students get an understanding of Zulu society in the late 19th and early 20th century, they were assigned to read and prepare Jeff Guy's historical overview "The Destruction and Reconstruction of Zulu Society". Zululand was a cohesive political system led by a king. Its unity was largely based on age regiments in which young men between puberty and marriage were recruited to fight, hunt and work on behalf of their king. The regiments served both as military forces and as means of state authority and control. In 1879, however, the Zulu were defeated by the British in the Anglo-Zulu war. The Zulu lost their centralised state which was divided into thirteen chiefdoms; their dynasty was ended and their king went into exile. As the title of Guy's article implies, the Zulu and the British subsequently attempted to reconstruct the administrative structure of Zulu society by drawing on elements from the old system and by introducing new, supposedly 'progressive' ones. By the 1890s, however, it is clear that this reconstruction is only a façade meant to conceal the massive changes Zulu society witnessed after the defeat and annexation by the colonial forces.

Instead of merely repeating the text's main arguments, the students were to imagine they lived in Zulu society. They were encouraged to adopt the respective roles of the Zulu king, chiefs, colonial forces, young men and members of age regiments, young women about to be married, husbands/fathers, wives/mothers, cattle, etc. By examining the military service, the organisation of a homestead and the social conventions of marriage, the students shed light on people's rights and obligations, on their social status, on power relations and on changes in Zulu society after the conquest.

With this preparation we approached *Zulu Woman* from literary and historical perspectives tackling issues such as the production and target audience, the character constellation with a special focus on gender and polygamy,[31] the representation of Christina Sibiya, of Solomon and of the royal household in general. The process of creating, editing and publishing *Zulu Woman* is characterised by an unequal distribution of power. In 1934, Christina Sibiya told Rebecca Hourwich Reyher her life story who, in turn, took down the story, later reworked her notes and published the text. In fact, the text is written in the third person singular, suggesting that it is about, rather than by Sibiya. Still, *Zulu Woman* is an extraordinary resource because, generally speaking, little information is available on the domestic lives of African kings. *Zulu Woman* fills this gap and provides insight into the everyday life of the royal Zulu family in the early 20th century. It thus triggers a debate about the significance of life writing for historical research.

To get a more complex understanding of Solomon as a historical figure, we dealt with Shula Marks's chapter "The Drunken King and the Nature of State",[32] in which she locates Solomon in the power structures in Zulu society after the Anglo-Zulu war. Although the Zulu kings were no longer officially recognised by the British, Solomon continued to exercise control over Zulu society and thus provided an alternative authority to the colonial powers.[33] With this account of Solomon's unstable political position in mind, we returned to *Zulu Woman* and studied in what ways Marks's historiographical analysis influences our reading of the life narrative.

Of course we could have gone on to study additional life narratives in order to explore the genre in greater detail.[34] Yet, we used a different strategy. Since the seminar was targeted at advanced students, it was our aim to engage them in independent studies. In keeping with this agenda, we provided them with time to develop their own interdisciplinary research or teaching projects on life writing in South(ern) Africa. My colleague and I put together a schedule so that related projects were presented in a panel (with about 10 minutes for each group), followed by a general discussion. The groups had to hand out relevant material in advance so that all seminar participants could think about the projects prior to the short presentations.[35] The diverse and well-planned projects ranged from lessons and extra-curricular projects at secondary schools to academic workshops and conferences. The teams were so motivated that they put much effort into their projects. The two teams planning conferences, for example, did not only think about the plenary speakers whom they would invite but they also created a leaflet with a schedule of panels, talks and authors' readings. Judging by the outcome and the feedback of the seminar participants, the independent-studies experiment was a success indeed.

4. Conclusion

The classes presented in this paper differed in terms of scope and subject-matter. While the seminar on life writing focused exclusively on Christina Sibiya's narrative, a variety of material – ranging from novels to films – was subject to investigation in 'Apartheid's Legacies'. Still, the general methodological set-up of the seminars was similar because both were designed as interdisciplinary classes, jointly taught by an historian and a literary and cultural studies lecturer. In keeping with Jameson's renowned statement, we placed the (contemporary) cultural products in their historical, political and social contexts. Setting the ground for this analysis, we dealt with historical documents and historiographical articles which enabled us to define and explore the locally specific circumstances in which the life narrative, the novels and films are produced and set. It became apparent in both seminars how much we can learn about present-day South Africa by engaging with its past.

Relying on the expertise of students and lecturers from History and from Anglophone Studies, we combined research questions from our own disciplinary background with new perspectives, thereby arriving at a complex contextualist reading of literary texts and films. It was one of the major merits of this interdisciplinary teamwork that all participants could thus further their understanding of the study objects. The different disciplinary viewpoints triggered a critical engagement with South Africa that has helped to confront simplistic and widespread stereotypes about (South) Africa. This objective justified the additional efforts it took for the lecturers to organise and for the students to attend an interdisciplinary seminar.

Notes

1. Jameson (1989: 9).
2. *Ibid.*
3. Moran (2010: 14).
4. At Leibniz University of Hanover, interdisciplinary endeavours have a long tradition. Scholars and students of history, sociology, religious, cultural and literary studies have cooperated in the research and study programme *Transformation Studies* for more than a decade. Exploring the 'global South' as well as its interrelations with the 'global North', they have focussed particularly on African, Latin American and Caribbean societies. For further information, please see the website: <http://www.transformation-studies.uni-hannover.de>.
5. Moran (2010: 14-15).
6. Grossberg (1997: 254).
7. *Ibid.* 255.
8. *Ibid.*
9. Thompson (1972: 45).
10. Giles & Middleton (2008: 91-92).
11. Pickering (2008: 202). Further information on historical research can also be obtained from the edited volume *Research Methods for History* (2012) by Simon Gunn and Lucy Faire.
12. Pickering (2008: 193).
13. *Ibid.* 195.
14. *Ibid.*
15. In her article "Archival methods", the historian Carolyn Steedman provides a helpful and short introduction to historical research methods and practices for non-historians (see Steedman 2005).
16. We taught the course on 'Apartheid's Legacies' in the summer term 2009 and 'Life Writing' in the winter term 2009/10.
17. See Marks & Trapido (1988). Further historical accounts, which are helpful for the seminar preparation and for further reference, include: Marx (2004) who combines overviews with case studies in order to explore the heterogeneous history of the African continent between 1800 and the present, Ross (1999) who focuses exclusively on South Africa and Beinart (2001) who, yet more specifically, addresses South African history of the twentieth century.
18. Marks & Trapido (1988: 45).
19. *Ibid.* 1.
20. The following are helpful introductions to film analysis: Bordwell & Thompson (2010), Monaco (2009), Steinmetz *et al.* (2005).

21 The historical context is introduced in the author's preface, see Magona (1998: v-vi).
22 Magona (1998: 48).
23 *Ibid.* 69.
24 *Ibid.*
25 Gordimer (1994: 315).
26 The film was co-produced by the German director Gisela Albrecht and the South African Angela Mai; it was shown at the *Berlinale* in 2004. Further information on the film is available online: <http://www.memories-of-rain.com/htm/home.html>.
27 On the relevance of life writing for postcolonial studies, see Döring (2008: 65-70) and Moore-Gilbert (2009). In South Africa, the genre has become a highly productive field since the abolition of apartheid in 1994, see Michael and Nuttall (2000). Compared to earlier decades in which autobiographies were often banned, the political transition has allowed for a plurification of voices.
28 Kadar (1992: 7).
29 For students and lecturers alike, I recommend the following material as a preparation for this debate: excerpts from Anderson (2001), especially the introduction; the relevant passage from Döring's introduction to postcolonial literatures (2008: 65-70); a special issue of *Wasafiri* on life writing with an editorial by Susheila Nasta (2006) and an historical overview of Western autobiography by Moore-Gilbert (2006).
30 To tackle these issues we worked with Bozzoli's introduction (1991).
31 We provided the students with secondary material about gender issues in Southern Africa, namely Hanretta (1998), Phoofolo (2005) and (2007). The students were divided into three groups and each group had to present the main arguments of the text they had prepared. Moreover, they had to reflect upon the question in what ways the texts were appropriate for approaching *Zulu Woman*. After all, the material did not explore exclusively the temporal and/or spatial setting of the life narrative.
32 Marks (1986).
33 See *Ibid.* 27.
34 Texts that would lend themselves to further investigation of Southern African life narratives are, for example, Elsa Joubert's *Poppie Nongena*, which depicts a black woman's struggle against apartheid, Margaret McCord's *The Calling of Katie Makanya*, briefly outlined in Kirsten Rüther's contribution to this volume, or Mpho 'M'Atsepo Nthunya's *Singing Away the Hunger. The Autobiography of an African Woman*, which explores Basotho society and culture.

35 We used the learning platform Stud.IP so that lecturers and students alike could upload material and make it accessible to all seminar participants.

Bibliography

Anderson, Linda: *Autobiography*, The New Critical Idiom, London & New York, 2001.
Beinart, William: *Twentieth-Century South Africa*, 2nd ed., Oxford, 2001.
Bordwell, David & Kristin Thompson: *Film Art. An Introduction*, 9th ed., New York, 2010.
Bozzoli, Belinda: "Introduction. Oral history, Consciousness, and Gender". – In B. B. (Ed.): *Women of Phokeng. Consciousness, Life Strategy, and Migrancy in South Africa, 1900-1983*, Johannesburg, 1991, pp. 1-15.
Döring, Tobias: *Postcolonial Literatures in English*, Uni-Wissen Anglistik – Amerikanistik, Stuttgart, 2008.
Giles, Judy & Tim Middleton: *Studying Culture. A Practical Introduction*, 2nd ed., Oxford, 2008.
Gordimer, Nadine: *None to Accompany Me*, London, 1994.
Grossberg, Lawrence: "Cultural Studies. What's in a Name? (One More Time)". – In L. G. (Ed.): *Bringing It All Back Home. Essays on Cultural Studies*, Durham, 1997, pp. 245-71.
Gunn, Simon & Lucy Faire (Eds.): *Research Methods for History*, Edinburgh, 2012.
Guy, Jeff: "The Destruction and Reconstruction of Zulu Society". – In Shula Marks & Richard Rathbone (Eds.): *Industrialisation and Social Change in South Africa. African Class Formation, Culture and Consciousness, 1870-1930*, London & New York, 1982, pp. 167-194.
Hanretta, Sean: "Women, Marginality and the Zulu State. Women's Institutions and Power in the Early Nineteenth Century", *Journal of African History* 39, 1998, 389-415.
Jameson, Frederic: *The Political Unconscious. Narrative as a Socially Symbolic Act*, London & New York, 1989.
Joubert, Elsa: *Poppie Nongena*, New York & London, 1980.
Kadar, Marlene: "Coming to Terms. Life Writing – from Genre to Critical Practice". – In M. K.: *Essays on Life Writing. From Genre to Critical Practice*, Toronto, 1992, pp. 3-16.
Keegan, Timothy: "Transformations in Boer Society". – In T. K. (Ed.): *Rural Transformations in Industrializing South Africa. The Southern Highveld to 1914*, Braamfontein, 1986, pp. 20-50.

Magona, Sindiwe: *Mother to Mother*, Boston, 1998.

Marks, Shula: "The Drunken King and the Nature of State". – In S. M. (Ed.): *The Ambiguities of Dependence in South Africa. Class, Nationalism, and the State in Twentieth-Century Natal*, Johannesburg, 1986, pp. 15-41.

Marks, Shula & Stanley Trapido: "South Africa since 1976. An Historical Perspective". – In Shaun Johnson (Ed.): *South Africa. No Turning Back*, London, 1988, pp. 1-51.

Marx, Christoph: *Geschichte Afrikas. Von 1800 bis zur Gegenwart*, Paderborn, 2004.

McCord, Margaret: *The Calling of Katie Makanya*, London, 1995.

Memories of Rain. Szenen aus dem Untergrund, dir. Gisela Albrecht & Angela Mai, South Africa & Germany, 2004.

Michael, Cheryl-Ann & Sarah Nuttall: "Autobiographical Acts". – In C.-A. M. & S. N. (Eds.): *Senses of Culture. South African Culture Studies*, Oxford, 2000, pp. 298-317.

Monaco, James: *How to Read a Film. Movies, Media, and Beyond*, 4th edition, Oxford & New York, 2009.

Moore-Gilbert, Bart: "Western Autobiography and Colonial Discourse. An Overview", *Wasafiri* 21:2, 2006, 9-16.

---: *Postcolonial Life-Writing. Culture, Politics and Self-Representation*, New York, 2009.

Moran, Joe: *Interdisciplinarity*, 2nd ed., The New Critical Idiom, London & New York, 2010.

Nasta, Susheila: "Editorial", *Wasafiri* 21:2, 2006, 1-2.

Norval, Aletta: "Reinventing the Politics of Cultural Recognition. The Freedom Front and the Demand for a *Volkstaat*". – In David R. Howarth & A. N. (Eds.): *South Africa in Transition. New Theoretical Perspectives*, London, 1998, pp. 93-110.

Nthunya, Mpho 'M'Atsepo: *Singing Away the Hunger. The Autobiography of an African Woman*. Ed. K. Limakatso Kendall, Bloomington & Indianapolis, 1997.

Phoofolo, Pule: "Female Extramarital Relationships and their Regulation in Early Colonial Thembuland, South Africa, 1875-95", *Journal of Family History* 30:1, 2005, 3-47.

---: "Holy Weddings, Unholy Marriages. Christian Spouses and Domestic Discords in Early Colonial Lesotho, 1870-1900", *Journal of Religious History* 31:4, 2007, 363-386.

Pickering, Michael: "Engaging with History". – In M. P. (Ed.): *Research Methods in Cultural Studies*, Edinburgh, 2008, pp. 193-213.

Promised Land, dir. Jason Xenopoulos, South Africa, 2002.

Reyher, Rebecca Hourwich: *Zulu Woman. The Life Story of Christina Sibiya*, New York, 1999.

Ross, Robert: *A Concise History of South Africa*, Cambridge, 1999.
Steedman, Carolyn: "Archival Methods". – In Gabriele Griffin (Ed.): *Research Methods in English Studies*, Edinburgh, 2005, pp. 17-30.
Steinmetz, Rüdiger *et al.*: *Filme sehen lernen. Grundlagen der Filmästhetik*, Frankfurt a.M., 2005.
Thompson, E.P.: "Anthropology and the Discipline of Historical Context", *Midland History* 1:3, 1972, 41-55.

Jana Gohrisch (Hanover)

Teaching West Africa.
Histories, Literatures, Cultures

1. Introduction

The following essay introduces a course on colonial West Africa, the first time taught by Jana Gohrisch alone as a literary and cultural scholar and the second time taught together with the historian Katja Füllberg-Stolberg, a specialist in West African and African American history. For methodological observations, the article will furthermore draw on the introduction into the theories and methodologies of Atlantic Studies jointly taught by Jana Gohrisch and the Africa historian Brigitte Reinwald, with an expertise in Francophone West Africa and Senegal.[1]

The courses began with a reflection on the methodological implication of their subject matter, 'Colonial West Africa/Colonial Nigeria in Historiography and Literature'. Here, we drew attention to the different levels of abstraction: while historiography designates an academic discipline, literature refers to the subject matter of yet another discipline, i.e. literary studies. From here we developed the central question of the course: what and how do we learn about colonial West Africa in general and about colonial Nigeria in particular? How exactly do we historicise, taking up Jameson's call? From the composition of the student body made up of both advanced Bachelor and Master students training to become teachers as well as of those studying for general interest, other challenges arose: why study colonial West Africa in the 21st century at all? What is the use of this kind of knowledge when there is no place for these issues in German school curricula and with Africa being so stereotyped and marginalised in the public sphere? How to motivate such a heterogeneous group of students and keep them going in a course that demands a lot of extra work due to its combination of two disciplines?

We suggested approaching this problem on the meta-level through a set of questions rather than answers: how do we produce knowledge about history? From which sources can we gain which kind of information? What do the disciplines have in common and where do they differ? What is it that historiography can do but literary studies cannot do given the type of material its scholars work with? What is it that literature can do but historiography cannot? And how can the two disciplines complement one other?

To prepare the interaction between the different types of textual sources assigned as course material, we looked into the factuality of literature and the fictionality of historiography to stress the common features. This approach challenges the wide-spread expectation as to the opposite and takes historiography's claim to objective factuality as what it is: an attempt at 'truth' based on the construction and subsequent interpretation of historical facts, a process that can be proven intersubjectively. While historiographic texts are usually aimed at special readers, literature targets a much more general readership. One of literature's defining characteristics is the ambiguity that sets it apart from expository (or referential) texts designed to give reliable answers to real questions. Literature relies on the imagination to construct an admittedly subjective version of the world which nevertheless has a certain claim to 'be true'. Literature operates on the basis of different conventions than historiography which suspend the expectations of 'truth' (or accuracy) on the factual level but indicate to provide it on the aesthetic level. Rather than document events or record historical developments, literature selectively represents social norms and ideals, affirming and questioning them at the same time. It offers fictional solutions to real conflicts and experiments with alternative options to unfulfilled desires. As a special kind of historical source, literature may be studied as to its "structures of feeling",[2] the aesthetically transformed experience of conflicting beliefs and value systems as they manifest themselves in the culture of a period. The term was coined by Raymond Williams, co-founder of the materialist school of British cultural studies, to capture historical change and the contribution of literature to understand the past:

> The most difficult thing to get hold of, in studying any past period, is this felt sense of the quality of life at a particular place and time: a sense

of the ways in which the particular activities combined into a way of thinking and living.[3]

This "felt sense" provides the readers with a special kind of knowledge – emotional rather than rational – asking them to re-live the very historical moment which gave rise to the literary text in question.

Inquiring into why some works of art have survived the original contexts of their production, the American new historicist scholar Stephen Greenblatt argues (writing about the English Renaissance) that these works have successfully absorbed "the social" which he locates in the aesthetics of a text: "artistic form itself is the expression of social evaluations and practices".[4] Commenting on Greenblatt, the British cultural materialist Kiernan Ryan continues (referring to *The Merchant of Venice*):

> The text, far from being a passive product of its world, emerges as a creative act of investigation in its own right, compelling a searching reassessment of what the history that made it possible actually involved.[5]

According to Ryan, the first task of the historically minded literary scholar is "to contextualise the inherent strategies of language and form which dictate how the plays conceive and judge their world".[6] This does not only apply to Shakespeare and his plays but to all literature as an aesthetic re-working of realities. It is here, that new historicist and cultural materialist literary scholars seek to transcend the 'old historicist' practice of matching the historiographic and the literary reconstructions of past and present realities. To do so, they study the politics of form, i.e. they contrast the particular aesthetic means of a text with the literary conventions of the time of production and establish their functions for the topics. Thus, the text emerges as part of a specific historical moment, not as a reflection of some kind of independently existing historical context. Most importantly, aesthetically encoded comments on historical realities may be found in contradictions and ruptures, paradoxical statements and inconsistencies of style which may indicate unease or even discontent with dominant norms and values. In order to appreciate gaps and things left unsaid, however, the reader needs to know what the text might have said which is only possible via comparison with other fictional, non-fictional and historiographic texts.

Using this methodological dialogue between related (but still different) theoretical schools of historically minded literary studies to develop our own approach, we merged the new historicist parallel reading of fictional and non-fictional texts from the archival continuum of the past with the political commitment of cultural materialists to the present (later to be supplemented by postcolonial approaches to power relations by Homi Bhabha). We decided to read the assigned literary texts against three temporal backgrounds: the time of production, the time of setting and the time of reception (then and now) to bring out personal implications for the participants.

From the historian's perspective, many of the points made above hold true as well – albeit to a different degree. Rather than follow the extreme new historicist understanding of history as text (derived from its poststructuralist heritage), the constructedness and subsequent relativity of all historical knowledge, we settled on a compromise: historiography, too, expresses conflicting political interests. These interests, however, need to be spelled out in the approximation to objectivity that defines an academic discipline. This allowed us to appreciate the contributions of African historians alongside European and American ones as well as their respective methodological backgrounds. Historiography thus emerges as a continued search for the past in its significance for the present arriving at intermediate stages of knowledge and pointing out what needs to be researched in the future.

2. West Africa. Colonial Nigeria in Historiography and Literature

The term 'colonial' in the course titles is ambiguous as there are no fixed dates to mark the advent of colonialism in West Africa and in Nigeria, which was formed by the British in 1914 and became independent in 1960. "Colonialism created Nigeria and Nigerians; neither had existed before European boundaries and European rule were established by force."[7] In the course on colonial Nigeria taught jointly with Katja Füllberg-Stolberg we assigned ten historiographic texts (each between 10 and 30 pages long and supplemented by maps and statistics) grouped chronologically and by topic: slave trade and slavery, the impact of abolition, colonisation in the 19th and 20th centuries, colonial administration in Nigeria, anti-colonial resistance and the Nigerian civil war.[8]

We selected three literary texts to investigate what and how literature can contribute to understand the contradictory processes of colonisation and the period's "structures of feeling" as well as those of the preceding period of the transatlantic slave trade. We read the first two chapters of the slave narrative *The Interesting Narrative of the Life of Olaudah Equiano, or Gustavus Vassa, The African, Written by Himself* (1789), Joyce Cary's colonial tale about *Mister Johnson* (1939) and Chinua Achebe's celebrated pre-independence novel *Things Fall Apart* (1958). As both Equiano and Achebe are of Igbo origin, we selected historiographic texts concentrating on south-eastern Nigeria including the Niger delta. In order to contextualise *Mister Johnson,* which is set among the Hausa-Fulani and the British, we read an essay on colonial administration accompanied by an archival source to understand the power structures under 'indirect rule' in the north.[9] Moreover, we discussed the economic, ethnic and political differences between the northern and the southern regions in the 19th and 20th century based on the assigned texts.[10]

2.1 *Olaudah Equiano's* Interesting Narrative

Our first set of topics included the slave trade, the struggle for its abolition, the transition to 'legitimate trade' and colonial rule. After having read two historiographic texts on slavery among the Igbo and on the period of the slave trade in Nigeria, we began our discussion of Olaudah Equiano (1745-1797) and abolition based on the paratexts, i.e. the title page, the frontispiece with Equiano's engraved portrait, the accompanying letter to the Houses of Parliament and the list of subscribers.[11] In accordance with Greenblatt's statement about artistic form as "the expression of social evaluations and practices" we analysed the strategies of Equiano's self-fashioning[12] as an African and a middle-class Englishman, a writer and an abolitionist. The *Interesting Narrative* was the first slave narrative written by a former slave himself and thus set the standards for the genre and its publication pattern. Inscribing a large readership into his text, Equiano combines the conventions of the (Protestant) spiritual autobiography with elements of the popular adventure story and the travelogue. The original title page proves Equiano's pioneering self-authorisation as a writer and publisher who entered his text into the Stationers' Register to protect its copyright rather than sell it straight away as was customary at the time. The motto below the title quotes the prophet Isaiah on salvation through faith which is both a gesture to the evangelicals among the first readers and a proof of Equiano's belief and literacy. The names mentioned in the long title signal the two most important identities Equiano negotiates: Olaudah Equiano refers to his African heritage and Gustavus Vassa is one of the names given to him as a slave, which he retains along with its link to the 16th-century Swedish king who freed his people from Danish oppression. The engraving shows a young African in the elegant dress of an affluent Englishman of the period with an opened Bible in his hands and looking confidently at the beholder. The next page (in the Norton edition) contains a letter to Parliament in which Equiano acknowledges the purpose of his publication along with his role as abolitionist. The following seven pages of subscribers demonstrate the aristocratic patronage and middle-class support Equiano was able to secure, especially among evangelicals, Methodists (John Wesley) and abolitionists (Thomas Clarkson, Granville Sharp, Henry Thornton, Josiah Wedgewood). With their signature they all pledged to buy a copy of the book (and, in Equiano's unusual case, paid some money in advance) which allowed the author to pay the printer and the book sellers.[13] Moreover, Equiano places himself into the emerging tradition of African writing in English by listing Ottobah Cuguano and Ignatius Sancho's son William. "The publishing success of his predecessors gave Equiano cause for believing that a market already existed for the autobiography of a black entrepreneur."[14]

In the first chapter Equiano designates his father as an elder or a chief of the Igbo and describes at length their social organisation and culture using the personal pronouns in the first person plural to identify himself with this culture. The style is educated and refined; the information corresponds to the ethnographic knowledge of the period. The second chapter recounts his experience of enslavement and the Middle Passage in a way that has become an almost classic eyewitness account of this experience. But what do we make of Vincent Carretta's finding that Equiano was not born in Igboland but in South Carolina?[15] How do we deal with an invented African eyewitness account? What about the relationship between fact and fiction in an autobiography? How do historians and literary scholars respond to this case of obvious 'fictional history'? Carretta convincingly refers us to the function of this former slave's narrative for the abolitionist movement which needed "an authentic African voice"[16] to tell the story from "the victim's point of view".[17] Equiano, who claims to have been born into a slave-owning family and was a slave and a slave-driver, styles himself as an expert on the issue and compares slavery among the Igbo to Western chattel slavery. From this, the Igbo emerge as the "Israelites in their primitive state"[18] which does not only prove Equiano's learning but serves to elevate the status of African cultures in the eyes of his Western and Christian readers. The Africans' "apparent inferiority"[19] is due to their situation as enslaved people who are denied education and equality. Keying into the late 18th-century middle-class culture of sensibility,[20] Equiano calls on his readers to show sympathy for and benevolence to their black brothers rather than discriminate against them because of their colour.[21]

The plea to compassion comes across even stronger in the chapter on the Middle Passage in which he tells vividly how he was kidnapped and sold time and again on his way from the interior of Africa to the coast. There he is confined below deck on a slaver bound for Barbados where he and his shipmates are finally sold to planters. The style is rational and matter-of-fact rather than emotional or sensational as in much of the sentimental and gothic literature of the time. Continuing in this sober and detached manner, Equiano concludes this chapter by indicting this new type of slavery as cruel beyond imagination and grounded only in the avarice of the whites.[22] But again, what do we make of a faked eye-witness account? How do we interpret this contradiction par excellence? Which elements of the social has the *Interesting Narrative* absorbed to survive as the classic account cited in all relevant textbooks down to German and French history school books?[23] The case demonstrates how history is constructed with a purpose and how the analytical deconstruction of the purpose can help us to understand the result and its very form. Equiano was the most famous black abolitionist at the end of the 18th century and had educated himself to the level of being able to write his autobiography (rather than dictate it). He fashioned the account of his own life to meet the political purpose by absorbing the stories of African enslavement and the Middle Passage to then re-create them as lived experience. Providing "this felt sense of the quality of life at a particular place and time", the fictional chapters of *The Interesting Narrative* have become the means to remind Western readers emotionally and rationally of their own past as well as of their present responsibility to confront this past and its effects on Africa.

2.2 Historiography on Colonialisation

The historiographic essays (by Gordon, Uchendu and Webster & Boahen) enabled us to evaluate Equiano's rendering of Igbo culture and gain insights into how the slave trade affected the regions of today's Nigeria. We saw how the historians' agenda changed over the decades observing how they stressed the active role of Africans when writing after Nigerian independence, from an African point of view and for African students (Uchendu, Webster & Boahen). We discussed the reasons for the abolition of slavery[24] and its economic and social effects on the delta states which moved to 'legitimate trade' in palm oil and palm kernels in the 19th century.[25] While the slave trade had been dominated by a small number of Africans, who used the whites' insatiable demand for cheap labour to make large profits, the oil trade was dominated by whites who penetrated the interior of West Africa in ever larger numbers, especially after the discovery of quinine in 1850.[26] By the 1890s, the African trading empires in the Niger delta were declining and colonisation was gaining momentum with British military support for merchants to gain control of the Niger River. Britain's colonial policy proclaimed "Christianity, Commerce, and Civilization"[27] as its goals but valued Nigeria primarily as a source of raw materials, valuable products and a market for British manufactured goods. The British made Lagos the first colony in Nigeria in 1861, stepping up their efforts after the Berlin conference in 1884 had inaugurated "the scramble for Africa".[28] To defend British commercial interests, the Oil River Protectorate was founded in 1885 (which comprised the delta of the Niger) and renamed Niger Coast Protectorate in 1893. At the beginning of the 20th century, the British established the Protectorate of Northern Nigeria and appointed Frederick Lugard as High Commissioner.[29] He subdued the Muslim Hausa peasantry and their Fulani rulers and introduced 'indirect rule', which meant ruling through the 'native authorities', i.e. the local rulers and the local system of government, to save costs and let colonialism appear more palatable.[30] Following the recommendations of Lugard, the northern and southern protectorates were amalgamated into the Colony and Protectorate of Nigeria in 1914. But "[d]espite the ideology of mutual benefit and minimal disruption of local cultures, British interference was extensive and in many ways far more negative than Lugard's writings indicate."[31]

2.3 Joyce Cary's Mister Johnson

It is exactly this contradiction between colonial ideology and colonial reality that Joyce Cary's *Mister Johnson* (1939) investigates and that produces the ruptures and inconsistencies of the text. The novel is set in northern Nigeria in the early 20th century where Cary (1888-1957) had served in the Nigerian Civil Service since 1913. From 1917 until he resigned in 1920, he worked as an (assistant) district officer, responsible for tax collection, education, legal affairs and road building. His first four novels (published in the 1930s) are set in Africa and aesthetically re-work the effects of British colonialism on the Africans. While most of Cary's work has lost its once numerous middle-brow readers, *Mister Johnson* lives on because Chinua Achebe's *Things Fall Apart* takes issue with its colonialist features. Before we compared the two texts for their respective contributions to historiography, we read Cary's novel for its ambiguously critical and affirmative representation of colonialism. The resulting aesthetic contradictions enable the readers to access the equivocal colonial "structures of feeling".

The narrative combines social realism with satire, farce and grotesque operating on contrasts and correspondences across gender, ethnic and class divides. It juxtaposes the British colonial authorities represented by (assistant) district officers and the resident and the native authorities represented by the Fulani emir and waziri, his prime minister. While both sides come across as corrupt, the Fulani rulers are also shown as weak and absurd. The social cosmos of the fictional northern provincial town of Fada[32] is completed by an English trader of working-class background who is stereotypically inclined to drink and become violent against his local employees and African lover. He stands for the private commercial interests of the British in the region; an endeavour judged as fatal by the novel's plot which culminates in his murder by the young African protagonist. Due to their professional association with the new rulers, the employees, situated on the intermediate social level, consider themselves socially and culturally superior to the local Hausa peasantry embodied by Mister Johnson's wife Bamu and her greedy family.

The character conception throughout the novel is static allowing for no character development. Moreover, the eponymous protagonist is conceived as a type rather than an individual representing the new generation of mission-educated southern Nigerians. His very young age of seventeen carries the connotations of childish innocence which feeds into the colonialist stereotype of Africans as children which runs through both the dialogue and the narrator's descriptions. In keeping with the conventions of satire, Mister Johnson (along with the other characters) is cast as one-dimensional. The authorial narrator endows him explicitly and repeatedly with exaggerated features to set him apart and make him the emotional centre of the novel and the driving force of the plot. Mister Johnson exhibits carefree exuberance, unbounded vitality and infinite optimism. At the same time he is ingeniously unreliable and professionally incompetent by European colonial standards. The vividness of the character is reflected stylistically by the present tense. Moreover, the text uses metonymy to bring Mister Johnson across as the classic mimic man with his generic English surname (leaving out the Christian name), white suit, patent leather shoes, hat and umbrella. On the one hand, the novel satirises his simplistic identification with the British. It makes fun of his exaggerated European values staging how he forces his unwilling Hausa wife to dress like "a government lady".[33] On the other hand, the novel shows him extensively as a poet, singer and dancer who in his song lyrics imagines a reversal of power relations between himself and the King whom he simultaneously worships.[34]

Mister Johnson's energetic resourcefulness contrasts sharply with the assistant district officer's lack of ideas, drive and personality. In contrast to Rudbeck, who "takes no pleasure in his own thoughts, which revolve in a good deal of confusion",[35] the narrative ascribes to Johnson both imagination and ideas which finally allow him to act as a creative collaborator.[36] The episodic plot begins with a satire on the middle-class idea of marriage (performed in the post office by a post office clerk) and on the culturally hybrid wedding celebration. It goes on with Mister Johnson's attempts to raise money to cover his ever increasing debts which involve him in embezzlement of funds, bribery and theft. The central episode revolves around the building of a road, the symbol of colonial modernisation to the colonial officer and of unwelcome change to the native rulers as well as to the district officer Blore. In addition, Blore fears Johnson's exuberance because it threatens the established order of things. "Johnson has no special interest in roads, but he is as sharp as a sharp child to know what pleases Rudbeck."[37] With his creativity, Mister Johnson generates the necessary money by convincing Rudbeck to embezzle government funds for which he later loses his job while Rudbeck gets away unharmed. The text employs the road motif to create a structural irony which underlines the ambiguity of the colonial endeavour to open up the country to commerce and Western civilisation. The road does not only bring 'progress' but – as both the emir and the resident predicted – crime and decay which eventually sweep away Johnson into his private tragedy. He stabs the local trader, who caught him stealing money, and is subsequently tried by the assistant district officer. In a final gesture of regard, the officer shoots his clerk (instead of hanging him as ordered) at Johnson's own request, who absurdly continues to cheer up his "friend"[38] despite his imminent death. Rudbeck's deed, however, is murder, too, which unites both sides of the colonial divide in crime with no (fictional) way out of the stalemate.

While the one-dimensional characterisation of Johnson is in keeping with the distancing strategies of satire, the ending clearly is not and thus causes an aesthetic inconsistency. Despite the colonialist traits of the representation, the exceptional African may be interpreted as an attempt at respect and appreciation but only up to the point when he murders the trader. From then on, the reader's basis for judgement is criminal law rather than the discrepancy between the ideal and reality of colonisation, making it impossible to read the murders as a grotesque element of satire. Thus, the subversive moment that Homi Bhabha located in colonial mimicry, i.e. in the metonymic imitation of the coloniser by the colonised, is lost. Rather than disrupt the authority of the colonial discourse, as envisioned by Bhabha[39] (and feared by the fictional district officer Blore), the murderous turn of the plot serves to stabilise the power structures because it calls for this very authority to punish the dangerously criminal African. Reading the novel as part of the historical moment of the late 1930s can help to explain this rupture as a contribution to negotiating the aims and forms of British colonialism in West Africa which were increasingly contested by Western-educated Africans themselves. They mainly came from the south, challenged both the traditional rulers and the British and demanded, from the 1930s onwards, an end to British rule. Cary's novel neither depicts Africans as political agents nor does it project any alternatives to their collaboration with the corrupt colonial administration. To contemporary readers, this gap considerably diminishes the anti-colonial thrust that the text undoubtedly possessed for its British readers in the 1940s.

2.4 Chinua Achebe's Things Fall Apart

Writing on the eve of Nigerian independence in the 1950s, Chinua Achebe (born in 1930) sets out to fill this gap in Cary's novel. Exploring pre-colonial and colonial Igbo culture from within, he contests the colonialist ideology that looked at Africans from the outside constructing them as traditional, primitive and static.[40] Achebe's "creative act of historical investigation" indeed compels "a searching reassessment of what the history that made it possible actually involved",[41] as Kiernan Ryan wrote. Why did the Igbo succumb to the British? How did they act in the historical moment of contact? Why would some of them collaborate while others resisted? How will the two types of agency in the face of colonialism affect the new Nigeria? Instead of answering these questions unequivocally, the novel suggests alternative modes of action through its character conception and constellation, through the handling of time and the interaction of story and plot.

The title *Things Fall Apart* is taken from the poem "The Second Coming" (written in 1919) by the modernist Anglo-Irish poet and playwright William Butler Yeats. Absorbing such developments as the imminent civil war in Ireland, the Russian revolution and the aftermath of the First World War, the poem imagines a profoundly disturbing return of Christ (envisioned by St. John at the end of the New Testament): Christ does not come back as a saviour but as an ominous beast. The metaphorically expressed notion of unstoppable dissolution from within comes across in the third and fourth lines: "Things fall apart; the centre cannot hold; mere anarchy is loosed upon the world".[42] The idea of collapse due to internal reasons serves as a leitmotif for Achebe's novel. The title joins the years of the setting in the late 1800s to the mid-1950s marking out both periods as times of crisis when old orders fall apart and new ones are not yet visible. The statement makes sense on the factual level as well because the Igbo had not created centralised states that could have unified and supported the people in their resistance to colonisation (which nevertheless was put up by the Aro in eastern and the Ekumeku in western Igboland). Rather, Igbo culture has developed in decentralised village communities of farmers with egalitarian traditions and a segmented political system.[43] Drawing on Yeats's poem, Achebe delineates the internal tensions that cause the communities to break down under external pressure. Rather than inaugurating a new civilisation with a new cultural centre, colonialism is the metaphorical beast that eventually destroys the indigenous ways of live. Moreover, the allusion to Yeats conveys the fear that independent Nigeria may turn out a beast in the image of the protagonist Okonkwo: violent and destructive in his desire to succeed individually in a highly competitive society.[44]

Achebe uses and challenges the aesthetic conventions of the European realist novel: the reliable authorial narrator focalises on the male protagonist but often digresses to explain social practices and cultural peculiarities. As Richard Lane has argued, "Achebe's narrator is a 'mediator' between the views of the individual and those of the community, whereas canonical European fiction creates 'individual introspection' as the norm."[45] The English novel is 'africanised' by (translated) Igbo words and concepts and many elements of oral story telling: stories from the Igbo archive, local metaphors and comparisons as well as structural, grammatical and morphological forms of repetition. The style is deceptively simple, emotionally sober and detached with its usually short, declarative sentences. Through these aesthetic means, the novel defines its inscribed readers as outsiders who are provided with 'objective' ethnographic information, a mode which alludes to the work of colonial anthropologists like G. T. Basden.[46] The tripartite structure of *Things Fall Apart* supports this impression: the seemingly plotless first part describes life in pre-colonial (fictional) Umuofia. It is twice as long as the action-filled second and third parts, which cover the initial contacts between missionaries and Igbo villagers and the post-contact world.[47] After having parodied the colonialist construction of the African 'Other' as timelessly static in the first part, the narrative time speeds up covering ever longer time periods in ever shorter chapters. The Yeatsian notion of cyclical time used to narrate the practices of Igbo culture gives way to linear time which suggests a world rushing to an apocalyptic ending. This, in turn, increases the reader's unease as things are falling apart.[48]

Right from the beginning, the character conception of the protagonist, however, unsettles the reader who is simultaneously being lulled into reading an 'authentic' story. The story unfolds chronologically alternating between telling and showing how Okonkwo carves out a position for himself in the village community where rank and prestige depend on wealth (demonstrated by numbers of titles and wives), age and ability.[49] Rejecting his less competitive (but musically gifted) father as a failure, the protagonist is determined to succeed as cultivator of yams, husband to many wives and father of many (preferably male) children, to serve his community as a warrior, to be heard in public debate and to influence decision making. The text contrasts this ambitious man, who lacks self-control and shuns all moderation as weakness, with characters such as his friend Obierika and his second wife Ekwefi. Using minor characters to point out alternatives to the protagonist's aggressive masculinity, the text enables its readers to imagine different trajectories for the plot. In his fear to fail on his way up, however, Okonkwo violates some cultural norms and practices and overfulfils others as when he blindly follows the oracle's demand to kill his ward Ikemefuna. In general, he does not question the traditions and goes into exile after having accidentally killed a man. After seven years in exile he returns to a drastically altered society: missionaries have built a church drawing a steadily increasing Igbo congregation. Among the new Christians is his son Nwoye, who has become estranged by Okonkwo's harsh treatment of his allegedly 'defective' masculinity and by the murder of Ikemefuna. Moreover, the British have established colonial administrative structures headed by a district commissioner who judges the locals for their offences. While Okonkwo wants to fight the strangers, Obierika rejects this as futile:

> "Our own men and our sons have joined the ranks of the stranger. They have joined his religion and they help to uphold the government. If we

should try to drive out the white men in Umuofia we should find it easy. There are only two of them. But what of our own people who are following their way and have been given power?"[50]

The creative collaborators of Mister Johnson's kind return here as one of the reasons why things were falling apart in the past and may continue to do so in the future. But rather than blaming individuals like Okonkwo or Nwoye, the novel draws attention to such features of Igbo culture that alienate some of its members. The readers are let into a culture that defines itself by ostracising seemingly 'deviant Others', such as twins and osu (slaves dedicated to a god); a culture that creates dysfunctional safeguarding rituals and consults oracles to decide on life or death of its members. At the end of the novel, Okonkwo, the outstanding male representative of Igbo culture, commits his last desperate act of violent resistance and then hangs himself. The concluding paragraph focalises on the district commissioner, the symbolic colonial official who sets out to convert his 'knowledge' of the case into a book, entitled *The Pacification of the Primitive Tribes of the Lower Niger*.

The result of Achebe's "creative act of investigation" into the history that made the novel possible is ambiguous. On the one hand, the text appreciates pre-colonial Igbo culture as complex and dynamic establishing Africans less as victims than as agents of their own history. On the other hand, it draws attention to its shortcomings which explain why the Igbo were unable to unitedly ward off the strangers that finally destroyed their institutions and practices. Rather than glorify Igbo culture as an unquestionable source the new Nigeria could build upon, it emerges as contradictory and full of fissures which need to be addressed in the present and in the future.

3. *Conclusion*

To conclude the course we evaluated the outcome of our analyses: what do we gain as historians and as literary and cultural scholars from unearthing the ambiguities and ambivalences in literary texts? What does it mean to access "this felt sense of the quality of life at a particular place and time" as Raymond Williams called it? On the epistemological meta-level we learned that all knowledge is constructed rather than given and that there is no such thing as 'truth'. On the contrary, there are 'truths' (in the plural) which change with the point of view of those who construct them as they follow certain aims. Rather than think of Equiano's accounts as 'true' in the literal sense of every detail, its abstract 'truth' becomes discernible when we deconstruct the political functions *The Interesting Narrative* had at the end of the 18th century and contextualise its audience. As there is no way of knowing 'how it really was' we need to take the trouble of reading and comparing various texts from and about a certain period. It is only this technique of parallel reading of various kinds of primary and secondary material that allows us to value what texts say in the light of what they withhold. Rather than reject Joyce Cary's *Mister Johnson* simply as a colonial artefact, we need to look into its aesthetics to locate the contradictions and ruptures that come with the historical moment of an empire under challenge. Rather than take Chinua Achebe's *Things Fall Apart* as a 'true' insider's report of Igbo culture, it is more useful to appreciate his re-writing of colonialist historiography and its potential for the present of the 1950s and the 2010s.

It is only through a historiographically informed approach to literary representation that we can challenge the stereotypes of Africa that Western mass media and educational institutions still perpetuate. The speaker in Dike-Ogu Chukwumerije's poem "Enduring Images" makes exactly this point addressing an imaginary African: no matter what he or she has achieved, they remain locked in devaluing Western stereotypes: "Till shining cities rise in Africa/ They will always prefer the landless farmer/ I see how the world sees you".[51] It is through interdisciplinary research and teaching that we can refute the stereotypes because we scrutinise who constructs them and for what purposes. Moreover, by listening to Africa and reading African fiction and non-fiction, we get to know alternative African self-images as well as images of us as the 'Other'.

Notes

1 Since 2009 the members of the research and study programme 'Transformation Studies' at Leibniz University of Hanover (see endnote 4 in Ellen Grünkemeier's contribution) have been offering the interdisciplinary two-years Masters programme 'Atlantic Studies in History, Culture and Society'. Its introductory course in methodology has so far been jointly taught by a historian and a sociologist or a literary scholar, respectively. Brigitte Reinwald and Jana Gohrisch offered it in the winter term 2011/12 for the first time and will repeat it in the winter term 2012/13. The courses on colonial West Africa (Jana Gohrisch) and colonial Nigeria (Jana Gohrisch and Katja Füllberg-Stolberg) were taught in the winter terms 2008/09 and 2009/10, respectively.
2 Williams (1971: 64).
3 *Ibid.* 63.
4 Greenblatt (1994: 33).
5 Ryan (1995: 26).
6 *Ibid.* 27.
7 Gordon (2003: 88).
8 The course taught by Jana Gohrisch alone offered only four historiographic texts, two theoretical ones (Edward Said on contrapuntal reading and Louis Montrose on new historicist practice) and four on British and West African literary history. Two historiographic essays were taken from *Nigeria's Diverse Peoples. A Reference Sourcebook* by April A. Gordon and two from Christoph Marx's *Geschichte Afrikas. Von 1800 bis zur Gegenwart*. As Ellen Grünkemeier has observed, without the advice of an historian well versed in the recent debates, literary scholars will prefer overviews and general outlines which they can locate easily and then manage in class without help.
9 The texts on the south-east and the Igbo as well as on the Niger delta are by Allen (a feminist essay on Igbo women's resistance from the early 1970s), Gordon (an overview by an American historian), Uchendu (a Nigerian historian's essay in a collection on *Slavery in Africa*), Webster & Boahen (one of the first history textbooks on the region for students in Nigeria co-authored by an American and a Ghanaian historian in 1970). Tamuno offers a thorough analysis of colonial administration from the point of view of a Nigerian historian writing for Nigerian students. He openly indicts the British morally for the corruption of local forms of organisation. To understand the archival source, i.e. the annual report of the assistant district officer of the Pankshin Division (in the northern provinces, south of the tin-mining city of Jos) for 1932, Katja Füllberg-Stolberg introduced us to the structures of colonial administration in Nigeria in general and in the north in

particular as well to the tax system (the types of taxes and the ways they were set and collected).

10 In the introduction to the theories and methodologies of Atlantic Studies, Brigitte Reinwald and Jana Gohrisch provided students with a handout on how to prepare a scholarly text for class. This handout asks students to first identify the topics and thesis statements on the content level and then to proceed to the formal level describing the syntactic and stylistic features of the text, i.e. the mode of presenting the contents. Thirdly, they are asked to tackle the conceptual meta-level and establish the central categories and theories the text relies on to classify the research traditions of which it partakes as well as those which it contests. The last step is to assess the text's usefulness for the assigned task and to summarise the knowledge gained. The conceptual level turned out to be a real challenge, especially identifying the thesis statements and theoretical approaches along with their influence on the presentation of the contents.

11 We used the Norton edition by Werner Sollors (2001) which prints these paratexts on the pages 5-15.

12 This term was coined by Stephen Greenblatt in his celebrated study *Renaissance Self-Fashioning. From More to Shakespeare* (1984).

13 In his essay on "Olaudah Equiano. African British Abolitionist and Founder of the African American Slave Narrative", the English studies scholar Vincent Carretta explains at length the publication process, including the significance of retaining the copyright and of publishing by subscription, which had already been out of use when Equiano revived it for his purposes (Carretta 2007: 52-56).

14 *Ibid.* 56.

15 *Ibid.* 46.

16 *Ibid.* 47.

17 *Ibid.* 48.

18 Equiano (2001: 30).

19 *Ibid.* 31.

20 Carretta (2007: 50-51).

21 Equiano (2001: 31). Contextualising this statement, we looked at one of the most wide-spread 18th-century visual representations used by the abolitionists in their campaigns. It shows a kneeling black man who raises his chained hands in supplication (to an imagined white man) claiming "Am I Not a Man and a Brother?" The image is shown in Füllberg-Stolberg's essay in *Hard Times* (2009: 5).

22 Here, Equiano directly addresses and accuses his – white – readers: "Is it not enough that we are torn from our country and friends to toil for your luxury

and lust of gain? Must every tender feeling be likewise sacrificed to your avarice?" (Equiano 2001: 43)

23 Hofacker & Schuler (1994: 202). The text was taken from the second chapter of Equiano's *Interesting Narrative* but is quoted anonymously (translated by the editors) from the tellingly titled collection *Black Voyage. Eyewitness Accounts of the Atlantic Slave Trade* (1971). The French history book for elementary school, *Histoire Cycle 3*, contains four quotes from Equiano (in French) under the heading of "Témoignage": his account of being kidnapped, of arriving on board the slave ship (the same as in the German textbook) and later in Barbados as well as a description of a domestic slave cruelly chained (Le Callennec 2002: 112).

24 There is a short and concise overview on "The British Abolition of the Slave Trade and of Slavery" by Claus and Katja Füllberg-Stolberg in *Hard Times* (2009). It was inspired by a course taught jointly by Claus Füllberg-Stolberg and Jana Gohrisch on "Representing Caribbean History in Anglophone Caribbean Literature" in the winter term of 2007/08.

25 The production of palm oil and kernels was promoted in the south to provide British industries with the raw material for soaps, candles and lubricants. The oil pressed from the palm kernels was used for margarine and chocolate confections. The north was encouraged to cultivate cotton (Gordon 2003: 55). The demand for cheap labour to produce the new crops caused an increase in domestic slavery while the struggle over trade routes brought about wide-spread political instability and war in the southern regions (*Ibid.* 57-58).

26 Gordon (2003: 58).

27 *Ibid.* 55.

28 *Ibid.* 64.

29 In *The Dual Mandate in British Tropical Africa* (1926) Lugard later "explains and justifies colonialism and describes administrative policy in Nigeria. The 'dual mandate' refers to the requirement of colonial administrators both to serve economic interests back in Great Britain and to promote the 'progress' of the 'native races' (in ways determined by the British policy makers)." (Gordon: 2003: 73) Lugard served as High Commissioner of Northern Nigeria from 1900 to 1906, then as Governor and Governor General of the whole of Nigeria, which he had united himself, from 1912 to 1919.

30 In the north, the British could build on the collaboration of the emirs and the established administrative structures. They became responsible for taxation and implementing colonial policies for which they gained the support of the British which, in turn, helped to keep them in power. In the south, however,

no such structures and rulers existed. Therefore, the British appointed warrant chiefs (among the Igbo) and obas (among the Yoruba). This did not only lead to wide-spread discontent because these rulers abused their power. Rather, the many decades of informal and formal colonialisation altered the social structures in both the north and the south laying the foundations for the many ethnic conflicts, economic and social problems Nigeria has been suffering from ever since (Gordon 2003: 75-84).

31 *Ibid.* 76.
32 There are at least two towns of this name in Burkina Faso and Chad. In Hausa, Fada means 'the chief's residence' which makes it an ironic comment on the colonial situation: there are two chiefs residing in the place – the British colonial and the native authorities.
33 Cary (1985: 46-47, 142).
34 *Ibid.* 41.
35 *Ibid.* 64.
36 To understand the interdependence of coloniser and colonised, we employed Homi Bhabha's concept of colonial mimicry that he developed to explain the subversive moment of metonymically mimicking the colonizer. The resulting parody undermines colonial authority by reflecting a refracted image of it. Bhabha defined mimicry, "almost the same, *but not quite*", as an effect of non-fictional colonial discourse (Bhabha 1984: 127; Bhabha's emphasis) which made it necessary to adapt it to analysing fiction.
37 Cary (1985: 66).
38 *Ibid.* 237.
39 Bhabha (1984: 129).
40 Gordon (2003: 81, 86).
41 Ryan (1995: 26).
42 Yeats (2012: 2099).
43 Webster & Boahen (1970: 166).
44 "Since everyone had a right to rise in society Ibo [sic] culture emphasized competition; competition between families, between lineages and between clans. […] Ibo society was, therefore, intensely democratic with a vigour characteristic of competitive, egalitarian societies. With this it also had the failings of wasted uncoordinated effort, slow decision-making and a lack of unity […]." (*Ibid.*)
45 Lane (2006: 37).
46 Lovesey (2006: 280).
47 Lane (2006: 36).
48 *Ibid.* 40. Lane here quotes an essay by Wole Ogundele on mythic and historical imagination in the postcolonial novel (2002).

49 Uchendu (1977: 124).
50 Achebe (2000: 124).
51 Chukwumerije (2008: 80).

Bibliography

Achebe, Chinua: *Things Fall Apart*, Oxford, 2000. [first published in 1958]
Allen, Judith van: "'Sitting on a Man'. Colonisation and the Lost Political Institutions of Igbo Women", *Canadian Journal of African Studies* 6:2, 1972, 165-181.
Bhabha, Homi: "Of Mimicry and Man. The Ambivalence of Colonial Discourse", *October* 28, 1984, 125-133.
Carretta, Vincent: "Olaudah Equiano. African British abolitionist and Founder of the African American Slave Narrative". – In Audrey Fisch (Ed.): *The Cambridge Companion to the African American Slave Narrative*, Cambridge, 2007, pp. 44-60.
Cary, Joyce: *Mister Johnson*, London, 1985. [first published in 1939]
Chukwumerije, Dike-Ogu: "Enduring Images". – In D.-O. C.: *The Revolution Has No Tribe. Contemporary Poetry on African History, Culture and Society*, London, 2008, p. 80.
Equiano, Olaudah: *The Interesting Narrative of the Life of Olaudah Equiano, or Gustavus Vassa, The African, Written by Himself*. Ed. Werner Sollors, New York & London, 2001. [first published in 1789]
Füllberg-Stolberg, Claus & Katja: "The British Abolition of the Slave Trade and of Slavery", *Hard Times* 85, 2009, 2-7.
Gordon, April A.: *Nigeria's Diverse Peoples. A Reference Sourcebook*, Santa Barbara, Denver & Oxford, 2003.
Greenblatt, Stephen: "'Invisible Bullets'. Renaissance Authority and its Subversion, *Henry IV* and *Henry V*". – In Jonathan Dollimore & Alan Sinfield (Eds.): *Political Shakespeares. Essays in Cultural Materialism*, 2nd ed., Manchester, 1994, pp. 18-47.
Hofacker, Hans-Georg & Thomas Schuler (Eds.): *Geschichtsbuch 2. Die Menschen und ihre Geschichte in Darstellungen und Dokumenten. Das Mittelalter und die Frühe Neuzeit*, Neue Ausgabe, Berlin, 1994.
Lane, Richard: *The Postcolonial Novel*, Malden & Cambridge, 2006.
Le Callennec, Sophie (Ed.): *Histoire Cycle 3*, Collection Magellan, Paris, 2002.
Lovesey, Oliver: "Making Use of the Past in *Things Fall Apart*", *Genre* XXXIX, 2006, 273-299.

Marx, Christoph: *Geschichte Afrikas. Von 1800 bis zur Gegenwart*, Paderborn, 2004.

Ryan, Kiernan: *Shakespeare*, 2nd ed., London & New York, 1995.

Tamuno, T. N. "British Colonial Administration in Nigeria in the Twentieth Century". – In Obaro Ikime (Ed.): *Groundwork in Nigerian History*, Ibadan, 1984, pp. 393-409.

Uchendu, Victor C. "Slaves and Slavery in Igboland". – In Suzanne Miers & Igor Kopytoff (Eds.): *Slavery in Africa. Historical and Anthropological Perspectives*, Madison, 1977, pp. 121-132.

Webster, J. A. & A. A. Boahen: *History of West Africa. The Revolutionary Years – 1815 to Independence*, Washington, 1970.

Williams, Raymond: *The Long Revolution*, Harmondsworth, 1971.

Yeats, William Butler: "The Second Coming". – In Stephen Greenblatt (Ed.): *The Norton Anthology of English Literature, vol. F, The Twentieth Century and After*, 9th ed., New York & London, 2012, p. 2099.

Dike-Ogu Chukwumerije (Abuja)

Enduring Images

I see how the world sees you

A broken woman sitting in the dust
A sad eyed man looking lost
Children without food, always crying
Villages without water, slowly dying
Vampire states with military faces
And empty continent of HIV cases

Though you work in the city
And carry all the trappings of prosperity
A sound financial plan
Weekends with children on the Isle of Man
A home in the suburbs, a life of affluence
A man or woman of considerable influence

Still, they will not let you be Africa
It will always be the landless farmer
They see you as the lucky one
The black person who escaped – the exception
Fortunate to have what the others do not
The opportunity of living in the North

Your success is an isolated case
Not enough to re-define the black man's face
Give him a new place in the gathering of all men
They will always prefer the dying children
Till shining cities rise in Africa
They will always prefer the landless farmer

I see how the world sees you

Dike-Ogu Chukwumerije has kindly allowed us to reprint this poem from his collection *The Revolution Has No Tribe. Contemporary Poetry on African History, Culture and Society*, London, 2008, p. 80.

Henning Marquardt (Hanover)

Anglophone Africa.
A Chronology of Events and Texts

	History	Literature and Culture
BC		
ca. 100000	Homo Sapiens spread from Africa to the world	
from 1000	development of proto-Bantu language	
ca. 500	beginning migration of Bantu-speaking peoples within southern Africa	
AD		
ca. 100	Indonesian sailors arrive at East African coast	
6th cent.	emerging Christianity in Nubia	
8th cent.	conquest of northern Africa by Arabs; Islam begins to shape Sudan	
1510	first slaves from Africa shipped to the Americas	
1652	foundation of Cape Town by Dutch	
1787	foundation of Freetown (Sierra Leone) as a refuge for freed slaves	

1788	Sierra Leone becomes British protectorate	
1806	British capture Cape of Good Hope from Dutch	
1807	abolition of slave trade on British ships	
1808	Sierra Leone becomes British colony	
1810	British capture Mauritius from French	
1811	British capture Seychelles from French	
1814	Cape Colony becomes British colony	
ca. 1815 - 1840	Mfecane in southern Africa	
1816	British military post established in eventual colony of The Gambia	
1821	Britain takes over administration of Gold Coast	
1822	American Colonisation Society buys land in western Africa that is to become Liberia	
1833	British enact abolition of slavery to be implemented in 1834	
1843	Natal becomes British colony	
1844	Gold Coast becomes British protectorate	
1847	Liberia gains independence	

1870	first finding of diamonds in southern Africa	
1874	Gold Coast becomes Crown Colony	
1879	British defeat Zulu	
1880/1881	First Boer War	
1883	British Central Africa Protectorate established, renamed Nyasaland in 1907	Olive Schreiner: *Story of an African Farm*
1884	Basutoland becomes British Crown Colony; Uganda becomes British protectorate	
1884/1885	Berlin Conference regulates Africa's colonisation	
1885	Bechuanaland becomes British protectorate; Britain establishes East Africa Protectorate	
1886	first finding of gold on Witwatersrand	
1887		Olive Schreiner: *Trooper Peter Halket of Mashonaland*
1888	The Gambia becomes British colony; Northern and Southern Rhodesia become British spheres of influence; British Somaliland protectorate established	
1890	Zanzibar becomes British protectorate	

1896-1897	Shona rebel against British rule (First Chimurenga)	
1899	Nubia incorporated into Sudan, virtually becomes British colony	
1899-1902	Second Boer War/South African War; British annex Orange Free State as Orange River Colony and South African Republic as Transvaal Colony	
from 1900	Britain exerts indirect rule over northern Nigeria	
1901/1902	Ashanti incorporated into Gold Coast	
1903	British claim Swaziland as part of the Transvaal; Seychelles become British colony	
1906	Swaziland separated from newly 'responsibly govern-ed' Transvaal	
1908		Stephen Black: *Love and the Hyphen* (drama)
1910	Cape Colony, Natal, Orange Free State and the Transvaal joined as South African Union and granted inde-pendence	
1912	South African Native National Congress founded as forerunner to African National Congress (ANC)	
1914	Nigeria united as British colony	Solomon T. Plaatje: *Native Life in South Africa*

1915	South Africa occupies German South West Africa	
1919	first Pan-African Congress in Paris; League of Nations assigns parts of Cameroon, Togo and Tanganyika to Britain; League of Nations assigns South West Africa Mandate to South Africa	
1920	East Africa Protectorate becomes Kenya Colony	
1923	Britain annexes Southern Rhodesia and grants self-government	
1924	Northern Rhodesia becomes British protectorate	Sarah Gertrude Millin: *God's Step-Children*
1925		William Plomer: *Turbott Wolfe*
1928		Rolfes Dhlomo: *An African Tragedy*
from 1929	global economic crisis increases exploitation of the colonies	
1930		Solomon T. Plaatje: *Mhudi*
1939		Thomas Mofolo: *Chaka*
1940		Tatamkhulu Afrika: *Broken Earth*
1941		Herbert Dhlomo: *Valley of a Thousand Hills* (poetry)
1945	fifth Pan-African Congress in Manchester demands independence for West African colonies	

1946		Peter Abrahams: *Mine Boy*
1948	apartheid regime established in South Africa by Afrikaner National Party	Peter Abrahams: *The Path of Thunder*; Herman Bosman: *Mafeking Road* (short stories); Alan Paton: *Cry, the Beloved Country*
1949		Donald Swanson (Dir.): *African Jim* (*Jim Comes to Jo'burg*)
1950		Peter Abrahams: *Wild Conquest*
1951		first issue of *Drum* magazine
1952		Amos Tutuola: *The Palm-Wine Drinkard*
1952-1956	Mau Mau uprising in Kenya	
1953	Northern and Southern Rhodesia joined with Nyasaland	
1954		Amos Tutuola: *My Life in the Bush of Ghosts*
1956	Sudan gains independence	
1957	Gold Coast and Western Togo gain independence to form Ghana	
1958	first All-African Peoples' Conference, Accra	Chinua Achebe: *Things Fall Apart*; Nadine Gordimer: *A World of Strangers*
1959		Wole Soyinka: *The Lion and the Jewel* (drama)

1960	second All-African Peoples' Conference, Tunis; ban of ANC after Sharpeville Massacre in South Africa; Cameroon and Nigeria gain independence; British Somaliland granted independence and joined with the former Italian Somaliland	Chinua Achebe: *No Longer at Ease*; Wole Soyinka: *A Dance of the Forrests* (drama); *The Trials of Brother Jero* (drama)
1961	third All-African Peoples' Conference, Cairo; Sierra Leone and Tanganyika gain independence	
1962	Uganda gains independence	Alex la Guma: *A Walk in the Night* (short stories)
1963	foundation of the Organisation of African Unity (OAU); Kenya and Zanzibar gain independence	
1964	Nyasaland gains independence, renamed Malawi; Northern Rhodesia gains independence, renamed Zambia; Zanzibar Revolution; Tanganyika and Zanzibar join to form Tanzania	Chinua Achebe: *Arrow of God*; Gabriel Okara: *The Voice*; Ngũgĩ wa Thiong'o: *Weep not, Child*
1964-1979	civil war in Southern Rhodesia (Second Chimurenga)	

1965	The Gambia gains independence; Southern Rhodesia unilaterally declares independence	Ama Ata Aidoo: *Dilemma of a Ghost* (drama); Wole Soyinka: *The Interpreters*; *The Road* (drama); Ngũgĩ wa Thiong'o: *The River Between*
1966	Basutoland gains independence, renamed Lesotho; Bechuanaland gains independence, renamed Botswana	Chinua Achebe: *A Man of the People*; Okot p'Bitek: *Song of Lawino* (poetry); Flora Nwapa: *Efuru*
1967		Ngũgĩ wa Thiong'o: *A Grain of Wheat*
1967-1970	Nigerian civil war (Biafran War)	
1968	Mauritius and Swaziland gain independence	Ayi Kweyi Armah: *The Beautyful Ones Are Not Yet Born*
1970		Ama Ata Aidoo: *Anowa* (drama); Okot p'Bitek: *Song of Ocol* (poetry)
1971		Taban lo Liyong: *The Uniformed Man* (essays); Christopher Okigbo: *Labyrinths with Paths of Thunder* (poetry)
1973		Athol Fugard: *The Island* (drama); Bessie Head: *A Question of Power*
1974		Nadine Gordimer wins Booker Prize for *The Conservationist*; Buchi Emecheta: *Second Class Citizen*;

			Athol Fugard: *Siswe Banzi is Dead* (drama); Wole Soyinka: *Death and the King's Horsman* (drama)
1975		Lomé Convention between European Community and African, Caribbean and Pacific Group of States (ACP)	André Brink: *An Instance in the Wind*
1976		Soweto uprising in South Africa; Seychelles gain independence	Meja Mwangi: *Going Down River Road*; Grace Ogot: *The Other Woman* (short stories)
1977			Ama Ata Aidoo: *Our Sister Killjoy*; Bessie Head: *The Collector of Treasures and Other Botswana Village Tales* (short stories); Femi Osofisan: *The Chattering and the Song* (drama); Ngũgĩ wa Thiong'o: *Petals of Blood*
1978			Dambudzo Marechera: *The House of Hunger* (short stories)
1979			André Brink: *A Dry White Season*; Buchi Emecheta: *The Joys of Motherhood*; Nuruddin Farah: *Sweet and Sour Milk*; Nadine Gordimer: *The Burgher's Daughter*

1980	Southern Rhodesia gains independence, renamed Zimbabwe	J.M. Coetzee: *Waiting for the Barbarians*; Dambudzo Marechera: *Black Sunlight*
1981		Nuruddin Farah: *Sardines*; Nadine Gordimer: *July's People*; Jack Mapanje: *Of Chameleons and God* (poetry); Wole Soyinka: *Aké*
1982		Buchi Emecheta: *Destination Biafra*; Athol Fugard: *'Master Harold' ... and the Boys* (drama); Mafika Gwala: *No More Lullabies* (poetry); Ngũgĩ wa Thiong'o: *Devil on the Cross*
1983		Harare International Book Fair established; J.M. Coetzee wins Booker Prize for *Life & Times of Michael K*; King Ampaw (Dir.): *Kuku-Rantumi – Road to Accra*; Nuruddin Farah: *Close Sesame*; Njabulo Ndebele: *Fools and Other Stories* (short stories)
1986		Wole Soyinka awarded Nobel Prize in Literature; J.M. Coetzee: *Foe*; Nuruddin Farah: *Maps*; Dambudzo Marechera: *Mindblast* (poetry, drama, prose);

		Marjorie Oludhe Macgoye: *Coming to Birth*; Ken Saro-Wiwa: *Soza Boy*
1987		Chinua Achebe: *Anthills of the Savannah*; Richard Attenborough (Dir.): *Cry Freedom*; Ngũgĩ wa Thiong'o: *Matigari*; Marjorie Oludhe Macgoye: *The Present Moment*; Zoë Wicomb: *You Can't Get Lost in Cape Town*
1988		Tsitsi Dangarembga: *Nervous Conditions*; Chenjerai Hove: *Bones*; Oliver Schmitz (Dir.): *Mapantsula*;
1989		Buchi Emecheta: *Gwendolen*; Euzhan Palcy (Dir.): *A Dry White Season*; Moyez G. Vassanji: *The Gunny Sack*
1989-1997	civil war in Liberia	
1990	Namibia gains independence from South Africa; unbanning of ANC; Nelson Mandela released from prison	Dakar Biennale starts with focus on literature; Nadine Gordimer: *My Son's Story*; Meja Mwangi: *Striving for the Wind*
1991		Nadine Gordimer awarded Nobel Prize in Literature; Ben Okri wins Booker Prize for *The Famished Road*;

		Ama Ata Aidoo: *Changes. A Love Story*; Biyi Bandele-Thomas: *The Sympathetic Undertaker and Other Dreams*
1992		Dakar Biennale renamed Dak'Art, focus: visual arts; Nuruddin Farah: *Gifts*; Yvonne Vera: *Why Don't You Carve Other Animals* (short stories)
1993		Lindsey Collen: *The Rape of Sita*; Tsitsi Dangarembga (Dir.): *Neria*; Haile Gerima (Dir.): *Sankofa*; Ben Okri: *Songs of Enchantment*; Yvonne Vera: *Nehanda*
1994	end of apartheid	Buchi Emecheta: *Kehinde*; Nadine Gordimer: *None to Accompany Me*; Abdulrazak Gurnah: *Paradise*; Yvonne Vera: *Without a Name*
1995	execution of Ken Saro-Wiwa	Ben Okri: *Astonishing the Gods*
1996		Dak'Art – Biennale de l'Art Africain Contemporain shifts focus to contemporary arts; Ingrid Sinclair (Dir.): *Flame*; Yvonne Vera: *Under the Tongue*

1996-1998	Truth and Reconciliation Commission investigates apartheid crimes	
1997	Kofi Annan (Ghana) becomes Secretary General of the UN	Taban Lo Liyong: *Carrying Knowledge up a Palm Tree* (poetry)
1998		Nuruddin Farah: *Secrets*; Jane Taylor: *Ubu and the Truth Commission* (drama); Yvonne Vera: *Butterfly Burning*
1999		J.M. Coetzee wins Booker Prize for *Disgrace*
2000	Lomé Convention replaced by Cotonou Agreement	first annual Caine Prize for African Writing awarded; Mandla Langa: *The Memory of Stones*; Zakes Mda: *The Heart of Redness*; Oliver Schmitz (Dir.): *Hijack Stories*; Zoë Wicomb: *David's Story*
2001	OAU becomes African Union (AU)	Phaswane Mpe: *Welcome to Our Hillbrow*
2002		Nadine Gordimer: *The Pickup*; Helon Habila: *Waiting for an Angel*; Yvonne Vera: *The Stone Virgins*
2003		J.M. Coetzee awarded Nobel Prize in Literature
2004		Chimamanda Ngozi Adichie: *Purple Hibiscus*; Chris Abani: *GraceLand*; J.M. Coetzee: *Slow Man*;

		Dickson Iroegbu (Dir.): *The Mayors*; Zola Maseko (Dir.): *Drum*; Niq Mhlongo: *Dog Eat Dog* Darrel Roodt (Dir.): *Yesterday*; Ramadan Suleman (Dir.): *Zulu Love Letter*
2005		first annual African Movie Academy Awards ceremony held in Nigeria; André Brink: *Praying Mantis*; Mark Donford-May (Dir.): *U-Carmen eKhayelitsha*; Gavin Hood (Dir.): *Tsotsi*; Andy Nwakalor (Dir.): *Rising Moon*
2006		first biennial Wole Soyinka Prize for Literature in Africa awarded; Cape Town Book Fair established; Chimamanda Ngozi Adichie: *Half of a Yellow Sun*; Tsitsi Dangarembga: *The Book of Not*
2007		J.M. Coetzee: *Diary of a Bad Year*; Izu Ojukwu (Dir.): *Sitanda*
2008		Emmanuel Apea (Dir.): *Run Baby Run*; Wanuri Kahiu (Dir.): *From a Whisper*

2009		Kunle Afolayan (Dir.): *The Figurine*; J.M. Coetzee: *Summertime*
2010	first football world cup on African continent held in South Africa	
2011	South Sudan gains independence from Sudan	Charlie Vundla (Dir.): *How to Steal 2 Million*

Henning Marquardt (Hanover)

Annotated Bibliography

1. General History

Collins, Robert O. & James MacGregor Burns: *A History of Sub-Saharan Africa*, Cambridge, 2007.
    This study introduces scholars, teachers and students to central themes of African history. It accounts for African history from the physical formation of the continent to the 21st century. Nearly half of the text is dedicated to the period before colonialism, thereby putting Africa's colonial history into perspective without neglecting it.

Reid, Richard J.: *A History of Modern Africa – 1800 to Present*, Malden & Oxford, 2012.
    In six roughly chronologically arranged parts this accessible overview concentrates on the colonial aspects of African history, including colonialism's legacy until today. The individual sections are organised thematically rather than geographically, which provides an integrated account of African history.

2. Literary History

Chapman, Michael: *Southern African Literatures*, London & New York, 1996.
    Chapman's standard work sets out to give a chronological account of Southern African literatures in various languages from Angola, Botswana, Lesotho, Malawi, Mozambique, Namibia, South Africa, Swaziland, Zambia and Zimbabwe. In practice, however, this originally broad approach is narrowed down to South African literatures in English leaving little room to the other regions and

languages. For readers interested in South African literatures in English the volume will nonetheless be very useful.

Heywood, Christopher: *A History of South African Literature*, Cambridge, 2004.

This well-written overview provides readers with a contextualised literary history of South Africa that is divided into the period before the Sharpeville massacre of 1960 and the period after it. Each section is subdivided into chapters on prose, poetry and drama. The helpful study is supplemented by a chronology, a glossary and a select bibliography.

Irele, F. Abiola & Simon Gikandi (Eds.): *The Cambridge History of African and Caribbean Literature*, Volume I & II, Cambridge, 2004.

On more than 900 pages, these two volumes provide a total of 40 essays, most of which deal with African literatures. The volumes work their way from oral to written literature with each chapter addressing a particular thematic aspect (e.g. orality or empire), a language and/or a region. What might look rather random at first sight turns out to be a most comprehensive collection on a large variety of African literatures in different languages from different regions.

Owomoyela, Oyekan (Ed.): *A History of Twentieth-Century African Literatures*, Lincoln & London, 1993.

This is a collection of articles on sub-Saharan African Literatures from different regions in different languages. The five chapters on English language literature are organised by genre and region, the three chapters on French language literature are organised by genre only. The volume is completed by a chapter on Portuguese language literature, one on literatures in African languages, one on women writing and two chapters on general issues concerning language and publishing. As its organisation already suggests, the volume is especially helpful for those readers who engage with Anglophone literatures.

3. Surveys/Introductions/Companions

Booker, M. Keith: *The African Novel in English. An Introduction*, Portsmouth & Oxford, 1998.
> Booker's helpful study combines two introductory chapters on the African novel and its history with eight case studies of canonical African novels: Chinua Achebe's *Things Fall Apart*, Buchi Emecheta's *The Joys of Motherhood*, Ayi Kwei Armah's *The Beautiful Ones are not yet Born*, Ama Ata Aidoo's *Our Sister Killjoy*, Nadine Gordimer's *Burger's Daughter*, Alex La Guma's *In the Fog of the Seasons' End*, Ngũgĩ wa Thiong'o's *Devil on the Cross* and Tsitsi Dangaremba's *Nervous Conditions*.

Breitinger, Eckhard (Ed.): *Theatre and Performance in Africa*, Bayreuth, 1994.
> This interesting collection of essays approaches multicultural idioms, grassroots and elite perspectives, political contexts and new forms of performance in African theatre. In doing so, the articles discuss theoretical and historical issues as well as individual plays and performances.

Döring, Tobias (Ed.): *African Cultures, Visual Arts, and the Museum*, Amsterdam & New York, 2002.
> Döring's collection of diverse essays is mainly dedicated to visual arts in Africa as well as to arts by Africans presented in Europe. Additionally, it includes articles on Francophone film and the interface between visual arts and literature, an interview with South African artist Sue Williamson and exhibition reports from Berlin and Paris.

Emenyonu, Ernest N. (Ed.): *Film in African Literature Today*, African Literature Today 28, Oxford, 2010.
> This issue of the annual journal *African Literature Today* mainly concentrates on West African films but also includes case studies from East, Central and South Africa. Focussing on Anglophone and Francophone productions, the insightful articles equally deal with video films and cinema.

Griffith, Gareth: *African Literatures in English. East and West*, Harlow, 2000.

In his helpful survey, Griffith applies a comparative approach to East and West African literatures. It is subdivided into sections on the development of East and West African literature, dominant themes as well as marginalised writings, such as English language writers from non-Anglophone countries or women writers, and their future. The volume is concluded by a section providing further references, including a chronology, a bibliography and notes on individual authors.

Gugler, Josef: *African Film. Re-Imagining a Continent*, Oxford *et al.*, 2003.

An illustrated survey introducing seventeen African films produced between 1970 and 1997. The films are arranged thematically according to six separate but interrelated socio-political categories. These informative case studies are framed by an introduction and an epilogue which provide insights into African film history, markets, distribution and their politics. Moreover, it raises questions about the responsibilities of viewers and producers.

Irele, F. Abiola (Ed.): *The Cambridge Companion to the African Novel*, Cambridge, 2009.

This companion directed at students and researchers comprises fifteen articles concerned with different aspects of the African novel. These include languages, regions, individual authors, orality, genre, gender, postcoloniality and critical receptions.

Killam, Douglas & Ruth Rowe (Eds.): *The Companion to African Literatures*, Oxford, 2000.

A comprehensive guide to African writing with articles on individual authors as well as topics and themes relevant to African literatures such as languages, genres, publications, orality etc.

Limb, Peter & Jean-Marie Volet: *Bibliography of African Literatures*, Lanham & London, 1996.

Limb and Volet offer researchers a comprehensive and useful bibliography that is organised by languages and subdivided by chapters on regions. Each chapter includes bibliographical references to bibliographies, anthologies, general studies and finally to individual authors. The sections on authors include references to mostly fictional works of major African writers.

Msiska, Mpalive-Hangson & Paul Hyland (Eds.): *Writing and Africa*, London & New York, 1997.
    This interesting collection of essays combines surveys of African literatures that focus on North African, West African and on East and Central African writing with an extensive section on "Issues and Problems" which is dedicated to the roles of ethnography, history, colonialism, orality and many other aspects. The volume is concluded by a short but useful collection of critical texts that can be included into analysis and teaching.

Okome, Onookome (Ed.): *Nollywood. West African Cinema*, Postcolonial Text 3:2, 2007.
    The term Nollywood refers to the Nigerian film industry – accordingly Okome's guest-edited issue of *Postcolonial Text* largely focuses on film productions from Nigeria, with Ghana and Cameroon only playing a minor role. The articles provide insight into production, markets, distribution and reception of West African films. In spite of the term cinema in the issue's title, however, the articles mainly revolve around video film productions and their reception.

Olaniyan, Tejumola & Ato Quayson (Eds.): *African Literature. An Anthology of Criticism and Theory*, Malden & Oxford, 2007.
    The two editors present an 800-pages collection of 97 abridged articles by distinguished scholars and writers originally published between 1965 and 2005. The comprehensive volume covers a wide thematic range including language, theory, gender, genre and much more.

Stone, Ruth M. (Ed.): *The Garland Handbook of African Music*, New York, 2000.
    This useful handbook provides readers with a variety of articles on African music, including technical aspects such as notation and instruments, the socio-cultural context such as dance, religion and HIV/AIDS. In addition, it contains a regional overview of the continent's music covering West, North, East, Central and Southern Africa separately.

Wright, Derek (Ed.): *Contemporary African Fiction*, Bayreuth, 1997.
This survey on sub-Saharan African literature since 1980 includes critical essays on individual authors and texts. The informative articles are arranged in three sections on Southern, East and West Africa.

4. Collections/Anthologies

Achebe, Chinua & C. L. Innes (Eds.): *African Short Stories. Twenty Short Stories from across the Continent*, Oxford, 1987.
This is a collection of short stories by mostly well-known African writers. It is organised by regions and covers West, East, North and Southern African Stories.

Banham, Martin & Jane Plastow (Eds.): *Contemporary African Plays*, London, 1999.
A collection of African plays including Femi Osofisan's *The Chattering Song*, Andrew Whaley's *The Rise and Shine of Comrade Fiasco*, Ama Ata Aidoo's *Anowa*, Percy Mtwa, Mbongeni Ngema and Barney Simon's *Woza Albert!*, Alemseged Tesfai's *The Other War* and Wole Soyinka's *Death and the King's Horseman*.

Browdy, Jennifer *et al.* (Eds.): *African Women Writing Resistance*, Madison, 2010.
This collection of short stories by African women is thematically arranged to account for the fields of tradition, sexuality, marriage, health, activism, exile and diaspora as well as visions of past, present and future.

Bruner, Charlotte H. (Ed.): *Unwinding Threads. Writing by Women in Africa*, Oxford, 1983.
A collection of short stories by African women representing western, eastern, southern and northern African women's writing.

Chapman, Michael (Ed.): *The 'Drum' Decade. Stories from the 1950s*, Pietermaritzburg, 1989.
In the 1950s, the South African magazine *Drum* was a symbol for black, urban life and for cultural resistance against apartheid.

Chapman's volume contains a selection of short stories by black South Africans from the heydays of the popular magazine.

Gray, Stephen (Ed.): *The Penguin Book of Southern African Stories*, London *et al.*, 1986.
Gray's collection contains a variety of short stories from Southern Africa, including some in translation. However, the stories can only be associated with certain regions or nation states via the authors' short biographies at the end of the book. Gray does not give reliable dates for many of the stories which complicates contextualised readings.

Gray, Stephen (Ed.): *The Penguin Book of Southern African Verse*, London *et al.*, 1989.
This collection of poems, which is roughly chronologically arranged by periods of the authors' works, includes many of the best-known Southern African poets. As was the case with *The Penguin Book of Southern African Stories*, working with the collection may become difficult because of the missing regions and dates.

Jeyifo, Biodun (Ed.): *Modern African Drama*, New York, 2002.
Jeyifo's Norton Critical Edition is especially suited for teaching African drama because the plays are accompanied by a large selection of background material and criticism. The plays included are Tawfik al-Hakim's *Fate of a Cockroach*, Kateb Yacine's *Intelligence Powder*, Athol Fugard, John Kani and Winston Ntshona's *Sizwe Bani is Dead*, Wole Soyinka's *Death and the King's Horseman*, Tsegaye Gabre-Medhin's *Collision of Altars*, Ama Ata Aidoo's *Dilemma of a Ghost*, Ngũgĩ wa Thiong'o and Ngũgĩ wa Mirii's *I will Marry when I Want* and Femi Osofisan's *Esu and the Vagabond Minstrels*.

Vera, Yvonne (Ed.): *Opening Spaces. An Anthology of Contemporary African Women's Writing*, Oxford, 1999.
This collection contains sixteen short stories by African women from all over the continent.

5. Teaching

Desai, Gaurav (Ed.): *Teaching the African Novel*, New York, 2009.
Desai's anthology provides teachers of African Literatures with thematically grouped essays on theories and methods, on regional issues as well as on mainly US-American pedagogical and institutional contexts. Especially the chapter on regional issues includes a number of non-English language texts and contexts. The volume offers general and theoretical debates and at the same time provides readers with discussions of canonical texts, such as Achebe's *Things Fall Apart* and Gordimer's *Burger's Daughter*.

Eisenmann, Maria, Nancy Grimm & Laurenz Volkmann (Eds.): *Teaching the New English Cultures and Literatures*, Heidelberg, 2010.
This broad collection of essays consists of two parts. The first one is dedicated to more general aspects of teaching New English Cultures in German secondary schools, including Gisela Feuerle's article on South African literatures. The second part contains literary case studies. Africa is represented here by Laurenz Volkmann's article on J. M. Coetzee's *Disgrace*.

Emenyonu, Ernest N. (Ed.): *Teaching African Literature Today*, African Literature Today 29, Oxford, 2011.
This diverse issue of the annual journal *African Literature Today* engages with various aspects of teaching African literature. The volume includes articles by scholars/teachers from Nigeria and the USA on teaching theory, teaching oral literature, using technology in the class room, online teaching and on teaching a number of canonical texts. Furthermore, the journal includes reviews of recent critical texts.

Contributors' Addresses

Dr. Anke Bartels
Institut für Anglistik und Amerikanistik, Universität Potsdam, Am Neuen Palais 10, 14469 Potsdam, E-Mail: anbartel@uni-potsdam.de

Dr. des. Claudia Böhme
Institut für Afrikanistik, Universität Leipzig, Beethovenstr.15, 04107 Leipzig, E-Mail: claudia.boehme@uni-leipzig.de

Dike-Ogu Chukwumerije
Abuja, Nigeria, E-Mail: dikeogu@yahoo.com

Prof. Dr. Rainer Emig
Englisches Seminar, Leibniz Universität Hannover, Königsworther Platz 1, 30167 Hannover, E-Mail: rainer.emig@engsem.uni-hannover.de

Prof. Dr. Susanne Gehrmann
Institut für Asien- und Afrikawissenschaften, Humboldt-Universität zu Berlin, Unter den Linden 6, 10099 Berlin, E-Mail: susanne.gehrmann @rz.hu-berlin.de

Prof. Dr. Jana Gohrisch
Englisches Seminar, Leibniz Universität Hannover, Königsworther Platz 1, 30167 Hannover, E-Mail: jana.gohrisch@engsem.uni-hannover.de

Dr. des. Ellen Grünkemeier
Englisches Seminar, Leibniz Universität Hannover, Königsworther Platz 1, 30167 Hannover, E-Mail: ellen.gruenkemeier@engsem.uni-hannover.de

Prof. Russell Harold Kaschula
School of Languages, Rhodes University, P.O. Box 94, Grahamstown, South Africa, E-Mail: R.Kaschula@ru.ac.za

Dr. Melanie Klein
Kunsthistorisches Institut, Freie Universität Berlin, Koserstr. 20, 14195 Berlin, E-Mail: melanie.klein@fu-berlin.de

Henning Marquardt
Englisches Seminar, Leibniz Universität Hannover, Königsworther Platz 1, 30167 Hannover, E-Mail: henning.marquardt@engsem.uni-hannover.de

Riaan Oppelt
Department of English, Stellenbosch University, Private Bag x1, Matieland, 7602, South Africa, E-Mail: roppelt@sun.ac.za

Dr. Uta Reuster-Jahn
Abteilung für Afrikanistik und Äthiopistik, Asien-Afrika-Institut, Universität Hamburg, Edmund-Siemers-Allee 1, 20146 Hamburg, E-Mail: uta.reuster-jahn@uni-hamburg.de

Prof. Dr. Kirsten Rüther
Institut für Afrikawissenschaften, Universität Wien, Spitalgasse 2, Hof 5, 1090 Wien, Österreich, E-Mail: kirsten.ruether@univie.ac.at

Prof. Dr. Anne Schröder
Fakultät für Linguistik und Literaturwissenschaft, Universität Bielefeld, Postfach 100131, 33501 Bielefeld, E-Mail: anne.schroeder@uni-bielefeld.de

Dr. des. Doreen Strauhs
Studienstiftung des deutschen Volkes, Ahrstraße 41, 53175 Bonn, E-Mail: doreenstrauhs@hotmail.com